Merleau-Ponty's Poetic of the World

Series Board

James Bernauer

Drucilla Cornell

Thomas R. Flynn

Kevin Hart

Richard Kearney

Jean-Luc Marion

Adriaan Peperzak

Thomas Sheehan

Hent de Vries

Merold Westphal

Michael Zimmerman

John D. Caputo, *series editor*

Perspectives in
Continental
Philosophy

GALEN A. JOHNSON,
MAURO CARBONE, AND
EMMANUEL DE SAINT AUBERT

Merleau-Ponty's Poetic of the World
Philosophy and Literature

FORDHAM UNIVERSITY PRESS
New York ■ 2020

Copyright © 2020 Fordham University Press

All rights reserved. No part of this publication may be reproduced, stored in a retrieval system, or transmitted in any form or by any means—electronic, mechanical, photocopy, recording, or any other—except for brief quotations in printed reviews, without the prior permission of the publisher.

Fordham University Press has no responsibility for the persistence or accuracy of URLs for external or third-party Internet websites referred to in this publication and does not guarantee that any content on such websites is, or will remain, accurate or appropriate.

Fordham University Press also publishes its books in a variety of electronic formats. Some content that appears in print may not be available in electronic books.

Visit us online at www.fordhampress.com.

Library of Congress Cataloging-in-Publication
DataNames: Johnson, Galen A., 1948– author. | Carbone, Mauro, 1956– author. | Saint-Aubert, Emmanuel de, author.
Title: Merleau-Ponty's poetic of the world : philosophy and literature / Galen A. Johnson, Mauro Carbone, Emmanuel de Saint Aubert.
Description: New York : Fordham University Press, 2020. | Series: Perspectives in continental philosophy | Includes bibliographical references and index. | Summary: "Merleau-Ponty has long been known as one of the most important philosophers of aesthetics, yet most discussions of his aesthetics focus on visual art. This book corrects that balance by turning to Merleau-Ponty's extensive engagement with literature" — Provided by publisher.
Identifiers: LCCN 2019058988 | ISBN 9780823288137 (hardback) | ISBN 9780823287703 (paperback) | ISBN 9780823288144 (epub)
Subjects: LCSH: Merleau-Ponty, Maurice, 1908–1961—Aesthetics. | Literature—Philosophy. | Language and languages—Philosophy.
Classification: LCC B2430.M3764 M474 2020 | DDC 801/.93—dc23
LC record available at https://lccn.loc.gov/2019058988

Printed in the United States of America

22 21 20   5 4 3 2 1

First edition

Contents

Preface — ix

Abbreviations of Works by Maurice Merleau-Ponty and Other Writers — xi

Introduction
Galen A. Johnson — *1*

PART I: MERLEAU-PONTY'S POETS

1. **"The Proustian Corporeity" and "The True Hawthorns": Merleau-Ponty as a Reader of Proust between Husserl and Benjamin**
   Mauro Carbone — *17*

2. **A Poetics of Co-Naissance: Via André Breton, Paul Claudel, and Claude Simon**
   Emmanuel de Saint Aubert — *31*

3. **From the World of Silence to Poetic Language: Merleau-Ponty and Valéry**
   Galen A. Johnson — *68*

Part II: Merleau-Ponty's Poetics

4 **The Clouded Surface: Literature and Philosophy as Visual Apparatuses According to Merleau-Ponty**
Mauro Carbone — *101*

5 **Metaphoricity: Carnal Infrastructures and Ontological Horizons**
Emmanuel de Saint Aubert — *121*

6 **On the Poetic and the True**
Galen A. Johnson — *159*

Acknowledgments — *191*

Notes — *193*

Index — *241*

Preface

The three authors of this book, Galen A. Johnson, Mauro Carbone, and Emmanuel de Saint Aubert, have collaborated over a period of ten years since the germ of the idea for the book was born, communicating electronically through email and Skype and in many face-to-face meetings in several locations: in France (Paris, Lyon, Nîmes, and Nyons), Switzerland (Bern and Basel), Italy (Milan), the United States (Providence, Fargo, Asheville), and Canada (Montreal and St. Catherines). A highlight was a sojourn in Nîmes, France, at the residence of Emmanuel de Saint Aubert with his family. That was June 2013. Our last meeting was in Nyons, France, a village south of Lyon, where we met at La Villa des Poètes. That was July 2017. The second location could not have been more apt, for both the name and the landscape lent themselves to the work of this project. We shared our chapters as they were finished in draft and redrafted and refined them in light of comments circulated among us.

This note is only to mark that *Merleau-Ponty's Poetic of the World* is not a collected work in the traditional sense of assembling the work of various disparate authors, but a genuine coauthorship and collaboration, quite rare in the discipline and history of philosophy. The processes involved have deferred completion of our project beyond that of a normal single-author book, and we three together express our gratitude to Fordham University Press for understanding and patience—in particular Tom Lay, Acquisitions Editor.

Abbreviations of Works by Maurice Merleau-Ponty and Other Writers

Works by Maurice Merleau-Ponty

After each passage cited from Merleau-Ponty, we indicate the pagination of the French edition, followed, where possible, by the pagination of the corresponding publication in English. In our references to unpublished manuscripts stored at the Bibliothèque Nationale de France (BNF), we specify the classification numbering established by that institution in square brackets, followed, when it exists, by Merleau-Ponty's manuscript pagination in round brackets. The letter "v" following the classification number of a folio page indicates that it refers to the verso of this page.

AD	*Les aventures de la dialectique*, written between July 1953 and December 1954 (Paris: Gallimard, 1955); *Adventures of the Dialectic*, trans. Joseph Bien (Evanston, IL: Northwestern University Press, 1973).
Brou	October 1960 manuscript, reworked in November to constitute the third chapter of the posthumous edition of *Le visible et l'invisible* (BNF, vol. 7). Partial transcription, under the heading "Brouillon d'une rédaction," in NC.
Caus	*Causeries 1948*, a series of seven talks broadcast between October 2 and November 13, 1948 ("Culture française" collection, INA Archives); text typed by Merleau-Ponty,

xi

	ed. Stéphanie Ménasé (Paris: Seuil, 2002); *The World of Perception*, trans. Oliver Davis (New York: Routledge, 2004).
ChRe	"Christianisme et ressentiment," review of French translation of Max Scheler's *L'homme du ressentiment*, in *La Vie Intellectuelle* 36 (June 10, 1935): 278–306; reprinted in *Parcours 1935–1951* (Lagrasse: Verdier, 1997), 9–33.
Desc	unpublished reading and working notes on Descartes (BNF, vols. 19 and 21).
EM	*Être et Monde* (unpublished, BNF, vol. 6). **EM1**: mostly autumn 1958, some pages from March 1959; **EM2**: various pieces of work from 1959; **EM3**: mainly April to May 1960, some rewritings in October 1960.
EP	*Éloge de la philosophie. Leçon inaugurale faite au Collège de France, le jeudi 15 janvier 1953* (Paris: Gallimard, 1953), reprinted in *Éloge de la philosophie et autres essais* (Paris: Gallimard, 1965 and 1989; we cite the later edition); "In Praise of Philosophy," trans. John Wild and James Edie, in *In Praise of Philosophy and Other Essays* (Evanston, IL: Northwestern University Press, 1988).
EtAv	"Être et Avoir," review of Gabriel Marcel's *Être et Avoir*, in *La Vie Intellectuelle* 45 (October 10, 1936): 98–109; reprinted in *Parcours 1935–1951* (Lagrasse: Verdier, 1997): 35–44.
FP	*Fondements de la psychologie*, course at the Faculté des Lettres de l'Université de Lyon (Autumn 1946), Merleau-Ponty's preparatory notes, unpublished.
HLP	*Husserl aux limites de la phénoménologie*, Monday course at the Collège de France, January–May 1960, Merleau-Ponty's preparatory notes (BNF, vol. 18); ed. Franck Robert, in *Notes de cours sur* L'origine de la géométrie *de Husserl* (Paris: Presses Universitaires de France, 1998); *Husserl at the Limits of Phenomenology*, trans. Leonard Lawlor and Bettina Bergo (Evanston, IL: Northwestern University Press, 2001).
HO	"L'homme et l'objet," unpublished lecture given by Merleau-Ponty at the Pavillon de Marsan as an introduction to a series on "L'objet et la poésie"; summarized by J.-L. Dumas, "Les conférences," in *La Nef* 45 (August 1948): 150–51.

HoXX	Merleau-Ponty's responses in the private and public discussion that followed his conference on "L'homme et l'adversité" (September 1951), in *La connaissance de l'homme au XXᵉ siècle* (Neuchâtel: La Baconnière, 1952); reprinted in *Parcours deux 1951–1961* (Lagrasse: Verdier, 2000), 321–76.
HT	*Humanisme et terreur: Essai sur le problème communiste* (Paris: Gallimard, 1947 and 1980; we cite the later edition); *Humanism and Terror: An Essay on the Communist Problem*, trans. John O'Neill (Boston: Beacon Press, 1969).
IP	*L'institution. La passivité: Notes de cours au Collège de France (1954–1955)* (Paris: Belin, 2003); *Institution and Passivity: Course Notes from the Collège de France (1954–1955)*, trans. Leonard Lawlor and Heath Massey (Evanston, IL: Northwestern University Press, 2010).
Mexico	Unpublished preparatory notes for the Conférences de Mexico (early 1949).
MSME	*Le monde sensible et le monde de l'expression*, Thursday course at the Collège de France, January–May 1953, Merleau-Ponty's preparatory notes (BNF, vol. 10); ed. Emmanuel de Saint Aubert and Stefan Kristensen (Geneva: MétisPresses, 2011). We would like to thank Bryan Smyth for his generous provision of translations for MSME passages from his translation of the entire volume, as *The Sensible World and the World of Expression* (Evanston, IL: Northwestern University Press, 2020).
NaPer	*La nature de la perception*, April 21, 1934, manuscript presented to the Caisse nationale des Sciences in support of a grant renewal; in *Le primat de la perception et ses conséquences philosophiques* (Grenoble: Cynara, 1989), 17–38.
NArn1	Unpublished lecture notes (probably 1957) on Rudolf Arnheim, *Art and Visual Perception: A Psychology of the Creative Eye* (BNF, vol. 21); **NArn2:** commentary on these notes, probably between April and July 1960.
Natu	*La Nature: Notes, cours du Collège de France* (Paris: Seuil, 1995); *Nature: Course Notes from the Collège de France*, trans. Robert Vallier (Evanston, IL: Northwestern University Press, 2003).

NC	*Notes de cours 1959–1961* (Paris: Gallimard, 1996).
NCorps	*Notes sur le corps*, 1956–1960, and especially 1960, unpublished (BNF, vol. 17).
NMS	*La Nature ou le monde du silence*, and other unpublished documents, pieces of work probably dating from autumn 1957, later placed in EM.
NPVI	Unpublished preparatory notes for *Le visible et l'invisible* (BNF, vol. 7).
NTi	Unpublished working notes from 1958–1960 (BNF, vol. 8).
OE	*L'oeil et l'esprit*, July–August 1960 (Paris: Gallimard, 1964 and 1985; we cite the later edition); "Eye and Mind," trans. Carleton Dallery, in *The Primacy of Perception* (Evanston, IL: Northwestern University Press, 1964); "Eye and Mind," trans. Michael B. Smith, in *The Merleau-Ponty Aesthetics Reader: Philosophy and Painting*, ed. Galen A. Johnson (Evanston, IL: Northwestern University Press, 1994); **OE-ms**: reading notes, preparatory notes, and various unpublished manuscript versions of *L'oeil et l'esprit*, spring and summer 1960, mostly July–August (BNF, vol. 5).
OntoC	*L'ontologie cartésienne et l'ontologie d'aujourd'hui*, Thursday course at the Collège de France, January–April 1961, Merleau-Ponty's preparatory notes (BNF, vol. 19); partial transcription by Stéphanie Ménasé, in **NC**. **NTontoc**: unpublished working notes accompanying the course preparation, December 1960–April 1961.
PbParole	*Le problème de la parole*, Thursday course at the Collège de France, December 1953–April 1954, Merleau-Ponty's preparatory notes (BNF, vol. 12); ed. Lovisa Andén, Franck Robert, and Emmanuel de Saint Aubert (Geneva: MétisPresses, 2020).
PbPassiv	*Le problème de la passivité: le sommeil, l'inconscient, la mémoire*, Monday course at the Collège de France, January–May 1955, Merleau-Ponty's preparatory notes (BNF, vol. 13); partial transcription by Stéphanie Ménasé in **IP**.
PhAuj	*La philosophie aujourd'hui*, untitled course at the Collège de France, January–May 1959, Merleau-Ponty's preparatory notes (BNF, vol. 18); partial transcription by Stéphanie Ménasé in **NC**.

PhDial — *La philosophie dialectique / Textes et commentaires sur la dialectique*, course at the Collège de France, January–May 1956, Merleau-Ponty's preparatory notes, unpublished (BNF, vol. 14).

PhP — *Phénoménologie de la perception* (Paris: Gallimard, 1945); *Phenomenology of Perception*, trans. Donald A. Landes (New York: Routledge, 2012).

PM — *La prose du monde*, 1950–1951, especially summer 1951 with some rewriting much later (BNF, vol. 3), text edited by Claude Lefort (Paris: Gallimard, 1969); *The Prose of the World*, trans. John O'Neill (Evanston, IL: Northwestern University Press, 1973); **PM-ms**: reading and working notes, outlines and plans relative to the preparation of *La prose du monde*, unpublished documents, various pieces of work, from 1950 to 1959 or even 1960 (BNF, vol. 3).

RAE — Centre de Documentation Universitaire de la Sorbonne version of the first part (1950–51) of the course on *Les relations avec autrui chez l'enfant*; reprinted in *Parcours 1935–1951* (Lagrasse: Verdier, 1997), 147–229; "The Child's Relations with Others," trans. William Cobb, in *The Primacy of Perception* (Evanston, IL: Northwestern University Press, 1964).

RC — *Résumés de cours: Collège de France, 1952–1960* (Paris: Gallimard, 1968 and 1982); "Themes from the Lectures at the Collège de France 1952–1960," trans. John O'Neill, in *In Praise of Philosophy and Other Essays* (Evanston, IL: Northwestern University Press, 1988).

S — *Signes* (Paris: Gallimard, 1960); *Signs*, trans. Richard C. McCleary (Evanston, IL: Northwestern University Press, 1964); **S-ms**: preparatory notes and various unpublished manuscript versions of the preface of *Signes*, February and September 1960 (BNF, vol. 4).

SC — *La structure du comportement* (Paris: Presses Universitaires de France, 1942 and 1990; we cite the later edition); *The Structure of Behavior*, trans. Alden Fisher (Boston: Beacon Press, 1963; London: Methuen, 1965, 1967; Pittsburgh: Duquesne University Press, 1983).

SNS — *Sens et non-sens* (Paris: Nagel, 1948; reprinted Paris: Gallimard, 1996; we cite the later edition); *Sense and*

	Non-Sense, trans. Patricia and Hubert Dreyfus (Evanston, IL: Northwestern University Press, 1964, 1992).
Sorb	Merleau-Ponty à la Sorbonne, résumé de cours 1949–1952 (Grenoble: Cynara, 1988); *Child Psychology and Pedagogy: The Sorbonne Lectures 1949–1952*, trans. Talia Welsh (Evanston, IL: Northwestern University Press, 2010).
TiTra	*Titres et travaux. Projet d'enseignement*, in support of candidature for the Collège de France (Paris: Centre de Documentation Universitaire, 1951); reprinted in *Parcours deux 1951–1961* (Lagrasse: Verdier, 2000), 9–35.
UAC	*L'union de l'âme et du corps chez Malebranche, Biran et Bergson*, new French edition, revised and augmented with a new unpublished fragment (Paris: Vrin, 1978); *The Incarnate Subject: Malebranche, Biran, and Bergson on the Union of Body and Soul*, trans. Paul B. Milan (Amherst, NY: Humanity Books, 2001).
ULL	*Recherches sur l'usage littéraire du langage*, Monday course at the Collège de France, January–May 1953, Merleau-Ponty's preparatory notes (BNF, vol. 11); ed. Benedetta Zaccarello and Emmanuel de Saint Aubert (Geneva: MétisPresses, 2013).
VI	*Le visible et l'invisible*, text edited by Claude Lefort (Paris: Gallimard, 1964); *The Visible and the Invisible*, trans. Alphonso Lingis (Evanston, IL: Northwestern University Press, 1968).

Works by Marcel Proust

Swann	*À la recherche du temps perdu*, vol. 1, *Du côté de chez Swann*, ed. Antoine Compagnon (Paris: Gallimard, 1988); *In Search of Lost Time: Swann's Way*, trans. C. K. Scott Moncrieff and Terence Kilmartin, revised D. J. Enright, vol. 1 (New York: Modern Library, 2003).
Jeunes Filles	*À la recherche du temps perdu*, vol. 2, *À l'ombre des jeunes filles en fleurs*, ed. Pierre-Louis Rey (Paris: Gallimard, 1988); *In Search of Lost Time: Within a Budding Grove*, trans. C. K. Scott Moncrieff and Terence Kilmartin, revised D. J. Enright, vol. 2 (New York: Modern Library, 2003).
Guermantes	*À la recherche du temps perdu*, vol. 3, *Le côté de Guermantes*, ed. Thierry Laget and Brian G. Rogers

	(Paris: Gallimard, 1994); *In Search of Lost Time: The Guermantes Way*, trans. C. K. Scott Moncrieff and Terence Kilmartin, revised D. J. Enright, vol. 3 (New York: Modern Library, 2003).
Temps retrouvé	*À la recherche du temps perdu*, vol. 7, *Le temps retrouvé*, ed. Pierre-Edmond Robert (Paris: Gallimard, 1990); *In Search of Lost Time: Time Regained*, trans. Andreas Mayor and Terence Kilmartin, revised D. J. Enright, vol. 6 (New York: Modern Library, 2003).

Works by Paul Valéry

C	*Cahiers*, vols. 1 and 2, ed. Judith Robinson (Paris: Gallimard, 1973–74).
CW	*The Collected Works of Paul Valéry*, ed. Jackson Matthews, 15 vols. (Princeton: Princeton University Press, 1956–75): 1. *Poems*, trans. David Paul. 2. *Poems in the Rough*, trans. Hilary Corke. 3. *Plays*. 4. *Dialogues*, trans. William McCausland Stewart. 5. *Idée Fixe*, trans. David Paul. 6. *Monsieur Teste*, trans. Jackson Matthews. 7. *The Art of Poetry*, trans. Denise Folliot. 8. *Leonardo, Poe, Mallarmé*, trans. Malcolm Cowley and James R. Lawler. 9. *Masters and Friends*, trans. Martin Turnell. 10. *History and Politics*. 11. *Occasions*. 12. *Degas, Monet, Morisot*, trans. David Paul. 13. *Aesthetics*, trans. Ralph Manheim. 14. *Analects*, trans. Stuart Gilbert. 15. *Moi*, trans. Marthiel and Jackson Matthews.
ILD	*Introduction to the Method of Leonardo da Vinci*, trans. Thomas McGreevy (London: John Rodker, 1929).
O	*Oeuvres*, vols. 1 and 2, ed. Jean Hytier (Paris: Gallimard, 1957 and 1960).

Works by Other Authors

M	Francis Ponge, *Méthodes*, vol. 2 of *Le grand recueil* (Paris: Gallimard, 1961).
MAT	Jean-Paul Sartre, "Man and Things," in *Critical Essays (Situations I)*, trans. Chris Turner (New York: Seagull Books, 2010), 383–465; French original: *Situations I* (Paris: Gallimard, 1947), 245–93.

NR	Francis Ponge, "L'objet, c'est la poétique," in *Nouveau recueil* (Paris: Gallimard, 1967).
PC	Edgar Allan Poe, "The Philosophy of Composition," in *Edgar Allan Poe: Critical Theory—The Major Documents*, ed. Stuart Levine and Susan F. Levine (Urbana: University of Illinois Press, 2009), 60–76.
T	Francis Ponge, *Le parti pris des choses* (1942), in *Tome premier* (Paris: Gallimard, 1965).
VT	Francis Ponge, *The Voice of Things*, ed. and trans. Beth Archer (New York: McGraw-Hill, 1972).

Merleau-Ponty's Poetic of the World

Introduction

GALEN A. JOHNSON

> But if, on the contrary, we consider the speaking word . . . that operative language . . . which is the language of life and of action but also that of literature and of poetry—then this logos is an absolutely universal theme, it is the theme of philosophy.
> —Maurice Merleau-Ponty, *The Visible and the Invisible*

Maurice Merleau-Ponty's writings display a deep love of literature, and they incorporate his literary reading, study, and thought into the heart of his philosophical reflections. The scope of his interest and writings on the arts ranged over modern painting to sculpture, photography, music, and cinema, and within these literature held a special place.[1] Near the beginning of Merleau-Ponty's oeuvre, the preface to *Phenomenology of Perception* ends by joining philosophy precisely with both modern literature and modern painting: "Phenomenology is as painstaking as the works of Balzac, Proust, Valéry, or Cézanne—through the same kind of attention and wonder, the same demand for awareness, the same will to grasp the sense of the world or of history in its nascent state. As such phenomenology merges with the effort of modern thought" (xvi/lxxxv). Near the end of his philosophical writing, a Working Note for *The Visible and the Invisible* from June 1959 reads, "Being is *what requires creation of us* for us to experience it. Make an analysis of literature in this sense: as *inscription* of Being" (251/197). In between this beginning and end, he wrote an essay on "The Novel and Metaphysics" (1945), and in "Indirect Language and the Voices of Silence" (1951–52) he discussed Saussure's diacritical theory of signs and offered an implicit critique of Sartre's *What Is Literature?* The lecture "Man and Adversity" is essential, and equally so the manuscript of *The Prose of the World*. Thus, throughout all his oeuvre, Merleau-Ponty's profound engagement with literary writers is readily apparent: Proust and Valéry, highlighted in the *Phenomenology* preface, and also Stendhal, Paul Claudel, Claude Simon, Baudelaire, Rimbaud, Breton, Balzac, Mallarmé, Francis Ponge, Sartre, and Beauvoir, to give an incomplete list.

Recently completed French transcriptions of Merleau-Ponty's first two 1953 courses given at the Collège de France have been published, both on questions of expression and literary language: *Le monde sensible et le monde de l'expression* (*The Sensible World and the World of Expression*) and *Recherches sur l'usage littéraire du langage* (*Research on the Literary Usage of Language*). The publication of the transcription of Merleau-Ponty's Thursday course of December 1953–April 1954, *Le problème de la parole* (*The Problem of Speech*), is imminent. These new resources energize this project.

If the mark of literature on the thought of Merleau-Ponty was profound, it remains a delicate matter to specify more precisely its nature and properly philosophical function. In his thought, the relation between philosophy and literature is more original, as well as more radical, than referring to literary works as philosophical illustrations or objects of study, and it offers an implicit conception of literature that makes the literary writer a partner of the phenomenologist. Merleau-Ponty deepens the dimensions of this partnership along many lines: in a wonderfully empathetic reading of writers who become in part mirrors for himself; in a conception of language in search for a delicate articulation of relationships and reality; but also by strategies of original expression that endeavor to respond to the requirements posed by the concepts of the flesh, being, and of philosophy itself. From Proust, the philosopher developed his conception of "sensible ideas"; from Claudel he conjoined birth and knowledge as "*co-naissance*"; from Valéry came "chiasm" and the "chiasma of two destinies." Therefore, Merleau-Ponty's engagement with literature goes far beyond creating a philosophy of literature or even an aesthetics or philosophy of art more broadly. Ultimately, it involves the creation and adaption of theoretical figures that appear at the threshold between philosophy and literature and enable the possibility of a new and radical, nondualist ontology. What is at stake is the very meaning of philosophy itself and its mode of expression.

More particularly and transversally, the task of writing in which the poet and the philosopher are jointly engaged inevitably implies the philosophical questions of a poetics in the philosophy of Merleau-Ponty. Thus arise the nature and meanings of expression, metaphor, and truth. This conjunction of poets and poetics gives the two main parts of our book project, Part I on Merleau-Ponty's poets, and Part II on his poetics.

Our use of the term "poet" is broad enough to include literary authors in general, be they novelists such as Proust or "poets" in the narrower sense such as Valéry, Baudelaire, and Mallarmé. Included are instances of literary language in their many forms and genres. Merleau-Ponty himself broadens the meaning of "poets" in this way in his course *Research on the Literary Usages of Language* to include not only verse as such but also all language that surpasses mere designation to become "symbolic."[2]

Our use of the term "poetics" is more complex and opens a vast field of inquiry that follows from Merleau-Ponty's own courses. A preliminary sketch here only opens the story that will unfold over the course of our book, an account of how radically Merleau-Ponty's sense of "poetics" contrasts with an outmoded husk of a voice of authority in which "poetics" merely meant rules and forms of composition. In *Research on the Literary Usages of Language* (1953), Merleau-Ponty specifies the goal of the course: not to study the professional problems of the writer but rather to understand literary language itself and to attempt, beyond literary theories, to clarify literary meaning and literary expression. The reason we should undertake this, he states, is to develop a philosophy of language and in general a philosophy of symbolism (ULL, 86–87). It is not without accident that Valéry clarifies the meaning of "poetics" in similar terms: "The name of *Poetics* seems appropriate to such a study if we take the word in its etymological sense, that is, a name for everything that bears on the creation or composition of works having language at once as their substance and as their instrument—and not in the restricted sense of a collection of aesthetic rules or precepts relating to poetry" (CW, 13:86/O, 1:1441). In contrast with rules and precepts, a modern poetics "investigates the expressive and suggestive inventions purporting to increase the power and penetration of the word" (ibid.). This is the first and fundamental point: poetry and all literary language is an "art of language." Should this seem a redundancy, it is at the origin and of the essence of what both Merleau-Ponty and Valéry mean by poetics, a theory of language. "An equally simple reflection," Valéry states, "leads us to believe that literature is and can be nothing else than a kind of extension and application of certain properties of language" (CW, 13:85/O, 1:1440).

In his course of 1953, Merleau-Ponty cites Valéry's "Opening Lecture of his Course in *Poetics*" at the Collège de France many times, and he cites in particular Valéry's reference to language itself as "the masterpiece of literary masterpieces": "a poet who makes repeated use of figurative speech is only rediscovering, within himself, the *nascent state* of language. Indeed, if we look at things at a sufficient remove, may we not consider language itself as the masterpiece of literary masterpieces?" (ULL, 129; CW, 13:86/O,

1:1440–41). The figures of poetic language are repetitions of nascent language, birth, and inspiration, and these are matters we do not fully understand. Merleau-Ponty emphasizes this point from Valéry's opening course: "A poem is a discourse that demands and induces a continuous connection between the '*voice that is* and the *voice that is coming* and *must come*': without us knowing exactly why" (ULL, 131; CW, 13:100/O, 1:1349). The poet and the philosopher share "the voice of no one, the very voice of the things, the waves, and the forest," as Merleau-Ponty incorporated the lines from Valéry's "La Pythie" ("The Pythoness") at the end of *The Visible and the Invisible* (VI, 204/155). In this sense, poetics involves itself with a mystery and even "indefinability" of a poetic language that is unhampered by practical use. The poets work with problems they "have to solve blindfold— but solve them they do (that is the essential), from time to time" (ULL, 126; CW, 13:108–9/O, 1:1356–57).

Nested in these Valéryan statements Merleau-Ponty introduced into his lectures are the central philosophical paradoxes about the nature of literary expression his poetics will study. He names four: the paradox of the true and the imaginary, of speech and silence, of the subjective (the most secret) and the objective, and of the relation of the author and the person who lives. These paradoxes are the "surprises," the "traps," that make literature appear as a problem to itself and cause the writer himself or herself to ask: "what is literature?" (ULL, 62). These paradoxes comprise the substance of a Merleau-Pontian philosophical investigation of literary language, and since the question "what is literature?" was that of Sartre prior to Merleau-Ponty's investigations, his poetics will also outline his responses to Sartre's philosophy and politics of "engaged literature" that preferred prose to poetry.

For a second and fundamental point, the meanings of "poetics" in Merleau-Ponty's studies of literary language also radically shift the meaning of the metaphor from a limited linguistic or semantic origin to an ontological one.[3] By the time of Merleau-Ponty's courses of 1959 to 1961, especially *Cartesian Ontology and Ontology Today*, in which we find commentary on Proust, Claudel, and Claude Simon, the philosopher grants to literature what may have been only implicit in the course of 1953—namely, he grants to literature an ontological meaning. It is doubtful, for example, if the later Merleau-Ponty would have spoken of the "usages" of literary language, implying a separation or gap between the writer and language, for in the introduction to *Signs* he spoke differently of language as the "element" in which we live. "To make of language a means or a code for thought is to break it. . . . It would not be our element as water is the element of fishes. . . . Things *are said* and *are thought* by a Speech and by a Thought which we do not have but which has us" (S, 24–27/17–19). Thus, the metaphor and other figures shared between philosophy and literature open a way for Merleau-Ponty's late ontology of Flesh, of its dimensions, lateral kinships, its tensions and differences. The etymology of the term *metaphor* itself,[4] referring to transfer or transport between things, bestows upon literary language its sense of movement, motion, and rhythm and thus gives it life and power. Metaphor thus opens the question of the space of literature and the kind and quality of this space, as well as its time and space-time, as must be the case since the truth of literature is the truth of a world and of the soul (*psyche*) of that world.[5] Perhaps it is Mallarmé who has made this most explicit in his "Un coup de dés" ("A Throw of the Dice"), with its enormous blank spaces in how the words are arranged on the pages, interspersed irregularly with words of different typeface and type size. Of this work, Valéry wrote: "He [Mallarmé] introduced a *spatial* reading, which he combined with the *linear* reading; it was equivalent to enriching the literary domain with a second dimension" (CW, 8:312/O, 1:627). He also wrote, echoing the language of Kant: "He tried . . . to raise a page to the power of the starry sky."[6]

In the course of 1953, immediately following Merleau-Ponty's recitation of "The Pythoness" with its emphasis upon the anonymity of voice, Merleau-Ponty recited the second stanza of Valéry's poem "Palm," the last poem of *Charmes*:

> For as much as it may bend
> Under its treasured abundance,
> Its form is fulfilled,
> Its heavy fruits are its bond.
> Wonder at how it sways,
> And how a gradual sinew
> Dividing a moment of time
> Unpretendingly apportions
> The attraction of the ground
> And the weight of the firmament![7]

In the commentary that follows, what interests Merleau-Ponty is the brevity and restraint of the poem within which the short lines and flowing rhythm create movement and "vibration" in space and time. The tree "bends" and "sways" in gestures that mirror the human body. The poem moves back and forth between the defining elements of the tree, its canopy and firmament above and the ground and roots below, creating an image of cosmic alternation "dividing a moment of time." In this context, Merleau-Ponty italicizes a definition of poetry: *"Poetry = the metamorphosis of one thing into another such that they have the same manner of modulating Being."*[8] He adds "poetry sees all things as never yet seen" (ULL, 141).

Thus, and above all, what is at stake with the meaning of poetics in the thought of Merleau-Ponty is a total and radical shift to an ontological significance of metaphor and figurative discourse, to a literary space-time of "metaphoricity." This ontological metaphoricity has a threefold sense articulated in this book by Saint Aubert's Chapter 5: anthropological, phenomenological, and epistemological. The ultimate ontological sense of metaphoricity expresses the movement and exchanges within Being itself among the visible and the invisible, not as separate realities but as an invisible that is the lining and depth of the visible. Depth is one of those figuratives that makes possible vision itself. This is the full and vast range of phenomenological, incarnate metaphoricity.

A feature of Valéry's poetic is his predilection for precision that led him to distrust philosophical words like space and time, nature and life, even though he could not do without them. He sought a poverty and spareness of poetic vocabulary quite different from the more ebullient poetic philosophy of Merleau-Ponty's late writings, though Merleau-Ponty admired it. In an address to the French Academy that included the President of the French Republic on the occasion of the third centenary of the publication of Descartes's *Discourse on Method*, Valéry spoke of the "extreme difficulty" of philosophy and its necessary alliance with the poets:

> What are we to make of terms that cannot be precisely defined unless we re-create them? *Thought, mind* itself, *reason, intelligence, understanding, intuition,* or *inspiration*? . . . You are aware at this point the philosopher becomes a poet, and often a great poet: he borrows metaphor from us and, by means of splendid images which we might well envy, he draws on all nature for the expression of his profoundest thought. (CW, 9:19/O, 1:797)

Part I: Merleau-Ponty's Poets

In this book, we have followed Merleau-Ponty's own studies of literary figures and literary texts with only minor exceptions; thus we emphasize the phrase, "Merleau-Ponty's Poets," which means the book's primary focus is on the literary authors whose works most explicitly and significantly influenced Merleau-Ponty's philosophy. Although his literary selections reflect judgments of value in much the same way that both gold and the *Iliad* are valued based on properties such as rarity and inimitability,[9] they already present a range of literary and philosophical study exceedingly large and demanding in scope.[10] We also have featured Merleau-Ponty's literary writers of modernity or modernism, which means beginning with the advent of the twentieth century.[11] Chapter 4, by Mauro Carbone, discusses two differing periodizations of the "modern" given by Merleau-Ponty, one of which does reach back into the nineteenth-century Romantic period. In *Causeries (The World of Perception)*, Merleau-Ponty drew the opposition that was important to his use of the term, namely, between the classical world of rationalism initiated by Descartes and sustained in philosophy through much of the seventeenth and eighteenth centuries as opposed to what he names the "modern world," apologizing for the vagueness of the term. "Modern thought displays the dual characteristics of being unfinished and ambiguous" (Caus, 63–64/106). Thus, the "modern" designates for Merleau-Ponty not so much a precise historical period but one of the ways in which Being, space, and depth appear within philosophy, science, and art as ambiguous and unfinished, or, as he says in "The Philosopher and His Shadow," as an "untamed" and "wild-flowering world and mind . . . upright, insistent, flaying our glance with their edges" (S, 228/181).

No doubt one of the most influential literary figures across Merleau-Ponty's philosophical career was Marcel Proust. In *The Visible and the Invisible* Merleau-Ponty famously wrote, "No one has gone further than Proust in fixing the relations between the visible and the invisible" (VI, 195/149). Thus, we begin from a study of Merleau-Ponty and Proust offered by Carbone, and to gain a fresh and original access to Merleau-Ponty's interpretation of Proust, it is helpful to place his views alongside those of another of Proust's great interpreters, Walter Benjamin. Such an optic has previously been omitted in Merleau-Ponty scholarship, and despite the absence of explicit references to Benjamin in the writings of Merleau-Ponty, certain intersections between the theoretical interests of the two thinkers are clear. For one thing, this comparative optic shows the originating importance of Husserl for Merleau-Ponty and Benjamin. Even though they make reference to very distant periods of Husserlian thought, they have in common at least a distrust with regard to experience understood as *Erlebnis*. Second, they each also give attention to the theme of essence and ideas, which, concerning artistic and literary works, are considered by the two thinkers as immanent within the works themselves. This suggests one of the most important contributions of Proust to Merleau-Ponty's aesthetic philosophy and overall ontology, namely, the concept of "sensible ideas." Third, both Merleau-Ponty and Benjamin demonstrate their common interest in the themes of perception and memory, sometimes focusing even on the very same pages of *À la recherche du temps perdu* (*In Search of Lost Time*) to deepen and exemplify, through the character of Marcel, the concept of "involuntary memory."

Merleau-Ponty's reading of André Breton, Paul Claudel, and Claude Simon allows Emmanuel de Saint Aubert to shed some light on the relations between Being and Flesh in his philosophy, as well as on how these relations promise a genuine poetic art. The poetic of Merleau-Ponty is, inseparably, a poetic of the *flesh* (poetic of the body and desire), a poetic of *mystery* (which is not primarily what is hidden, but what expresses itself inexhaustibly), and a poetic of the *visible* in its relation to the invisible. These three dimensions touch respectively on the overdetermination Merleau-Ponty gives to the questions of *desire*, *expression*, and *perception*— and they are deployed in their corresponding horizons, the first more anthropological, the next more epistemological, and the last more ontological. The bold and broad inspiration that Merleau-Ponty finds in the conception of "the flesh of the world" taken from Claude Simon and in the conception of "*co-naissance*," meaning simultaneously both birth and knowledge drawn from Paul Claudel, is a particularly rich leading thread in the exploration of this poetic, which plunges us in the heart of the unfinished work site of the philosopher's last manuscripts, published and unpublished. Equally important to this poetic of the flesh is the literature of surrealism, especially André Breton's conception and figuration of the "sublime point."

My own offering to the study of Merleau-Ponty's poets makes explicit the influence of Valéry, whose poem "La Pythie" ("The Pythoness") is cited without attribution in the penultimate sentence of *The Visible and the Invisible*, thereby according a certain authority to his writing.[12] Merleau-Ponty discussed the work and life of Paul Valéry (1871–1945) for the entire first half of the first course of 1953, *Recherches sur l'usage littéraire du langage*. After early poetic successes, Valéry experienced a deep personal crisis that led him to impose a silence upon himself that lasted for a period of twenty-five years, from 1892 until 1917, after which he emerged reborn as a writer. Merleau-Ponty recognizes the power of silence to nourish both poetic and philosophical language and he situated philosophical interrogation in relation to three orders or dimensions: first, the world of silence; second, the universe of speech; and third, the world of thought, especially philosophical thought. He argues that these are not parallel orders among which we would search for point by point coincidence, but rather they are three dimensions of the same Being in which there is an "exchange" or "chiasma" (NC, 377) made possible by their overlapping horizons: "the horizon of the visible, the horizon of the nameable, and the horizon of the thinkable" (NC, 378). The notions of the "chiasma of two destinies" and the "implex of words" derive directly from Valéry, who leads on to Mallarmé and Baudelaire together with Edgar Allan Poe, as well as to Francis Ponge, who captured this overlapping exchange among the dimensions of Being in *Taking the Side of Things* (*Le parti pris des choses*):

> Poetry as such does not interest me, in the sense that raw analogical magma is called poetry today. Analogies are interesting, but less so than differences. What is important is to grasp, through analogies, the differential quality. When I say that the inside of a walnut is similar to a praline, that is interesting. But even more interesting is their difference. To make one feel analogies, that is something. To name the differential quality of the walnut, that is purpose, that is progress.[13]

Part II: Merleau-Ponty's Poetics

As consideration of the relationships among Merleau-Ponty's thought and the writers and poets necessarily begins from Proust, so reflections on the poetic and philosophic ideas that are at stake also begin from Carbone's study of Merleau-Ponty's readings of *À la recherche du temps perdu*. He offers us for the first time in the history of Proust scholarship an analysis of the three different readings by Merleau-Ponty of one of the main passages of Proust's first volume, the scene in which Swann happens to listen to the "little phrase" from Vinteuil's *Sonata*.[14] In each of these readings, Merleau-Ponty's attention and focus shift in significant ways, together gathering the main elements of what Carbone proposes to interpret as the *visual apparatus* Merleau-Ponty finds at work in Proust's pages in order to "make us see by words"—rather than intellectually possessing—our relationship to ourselves, to others, to things, and to the world.

Before we turn to these varied readings of Proust explicitly, the context that extends from *Sense and Non-Sense* through *The Visible and the Invisible* should be noted as it pertains to the relation of words and seeing. In what Merleau-Ponty designates as the *modern* era (about which Carbone also points out the different periodizations that Merleau-Ponty proposes), he states that "the tasks of literature and philosophy can no longer be separated" (SNS, 36/28) precisely because "philosophical expression assumes the same ambiguities as literary expression, if the world is such that it cannot be expressed except in 'stories' and, as it were, *pointed out*" (SNS, 36–37/28), that is to say, literally *made seen*. This theme continues in what Merleau-Ponty has to say about cinema in the essay "Film and the New Psychology," also found in *Sense and Non-Sense*, and it appears again in *The Visible and the Invisible*, in the passage in which Merleau-Ponty evokes the inadequacy of philosophy's traditional conceptual characterization and adds: "it makes us see by words. Like all literature" (VI, 313/266).[15] Using an expression that originated in film studies, both philosophy and literature are interpreted as convergent *apparatuses* (*dispositifs*) of vision, understood as *bodily* and not merely *ocular* practices.

Merleau-Ponty's readings of Proust produce the notion of the "sensible ideas" appearing on what Proust qualifies as "a clouded surface," namely, a surface that, despite its opaqueness and even for this very feature, *allows us to see on or through itself.* Therefore, such a surface is no longer supposed to be removed or even pierced in order to make our vision possible, contrary to what the tradition of Western metaphysics supposed. Typically, Merleau-Ponty evokes the "watermark [*filigrane*]" in order to signify that "it is essential . . . to truth never to be possessed, but only transparent through the clouded [*brouillée*] logic of a system of expression" (PM, 52–53/37). The complexities the sensible ideas and clouded surfaces introduce lead to considerations of the veil and the screen as components of different visual apparatuses implying different relationships between hiding and showing, seeing beyond or not seeing beyond.

Likewise, we find manifest and multiple ties between Merleau-Ponty's philosophy and the question of metaphor. Saint Aubert's study of these linkages invites an examination of the philosopher's original manner or style of writing, especially in the late texts. It also leads to a reading of what Merleau-Ponty says explicitly about metaphor. Finally, and especially, it promises an evaluation of what his philosophy brings to us for a renewed understanding of metaphoricity. Particularly, we need to understand its natural inscription and its expressive power, its anthropological foundations and its ontological horizons: why metaphor is typical of our carnal being-in-the-world, as well as what it says to us about being human, about the world, and even about Being. Metaphor is not a preexistent linguistic meaning that becomes incarnate, that dons a sensible garb; the body itself generates and orchestrates metaphoricity through its own fundamental analogicity. In the framework of this philosophy of the flesh, then, we might speak of the metaphorical power of the body, of the metaphoricity of the body, yet above all, of the metaphoricity of Being in its transferences, exchanges, kinships, displacements, and differentiations.[16]

Merleau-Ponty's writing style evolves along with his conception of the flesh through the gradual relinquishment of classical concepts in favor of the descriptive power of certain "figures."[17] Aware of the semantic density of familiar words in his native tongue, Merleau-Ponty sets out to choose nonsubstitutable, new terms, without borrowing them directly or exclusively from any philosophical vocabulary, avoiding as well neologisms or concatenated terms. As is the case with original terms such as "flesh," "encroachment," "promiscuity," and many others, they are never severed from their moral, political, or spiritual meanings or from their psychological, erotic, or literary dimensions.[18]

My own chapter studying Merleau-Ponty's poetics takes up the topic of the "origin of truth," one toward which Merleau-Ponty frequently directed himself but never explicitly fulfilled, leaving us threads without an entire fabric. Two of the working titles he had considered for his posthumously published last work, *The Visible and the Invisible*, were *Genealogy of the True* and *The Origin of Truth*. As well as offering us a genealogical critique of any reduction of truth to a single absolute origin, his philosophy also strongly contests against giving in to notions of skepticism, Pyrrhonism, deception, and illusion. He contests equally against notions of "eternal truth" based upon a forgetting of the "retrograde movement of truth," which means remembering that things and events happen at certain moments in time, that what is real is movement and duration. There were two moments of Merleau-Ponty's thought and work when the questions of truth were at the forefront of his attention, the time of *The Prose of the World* with the related course at the Collège de France, *Research on the Literary Usage of Language*, and the time of his work on *The Visible and the Invisible* with the related essays in *Signs* and *Eye and Mind*. The focus of the first moment concerns clarifying the "mystery of language" in both literary and mathematical expression while the second moment introduces us to a new idea of truth and new vocabulary of truth centering on Merleau-Ponty's introduction and increasing use of the term *éclatement* (breaking forth, burst, spark, sparkle, shining). In a Working Note about literary "pregnancy (*prégnance*)," Merleau-Ponty spoke of a "power to break forth, productivity, fecundity [*pouvoir d'éclatement, productivité (praegnans futuri), fécondité*]" (September 1959; VI, 262/208). Merleau-Ponty paired this literary "pregnancy"[19] with the new ontological term, the "dehiscence" of Being. If Being is a becoming, truth is also event and happening, the movement of thought and life. Like Heidegger, Merleau-Ponty is not interested in tests for the mere truth of statements as secondary language, rather in originary speech and writing, both philosophical and literary, that expresses a more "militant truth," marked by its nobility, mobility, subtlety, suppleness, depth, and richness.

We can do no better in concluding the introduction to this study than to cite the philosopher's own reflections on literature, literary language, and philosophy. Reflecting upon the proper approach to ultimate things, in Chapter 2 of *The Visible and the Invisible*, titled "Interrogation and Dialectic," he wrote that "the effective, present, ultimate, and primary being, the thing itself":

offer themselves therefore only to someone who wishes not to have them but to see them, not to hold them as with forceps, or to immobilize them as under the objective of a microscope, but to let them be and to witness their continued being—to someone who therefore limits himself to giving them the hollow, the free space they ask for in return, the resonance they require, who follows their own movement . . . from which it obtains not an *answer*, but a confirmation of its astonishment. (VI, 138/101–2)

Reflecting upon the linguistic "paradox of philosophy" caught between muteness and the demand for an "eloquent language" in the same chapter of *The Visible and the Invisible*, he wrote, "the philosopher knows very well that, whatever be his effort, in the best of cases it will take its place among the *artefacts* and products of culture, as an instance of them." The passage continues:

If this paradox is not an impossibility, and if philosophy can speak, it is because language is not only the depository of fixed and acquired significations, because its cumulative power itself results from a power of anticipation or of prepossession. . . . From this it follows that the words most charged with philosophy are not necessarily those that contain what they say, but rather those that most energetically open upon Being, because they more closely convey the life of the whole and make our habitual evidences vibrate until they disjoin. Hence it is a question whether philosophy as reconquest of brute or wild being can be accomplished by the resources of the eloquent language, or whether it would be necessary for philosophy to use language in a way that takes from it its power of immediate or direct signification in order to equal it with what it wishes all the same to say. (VI, 139/102–3)

This text opposes the secondary deposited, "fixed and acquired significations" over against originary language that Merleau-Ponty had first articulated in *Phenomenology of Perception* and again in *The Prose of the World*. He contends it is "the error of the semantic [analytic] philosophies to close up language as if it spoke only of itself," thereby rendering the philosophy of language "only a regional problem" pertaining to "the ready-made language, the secondary and empirical operation of translation, of coding and decoding, the artificial languages, the technical relation between a sound and a meaning which are joined only by express convention and are therefore ideally isolable" (VI, 167–68/126). Yet, "it is by considering language that we would best see how we are to and how we are not to return to the things themselves" (VI, 166/125). Originary, genuinely creative poetic and philosophic language seeks

> a manner of making the things themselves speak ... a language of which he would not be the organizer, words he would not assemble, that would combine in him by virtue of a natural intertwining of their meaning, through the occult trading of the metaphor—where what counts is no longer the manifest meaning of each word and of each image, but the lateral relations, the kinships that are implicated in their transfers and their exchanges. (VI, 167/125–27)

The "occult trading of the metaphor" is resonant of Merleau-Ponty's reference to "the oneiric world of analogy" (OE, 41/132) in *Eye and Mind*, which, he argued, the Cartesian philosophy had abandoned in favor of univocal meanings, thereby banning from philosophy shadow, dream, latency, and depth. In contrast, "We need only take language too in the living or nascent state ... with its movement, its subtleties, its reversals, its life, which expresses and multiplies tenfold the life of the bare things. Language is a life, is our life and the life of the things" (VI, 167/125).

Finally, in reflection upon Husserl's reconfiguration of the meaning of reason, the crisis of European sciences, and the limits of phenomenology, Merleau-Ponty noted the meaning he accorded philosophy: "Philosophy seeks in the archeology of the ground, in the depth and not in the height (the ideas).... philosophy as poetry" (HLP, 81/67).

We recall again the Working Note titled "Philosophy and Literature" cited at the beginning of this introduction:

> Philosophy, precisely as 'Being speaking within us,' expression of the mute experience by itself, is creation. ... art and philosophy *together* are precisely not arbitrary fabrications in the universe of the "spiritual" ("of culture"), but contact with Being precisely as creations. Being is *what requires creation of us* for us to experience it.
>
> Make an analysis of literature in this sense: as *inscription* of Being (VI, 251/197).

Inscription, that is to say, writing from the place of the "in," "within," "inside" is equally "exscription"[20] as philosophy reads and responds to its "outside," philosophy with and as non-philosophy, philosophy with and as poetry. Responding to this demand for the inscription and exscription of Being is precisely what *Merleau-Ponty's Poetic of the World* undertakes.

PART I

Merleau-Ponty's Poets

"The Proustian Corporeity" and "The True Hawthorns"
Merleau-Ponty as a Reader of Proust between Husserl and Benjamin

MAURO CARBONE

> It is there that I have lived in calm voluptuousness,
> In the center of the blue, amidst the waves and splendors.
> —**Charles Baudelaire**, *Previous Existence*

The work of a great novelist always rests on two or three philosophical ideas. For . . . Proust, [these are] the way the past is involved in the present and the presence of times gone by. The function of the novelist is not to state these ideas thematically but to make them exist for us in the way that things exist. . . . It is nonetheless surprising that, when writers do take a deliberate interest in philosophy, they have such difficulty in recognizing their affinities. . . . Proust sometimes translates his intuition about time into a relativistic and skeptical philosophy and at other times into hopes of immortality which distort it just as much. . . . For a long time it looked as if philosophy and literature not only had different ways of saying things but had different objects as well. Since the end of the 19th century, however, the ties between them have been getting closer and closer. (SNS, 34–35/26–27)

This is how, at the beginning of his 1945 article "Metaphysics and the Novel," Merleau-Ponty formulates some fundamental ideas, which I find particularly important. In Chapter 4, I will focus on this article with respect to Merleau-Ponty's coeval and successive writings on related topics, like the supposed mutations of the relationship between "philosophy and literature . . . since the end of the 19th century" (SNS, 35/27). I will also take into account Merleau-Ponty's evolving reflection on Proust's peculiar description from *In Search of Lost Time* of how some *actual* ideas "exist for us in the way that things exist," to use a meaningful expression from the aforementioned quotation. In the present chapter, I will focus my attention on what Merleau-Ponty indicates as one of the core "philosophical ideas" of Proust's oeuvre, namely, "the envelopment of the past in the present and the presence of lost time" (SNS, 34/26).

"The Function of the Body in Memory"

In *Phenomenology of Perception*—namely Merleau-Ponty's most important achieved book, published in the same year of "Metaphysics and the Novel"—such a "philosophical idea" seems to be mainly traced in what he calls "the function of the body in memory" (PhP, 211/187). In fact, it is precisely about this topic that Merleau-Ponty quotes the largest Proustian passage included in his book:

> when I awoke like this, and my mind struggled in an unsuccessful attempt to discover where I was, everything revolved around me through the darkness: things, places, years. My body, still too heavy with sleep to move, would endeavor to construe from the pattern of its tiredness the position of its various limbs, in order to deduce therefrom the direction of the wall, the location of the furniture, to piece together and give a name to the house in which it lay. Its memory, the composite memory of its ribs, its knees, its shoulder-blades, offered it a series of rooms in which it had at one time or another slept, while the unseen walls, shifting and adapting themselves to the shape of each successive room that it remembered, whirled round it in the dark. . . . My body, the side upon which I was lying, faithful guardians of a past which my mind should never have forgotten, brought back before my eyes the glimmering flame of the night-light in its urn-shaped bowl of Bohemian glass that hung by chains from the ceiling, and the chimney-piece of Siena marble in my bedroom at Combray, in my grandparents' house, in those far distant days which at this moment I imagined to be in the present without being able to picture them exactly. (PhP, 211n1/530n11)[1]

According to Merleau-Ponty, the experience described in this Proustian page reveals that "memory is not the constituting consciousness of the past, but rather an effort to reopen time beginning from the implications of the present," and that "the body, being our permanent means of 'adopting attitudes' and hence of creating pseudo-presents, is the means of our communication with both time and space" (PhP, 211/187). This happens also when our experience is "unreflected," like the one Proust describes. Indeed, in this case too, our body lives in an uninterrupted relation with a spatiotemporal totality. Edmund Husserl defined this kind of relation as *intentionality*, which he considered to be *unbreakable*. This is what one should keep in mind when reading his famous claim according to which "consciousness is always consciousness of something." In other words, for Husserl, *intentionality* qualifies the very essence of consciousness (understood in its insuppressible link with our body) and characterizes it in terms of relationship.

As showed by the Proustian description, such a relation is first of all outlined in the encounter by which the sensible world gives itself to our living body (*Leib*). Concerning such an encounter, in the preface to *Phenomenology of Perception*, Merleau-Ponty highlights that

> Husserl distinguishes between act intentionality—which is the intentionality of our judgments and of our voluntary decisions ... —and operative intentionality (*fungierende Intentionalität*), the intentionality that establishes the natural and pre-predicative unity of the world and of our life, the intentionality that appears in our desires, our evaluations, and our landscape more clearly than it does in objective knowledge. (PhP, XIII/xxxii)

This second intentional mode is the one at work in our unreflected life, that is to say, precisely operating in the originating and always renewed relation between our living body and the sensible world. Indeed, "operative" intentionality is defined by Husserl as "life experiencing the world [*welterfahrendes Leben*]"[2] through a relation that is "operating" without being thematized by any act of consciousness. In paragraph 28 of *The Crisis of European Sciences and Transcendental Phenomenology*, Husserl characterizes the "operative" as "a residuum that remains unthematic—remains, so to speak anonymous."[3] In other words, he characterizes the "operative" as that peculiar relation with things that has not been *thematized* as an explicit thought, and hence maintains its feature of "passive synthesis," since the synthesis of the sensible in virtue of which such a relation is given has not been posited by an act of consciousness, but works as a "passive having of the world [*Welthabe*]."[4]

Since *Phenomenology of Perception*, this operative intentionality is at the core of Merleau-Ponty's philosophical enquiry and constitutes one of the main reasons for his interest in the *Recherche*. In fact, Merleau-Ponty traces the description of operative intentionality, which is at work in the unreflected mutual exchange between our body and the sensible world, in pages such as the aforementioned. Therefore, he explicitly refers to it in order to highlight how the living body, as we already read, is precisely "the means of our communication with both time and space."

In this light, Merleau-Ponty's remarks, like Proust's, reveal a tendency to accentuate the corporeal tonality of temporal experience with respect to Husserl's phenomenology of the constitutive ego and the related notion of *Erlebnis*,[5] as well as with respect to the conception of memory that sprang from Husserl's own theories. Indeed, in a Proustian way, Merleau-Ponty writes that protensions and retentions "do not emanate from a central I, but somehow from my perceptual field itself" (PhP, 476/439). Still, at this stage of Merleau-Ponty's meditation, the difference between Proust's, Husserl's, and his own perspective is not yet clear to him. This is the reason why, in *Phenomenology of Perception,* he tends to assimilate the reminiscences produced by the involuntary memory to the notion of *retention* elaborated by Husserl, as he writes in the chapter titled "Temporality":

> When I uncover the concrete origin of the memory, this is because it again takes its place in a certain current of worry and hope that runs from Munich to the war, because I rejoin *lost time*, because, from the moment at issue right up until my present, the chain of retentions and the interlinking of successive horizons assures a continuous passage. (PhP, 478/441; my emphasis)[6]

Merleau-Ponty draws attention to the aforementioned corporeal tonality of our temporal experience by quoting precisely the Proustian description of the half-sleep to which another philosopher, Walter Benjamin, also made reference for similar reasons.

"No explicit trace" of Benjamin's work is present "in the whole body" of Merleau-Ponty's own texts, "unpublished writings included."[7] Moreover, Benjamin's somehow suspicious attitude concerning notions such as that of *intention*[8] has contributed in qualifying his thinking as resolutely antiphenomenological. Nevertheless, in a footnote to his essay titled "On Some Motifs in Baudelaire," Benjamin points out how the most famous Proustian discovery, that of involuntary memory, roots such memory in our corporeity. He recalls that Proust

> recurs with a particular predilection to the body parts, and does not cease to evoke the images of memory that are thereby gathered, show-

ing how, without obeying to any sign of whatever consciousness, such images immediately impose themselves on consciousness itself, as soon as a sleeper's thigh, arm, or scapula involuntarily regains the position it had before. The involuntary memory of body parts is one of Proust's favorite topics.[9]

Differently from Merleau-Ponty, who traces in Proust's excerpt the phenomenological configuration of the *Leib*, Benjamin interprets the same passage as a characterization of involuntary memory that does not seem to refer to a unitary experience of the body, such as the one that phenomenology traditionally tends to take into account; instead, the involuntary memory is autonomously fragmented in the different parts of the body in which it has been sedimenting: "its ribs, its knees, its shoulder-blades."[10] Still, it is important to remark that both Merleau-Ponty and Benjamin highlight the corporeal feature of involuntary memory as it is described in the Proustian passage; hence, they both propose the *autonomy* of such memory from the activity of consciousness.

Hence, on the one hand, in *Phenomenology of Perception* Merleau-Ponty tends to find that the Proustian descriptions do not have divergent characteristics with respect to the teachings of Husserl's phenomenology. Indeed, he mainly tends to interpret such teachings precisely according to those characteristics, as we saw both in the case of the corporeal tonality of temporal experience, and in the case of the unitary configuration of the corporeal experience. And anyway, Merleau-Ponty sees no contradiction between them, as it happens with the phenomenological conception of temporal continuity with respect to the famous and celebrated "intermittences" of the Proustian time.[11]

On the other hand, in prolonging the comparison between Merleau-Ponty and Benjamin as readers of Proust, it is important to highlight that Merleau-Ponty's interpretation of intentionality, which I summarized earlier, has nothing to do with the critical reasons that, in *The Origin of German Tragic Drama,* had urged Benjamin to define truth as "an *intentionless* state of being, made up of ideas. The proper approach to it is not therefore one of intention and knowledge, but rather a total immersion and absorption in it. Truth is the death of intention."[12] Or, we could add, at least the *sleep* of "act intentionality." In this sense, both Merleau-Ponty and Benjamin were trying to find and describe an approach to the being of truth and to Being itself not centered on consciousness. This is why they were both so deeply interested in the experience evoked in the aforementioned Proustian passage, which recurs in many other passages from the *Recherche*: namely, the experience of "loss of consciousness."[13]

In the Merleau-Pontian interpretation of that excerpt, the experience of corporeity is not *desubjectified* by its fragmentation, in the sense suggested by Benjamin's attention to "the involuntary memory of body parts." According to Merleau-Ponty, the experience of corporeity is rather *desubjectifying* precisely by remaining unitary, since it allows the body itself to be assigned to features that used to be assigned to the subject. The subject eventually recognizes in the body skills that it considered to be its own, and thus discovers the *improper* side of that very *Leib*, which, for far too long, has been translated as "body proper."[14] This is why the reference to "the Proustian corporeity as guardian of the past" (VI, 297/243) inspired by the preceding passage will incessantly return in Merleau-Ponty's reflection.[15]

The weakening of subjectivity due to the attention cast on corporeity is precisely what, in his 1951 lecture titled "Man and Adversity," Merleau-Ponty considers a fundamental characteristic of certain examples of French literature of the first half of the twentieth century.[16] In this lecture—certainly not by chance—we find an echo of the recurring reference I just evoked. Even before that, Merleau-Ponty highlights the improper feature that belongs to the living body:

> With Proust, with Gide, an unwearying report of the body begins. *It is confirmed, consulted, listened to like a person.* The intermittences of his desire and (as they put it) its fervor are spied on. *With Proust, it becomes the guardian of the past*; and it is the body which, in spite of the deteriorations which render it almost unrecognizable itself, maintains from one time to another a substantial relationship between us and our past in the two inverse cases of death and awakening. Proust describes the meeting-point of mind and body, showing how, in the dispersion of the sleeping body, our gestures at awakening renew a meaning from beyond the grave; and how on the contrary *meaning* is undone in the tics of the death agony. (S, 292/230–31, trans. modified; my emphases)

In *The Visible and the Invisible*, the formulation "the Proustian corporeity as guardian of the past" appears again in a Working Note dated April 1960 and titled "'Indestructible' past, and intentional analytic—and ontology," where Merleau-Ponty develops a meditation further deepened and rectified in the light of ontology. However, in order to refer to this particular reappearance of the formulation, we shall wait for the final part of the following paragraph.

The Experience of Involuntary Memory between Benjamin and Merleau-Ponty

As we read in *Phenomenology of Perception*, the body is for Merleau-Ponty "the means [*le moyen*]," *the medium* of our sensible relationship to the world. Within such a relationship—just as in Marcel's half-sleep—emerges what Merleau-Ponty defines in the concluding lines of the preface as "the sense of the world . . . in its nascent state" (PhP, XVI/xxxv), which elsewhere he calls, by a Husserlian expression, the "logos of the aesthetic world,"[17] to be understood according to the etymological meaning of the word *aesthetics*. In his essay on painting written a year before his death, *Eye and Mind*, Merleau-Ponty characterizes such a logos as a "conceptless universality" (OE, 43/133). This universality is exhibited on the canvas by colors, for example—which Descartes ignored, therefore missing the "oneiric world of analogy" (OE, 41/132), which for Merleau-Ponty is the aesthetic (i.e., sensible) world itself.

Similar to the Merleau-Pontian expression, Walter Benjamin also strictly connects "the world distorted in the state of analogy"[18] to the world of dreams in his 1929 essay on Proust. Indeed, in Benjamin's opinion, the value of truth that Proust attributes to "the world distorted in the state of analogy"[19] finds its ultimate depth in the world of dreams. This is what "Proust's frenetically studying . . . his impassioned cult of analogy"[20] are for:

> The true signs of its hegemony do not become obvious where he suddenly and startlingly uncovers analogies in actions, physiognomies, or speech mannerisms. The similarity of one thing to another which we are used to, which occupies us in a wakeful state, reflects only vaguely the deeper analogy of the dream world in which everything that happens appears not in identical but in similar guise, opaquely similar to itself.[21]

We see how Merleau-Ponty's "world . . . in its nascent state" seems to be just another way to outline what Benjamin characterizes as "the world . . . in the state of analogy." Benjamin explains that such a world is dominated by "correspondences," which "the Romanticists were the first to comprehend . . . and Baudelaire [to] embrace . . . most fervently, but [which] Proust was the only one who managed to reveal . . . in our lived life" by showing "the work of the *mémoire involontaire*."[22]

On this subject, it is important to recall that, in his philosophical essay on Baudelaire, Benjamin connects the Proustian characterization of the voluntary and of the involuntary memory to two different modes of experience, which he calls respectively *Erlebnis* and *Erfahrung*. By the first term, he designates the "explicitly and consciously"²³ *lived experience*—which is how the term *Erlebnis* may be translated. Precisely in virtue of such characteristics, this kind of experience cannot be connected in memory to any "sensible impression," comparable to the ones that the narrator of *Recherche* feels when tasting his tea or the madeleine, which, as we know, are related to the experience of his childhood holidays in Combray. Hence, the souvenir of the voluntary memory will not be characterized by any "auras." In other words, it will not be surrounded by a halo characterizing it as "unique" and "inapproachable."²⁴ Indeed, the kind of experience referred to by the souvenir completely lacks the "cult character,"²⁵ which, in turn, specifically qualifies the other kind of experience, *Erfahrung*. This is why, according to Benjamin, Proust wrote, concerning the voluntary memory, that "the information [*renseignements*] which that kind of memory gives us preserve nothing of the past itself."²⁶

In one of the coeval fragments on Baudelaire, which are gathered in "Central Park," Benjamin summarizes as follows the essential link he sees between voluntary memory and *Erlebnis*: "The souvenir is the complement to 'lived experience.' In it is precipitated the increasing self-estrangement of human beings, whose past is inventoried as dead effects."²⁷

On the other hand, for Benjamin, an "aura" accompanies the reminiscences that belong to *Erfahrung*, and presents them as "the unique manifestation of a distance."²⁸ He borrows his definition of "aura" in "On Some Motifs in Baudelaire" from the writing he had devoted to "The Work of Art in the Age of Its Technological Reproducibility."²⁹ He explains that this kind of experience "is less the product of facts firmly anchored in memory than of a convergence in memory of accumulated and frequently unconscious data."³⁰ Hence, we may state that such a kind of auratic experience forms itself in the *indistinction of activity and passivity*.

Thus, both Merleau-Ponty's "world . . . in its nascent state" and Benjamin's "world . . . in the state of analogy" imply a critique of the idea of *Erlebnis*, since each of them refers to what Benjamin described as "what has not been experienced explicitly and consciously"³¹ and what hence Merleau-Ponty would consider to be imbued with an operative intentionality.³² Therefore, although forgetfulness appears as *the contrary* of what Proust calls "voluntary memory"³³—that is, as a passivity *opposing* a resistance to our activity of remembering—Benjamin's 1929 essay on Proust describes *involuntary memory and forgetfulness as working together* in order to produce overnight "the tapestry of lived life" that the voluntary memory undoes during the day.³⁴

Similarly, Merleau-Ponty returns to the question of memory in his course delivered at the Collège de France in 1954–55, the title of which evokes this very problem. His course notes include once more, yet in a broader transcription, the Proustian passage he had already quoted in *Phenomenology of Perception*, as well as other passages concerning the same subject.[35] By referring once more to that passage, Merleau-Ponty focuses on what he defines in *Phenomenology of Perception* as "the function of the body in memory." Even in the course notes, he insists that "the body [is] an apparatus not only for perceiving space, but also time" (IP, 255/196); in fact, both space and time are literally *incorporated* in *the body's own* memory, as Proust makes clear by evoking the figure of "embodied time,"[36] which Merleau-Ponty mentions precisely in these course notes.[37] With respect to *Phenomenology of Perception*, in his course notes Merleau-Ponty looks deeper into the "function of the body in memory," and concentrates on the role that its "postures" (IP, 255/196) when asleep—and not its fragmentation, as it happened in Benjamin—play in that function, allowing us to get our bearings in time and space as we get closer to the world of awakeness. Moreover, differently from what we saw in *Phenomenology of Perception*, and similarly to what we read in Benjamin's essay on Proust, Merleau-Ponty's reflection on the involuntary memory—characterized as a "memory of the body" (IP, 273/211) and capable of evoking our past more than our mind can—is now focused on the decisive role that *forgetfulness* plays in it. Indeed, Merleau-Ponty points out that "it is forgetfulness that preserves, not absolute forgetting, as if the past had never been lived, but . . . the forgetfulness which is disclosed as forgetfulness and thereby even as secret memory" (IP, 256/197).

In the summary to this course, by implicitly referring to such a conception of forgetfulness, which he finds in Proust's texts as well as in the writings by Freud he evokes in the course, Merleau-Ponty remarks that if one conceives—as he suggests—the field of presence according to the figure-ground model,

> then *memory [mémoire] would not be the opposite of forgetfulness*, and it might be seen that true memory [*mémoire*] has to be found at the intersection of the two, at the moment where memory [*souvenir*] [is] forgotten and kept by forgetfulness returns. It might then be clear that forgetfulness and explicit memory [*souvenir*] are two modes of our oblique relation with a past that is present to us only through the determined void that it leaves in us. (RC, 72/119, trans. modified; my emphasis)

Important and evident traces of these reflections will have their ontological maturation in the later phase of Merleau-Ponty's production. In a Working Note of *The Visible and the Invisible* dated May 20, 1959,[38] he distances himself from the Husserlian conception of retention to which he had adhered in *Phenomenology of Perception*. If in that work, he had defended the characterization of temporality meant as continuity, here that very characterization becomes problematic for him. Actually, Merleau-Ponty thinks that the Husserlian retention cannot account for the discontinuity that characterizes the phenomenon of forgetfulness, which in turn contributes to radicalize the dispossession of subjectivity. Rather than "Husserl's diagram" (VI, 248/195), Merleau-Ponty instead prefers the Gestaltic figure-ground model, which seems to place itself *on this side* of the opposition between continuity and discontinuity, thus outlining forgetfulness as the reverse of memory.

More generally, in the last phase of his thought, Merleau-Ponty's conception of temporality is thematized and developed on motifs of reflection provided once again by Proust's *Recherche*, leading him to criticize Husserl's idea of time as well as the ontology that subtends it. Indeed, in the very important Working Note of *The Visible and the Invisible* dated April 1960, to which I referred at the end of the previous section of this chapter, Merleau-Ponty invokes the "Proustian corporeity as guardian of the past" (VI, 297/243) against what he calls "the common idea of time as a 'series of *Erlebnisse*'" in that same passage (VI, 296/243). According to Merleau-Ponty, this idea "blocks" the Husserlian analysis of temporality.[39] By alluding to the same inspiration for Benjamin's essay "On Some Motifs in Baudelaire," on the one hand, Merleau-Ponty delivers a Freudian interpretation of the temporality at work in the involuntary memory; on the other hand, he also refers to Proust and to Baudelaire's *The Flowers of Evil*. Indeed, he echoes the title of Baudelaire's poem "Previous Existence" ("La vie antérieure") and mentions a line from "Grieving and Wandering" ("Moesta et Errabunda"). Here are the first, programmatic lines of the Working Note from *The Visible and the Invisible* to which I am referring:

> The Freudian idea of the unconscious and the past as "indestructible," as "intemporal" = elimination of the common idea of time as a "series of *Erlebnisse*"—There is an architectonic past. cf. Proust: the *true* hawthorns are the hawthorns of the past—Restore this life without *Erlebnisse*, without interiority . . . which is, in reality, the "monumental" life, *Stiftung*, initiation. This "past" belongs to a mythical time, to the time before time, to the prior life [*la vie antérieure*], "farther than India and China." (VI, 296/243)[40]

"The *True* Hawthorns Are the Hawthorns of the Past": Memory and Initiation

In his course notes devoted to Proust on "The Problem of Passivity," Merleau-Ponty's deepened reflection on the function of the body in memory results in his highlighting of the central role of forgetfulness. More important, his emphasis on the body urges him to concentrate on another decisive "philosophical idea" emerging in the *Recherche*: the relation between reality and memory. Merleau-Ponty finds this "philosophical idea" remarkably condensed in the Proustian sentence that he will recall and refer to in a Working Note of *The Visible and the Invisible* dated April 1960: "Whether it is because the faith which creates has ceased to exist in me, or because reality takes shape in the memory [*mémoire*] alone, the flowers that people show me nowadays for the first time never seem to me to be true flowers."[41]

This Proustian passage dedicated to the hawthorns on the Méséglise Way[42] seems to describe an experience of "initiation," as Merleau-Ponty highlights in his aforementioned Working Note. This very sentence had been previously evoked, along with others, in the first of the "reading notes" on Proust from the course on "The Problem of Passivity." Here Merleau-Ponty explains the sentence's dense implications as follows:

> It makes no sense to search for the equivalent of recollection [*souvenir*] in reality—(The recollection [*souvenir*] is neither the past that is reproduced or preserved nor a falsified past.)—Memory [*mémoire*] deforms reality, which nevertheless is formed as reality only in memory [*mémoire*]. And yet, there is a memory [*mémoire*] which gives the past "itself": that of, for example, provisionally forgotten recollections [*souvenirs*]. (IP, 271/210)

In the notes on the *Recherche* prepared for the course titled "The Cartesian Ontology and the Ontology of Today" (1960–61)[43]—that is to say, one of the two courses interrupted by his sudden death—Merleau-Ponty returns twice to the Proustian passages dedicated to the hawthorns on the Méséglise Way and focuses particularly on the sentence quoted above. The second time these course notes refer to it, the focus is exclusively set on the claim according to which "reality takes shape in the memory alone." Besides, this very claim can also be found in a letter Merleau-Ponty addressed to Claude Simon,[44] whom, in the same course, he considered to be one of the heirs of the literary line opened precisely by Proust.[45] As Merleau-Ponty explains in these notes, such a line is characterized by the "reversal of the relations between the visible and the invisible; of flesh and mind" (NC, 392). I will discuss this point further in Chapter 4.

The Merleau-Pontian notes we are considering hence take into account the aforementioned Proustian quote and point out that—although the narrator's hypothesis is that "reality takes shape in the memory alone"—we are still not dealing with "an *illusion* of reality. No, one remembers precisely what once was. Through distance, the present 'develops' all of its meaning" (NC, 202). Further on, he indicates the way in which that *development* placed between inverted commas should be understood: "flesh that has become essence" (ibid.). The "development" distancing the past from the actual lived experience places it in the "mythical" and hence "indestructible" temporality mentioned in the aforementioned Working Note from *The Visible and the Invisible*. Such a past will become its own "carnal essence," its "sensible idea," in other words, "a dimension that can never again be closed" (VI, 198/151). In this sense, it will become an *empirical turned into transcendental*, as I have defined elsewhere,[46] as well as retrojected as an a priori.[47] Hence, the main character of the *Recherche* ends up feeling that the hawthorns on the Méséglise Way incarnate the essence of a past that "belongs to a mythical time, to the time before time, to the prior life" (VI, 296/243).

In turn, the first remark on the aforementioned Proustian passage in these notes considers both the hypotheses outlined therein: "Whether it is because the faith which creates has ceased to exist in me, or because reality takes shape in the memory [*mémoire*] alone." Here Merleau-Ponty highlights the crucial role played by language in that "development" for which the flesh becomes essence: "The past is lost,—however, strange resurrection by means of the speech" (NC, 197). As explained only a few lines earlier, the speech "comes to awaken and restart this wonder [i.e., of the sensible] by touching within me what I considered as most hidden, and which reveals to be sharable and, as such, an 'idea'" (ibid.).

Such considerations recall the reflections on the mutual implication of the *logos endiáthetos* and the *logos prophorikós* that Merleau-Ponty registered in some Working Notes from *The Visible and the Invisible*, such as the one in which he alludes precisely to the creative operation Proust evokes also in the passage I just mentioned. This note, dated January 1959, indeed points out that the sensible world, ontologically understood as brute or wild Being, aliments painting and philosophy as it "appears as containing everything that will ever be said, and yet leaving us to create it (Proust): it is the λόγος ἐνδιάθετος [implicit *logos*] which calls for the λόγος προφορικός [spoken *logos*]" (VI, 224/170). However, in his last phase of thought, Merleau-Ponty does not consider the functions of sedimentation and ideation to be an exclusive privilege of language or of a "spoken logos." Hence, by adhering to the structure of the Proustian passage we are considering, the course notes assume both its possibilities: "No matter whether it happens by means of the body and memory or through speech, Time becomes something other than succession: a pyramid of 'simultaneity'" (NC, 197).

The first of these two possibilities indicates the crucial role of the Proustian "memory of the body" in promoting the becoming "essence" of the "flesh," or—in the terms I previously matched with these—in the becoming transcendental of the empirical. This is the "true memory" we found mentioned in the summary of the Collège de France course on "The Problem of Passivity." As we read earlier, Merleau-Ponty places the "true memory" on this side of the opposition between forgetfulness and memory as it is traditionally conceived, namely, on this side of "any alternative between conservation and construction" (RC, 71/119). Therefore, according to the hypothesis formulated by the Proustian narrator, "reality takes shape" in the memory hence understood. In other terms, by operating in the indistinction of activity and passivity, the experience of reality becomes its own transcendental, just as the hawthorns on the Méséglise Way turn into the "*true* hawthorns." According to Merleau-Ponty, the intertwining of memory and forgetfulness that Proust calls *involuntary memory* makes certain experiences that had arisen within our operative relationship with the world decant into the body, where they become those *sensible ideas* on which I will focus in the second of my chapters. Rather than an opposition, such memory is a *chiasm* of remembering and forgetting—that is to say, not an alternative between conservation and construction, but a *chiasm* implying both, since in such memory "past and present are *Ineinander,* each enveloping-enveloped" (VI, 321/268). Hence understood, memory prevents from conceiving the "initiation" we found evoked in the opening of the Working Note of *The Visible and the Invisible* dated April 1960 as a metaphysical and punctiform *beginning*. Instead, Merleau-Ponty still tends to assimilate *beginning* and *initiation* when, in the same manuscript, he writes that "with the *first* vision, the *first* contact, the *first* pleasure, there is initiation" (VI, 198/151). Thus, what he seems to affirm in one of his "five notes" concerning, once more, the writer Claude Simon acquires a special interest in this perspective. I am referring to the note dated March 1961, significantly titled "The 'Association' as Initiation," which I shall quote entirely:

> The red of the gunner's badges (Claude Simon: text in *Lettres françaises*)—it says this and that to him—one says: by association. It's not that, nor *Verschmelzung* etc. It's that there is a signifying virtue in the texture of this red, a qualitative texture, first of all. Then, the experiences of which it reawakens the feeling have been lived *through*

it (as things are experienced through their names) and that's the reason—that archaic structure is the reason—why it will always be the mediator of those experiences. Because our experience is not a flat field of qualities, but always subject to the invocation of some fetish or other, always reached through the intercession of some fetish or other.[48]

Differently from what a too-simple association between *beginning* and *initiation* may suggest, the note we just read makes clear that an initiation only gives itself "*through*" the *repetition* of an experience within another. Yet, the initiation cannot be considered accomplished in the mere *association* of the two, since it is *always* a matter of a *creative* repetition, even if, in virtue of what Bergson defined as "retrospective illusion," one tends to consider their sense as *preexisting* in that *first* experience, whose "signifying virtue" actually looks just like an *anticipation* in the light of the second experience. The initiation thus happens *in-between* an experience and the one that we successively associate with it, which is why it gives itself as an *overdetermination* with respect to both.[49] In other words, if the initiation can found a mythical time, it is precisely because *it happens in the chiasm between past and present*, and for this reason it is *always already given*, since it is the institution of a field of experience that—precisely in a mythical way—"is always behind us" (RC, 67/115).

It is in this sense that Proust could write that "reality takes shape in the memory alone." In turn, it is in this very sense that Benjamin could hazard a vertiginous formulation so as to condense the dynamics of the mutual precession[50] of such reality and such memory: "On the knowledge of the *mémoire involontaire*: not only does its images come unsummoned, but it is a matter of images *we never saw before remembering them*."[51]

Translated by Marta Nijhuis

2

A Poetics of Co-Naissance
Via André Breton, Paul Claudel, and Claude Simon

EMMANUEL DE SAINT AUBERT

In the two chapters entrusted to me in this book, I will attempt to shed light on how Maurice Merleau-Ponty's philosophical exploration of the relationship between being and flesh engages the author's poetic artistry—a *poetic* art that remains first and foremost *philosophical*. In the course of his work, Merleau-Ponty discovers that we cannot describe the flesh, our being-in-the-world interwoven with perceptions and desires, without drawing our concepts from the sensorial world and the ever-pulsating roots of our imaginative relationship with the real. Whence a style of writing that makes increasing use of metaphors and metaphorical figures, where the poetic dimension is considered, not a cop-out or avoidance of serious thought, but, to the contrary, as important, necessary even, in our philosophical approach to the ontological mystery embedded in the flesh. These metaphorical figures hint at a universal significance while continuing to express and convey the uniqueness of our being-in-the-world, its personal and interpersonal dimensions, its configurations through experiences, personal encounters, things we have read. Merleau-Ponty's literary involvements accompany the progressive development of his figural universe, a cohesive fabric of which more than one node will be explored in the pages that follow. This fabric is so expansive, so expressively cohesive, that it seems to embrace Merleau-Ponty's entire anthropology and ontology, as though bearing a profound comprehension thereof so that the poetic dimension of Merleau-Ponty's thought cannot be considered as merely one dimension among others, but as the mark of a true poetic artistry, flowing through and animating the core issues of his philosophy.

To risk an overly condensed initial synopsis: Merleau-Ponty's poetics is, somewhat indistinguishably, a poetics of the *flesh* (a poetics of the body and desire, as well as the flesh of the world), a poetics of *mystery* (which is not solely, or even primarily, that which is hidden, but that which expresses itself), and a poetics of the visible in relation to the *invisible* (the invisible that *renders visible*, the infrastructure and latent matrix of the manifest, up to and including linguistic expression). These three dimensions correspond to the overdetermined themes of *desire, expression*, and *perception*—and their respective anthropological, epistemological, and ontological horizons. All three are implicated and intimately involved in a poetics of *depth*, one of this philosophy's most consistent transversal motifs. And all three eventually accompany the later Merleau-Ponty's original conception of the unconscious. Coextensive with the tightly woven fabric of our perceptual, expressive, and desirous life, the unconscious, like mystery, is not that which is hidden, but that which expresses itself. That alone is capable of espousing the depth of the other and the world, of letting being *be*: not representing being, but letting it emerge and express itself; configuring itself to being, while letting being en-figure (*figurer*) (us) and express (us). Letting it bear us and co-conceive us (*nous co-naître*). This complex ensemble allows for the budding and growth of one final, transversal dimension—that is, ultimately, a poetics of *nascence* and *co-naissance*,[1] where desire is entwined with the lift (*portance*) of being.

Such a complex configuration of ideas is obviously not delivered in one thetic block; it is forged at the crossroads of various thematic lines and issues, marked by a conceptual progressivity, as well as by tensions, hesitations, even those of Merleau-Ponty, which in turn engender our own, those of the reader. We will thus begin to flesh out this all-too-synoptic overview, outlining this progressivity as well as some of its tensions.

From the outset, anyone would accept our evocation, with regard to this author, of a *poetics of the flesh*. But we still need to understand the sense (and senses) of *flesh* in Merleau-Ponty's work, an idea that implicates his thought as a whole.[2] The concept of flesh, of the animated and animating body, comes to encompass what Merleau-Ponty refers to as the "generality of the body": the capacity for expression and extension of a human corporeity accomplished in its self-surpassing, in an extraordinarily tight game of passivity and activity, the body letting itself be configured by the structures of a world that it dresses with its own contexture. Merleau-Ponty's *flesh* qualifies in turn, or at once, as *my body* (my body schema, from its sensorimotor foundations to the most subtle dimensions of its animation mingled with desire and intelligence); as *way* or *style of being* (the flesh as relation to . . . as demeanor or attitude, starting from the characteristic features of my flesh in relation to others and the world); and as the *flesh of the world* (where the world is related to the flesh, wearing it, or weaving it in turn, convoking and provoking it, carrying it toward emergence and desire).

Merleau-Ponty's poetics must thus be understood as a poetics of the flesh *in relation to the world and to others*, and in accordance with the primary experiential modes privileged by the phenomenologist. First and foremost is perception, a perception that, as Merleau-Ponty discovers, is always already expression and desire. Yet, while the flesh is essentially relational, our relationships are themselves understood as more carnal than we might initially imagine. Merleau-Ponty enjoys portraying them, in his writing as well as his imagination (*imaginaire*), in diametric opposition to the *partes extra partes* of the Cartesian extension, to the juxtaposition and *poser-contre* of the Sartrean flesh: encroachment, *Ineinander*, intertwining, chiasm, and many other metaphorical figures evoke the carnality of relationship, drawing us ever closer to *a poetics of incorporation and intercorporeity*.

Incorporation and intercorporeity: This is, in a sense, the Merleau-Pontian anthropology in a nutshell. With his psychoanalytic understanding of incorporation—as a ballet of projection and introjection—Merleau-Ponty's conception of the unfolding relationship between flesh and world assumes a radically generalized "anthropological projection": the flesh is capable of making anything flesh, and the world itself becomes the oneiric *développé* of a body schema animated by desire.[3] Whence this bold line of thinking, which goes so far as to announce the "flesh of the things," and later, the "flesh of the world." This conceptual development regularly crosses paths with an author whom we will not discuss further here, but who should nonetheless be mentioned as having had a significant influence on Merleau-Ponty's poetics: Gaston Bachelard, and his psychoanalysis of the "elements."[4] Just as Bachelard's "elements" are experienced as flesh in relation to our own flesh, in a complex relationship of resistance and adversity, desire and lift (*portance*)—so Merleau-Ponty's poetics might in places be described as a *poetics of the elements*, and later, as a *poetics of the flesh of the world*.

From a poetics of the flesh to a poetics of carnal relationship and finally, a poetics of the flesh of the world—the first unfolding into the second, culminating in the last—one might be tempted to leave it at that. To interpret the merry-go-round of this carnal articulation between the flesh and the flesh of the world as a reciprocal and generalized incorporation, in which some critical eyes have (not unjustifiably) discerned a vertiginous fusion and confusion. Perhaps even the vertigo of a latent fleshly monism that resolves all separation into a molluscan ontology, with hints of pantheism, resulting in a neglect of the tragic dimension of our condition—at risk of erasing man along with adversity, thus ratifying the failure of the entire Merleau-Pontian endeavor. This critical position is not completely unwarranted, yet while thought provoking, it is too comfortable, too lazy even, to escape our suspicion. It frees us at little cost from fully garnering the best of Merleau-Ponty's thought, from grappling with its demands and destabilizing implications.

Because for Merleau-Ponty, the *flesh* can only exist in relation to the world or others if it is open to . . . *being*. But *being* is not the *world*; if these were synonymous, the phenomenologist would not have entitled his last great work "Being and the World." Being is the depth of the world, which is not the same thing. Being, in a sense, is the "flesh of the world," but it is neither world . . . nor flesh. And the full import of Merleau-Ponty's poetics can only be grasped as a poetics of the *flesh* in relation to *being*. This is precisely what we discover as we examine how this French phenomenologist seeks inspiration in three of his favorite authors, and as we explore his contribution to our understanding of the carnal infrastructures and ontological horizons of metaphoricity. Existentially oriented from the outset, Merleau-Ponty increasingly understands that his anthropology must be *ontologically* grounded and fulfilled. This understanding and assumption is evident in his conception of desire and perceptual faith as openness to *being*.[5]

André Breton, Paul Claudel, and Claude Simon accompany the development of this poetics of incorporation, which, in its traversal of the circle of *Ineinander*'s relationship with the world and others, traces the existential structures of desire, and metaphorical figures of being. Through his reading of these three authors, Merleau-Ponty finds a way of describing our *corps-à-corps* with the world; with them he becomes steeped in figures of the flesh, which are also, and equally, figures of what drives the flesh—desire—and of what bears the flesh, and is thereby expressed—being. From each, he acquires a specific image of the corporeal unity of the manifold: Breton's *crystallization*, Claudel's *simultaneity* and Simon's *ubiquity*: that is, the "crystallization of desire," a variant of Stendhal's crystallization (also discussed by Merleau-Ponty); the *simultaneity* of "all these things existing together," "co-emerging" with us; and the *ubiquity* of intercorporeity, the "ubiquitous space where bodies are superimposed on each other."[6] It is in these poetic conjunctions that Merleau-Ponty discovers how each author's imagination and writing are haunted by a topology of reciprocal envelopment. The "sublime point" of the enveloped-enveloping underlies the privileged figures of love, coupling, and pregnancy—in a dynamic that leads from the former to the latter, from envelopment to engendering. This later leads to a third figure in Merleau-Ponty's poetics: *surrection* ("upsurge"),[7] which is a metaphorical figure of desire as well as of being: a figure of desire, its insurrections and resurrections, lifting and pushing us up through frustration and adversity, until we stand erect, before being and within being, borne by this "vertical being," this being that affirms itself and affirms us, that interrogates and expresses us.

Desire leads to the reversibility of inside and outside, a reversibility that is already a pregnancy: The reversibility at work in the enveloped-enveloping unfolds into the engendering-engendered and this pregnancy culminates in birth, the co-birth (*co-naissance*) of myself and the world, myself and others. If the *surrection* of desire is extended into the *surrection* of beings, this is only because we are open to being and the upward lift (*portance*) of being. The *co-naissance* of beings is thus secretly accompanied, and intensified, by the *surrection* of being within us, and of ourselves within being: the sublime point of desire's phenomenality—the enveloping-enveloped of two fleshes, until the *co-naissance* of beings—with the *co-naissance* of the flesh and of being as both foundation and ultimate fruit.

The Quest for the Sublime Point

The Sublime Point

Apart from a fleeting mention in *The Structure of Behavior*, it is not until 1945 that Merleau-Ponty explicitly engages with surrealism.[8] In 1947 he participates in a radio program dedicated to the subject,[9] and after this we find references in *Man and Object, Causeries* (the radio talks of 1948), his Mexico lectures—and then in a 1949 talk delivered at the Collège Philosophique entitled "Surrealist Humanism and Existentialist Humanism."[10] From this point onward, we find recurrent references to surrealism in Merleau-Ponty's work, until the final rereading of *The Prose of the World*, where he indicates that he will devote an entire chapter to Breton.[11] Again in 1959 we find the philosopher addressing the issue in his interviews with Georges Charbonnier.[12]

Merleau-Ponty's interest in surrealism essentially revolves around the work of André Breton.[13] Breton and Merleau-Ponty share, at the end of two different wars, the same concern with salvaging thought from its ruins, after a time of crisis, after the collapse of all the old categories. Breton's 1930 *Second Manifesto of Surrealism* announces itself from the outset as a reflection on the experience of war, beginning a defiant discourse of which we find more than one analogous expression in Merleau-Ponty's work from 1945 until *The Visible and the Invisible*. The following lines, for example, might very well have been written by the author of *Eye and Mind*:

> It was, and still is, a question of testing by any and all means, of demonstrating at any price, the factitious nature of the old antinomies.... Everything leads us to believe there is a certain point in the mind, where life and death, the real and the imaginary, past and future, the communicable and the incommunicable, high and low, are no longer perceived as contradictions. One would search in vain for any other motivating factor in the surrealist's activity, than the hope of nailing down this point.[14]

Merleau-Ponty shares this objective; on occasion, he even adopts the manifesto format. The first few pages of *Man and Adversity*, some passages of the *Introduction to Ontology* (unpublished, 1958), *The Visible and the Invisible*, and again, *Eye and Mind*, are an expression of a *philosophical Art* that seeks to cultivate, to the point of exasperation, this hope for unexpected encounters. "Essence and existence, imaginary and real, visible and invisible—a painting mixes up all our categories in laying before us its oneiric universe of carnal essences, of effective likenesses, of mute meanings."[15]

But what is this "point" where the "old antinomies" are "no longer perceived as contradictions," where, contra Sartre in particular, "the real and the imaginary" communicate? Through his preferred metaphorical figures (encroachment, chiasm, enveloped-enveloping . . .), Merleau-Ponty attempts to describe this singularity, occasionally referred to as the "sublime point." This sublime point is not a preestablished harmony, but a permanent *revolution*.[16] "If inner and outer are reunited, their meeting will not be harmonious or beautiful but will have, rather, the violence of the sublime."[17] Merleau-Ponty acknowledges that he takes this image of the Sublime Point from Breton[18]—a privileged geographic location where visual perception allows itself to be seized by the impossible meeting of two depths, like two vertiginous gorges; an extreme, intense, and exemplary version of the tension inhabiting our vision of depth.[19]

> I have spoken of a certain "sublime point" on the mountain. It was never a question of establishing my dwelling on this point. It would, moreover, from then on, have ceased to be sublime and I should, myself, have ceased to be a person. Unable reasonably to dwell there, I have nevertheless never gone so far from it as to lose it from view, as to not be able to point it out. I had chosen to be this guide, and there-

fore I had forced myself not to be unworthy of the power which, in the direction of eternal love, had made me *see* and granted me the still rarer privilege of *having others see*. I have never been unworthy; I have never ceased to identify the flesh of the being I love and the snow of the peaks in the rising sun.[20]

Seeing and rendering visible the coexistence of incompossibles; the flesh of the beloved and the depth of being, all held together within the unity of a single desire: The overlap with Merleau-Ponty's philosophical gesture is self-evident. In this first phase of the surrealist revolt, Merleau-Ponty re-reads his own initial contestations. For Merleau-Ponty, surrealism, as "a distortion of subjectivity,"[21] is valid, even in its obscurity, and this is defended against the "rationalist spirit" of Sartre's *Qu'est-ce que la littérature?* ("What Is Literature?").[22] Yet the motivation behind this rebellion is less the pleasure of destroying a world, than the desire to construct another.[23] Thus, "destruction" here might be reinterpreted as a reconquest, an attempt to "restore" a certain usage of vision, speech, and writing, in stark contrast to Mallarmé's essentialist project.[24]

The Omnipotence of Desire

Merleau-Ponty agrees that we cannot abide in the sublime point, that this point needs to be traversed through a dialectical movement—a "hyperdialectic"—undergirded by the desire to see "in depth," as though vision might hold incompossible monocular images together. A movement oriented in "the direction of eternal love" inhabiting the being of desire, lining even the least perceptible thing. Breton follows this path, his poetic oeuvre infused by his own concrete experience of man, in particular his experience of the manifestations of madness, of disorders of desire in hysteria.[25] Merleau-Ponty is struck by *L'amour fou*'s exploration of "the omnipotence of human desire."[26] He associates this potency with desire's *insurrectional* power, a power essential to human freedom, its capacity for *resurrection* in adversity, our faith in desire's "indestructibility."[27] This faith is not based on the evidence of the understanding, but stems from the cohesive strength of a flesh reinforced by the consistency of being itself. Through its insurrections and resurrections, human desire reveals its radical capacity for *surrection*: its capacity for delivering us, for opening us up to the surreal. Breton locates the latter's emergence, not primarily in the realm of ideas, but like Merleau-Ponty, in the radiance of the *sensible*. *L'amour fou* develops "this sensible realm that spans all areas of my mind, and thus resides in a handheld sheaf of rays."[28] Surreality is thus not lurking in the back-world but infused within the real itself. As Breton states in his entry on "philosophy" for the *Abridged Dictionary of Surrealism*:

> Everything I love, everything I think and feel, inclines me towards a particular philosophy of immanence, from which it follows that surreality would be contained in reality itself and would not be superior or external to it. And reciprocally, since the container would also be the content. It would be a question, almost, of a communicating vessel between the container and the content.[29]

This is the same immanent transcendence, the same structural dynamics of enveloping-enveloped we find in Merleau-Ponty, reaching its climax in the latter's conception of the relation between the visible and invisible: the idea of a flesh accessing an invisible that is neither superior to, nor external to the visible, but infused within the visible itself. The visible is not only *pregnant* with the invisible but is also, conversely, *borne* by it: The invisible is the infrastructure of the visible.

Merleau-Ponty endorses this dynamic "insurrectional" surrealism, in relation to the theme of desire's omnipotence—an insurrection that aims to "restore some profound and radical usage of speech";[30] to redirect speech and writing back to their original vocation, where the flesh expresses being, and lets being express itself. Yet while Merleau-Ponty repeatedly defends surrealism against its critics, he is equally anxious about its potential drift into "occultism,"[31] as he warns in *Man and Object*. This would in fact be a drift away from the sublime point, the unstable point of miraculous expression, where the human being is revealed[32]—and outside of which ontological mystery is reduced to a petrified Gnosticism.[33] Surrealism would then relapse, from the insurrectional heights of an all-conquering desire, to a conservative regressive drive, "from the surreal to the puerile," from the sublime point to the nostalgia of lost origins.

Breton's radiance of the sensible is inseparable from the flesh's reciprocal radiance on things; a projective dimension illustrated notably in the example of the "find" (*la trouvaille*). In each and every thing, even the most mundane or utilitarian artifact, so long as we can relate to it, "we can recognize the wonderful precipitate of desire," which in turn allows us to "discover therein some extraordinary resources for concealment."[34] Merleau-Ponty's 1948 lecture, *Man and Object*, emphasizes this projective aspect of desirous incorporation, where our own complex constitutional structure is found inscribed, legible, in the flesh of the object:

> Like Breton, we must be aware that a lamp has a physiognomy, a "convulsive beauty." It is up to literature to remind us of this, to

prevent a utensil from becoming a rigid and dead thing. An object found at the flea market, whether mask or spoon, is a "wonderful precipitate of the human face," fraught with reminiscences. Without stretching this to the point of occultism, we must admit that every object is also a 'find' that allows us decipher ourselves. Objects are our own possibilities projected into space; as such, they can always return consciousness to itself.[35]

In a series of radio talks the following autumn, Merleau-Ponty comes back to this "surrealist experiment," to this search for what André Breton refers to as the "catalysts of desire" within objects—"the place where human desire manifests itself, or 'crystallizes.'"[36] Throughout these talks he insists that man is "a being who can only get to the truth of things because its body is, as it were, embedded in those things," that, "we can only gain access to them through our body"—"clothed in human qualities, they too are a combination of mind and body"[37]—they, too, are flesh. Our relationship with the world is thoroughly forged in this mixing, which itself participates in the expression and edification of our flesh.

> Our relationship with things is not a distant one: each speaks to our body and to the way we live. They are clothed in human characteristics (whether docile, soft, hostile, or resistant) and conversely, they dwell within us as emblems of forms of life we either love or hate. Humanity is invested in the things of the world and these are invested in it.[38]

Merleau-Ponty comes back to these references and ideas a few months later in his Mexico Lectures,[39] once again concluding that it is "impossible to disentangle" the respective debts that bind man and things in this communal flesh of desirous incorporation.[40] Never before affirmed so radically, Merleau-Ponty never hereafter abandons the reciprocal envelopment of *flesh* and *world*, later even pushing it to extremes in his daring concept of the "flesh of the world." We will return to this in our discussion of Claude Simon.

In sum: Both Breton and Merleau-Ponty add—to the enveloping-enveloped of the real and the surreal, of the visible and the invisible, of the *world* and *being*—another reciprocal envelopment, one forged through the power of desire: of ourselves and the world—of our *flesh* and the flesh of the *world*. The former becomes accessible to us via the latter, and this is how we are opened to being.[41] To the point of weaving a final mutual envelopment: that of *flesh* and *being*. Suffice it to say that we cannot grasp Merleau-Ponty's poetic art, in its full significance, without discerning these different levels of envelopment, all of which are initiated and sustained by the power of desire and its overdetermination of the sensible. These three levels lead us from the flesh, to the world, and to being—or, more precisely, from our flesh to the flesh of the world, and from the flesh of the world to the depth of being; a gesture in which the desirous opening of our flesh to the depth of being, is understood as both ground and horizon.

If access to the sublime point is played out in this ballet of desirous incorporation, in which our *flesh* is bound to the flesh of the *world*; and if the sublime point opens us up to the reciprocal envelopment of the visible and the invisible, of the *world* and *being*,[42] it both sustains and is sustained by our openness to being, it forges the mutual envelopment of *flesh* and *being*. An enveloping-enveloped, which, as we will see, is also an engendering-engendered: the *co-naissance* of flesh and being. We end this brief exploration of Merleau-Ponty's surrealist inspiration with a last—but certainly not least—entry from the *Abridged Dictionary of Surrealism*: that is, the entry on "Surrealism," and its significant resonance with *Eye and Mind*'s "secret and feverish genesis of things":

> Surrealism, in its broadest sense, represents the latest attempt to break with *things as they are*, to substitute them with things in mid-action, in mid-genesis, things whose shifting contours are implicitly inscribed in the very foundations of being. . . . Never before in France has a school of poets so consciously blended [*confondu*] the problem of poetry and the crucial problem of being.[43]

Toward a Phenomenology of Co-Naissance

In his own pursuit of the quest for the sublime point, where visible and invisible are mutually enveloped, in his search for this node in the overdetermination of the sensible under the omnipotent effect of desire, Merleau-Ponty is inspired not only by Breton but also by another of Rimbaud's self-professed heirs: Paul Claudel. Merleau-Ponty's engagement with Claudel not only has a longer history, but it also remains an active influence right until his last writings and takes his thought much further.[44]

Merleau-Ponty's library contains, to this day, some twenty works by Claudel,[45] a number of which are dated and signed (the first in 1928 and 1929). Among them, *Art poétique*[46] is the most worked over—in fact, one of the most annotated volumes in the whole library. Merleau-Ponty discovers this essay in October 1935,[47] at a time when he is forging his own conception of philosophical knowledge against Brunschvicg's idealism, under the influence of Gabriel Marcel and Max Scheler, as that of a "direct commerce with the world and with things."[48] The strange metaphysics of *Art poétique* supports Merleau-Ponty's approach here, through its central text, the "Treatise on Co-Naissance."

Co-naissance, an original term that combines "birth" (*naissance*) and "knowledge" (*connaissance*) in a conception of generalized coexistence, appears repeatedly throughout Merleau-Ponty's work from *The Structure of Behavior* onward. *Phenomenology of Perception*, for example, evokes "a relation of *co-naissance*,"[49] and the chapter devoted to *Sensing* is largely based on Claudel's *Treatise*, though the poet is never named. These pages in *Phenomenology*, which anticipate his later work, are concerned with "the relations between sentient and sensible"[50]—with "*co-naissance*" here referring to the fact that the subject of sensation is both active and passive: "neither a thinker who notices a quality, nor an inert milieu that would be affected or modified by it," but "a power that is born together in a certain existential milieu."[51] Much later again, at the start of autumn 1958, Merleau-Ponty sets out to define his ontology in an unpublished volume, part of the joint project of *Being and World*, *The Visible and the Invisible*, which opens with the assertion that ontology consists of a "formulation" of man as "nascence and *co-naissance*."[52]

More than simply a neologism borrowed from *Art poétique*, we find in Merleau-Ponty's work—and to this we will return—most of the general equations that shape Claudel's theoretical discussion of *co-naissance*, as well as some of the latter's preferred descriptions. Through the course of his regular consultations of the French poet and playwright, the latter's influence is soon transformed into a somewhat liberal inspiration. And if some of the late manuscripts reproach Sartre for having ignored "*co-naissance*,"[53] this in a sense also sums up Merleau-Ponty's opposition to the latter—for Merleau-Ponty, Sartre's analysis of "double incarnation" (in the *poser-contre* of bodies and the impotence of desire) represents the *failure* of *co-naissance*.

Merleau-Ponty's Claudelian infusion, so obvious to those immersed in both authors' worlds of thought, is difficult to demarcate precisely, given the extent and subtlety of the poet's influence on the philosopher.[54] The difficulty is compounded by the status of Claudel's writing, which is less conceptual and more figurative than that of Merleau-Ponty. The "theoretical" stance of *Art poétique* is particularly disconcerting. Extracting its meaning requires a certain amount of patience, like extricating a diamond from graphite, with the most dazzling ideas often contained within the most confusing analogies. The encounter reaches its limits in the two men's different attitudes to religious faith. For Claudel, the freedom of poetic reverie, while restoring the prodigality of sentient life that Merleau-Ponty so appreciates,[55] is nevertheless inseparable from the light of his faith. For

Merleau-Ponty, on the other hand, the religious descends into the oneiric. He confirms philosophy's autonomy with regard to theology, although this does not exclude a spiritual dimension from his work.

Existence and Perception

André Vachon, a disciple of Georges Poulet and author of a remarkable thesis on space and time in Claudel, is probably the first Claudel specialist to have highlighted the latter's proximity to phenomenology, especially that of Merleau-Ponty.[56] Claudel, for his part, never read any phenomenology. As he himself points out, it is from Rimbaud that he draws his fundamental concern with expressing the union of soul and body, in the preferred modality of sentient life—and against the dominant intellectual currents of Kantian idealism and positivism.[57] This starting point is not dissimilar to the origins of Merleau-Ponty's own philosophical reflections toward the end of the 1920s and during the 1930s.[58]

The shared general framework where we find, in both authors, the concept of *co-naissance*, involves a radical conception of perceptual life as an experience of being—in the dual sense (passive and active) of the French verb *éprouver*: to feel and to put to the test, to sense and to interrogate. Jean Wahl, an avid reader of both Claudel and Merleau-Ponty, a privileged witness to the poet's influence on the philosopher, sums up the main principle shared by both authors: "Dearest Merleau-Ponty . . . Both you and Claudel take as fundamental a universal perception made within us rather than by us, you both affirm that to *perceive*, is to *be*."[59] André Vachon, for his part, emphasizes how Claudel cultivates "a rigorous equation of *being* and *being perceived*."[60] These two equations—to perceive is to be, to be is to be perceived—are equally true for the author of *Art poétique*. For Claudel, to be is to be inscribed in time and space and to feel oneself thus inscribed in a *corps à corps*.[61] But human beings perceive, and perceive themselves, only insofar as they are perceived—we (re)cognize things, and ourselves, through contact with that which recognizes us. This perception-as-co-perception reaches its fullest expression in our relationship with others: a person experiences their existence when their body is viewed and touched by another.[62] This can in turn be extended to everything, which seems to come alive, returning our gaze and our touch, seeming to perceive us in return. As Merleau-Ponty comments on Claudel, in his preparatory manuscripts for *Eye and Mind*: "The visible is a kind of seeing (things are watching us)."[63] It is not difficult to imagine why the poet's ideas were able to capture the attention of a philosopher dedicated to the idea of the seen-seer and, more generally, the sensing-sensed.

This Claudelian marriage of existence and co-perception results in a profound equation of existence and coexistence. Perception is proof (*épreuve*) of my existence insofar as it experiences (*éprouve*) my coexistence with all things, as well as the coexistence of all things with each other. Claudel never ceases to celebrate this ontological *simultaneity*, a constant source of wonder:

> "I exist among the things that are."[64] "How I love the million things that exist together!"[65] "All these things that exist together!"[66] "Here, again, Life! . . . this assiduous, multiple, interweaving activity, in which all things exist together."[67] "I exist this ensemble . . . this unity in diversity, this powerful, delicate, and wonderful harmony . . ."[68] "this general communication, this infinitely subtle and diverse flow of things, existing together, all around us."[69] Etc.

This system of equivalences, wherein perception is granted an ontological significance, is the cradle of the Claudelian notion of *co-naissance*, having an ultimate equation of being and co-birth (*être et co-naître*) as horizon. For Claudel, a being is not held together except *in movement*, in an ever-nascent state of coexistence.[70] Forever incomplete, it never ceases to be swollen with being and connection, never ceases to be born and co-born. This idea obviously reaches its greatest significance in application to the living being—"To live is to be [perpetually] born."[71] At every moment, in every perception, the human being and its other (person, nature, or God) co-emerge into visibility, simultaneously nascent, one from the other and one into the other, thus coming to know each other.

> We are not born alone. For everything, to be born is to be co-born [*co-naître*]. All birth [*naissance*] is a form of knowledge [*connaissance*]. . . . as we are co-born with *nature*, so we know it. . . . To know [*connaître*] is therefore to be: that which is lacking in everything else. Nothing ends with oneself alone.[72]

Merleau-Ponty develops, in his own way, a conception of coexistence that takes up this network of equivalences. Entering himself into "this Being where everything exists together,"[73] the philosopher consciously cultivates one of Claudel's most iconic formulas. In his unpublished *Nature, or the World of Silence*, Merleau-Ponty presents nature as a being that "bears us, that bears us pell-mell with other people," that "holds everything together."[74] In the preface of *Signs*, we read that "man exists only in movement," to which he immediately adds: "Similarly the world and Being hold together only in movement; it is only in this way that all things can be together."[75] *The Visible and the Invisible*, in turn, reads an "appeal for totality" into perception, a sense of wonder at the sheer measure of the "immense simultaneity of the world."[76] It is not until 1961, however, during the final year of his Collège de France courses, that Merleau-Ponty finally acknowledges the Claudelian origins of this theme in his talk dedicated to the poet,[77] entitled "The Cohesion of Being and Simultaneity: Claudel."[78]

In a radio tribute to Merleau-Ponty, broadcast a few days after the philosopher's death, Jean Wahl treats these lessons on Claudel as emblematic of the philosopher's entire oeuvre: "Claudel's simultaneity of vision, the great simultaneity of all things, not before God, as for Claudel, but before man, who strives to see things in a divine way, beyond subject and object."[79] This requires some effort, the challenge of overcoming the separation that continues to haunt Merleau-Ponty: This simultaneity is not a preestablished harmony. It is no different for Claudel. "Separation is irremediable, everything seems distant, I am connected only through vision,"[80] says the poet, and it is this same visual power that underlies the effort of perceptual simultaneity in Merleau-Ponty's work, from the *Phenomenology of Perception*,[81] all the way to *Prose of the World*[82] and *Eye and Mind*. According to this last essay, only vision teaches us that "beings that are different, 'exterior,' foreign to one another, are yet absolutely *together*."[83] Like Claudel, Merleau-Ponty wants to account for everything in the human being that is capable of this "unity forged in separation,"[84] this miraculous "coexistence of incompossibles"[85] brought about by a desiring flesh, up to the challenging coexistence of human beings with each other.

Being and Knowing

Through this phenomenology of perception and its supporting ontology of coexistence, Merleau-Ponty maintains a subtle objective, at work since his earliest projects: to renew the question of *knowledge*. Already in his 1930s thesis projects, we find the promise of "a theory of knowledge absolutely distinct from criticism."[86] Shortly after this, *The Structure of Behavior* makes a first reference to Claudel's *co-naissance*, in direct contrast to the criticist conception of knowledge, which "detaches from a thing," refusing to "live" in the thing, refusing any "participation in its existence."[87] Merleau-Ponty distinguishes himself from a philosophical tradition that, he says, takes "the contemplation of inanimate objects as the type and ideal of human knowledge, indifferent things, which do not *touch* us."[88] The philosopher of encroachment is obviously not satisfied with the cool distance in which this objectivist ontology encloses itself, constructing the known through projection and view from above, observing it from the height of the window of the *Second Meditation*. He denounces intellectualism, according to which "being only exists for someone who is capable of stepping back from it and is thus himself absolutely outside of being," a philosophy requiring that one "[cease] to exist in order to know."[89] Merleau-Ponty, on the contrary, wishes to recover the profound unity of the attitudes of *being* and *knowing*; to rediscover their unity in the carnal, quasi-organic infrastructures of knowledge, which cannot be considered merely a waiting room for form or information, but as an interrogation of our *connection* with all things: the amazed quest for a connaturalness that unites our self-awareness with the testing perception of the world's birth.

The unpublished manuscripts of 1948–49, influenced by Claudel, insist on this living experience of our attachments. Perception awakens a "connatural connection" between man and things, a "relationship of the subject to [the] world that is not of [an] intellectual constitution, but [a] more organic connection":[90]

> Our relation to a thing in perception ≠ relation of pure knowledge, but of living experience. . . . A thing is not in front of us, but with us, it wounds our body. We might even say that it is in us, it speaks to us and we respond without analyzing. . . . We are completely within things, and they are within us . . . things do not offer themselves to someone who is not connatural with them.[91]

As we hear in the radio talks of autumn 1948, this connaturalness is revived in modern art, which knows how to "recapture and reproduce before our very eyes the birth of the landscape,"[92] to "give birth to the outline and shape of objects in the same way that nature does."[93] But art possesses this power only to the extent that, like the painter, we give our body over to these metamorphoses, consenting to that which resonates in it, to the diapason of the modern artwork, our own coming into visibility, our own birth.

These ideas bring Merleau-Ponty closer to the Claudelian perspective, to the latter's conception—neither realistic nor idealistic—of a general and generative knowledge that precedes man, mobilizing his entire being, investing him with the *co-naissance* of things.[94] "I, man . . . I am in the world, I exercise my knowledge everywhere. I know all things and all things know themselves in me."[95] Knowledge does not arise in our capacity for projective withdrawal, but in our engagement with a sensible simultaneity that pushes us toward *co-naissance*. "Beyond all logic," says Jean Wahl, "there is a conversation between things, due solely to their coexistence and their interpenetration."[96] This is precisely the conversation the poet wishes to join.

It is through a kind of projection of his whole being that man comes into contact with different objects and takes advantage of them. This is the first point. In all knowledge, it is a case of something total engaging with the whole being. But the second point . . . is that this knowledge is something, we might say, in the things themselves; there would be no knowledge like ours if there were no coexistence inside things, what Claudel specifically refers to as a "*co-naissance*."[97]

For Claudel, Jean Wahl resumes, the problem of knowledge should begin not with an analysis of *our* modes of understanding but with an ontological study. "First, we must understand how things know each other; and it is only when we understand this profound knowledge relation that is in things, that we will be able to comprehend our own knowledge."[98] Wahl emphasizes the extent to which this approach breaks with the classical theory of abstraction, falling more in line with Alexander's *co-presence*, or Whitehead's *comprehension*.[99]

Metaphorical Figures of Passivity-Activity

For Merleau-Ponty, as for Claudel, man can know things in a fundamental way, a way of knowing that cannot be reduced to an (active) contemplation, where meaning is attributed to that which otherwise would not have had it, or to its (passive) alternative, the mere recording of a meaning that is already constituted. Claudel uses some choice poetic figures to describe this knowledge, markedly free from this alternative in their cultivation of a reciprocal tension that is dynamic (passive-active), topological (enveloping-enveloped) and archaeological (engendering-engendered). The most significant of these are *communion* (understood as mutual manducation and incorporation), *coupling* (in the sexual sense), *vibration*, and even *respiration*.

Merleau-Ponty regularly deploys these figures of passive-active reciprocity, from *Phenomenology of Perception* and the unpublished manuscripts of the late 1940s, right until his final work. Such is the case with *communion*, the Eucharistic manducation, where the consecrated bread is assimilated and assimilating in equal measure. Merleau-Ponty evokes this sacramental communion in *Phenomenology* to describe the relationship between sentient and sensible. In the corresponding pages, he presses his point through multiple references—Bergson's emerging movements, Goethe's classic texts on color, those of Kandinsky, the pathologies described by Goldstein—although he glosses over Claudel, from whom he borrowed this radical idea of sensation as *co-naissance* in the first place. The reference is transparent, however, in his use of the verb *co-naître*,[100] and, more than this, in his adoption of the very style of the author of *Art poétique*. The following passage, particularly indicative of his Claudelian osmosis, is one of the most daring in the whole of *Phenomenology of Perception*. It is an astonishing anticipation of the ontology of the sensible found in his later work, particularly in certain passages of *Eye and Mind* concerning the respiration of being, vibration, and "possession" by the sensible.

> The relations between sentient and sensible are comparable to those between the sleeper and his sleep: sleep arrives when a certain voluntary attitude suddenly receives from the outside the very confirmation that it was expecting. I breathe slowly and deeply to call forth sleep, and suddenly, one might say, my mouth communicates with some immense external lung that calls my breath forth and forces it back. A certain respiratory rhythm, desired by me just a moment ago, becomes my very being, and sleep, intended until then as a signification, turns itself into a situation. Similarly, I offer my ear or my gaze with the anticipation of a sensation, and suddenly the sensible catches my ear or my gaze; I deliver over a part of my body, or even my entire body, to this manner of vibrating and of filling space named "blue" or "red."

Merleau-Ponty continues the analogy:

> This is just as the sacrament does not merely symbolize, in a sensible way, an operation of Grace, but is the real presence of God and makes this presence occupy a fragment of space and to communicate it to those who eat the bread, given that they are inwardly prepared. In the same way, the sensible does not merely have a motor and vital signification, but is rather nothing other than a certain manner of being in the world that is proposed to us from a point in space, that our body takes up and adopts if it is capable, and sensation is, literally, a communion.[101]

Sensation as *co-naissance*: an idea as radical as that of *sacramental communion*, body and soul, from the flesh of man to the flesh of God, of the manducation of (the) Being via the visible transubstantiated bread, where man contributes the effort of his body, and where the Invisible is present within the visible, in a total imminence.[102]

These same pages of *Phenomenology of Perception* take up the biblical sense of "knowing" as *coupling*, which is reminiscent of *Art poétique*, especially the famous passage at the start of the "Treatise on *Co-Naissance*": "Blue truly knows the color orange, the hand truly knows its shadow on the wall . . . in the same sense that Isaac 'knew' Rebecca."[103]

> If qualities radiate a certain mode of existence around themselves, if they have a power to enchant, or if they have what we called earlier a sacramental value, this is because the sensing subject does not posit them as objects, but sympathizes with them, makes them its own, and finds in them his momentary law. Let us be more precise. The sensing being and the sensible are not opposite each other like two external terms, and sensation does not consist of the sensible invading the sensing being. My gaze subtends color, the movement of my hand subtends the form of the object, or rather my gaze pairs off with the color and my hand with the hard and the soft. In this exchange between the subject of sensation and the sensible, it cannot be said that one acts while the other suffers the action, nor that one gives sense to the other.[104]

This is the first time in his entire corpus that Merleau-Ponty evokes the idea of "coupling"—an image that becomes central to the philosophy of the flesh in the later manuscripts. We find this term employed only once again in *Phenomenology of Perception*, in a proposition serving as a summary of Merleau-Ponty's thesis, a definition of perception involving the intersection of erotic and sacramental overtones (the coupling and communion) of Claudel's *co-naissance*.[105]

> Every perception is a communication or a communion, the taking up or the achievement by us of an alien intention or inversely the accomplishment beyond our perceptual powers and as a coupling of our body with the things. If this was not noticed earlier, it is because the becoming aware of the perceived world was made difficult by the prejudices of objective thought.[106]

Under the influence of psychoanalysis, Merleau-Ponty gradually integrates these Claudelian resonances into an analysis of knowledge as *incorporation* (projection-introjection). And it is within the context of this same analysis that, from the fifties onwards, we find the development of his famous use of "coupling" as the overdetermined translation of "*Paarung*" (pairing) in the fifth of Husserl's *Cartesian Meditations*.[107] Such a combination—a poet's taste for the flesh and the mystical, the influence of psychoanalysis, as well as phenomenology—might seem audacious, risky even, but this is no less typical of the impression Merleau-Ponty leaves on his own culture, thus making his way, via the twists and turns of these borrowings, toward the original and dense identity of his concept of *flesh*.

To the vital corporeal themes of food and sexuality, Merleau-Ponty adds a third, more spiritual and musical carnal metaphorical register: that of *vibration*, also to be found in the pages of *Phenomenology of Perception* just mentioned. For Claudel, vibration is the image of *co-naissance* par excellence, given its capacity for forging difficult alliances: that of sensing and sensed in sensation,[108] as well as the force and form in the animal being,[109] of being and nothingness in desire's openings.[110] Vibration is the "element" of life itself,[111] the fundamental state of being, as moving, sensing, co-nascent.

> I believe that being is in a constant state of vibration. . . . What does this sort of emission resemble? . . . A birth! Being never ceases to be born. . . . We do not cease to be co-born with the world; our knowledge is the result of the circular flowering of our being, in constant state of vibration . . . whether to a greater or lesser extent, more or less enduring, the systole and the diastole of the heart: one always finds this vibrational movement in nature, especially in the living being, this rhythm of relaxation and tension. This is the whole idea behind *Art poétique*.[112]

In addition to portraying the passive-active complexity of our relationship with the world, *vibration*, for Claudel, also symbolizes the active union of soul and body.[113] Claudel takes the "spiritual body" of Saint Paul as a paradigm of the *actual* animated body:[114] not two separate and mutually articulating metaphysical moments, but a single movement. Vibration is the very mode of existence of this spiritual flesh that only *is* in its simmering contact with being, in its *co-naissance* with other bodies.[115] Vibration is not the joint act of a soul and a body, even less the preestablished harmony of two synchronized clocks. It is animation per se.

In his 1948–49 lectures, Merleau-Ponty places Claudel among the "artists of today" who reject the idea of a "preestablished harmony," and are "particularly sensitive to this vibration that form generates by taking possession of matter."[116] His own use of vibration retains its dense Claudelian sense.[117] Merleau-Ponty uses vibration to refer to the simultaneous movements or on-site shifts of force that wound a painting's forms, bestowing upon it its operating lines and radiant body.[118] This is precisely the vibration that Cartesian perspectivism would erase, with its tendency to reduce the flesh of the sensible into a lifeless wrapping.[119] Because if perception is neither the pure incursion of spirit into matter, nor, conversely, the simple invasion of the sensible into myself, then it is the communal vibration of perceiving and perceived spread throughout my body as in the world.[120] In a broader sense, vibration refers to being in the process of becoming.[121] This ontological vibration is "the cradle of things,"[122] "the nodes and anti-nodes of the same ontological vibration,"[123] the fundamental aim of philosophical inquiry.

As an image of life, of flesh as movement, as metaphor of being in the process of becoming, *vibration*—for Merleau-Ponty, as for Claudel—ultimately serves as an image of the encounter of desires, and desire's fulfillment. Under desire's influence, the flesh listens to the vibration of another's flesh, so as to know it, to comprehend it. In this vibration-in-unison of two desires, the passivity and activity of each forms the nodes and anti-nodes of the same wavelength, in a mutual comprehension that drives coupling and communion toward a radical co-birth (*co-enfantement*). The technical vocabulary of "nodes and anti-nodes" is intended to prevent a conception of desire's passivity and activity as a mutually static equilibrium—a summative cancellation of the dynamics of each, a final collapse of the tension of each into the immobile adjustment of the *poser-contre*. What we have, instead, is a dynamic continuous precession, in which the passivity of the one tunes into the activity of the other and vice versa, each reaching a higher point of passivity and activity, in a resonance that maximizes the tension and intention of these desires, as well as the unity of their communion.

Along with communion, coupling, and vibration, there is another Claudelian figure that should be mentioned here: *respiration*,[124] which is highlighted by Merleau-Ponty in *Eye and Mind*, the heir *par excellence* of his pre-ontological writings of the late 1940s. Emblematic of the reciprocal passivity-activity that Merleau-Ponty finds in Claudel's notion of *co-naissance*, respiration appears at the heart of those pages dedicated to the "continuous nascence" lived by perception—"this secret and feverish genesis of things in our body," which the painter attempts to render visible, "according to an efficacious similarity which is the parent, the genesis, the metamorphosis of Being in his vision."[125] Merleau-Ponty's debt to Rimbaud's heirs, Claudel and Breton, once again shines through in his affirmation of the role of the poet as seer, as the one who sees the invisible in the visible,[126] in the experience of all his senses. Everything is here: Rimbaud's seer, surrealism, Claudel's round-eyed mirror that returns our gaze, pregnancy and birth, the inspiration and expiration of Being.[127] While possibly too swift, the resulting text becomes clearer if we remember, as Jean Wahl remarks a few months later, that Merleau-Ponty is "faithful to the lessons of both Rimbaud and Claudel."[128]

> "I expect to be inwardly submerged, buried. Perhaps I paint to break out." We speak of "inspiration," and the word should be taken literally. There really is inspiration and expiration of Being, respiration

in Being, action and passion so slightly discernible that it becomes impossible to distinguish between what sees and what is seen, what paints and what is painted. It can be said that a human is born at the instant when something that was only virtually visible, inside the mother's body, becomes at one and the same time visible for itself and for us. The painter's vision is a continued birth.[129]

In this passive-active respiration, it is not strictly possible to distinguish knower from known, enveloping from enveloped, generating from generated. *Co-naissance* thus provides us with an image of Breton's longed-for sublime point, where the enveloping virtues of knowledge are always already intensified, taken over, by an emergence or birth that are being itself. Being is the nonobjectifiable depth that envelops us while compounding our desire to know, announcing itself in its appeal to be enveloped in return, to be named and known. So it is not surprising to find the use of unmistakably Claudelian qualifiers in Merleau-Ponty's ontology: a "deep" being,[130] a "cavity" (*creux*), "beneath" us, which "needs us"[131]— opposed to Descartes's and Sartre's being as "absolute fullness and complete positivity."[132]

In its drive for absolute clarity, the ontology of the object is paradoxically led into a blind alley: Completely erasing the invisible that was about to be seen from the thus petrified thing, it appears eminently repressive. In the strange light of this ontology, the subject seems to have no goal other than to hide behind the object, slipping into the irrevocable status of an irreversible invisibility, as though it became a subject, only never to be born, never to exist. In the unpublished volume of his *Introduction to Ontology*, Merleau-Ponty, to the contrary, resituates

> The problem of Being, in this fold [*pli*] where we appear, arising from being and destined for being. . . . Ontology is the attempt to formulate this nascence and *co-naissance*, to find that which is beyond naturalism and idealism, to portray man as he really is: not the sketch of an absolute subjectivity, but a *surrection* (upsurge), a light at the top of this incredible arrangement that is the human body.[133]

If we are sincere in our renunciation of the face-to-face encounter of subject and object, where we are sooner or later lead by realism and idealism, then we cannot escape this passive-active respiration, this irreducible circularity that sustains being itself. To be, is to be born and to arise: to come to visibility. But this applies to our own being, and it is inconceivable without our own coming into being—without our own birth.

Desire and Flesh of the World

Claude Simon's "Profound Novelty"

While Breton and Claudel profoundly influenced Merleau-Ponty's imagination and his conception of desire—most notably concerning the structural formulations of the enveloping-enveloped and engendering-engendered—we should also mention a third author who was equally influential in this regard: Claude Simon. This late influence, in many ways quite remarkable, is most noticeable in the development of Merleau-Ponty's famous notion of the "flesh of the world." An idea that, as we have seen, is already prefigured in Merleau-Ponty's engagement with surrealism.

Merleau-Ponty first uses the expression "flesh of the world" in the second chapter of *The Visible and the Invisible*, which he composed in the spring of 1959.[134] The expression crops up again a year later, marking the start of an effusive outpouring that continues until the last year of Merleau-Ponty's life. The expression "flesh of the world" can also be found in the writings of various contemporaries, most of whom were friends of Merleau-Ponty: Aimé Césaire,[135] Emmanuel Mounier,[136] René Huyghe,[137] and Claude Simon. A comparison would be pertinent in each case, although Claude Simon deserves most attention here, if only because of Merleau-Ponty's extensive references to this author in his course, "Cartesian Ontology and Ontology Today." It is here that we find the affirmation that, "we are flesh, within the 'flesh of the world' (*Le Vent*, p. 98)"—with an explicit reference to a specific page of Simon's novel, *Le Vent: Tentative de restitution d'un retable baroque* (1957).[138]

The courses of March 1961 insist on Claude Simon's "profound novelty."[139] Simon, we are told, does not compose things "from the outside," by "external contours and perspectives," but rather, like children's drawings or certain modern paintings: "like transparent presences without contours," like samples of a totality of existence, a totality "always showing itself as a kind of englobing, a kind of magma."[140] Claude Simon's "novelty" is thus, for the most part, formulated in markedly Merleau-Pontian terms, taking us back to what the philosopher had written ten years earlier in the *Prose of the World*. Only the metaphorical figure of *magma* is indeed novel and specific to the author (Simon in fact uses this term to describe his own work in his 1985 Stockholm speech after receiving the Nobel Prize). Through his own presentation of the writer's work, then, Merleau-Ponty turns Simon into a perfect ally in his opposition to the Cartesian ontology, and in his search for a "modern ontology."

Cl. Simon, speaking about *La Route des Flandres*: "everything came to mind, everything, all at once, like a sort of violent flash" (Madeleine interview).[141] "All that remained was to write down the . . . perception or the . . . I wouldn't say it was a thought, I do not believe I was thinking . . ." (Madeleine interview). He thinks in the same way that Cézanne "thought in painting;" he speaks with his voice and presents the world, renders it visible in a certain gesture—but this unveiling of the world, without separated thought, this is modern ontology.[142]

This perception-expression thinks, "without separated thought." It thinks through gesture and speech, or more generally, as in the case of the painter, through the entire body, in this way preserving the density of things themselves, rendering transparent their living topological structure. Leaving things "to bleed," to show that they are nonobjectifiable—the surrealist image of the "blood of things," first mentioned in the 1948–51 manuscripts, can be seen as a first step toward this idea of the "flesh of the world."[143] Things are left to express themselves, to reveal their own style, a way of being that provokes our own: things also have a "flesh." This strange phenomenological reduction is poles apart from Sartre's own reduction to define the flesh, as invoked in the latter's interpretation of Ponge's *Le parti pris des choses*.[144] Merleau-Ponty sees in the writer and artist's expressive work a possible essential contribution to the return to "the things themselves," at least to the extent that this expression is the co-expression of my flesh and the flesh of the world—neither could exist without the other. In this non-Leibnizian co-expression, the thing, as a "crystallization of desire," is expressed and expresses itself, because the phenomenologist, the painter, and the writer bring their bodies. Far from Claude Simon's "profound novelty," then, the late proposal of the "flesh of the world" is in fact the final logical step in Merleau-Ponty's series of proposals that punctuate the development of his philosophy of expression—from the "blood of things" to the "flesh of the sensible," via the "sensible world" and the "flesh of the thing."

In 1961, as in the unpublished manuscripts of 1948, Merleau-Ponty is seeking a "modern ontology" in response to a "Cartesian" ontology characterized as embarrassed by the idea of ontological mixing,[145] protecting itself against this embarrassment by its own imaginary infrastructure (where the projective and metric structures of the "extension" erase the carnal crystallizations that drive the originally topological structuring of the world). The lessons on Claude Simon consistently return to this idea of mixing:

"Mixing is chaos, but it is also the proliferation of meaning. The mixing of past, present and future, of the imaginary and the real . . ."[146] This is perhaps not the fairest presentation of Claude Simon's "profound novelty." Merleau-Ponty's reflections on "mixing" are perhaps more typically akin to Breton's *Second Manifesto of Surrealism* (1930), whose influence we have already examined.[147] The *Second Manifesto*, we recall, inherits, in part, a reflection on the experience of war: both Breton and the author of "The War Has Taken Place" are living in the wake of two different wars; the old categories have collapsed, and both are hoping to salvage thought from the ruins. Claude Simon is also deeply affected by the experience of war—perhaps even more so. But this does not lead him to the Merleau-Pontian coupling of sense and nonsense, or to the "proliferation of meaning."[148]

Intercorporeality and Promiscuity

Yet even if Claude Simon's "novelty" is immediately co-opted into the service of Merleau-Ponty's own thought,[149] this does not diminish the philosopher's genuine surprise at discovering a bold expression of intercorporeality in another author's work, especially one bearing such a remarkable resemblance to his own conception of the flesh. Consider the following passage, where Simon refers to the "flesh of the world," cited by Merleau-Ponty in his course on March 16, 1961:

> . . . or undressing, stretching their tired bodies, or already in bed, inert, sweating, and some struggling for pleasure with sighs and gasps . . . and it was as if I could hear something in all of it, something like breathing, like the respiration of her own flesh—that same secret multifarious mysterious palpitation—because the world's flesh is female by the very fact that it can engender and create without even knowing it . . . [150]

As in many other passages of his work, Claude Simon here delivers a condensed illustration of the polymorphic sense of the French *chair*: as that which is both meat (*Fleisch*) and living tissue, both maternal and erotic, mortal and fertile. Merleau-Ponty's furtive engagement with these diverse significations reveals a clear preference for one of them. In Simon's work he finds, above all, a surprising proximity to his own approach to the body's spatiality. Suffice it to say that Claude Simon's "profound novelty" lies in his deployment of a metaphorical and synthetic literary style, illustrating one of the philosopher's oldest and most transversal themes, that is, the body schema.

... nested space, vegetative space, like that of the bud's power, space of proliferation, akin to our flesh.... We are flesh, in the "flesh of the world" (*Le Vent*, p. 98). Space is the relation between our flesh and the flesh of the world. Whence this extraordinary description (in *L'Herbe*, pp. 181–184) of bodily space. A ubiquitous space, where bodies are superimposed on each other ...[151]

This carnal spatiality ties in with what Merleau-Ponty gleans from his study of Paul Schilder from 1953 onward—a spatiality thoroughly marked by the relational and desiring dimensions of the body schema, expressed in the *Ineinander* of body images.[152] More than this, it perfectly expresses Merleau-Ponty's favored image of carnal space as "promiscuous," as always already intercorporeally interwoven.[153] "Flesh of the world" appears in his work at the exact moment when, having just reread his lecture notes from 1953, 1955, and 1957, Merleau-Ponty devotes himself to the largest of his three folders on *Being and World*, choosing to entitle the second chapter, "Intercorporeality—Promiscuity."[154] The preparation of this same chapter is extended a year later in his *Notes on the Body*, as well as the 1960 course on *Nature*, where he addresses the Schilderian theme of the entanglement of body images, which is also supported by his reading of Melanie Klein's treatment of incorporation. As we can see, the regime of the "flesh of the world" is in full swing.

A carnal spatiality, expressed as promiscuity, incorporation, *Ineinander* of body schemas: In 1960 Merleau-Ponty discovers an extraordinary description of this while reading Claude Simon's *La route des Flandres*—especially in the third part, where Simon combines the evocation of an erotic scene with the proximity of dying bodies in the trenches. Here are three brief excerpts:

> I kept running over her crawling under her exploring in the darkness discovering her enormous and shadowy body as though under a milk-giving goat ... sucking the perfume of her bronze breasts finally reaching that warm tuft lapping intoxicating myself ... feeding on me becoming me or rather me becoming it and then there was nothing left of my body but a shrunken wizened foetus lying between the lips of a ditch as if I could melt into it disappear there engulf myself there.[155]

> feed on me my flesh nourishing the earth ... far back in her mouth like a greedy child it was as if we were drinking each other slaking each other's thirst gorging on each other feasting famished.[156]

> I carefully stepped over the interlocking bodies (they looked like corpses). . . . We lay trembling all our limbs shivering closely interlaced entwined . . . groping for her flesh for the entrance for the opening of her flesh among that tangled . . . [157]

We find two complementary correlations with Merleau-Ponty's thought here, as distributed throughout the latter's oeuvre. The first is, again, that of *promiscuity*, as emphasized by Merleau-Ponty in his course on Claude Simon.[158] A polymorphic promiscuity expressed in the most fundamental of carnal reversibilities (and highlighted by Claude Simon's technique of literary superimposition).

Promiscuity is conjugated in a double sense, spatial and temporal, worked on by the philosopher from 1955, extended to the ideas of coupling and pregnancy in the final manuscripts. Mixing (to the point of becoming "magma"), interweaving, intertwining,[159] presented on the one hand as a topological or spatial layering, as enveloping-enveloped, and, on the other, as a temporal or archaeological layering, as engendering-engendered. The enveloping-enveloped reveals itself in its most archaic, vegetative or animal aspects—as respiration,[160] as nutrition[161]—and as coupling. The temporal aspect, the engendering-engendered, culminates in pregnancy,[162] although this has already begun at the level of the enveloping-enveloped: respiration, food, and coupling all involve the engagement of vital reversibilities (between active and passive, inside and outside, myself and others) that participate in the generation of ourselves and others. This conjugation of promiscuity is echoed, it should be noted, in the images of passive-active reciprocity Merleau-Ponty draws from Claudel[163]—although this convergence should nevertheless be qualified, and we will return to this, by each writer's very different treatment of the same poetic figures of the flesh.

The Existential Structures of Desire

The second area of correlation, between Claude Simon's descriptions and Merleau-Ponty's approach to the flesh, concerns the questions of drive and desire. The correlation here lies mainly at the level of literary imagination; on a conceptual level, there are significant differences. Given the texts we have just read, we would expect Merleau-Ponty to eventually consider the drive, or the pair Eros/Thanatos, in his commentary on Claude Simon.[164] Merleau-Ponty's writing on the "flesh of the world" betrays a conceptual ambivalence between desire and drive; the concept of flesh simultaneously contains and retains these two dynamics, each fully expressed, although not fully thought through.[165]

In the spring of 1960, Merleau-Ponty furtively evokes the Freudian pair, *Eros* and *Thanatos*:

> Freudian *Eros* and *Thanatos* rejoin our problem of the flesh with its double sense of opening and narcissism, mediation and involution.
> —Freud truly saw with projection-introjection and sadomasochism the relation of the *Ineinander* of ego and world, of ego and nature, of ego and animality, of ego and *socius*.[166]

In its spontaneity, the formulation of these lecture notes betrays a somewhat inverted personal perspective: "Freud's *Eros* and *Thanatos* share our problem of the flesh." Furthermore, the Freudian Thanatos, or death drive, is noticeable for its absence from the Merleau-Pontian anthropology, and this absence is felt in the philosopher's reading of Claude Simon. Merleau-Ponty is also spontaneously selective in his consideration of Claude Simon's polymorphic flesh: while both maternal and erotic, the Merleau-Pontian flesh is nevertheless more fertile than it is death-bearing, more unified and unifying than split, fragmented, or fragmenting.[167] It remains inextricably linked to an anthropology haunted by the opportunity and growth of connection with others—a "binding principle" that, at the heart of the life drive, impedes the very notion of drive itself.

Despite this important difference, there is a genuine proximity between Claude Simon's descriptions and Merleau-Ponty's poetic figures (in their multiplicity as well as their detail), in their eventual adumbration of a picture of the existential structures of desire.[168] If desire is fundamentally the desire *to be*, it is also inextricably the desire *to be with*, in a reciprocal sense. The desire *to be with* what is—and to a greater extent, with others—in the experience of a communal lift (*portance commune*) (so that the *communion* that fundamentally *desires* desire, is not a fusion of two beings, but involves being itself as an included third, as the bearer of their coexistence). To be *with beings* who are with me *in being*—and Merleau-Ponty often writes "Being" with an enigmatic uppercase, so as to better distinguish it from "beings."[169]

The desire to be with (another) can be so strong that it turns into a desire to *be* this other. A desire to *be* that is not without *having*, so much is it traversed by the incorporation process. So that the "me with you, and you with me," which we find at the inauguration of desire's chiasmatic adventures, becomes a "me in you and you in me": a "being with the other," where *being* is radicalized (in the sense of an act, that also plays out with all the intensity of a *becoming*), just as the reciprocal "together-with" is radicalized, to the point of "being one *in* the other" *Ineinander*. "As soon as our gazes meet," the chiasmatic life of desire has already begun, "making an inside of its outside, and an outside of its inside." Incorporating another, one incorporating the other: the existential structure of desire, as sustained by its most libidinal and erotic dimension (a dimension that is equally fantastical—an originary fantasy that might very well be the origin of all fantasy)—yet without being reducible to this.

The same structure inhabits the very foundations of knowledge: from our first epistemophilic relationships with the world, as Merleau-Ponty interprets Melanie Klein's analysis;[170] from the most corporeal learning processes (the "habits" described by Merleau-Ponty as an intimate articulation of being and having, a full expression of the body schema's incorporative strategies,[171] with desire proving itself inseparable from the sensorimotor foundations of intelligence); and from "coupling," in the archaic and ultimate sense of a "knowing" relationship with the sensible world, also echoing the biblical sense of "knowing."

Being one *in* another: in addition to its erotic and knowing dimensions, this existential structure of desire also includes a mystical horizon, as in the Johannine art of the chiasm.[172] From the most erotic, to the most intellectual and spiritual—while still conveying the archaic maternal oral dimension—desire's "being another" touches on the fantasy of "eating another" and being eaten by another—with "being" here almost indistinguishable from "having." Eating another, an act of assimilation in which the other becomes my substance—without actually losing his own substance, since he thus goes all the way of his being-with, since we thus go all the way of our communion.[173]

This description of relationship as substantial exchange is a theme that runs throughout the later manuscripts—the famous "passage of myself in another and another in me," as thematized from the Mexico lectures onward.[174] A substantial relation that affects my own and the other's substance, a substantial communion that becomes a transubstantial relation, coupling as mutual manducation: This is still a matter of describing the "relation of being" that Merleau-Ponty finds in the most perceptual and desirous aspects of our being-in-the-world. Yet we should not be fooled by the apparent metaphysical coloring of such terminology ("being," "substance"); in fact, it is precisely the (typically metaphysical) separation between substance and relation that is reversed by such descriptions. The expression, "relation of being," eloquently expresses this nonseparation. By "substance," Merleau-Ponty is referring to "my" and not "the" substance, in resonance with the visceral oneirism of the "substantial," in the sense of "substantial nutrition."

This same oneiric idea of "feeding off another" effects a transition, once again, between the enveloping-enveloped topology of desirous incorporation, and the engendering-engendered, which is also subject to the existential structure of desire, pushed to its peak by the carnal reversibility that animates it.[175] To feed off another, to the point of being engendered by this other, born of this other; to feed another to the point of engendering this other, giving birth to this other. As though all desire were essentially a desire to be co-born (*co-naître*)—from its most cognitive to the most affective dimensions, and of course beyond this differentiation—from the existential dimensions of perception: to be with "all these things existing together," to be with things that exist and coexist, to be born with things that are co-nascent, to see them and conceive of them, to be seen by and conceived by them. To know (to be born with) (*co-naître* [*avec*]) the world.

But this redoubling of the enveloping-enveloped in the engendering-engendered, this accomplishment of pregnancy in birth, transforms in turn the spatiality of the flesh, as well as its possible conception. The *Ineinander* thus loses its descriptive privilege in favor of a new schema, which begins to make a discrete appearance from the 1955 course on passivity onward, in Merleau-Ponty's reflections on "the fertility of desire" within the realms of the oneiric and the unconscious, and in relation to an anti-Sartrean conception of freedom: *surrection*—"*surrection* or insurrection or resurrection . . . this fertility or productivity."[176] This fertility, "is the power of what we have desired, all the greater since we have also repressed it. . . . The unconscious = modality of embodiment, i.e., of repressed desire—Upheaval [*Surrection*] of the unconscious and erection of the body."[177] The *surrection* of the unconscious, and the erection of the body, in the insurrection of desire: At the heart of these daring formulations lies an intimate relationship between the unconscious, corporeity, and desire, the tracing of a combined image of birth and of freedom.[178] This "surrection" has an existential dimension, as resumed from its most corporeal roots. The desire to be born, the desire to give birth, the desire for the other, to make him flesh and to give birth to his desire, in the animation of various *surrections* and resurrections, from the substantial to the subtle, from the most organic to the most linguistic.

In Merleau-Ponty's late writing, partially inspired by Teilhard de Chardin's own oneirism, "surrection" also becomes the symbol of a humanity that rises every morning, straightening itself up on the constellations of the world, rising up in the face of adversity and nonsense, who stands, upright, in the depths of a vertical being. "Man appears as an awake being, we cannot talk about him as though he were not born, as though he were never asleep."[179] Against Sartre's conception of divine freedom transposed onto man—entrusted with the full powers of consciousness and thus protected from the invisible, armed with creations that detonate in front of him, serving as protections from the past—Merleau-Ponty emphasizes a perpetual birth and *surrection*. In the flesh, creation is respiration of the invisible and emergence of the invisible within the visible,[180] and freedom opens up the future in a *surrection*, insurrection, and resurrection of the past, which can only thus be surpassed.[181]

This understanding of the flesh, now described as a vital dynamic of *surrection*, destabilizes Merleau-Ponty's privileged treatment given to incorporation and intercorporeality. It demands, at least, a change in their usual understanding, as expressed in the patterns of encroachment, *Ineinander*, or even circularity. The spatiotemporality of the flesh remains forever an interwoven intercorporeality, yet it no longer plays out merely in the enveloping-enveloped of coupling and pregnancy. Flesh *arises* in the depths of the world, in "the real outside."[182] The Copernican revolutions experienced at each of its multiple births release it from its enclosure, freeing it to proceed and progress, beyond the flesh, in the "*native* arising of being."[183] Ontology, as Merleau-Ponty writes at the start of the first folder of *Being and World*, must "portray man as he really is," as "surrection," "in this fold [*pli*] where we appear, arising from being and destined for being." Ontology, he says, is "the attempt to formulate this nascence and *co-naissance*."[184]

The Flesh of the World: Impasses

While deploying Claude Simon's "flesh of the world," Merleau-Ponty's poetics of the existential structures of desire nevertheless leads to a further disparity with the writer: his poetics seems to traverse the "flesh of the world" to the point of burdening it with a load that exceeds its capacities. I have shown elsewhere how this concept forms a culminating point in Merleau-Ponty's attempt to think the "general body," the ability of the body schema to extend itself into the world and others, particularly in its strategies of incorporative desire.[185] Understanding the *flesh* as the *body's generality* leads to a generalization of the second-degree: that is, from the flesh itself, to the flesh of the world. For Merleau-Ponty, our being in the world is borne by (and via) an incorporative regime, from the outset animated by the concerns of a radical intercorporeity, so that incorporation becomes "relation of being," with the *flesh* at risk of becoming the result of a ceaseless polymorphic introjection, and the *flesh of the world*—this "other side" . . . of the same—seeming to become the result of a massive projection . . . of the flesh.

The vertigo of the enveloping-enveloped, of an *Ineinander* regime with an unlimited appetite for extension, seems to blur all differentiations.

Merleau-Ponty so systematically overvalues "encroachments" that the dynamic of encroachment is itself threatened: With no boundaries to transgress, all separations are reduced. Conforming to the ordinary French use of the term, Merleau-Ponty initially uses "encroachment" (*empiétement*) to refer to a form of intrusion into another's flesh: Its violence and possible fruit of coexistence remain the modes of a bond that connects two beings, two part-strangers. But what happened to the "blood of others," which marked the beginnings of "encroachment" and "flesh" during the philosopher's existentialist period? What remains of the "blood of things," which marked the first lineaments of his ontology around the same period, anticipating the "flesh of the world" itself?[186] "Objects bleed," that is, they have a flesh; they express themselves and express us, and it is here, in their separation and strangeness, that they demand an unexpected kinship with us. Twelve years after the Mexico lectures, where is this injury and otherness? Ten years after *Man and Adversity*, what remains of the adversity that played, yet again, such a major role in Merleau-Ponty's drafted introduction to his ontology at the end of 1957 (*Nature or the World of Silence*)? This is not to say that everything is cauterized and closed off in a preestablished harmony—far from it. Merleau-Ponty indeed considers the question of death, and the "flesh of the world" is not the best of possible worlds. But the "promiscuity of birth and love and death"[187] that Merleau-Ponty asserts in March 1961, while remaining faithful to Claude Simon's imaginative universe, deserves further commentary from the philosopher, that is, more than a repeated observation of a generalized encroachment, in a repetitive style of writing that makes use of a number of overlapping terms, all of which express the same imaginative nucleus: mixture, chaos, proliferation, magma, promiscuity, nesting, encroachment, and so on.[188]

The metaphor of the "flesh of the world," starting with Claude Simon, touches on some significant oneiric roots of the very concept of "world," as strongly associated with an oral and uterine imagination, cultivating the coming-and-going, the departing and return movement of an erotic ballet of introjection and ejection, all the way to the reversibility of *surrection* and burial, birth and death.[189] These same oneiric dimensions are found in the later Merleau-Ponty, in his occasional suggestions of the equivalence of coming and going, birth and death—an equivalence that is nevertheless contestable: because one can never escape birth, the experience of becoming separate. Separation is an irreplaceable ordeal, played out in the flesh from the moment of the corporeal and existential experience of birth, from the *corps à corps* with the mother and its inevitable splitting.[190] Along with *encroachment* and *circularity*, separation offers a third fundamental dimension of the flesh in its desirous experience of being. According to an undeniable lacuna, Merleau-Ponty's endo-ontology fails to sufficiently incorporate this dimension, which occasionally drives the flesh—notably, in the experience of another's death, and the grieving process that ensues—to the silence of feeling, a desire of being without content and without world.

It seems that the critical (notably anti-Cartesian and anti-Sartrean) intentions behind his formulation of the concept of flesh take Merleau-Ponty a step too far. His opposition to the *partes extra partes*, to the encounter between consciousness and object, to a mineral imagination where separations are such that one can no longer conceive the strength of our relationships with others and our ontological attachments, at times leads the philosopher of the flesh to an opposite excess. To the excess of an overgeneralized encroachment, which risks dissolving into its own generality; an ontology of the flesh of the world already containing all relations within itself—contained and retained, preserved, as a fetish protected from time—within a pregnancy too all-embracing to lead to any genuine birth.[191] To a true separation, without which persons cannot achieve identity, without which we cannot go beyond the world's pregnancy, toward that which constitutes its very accomplishment: an experience of the upward lift of being.

A late addition, the "flesh of the world" was perhaps meant to be provisional. "Flesh" and "world" are insufficient in our attempts to think through the structures of perception, expression, and desire that sustain the transcendence of our being-in-the-world: Our flesh, being connected to the world and others, and so as to be related to them, needs to be related to being, and not just the world. So the question remains as to whether *being* can be thought of as *flesh of the world*, without being reduced to a fleshly circularity, insufficient for our attempts to consider the horizons of desire, which are opened at the slightest perception. In other words, if the "ontological mystery which is enclosed in the flesh of the sensible"[192] is really contained in it, then it cannot be assimilated to it. To express this mystery, Merleau-Ponty's ontology follows other tracks, not least: those of the invisible, depth, the incorporeal, or the shadow. These metaphorical figures of being cannot be assimilated to the "flesh" of the world, because they refer less to the flesh than to what expresses the flesh and what is expressed by it, to what sustains it and what it desires, what carries the flesh within being, and what carries it toward being.

Epilogue: Being and Desire

We return to these "other tracks" in our chapter devoted to metaphor. Before this, and in preparation for it, we might do Merleau-Ponty justice not only by pointing out that these "other tracks" are also present alongside his analysis of Claude Simon, but to comment on another writer: Paul Claudel—a completely different writer of the flesh, although this does not mean we should characterize Claudel and Simon as alternatives. Merleau-Ponty never makes this mistake, and neither does he oppose these two writers. The overall dynamic that moves from the flesh of the world to metaphorical figures of being is not formulated in a movement from Claude Simon to Paul Claudel, as though these authors simply provided an allegorical literary support to two alternative philosophies of the flesh. Neither can we locate Merleau-Ponty somewhere between Simon and Claudel, or as moving from one to the other, even if their impossible conjunction seems to hold together in his thought, as reflected in the hesitation, even ambivalence, of certain aspects of his thinking. Because these same tensions are also found within Claudel's thought, which has always inspired Merleau-Ponty, who finds therein so many possibilities for his own philosophy, both in the rich meaning of the concept of flesh and in the complexity of our relations to the world and to others.

At the intersection of the themes of the flesh of the world, fantasy and loss, of the link between the pleasure principle and the reality principle, and also, above all, of separation and desire, Merleau-Ponty is particularly fond of a certain Claudelian text: the scenes of the Moon and Double Shadow in *Le soulier de satin*.[193] Of all the playwright's works, these scenes offer probably the most beautiful of his many reworkings of personal pain, distanced through mythologization: specifically, his love for Rosalie Vetch, already transposed into "Ysé" (Yseult or Isolde . . .) in *Partage de Midi*. Rodrigue and Prouhèze love and desire each other, at the heart of an impossible relation. Claudel presents them as borne by the same shadow that cries their union as well as their separation, and then as bathing together in the depth of the Moon, the lunar being, the flesh of the world that reunites them, a maternal being in whose envelopment they commune with each other in the depths of their flesh. Rodrigue and Prouhèze are born together and reborn through their carnal union, they are *co-naissant* to the point of conception. The being in which they are enveloped is pregnant with their coupling; they are pregnant with the being they engender through their union: Being is the enveloping-enveloped and engendering-engendered of their desire, their relationship, their story even.

It is no coincidence that Merleau-Ponty comments on these scenes several times; emblematic of his own figural universe, they are also emblematic of important dimensions of his anthropology and his ontology. They seem to provide the perfect example of the staging of a fantasy in which the pleasure principle encourages a rejection of separation and leads desire toward a hallucination of its own fulfillment. Such a reading nonetheless misses the potentially deepest significance, which Merleau-Ponty indeed explores in his own way.

Having already mentioned these scenes in his course on passivity (1955), the philosopher returns to them in greater length in the ontology lectures of March 1961. He points out the obvious impossibility of Rodrigue and Prouhèze's relationship, the visible reality of their separation, while also affirming the effective reality of an invisible connection—a connection that is real and not fantastical—and he tries to express that which is most difficult: the subtle articulation of these two dimensions, one visible, the other invisible, both seemingly contradictory, yet perfectly real. An articulation concerning our relationship with others, of which Merleau-Ponty finds the originary inscription in perceptual life and the sensible world. As usual, this is not so much a fair exegesis of the author's text as an attempt to find therein and deepen some essential dimensions of his own thought, in its two inextricably connected sides: (1) a *phenomenological ontology* preoccupied with the relations between visible and invisible, between perception and image, reality and the imaginary; (2) a *phenomenological anthropology*, concerned with thinking the possibilities and modalities of interpersonal relationship across these same dimensions. These two concerns are dealt with in the later manuscripts in the form of some original reflections on the role of the invisible and depth, the incorporeal and shadow—in perception, painting, and speech.

As we have already seen, Merleau-Ponty acknowledges the distance between Claudel and the rationalistic harmonies of Leibniz.[194] Claudel's approach to simultaneity and *co-naissance* is that of the "modern world," not of the "classical world." Like the "encroachment" of Merleau-Ponty's existentialist period, it speaks of a coexistence interwoven of desires, of violence and contradictions, of relationship forged in distance. The separation between the two lovers is effective: "In the visible, Rodrigue and Prouhèze are separate,"[195] and "each is impossible for the other."[196] Yet while impossible, their union is indeed real; not satisfied with a visual connection, an imaginary relationship, nor a purely spiritual connection, a union "in God," it is a union of the flesh (in the same radical sense, we recall, that Claudel attributes to "*co-naissance*," as implying the biblical sense of "knowing" as sexual union: "Adam knew Eve," the "flesh of his flesh"). This is also a union of flesh within the Merleau-Pontian ontological horizon of flesh and desire: Through their involvement in this desirous relation, each transfers their "indistinction with all the being" to the other and accedes, in the other, to his own relationship with everything. So that being is plunged into the heart of this relationship, yet without adding itself as an extra entity.[197] This radically carnal and ontological relationship extends all the way to engendering: "In an instant, passion creates a 'new being.'"[198]

And both—separation and union—are intimately related: "a unity forged in separation i.e. possible death, cf. Claudel's double shadow, the moon as inscription of the irrevocable."[199] This union is not forged *in spite of* separation, but *in* it, and partly *because of* it—"this adherence to the other, and all things, can only be maintained through distance."[200] In his commentary on the *Song of Songs*, the biblical book profoundly marked by desirous knowledge, unto its erotic dimensions, Claudel summarizes this dialectic tension, poles apart from a regressive fusion:

> What we call a high wall is precisely the connection, the supersubstantial communication that unites us, the blissful separation that allows us to be one, while yet being two. . . . We are unified, not by fusion, but by difference. We draw blissfully on each other our reasons forever to differ.[201]

Le soulier de satin presents us with a representational limit, one of the secret devices of Claudelian theater: a "supersubstantial" union in separation. "But I, whose shadow do they say I am? Not of this separate man and woman, but of both at once, one in the other, in me submerged."[202] Where we find the diffuse and discreet existence of an included third: this shadow, which is not an extra being, but that which is included in both union and separation, in their hidden coherence. Rodrigue and Prouhèze are united in "the land of shadows," in "the night sun," in "the brightness of the Moon."[203] Merleau-Ponty asks: "What exactly is the land of shadows, the night sun? Reconciliation in death?"[204] His response, both challenging and surprisingly powerful, is without a doubt the peak of his commentary:

> No, on the contrary, it is the most real: the "indestructible archives," "the page of eternity." The being-no-longer is founded on "having been"—anti-Platonism: the visible is certainly not everything, but truer still is its double, the shadow that "alone exists." Each is for the other the impossible, and though their union lasted but "a single second," this being behind the present, which could not remain there, was inaugurated and created in the present. . . . It is not an *illusion* of reality.[205]

The invisible in question, then, is not an illusion. It is not simply the remains of the visible (assuming that "the visible is not everything"): it is "truer" than the visible, "the most real," an "indestructible" reality even, that "alone exists." Merleau-Ponty also speaks of a dimension that is "forever inscribed,"[206] of an "inerasable" shadow.[207] But this shadow is not, symmetrically, a hidden reality, turning the visible into a false appearance, an illusion—and Merleau-Ponty defends against this: "Not spiritualism, but a philosophy of the flesh and the incorporeal as two sides of the same Being."[208] If the shadow of the visible is "truer" than the visible, if in a sense it "alone exists," this does not mean that it exists without the visible. Suffice it to say that once introduced, these difficult ideas, each of which is brimming with significance, are still far from being fully developed. They draw on certain ultimate and original lines of Merleau-Ponty's phenomenology of perception, notably what the philosopher will later refer to as "figuratives" (*les figuratifs*)—to be addressed in Chapter 5, on metaphor.

The Claudelian scenes of the Moon and the Double Shadow, and the inspiration Merleau-Ponty draws therefrom, provide a remarkable converging point for the ideas pioneered over this chapter. The *shadow*, whose physical status is but a consequence and weaker version of the being of which it is the shadow, is reclaimed and overdetermined by Merleau-Ponty in a completely different way. No longer the projected shadow, but a sustaining shadow, a being even stronger for its discreet effectiveness, the perfect example of an incorporeal dimension that bears the flesh and its relations. No longer the shadow of a singular being, but the shadow that bears beings together, attesting to an invisible and surreal union that nevertheless does not erase our visible and real separation.

The depth and the light of lunar being are themselves figurations of being as the connection between beings, accentuating complementary tonalities. They illustrate this "flesh of the world," which is neither flesh nor world, the designation of an enveloping element wherein desirous beings couple and commune their entire being with each other. But this depth and light are an element enveloping their mutual desire, while also radiating from this communion itself. Not as an external third party, but as an included third in their desirous relationship, functioning as an ontological milieu, itself generative of, and generated by, this relationship. Their communion of desire comes to surpass them, as a redoubling of desire that carries and comprehends them, transports and exceeds them, in a communal rapture. This opens a subtle transcendence within their reciprocal exchange: transcendence at the heart of their greatest intimacy, an opening within the most intoxicating circularity. Without any alienation other than this communal ecstasy, this mutual surrender to a circulation that exceeds them, deepens and relaunches their desire. A communal *surrection*, which is nothing less than being itself.

We are reminded of that beautiful passage in the *Visible and the Invisible*—"coupling with the flesh of the world"—where the human being is portrayed as "fascinated by the unique occupation of floating in Being with another life, of making the outside of its inside and the inside of its outside," with "movement, touch, vision, applying to the other and to themselves, return toward their source," "in the patient and silent labor of desire."[209] It is easy to see why this poetic text, with its patently erotic overtones, is often interpreted as expressing a regressive fantasy, with "floating in Being" referring to the intrauterine and amniotic fluid. Perhaps. But this is to dismiss it too easily out of hand, as offering us nothing important to think about, while glossing over that which is most difficult to articulate: the phenomenality of desire, the discrete introduction of being as milieu, as source and fulfillment: as the milieu of life, and as source of the *surrection* and horizon of desire, the desire that *desires* in both, as well as the desire *desired* by both. In this *poetics of being*, of being in relation to (the relations of) the flesh, we are faced with what might be considered the most beautiful possibilities of Merleau-Ponty's thought, his anthropology's fulfillment in ontology, and the best of what phenomenology has to offer.

"As soon as gazes meet," we are "no longer wholly two, and it is hard to remain alone."[210] Because we are already opened upon being, the included third in our relationship, the "common framework"[211] of our worlds, matrix of our desires and offspring of their chiasm. This economy of exchanged desire is not merely a face-to-face encounter between two beings, but a movement toward being itself, which is not a separate additional entity, but the very enveloping-enveloped of both desiring and desired, the very engendering-engendered of their coupling. This liturgy of desire's communion thus points us toward something other than desire: toward a double impregnation—of our union within the being that envelops us, and of the being within us, that is generated through this union—which is also a double bearing. Love is the climax of relationship, because it engages, at both the origins and limits of desire, a *co-naissance*, the source and fulfillment of being-together.

Translated by Janice Deary

From the World of Silence to Poetic Language
Merleau-Ponty and Valéry

GALEN A. JOHNSON

Near the end of Merleau-Ponty's *Notes de Cours 1959–1961* is a rough draft of an unpublished essay ("*Brouillon d'une rédaction*") dating from October–November 1960. It was omitted from *The Visible and the Invisible*, but it nevertheless bears much interest for its last section, titled "The Voice of Silence, or the Philosophical Question (*La voix du silence ou la question philosophique*)." Here Merleau-Ponty situated philosophical interrogation more precisely in relation to three orders or three dimensions: first, the world of silence; second, the universe of speech; and third, the world of thought, especially philosophical thought. He argues that these are not parallel orders among which we would search for point by point coincidence, but rather that they are three dimensions of the same Being in which there is an "exchange" or "chiasma" (NC, 377) made possible by their overlapping horizons: "the horizon of the visible, the horizon of the nameable, and the horizon of the thinkable" (NC, 378). Philosophy is able to speak of the world of silence because it lets the things say what they themselves want to say ("*leur laisse dire ce qu'elles-mêmes veulent dire*"). Precisely in this context, Merleau-Ponty then cites the last five lines of the last stanza from Paul Valéry's poem "La Pythie" ("The Pythoness"):

> Now a Wisdom makes utterance,
> And rings out in that sovereign voice
> Which when it rings can only know
> It is no longer anyone's
> So much as the woods' and the waters' voice![1]

In this chapter, we will explore and clarify the meanings of silence in both poetic language and in Being, doing so through a focus on Merleau-Ponty's appropriations from Valery's poets and poetics. Among those poets, we will have the opportunity to consider the links among Valéry, Baudelaire, Mallarmé, and Edgar Allan Poe, as well as Valéry's critique of Proust and the novel. Differences between Valéry and the poetry and poetic of Francis Ponge, another of France's great poets of the twentieth century, will throw light upon the parallel differences between Merleau-Ponty and Sartre regarding poetic language. Throughout, our theme of silence will lead us to Valéry's greatest poetic concepts, according to Merleau-Ponty: embodied form, semantic thickness, and implex.

Merleau-Ponty, Valéry, Proust

We know that Merleau-Ponty also cited Valéry's "La Pythie," though without attribution, in the penultimate sentence of *The Visible and the Invisible*, thereby lending a certain authority both to this impersonal and anonymous "Wisdom" and "Voice" and to their poet, Valéry: "And in a sense, as Valéry said, language is everything since it is the voice of no one, since it is the very voice of the things, the waves, and the forests" (VI, 204/155). By the time of the late writings, Merleau-Ponty had pursued the significance of silence beyond the silent art of painting where he had first addressed it in "Indirect Language and the Voices of Silence."[2] He was now interested in the ontological question of silence, or the "world of silence," as he named it in his 1957 unpublished manuscript *La Nature ou le monde du silence*.[3] The unpublished rough draft included in *Notes de Cours 1959–1961* from which we began has for its context the third chapter of *The Visible and the Invisible* titled "Interrogation and Intuition." Here Merleau-Ponty discusses at greater length the question of the coincidence or noncoincidence between language and things. On the one hand, from the point of view of a philosophy of intuition that seeks coincidence with the world, the philosopher who speaks displays "an inexplicable weakness: he should keep silent" for his language is only a "power for error" that cannot state his contact with Being (VI, 166/125). However, on the other hand, if we abandon the demand of coincidence, and furthermore, if we say, "language is a life, is our life and the life of things" (VI, 167/125), as Valéry had said, then language is not closed in upon itself. This living language "is not a mask over Being, but—if one knows how to grasp it with all its roots and all its foliation—the most valuable witness to Being" (VI, 167/126). Merleau-Ponty suggests the qualities of this living language: metaphor, lateral relations, kinships, transfers, and exchanges. He affirms that this "language of life" is also the language of literature and poetry and, moreover and above all, this "language lives only from silence" (VI, 168/126). Poetic language is "open upon the things" only because it is "called forth by the voices of silence" (VI, 168/126–27). Thus, Merleau-Ponty argues that silence is necessary for speech as its living background and horizon; the power of speech and writing, indeed of all genuine expression, is born from silence. Without its nourishment, language is only a weakness and a mask over Being.

When Merleau-Ponty writes in this way of language as a "power for error" and an "inexplicable weakness," the unstated reference is to Paul Valéry, whose work and life Merleau-Ponty discusses in his 1953 course at Collège de France, *Recherches sur l'usage littéraire du langage.* At the beginning, Merleau-Ponty says, Valéry could write only "through weakness or cynicism" (ULL, 63, 93). Writing was a "compromise between the rigor of silence and the stupidity of life" ("*écrire = compromis entre rigueur qui est silence et vie qui est bêtise*") (ULL, 77–78). Valéry made this the opening of *Monsieur Teste,* a work we will discuss in more detail below: "Stupidity is not my strong suit" (CW, 6:8/O, 2:15). The journal edited by André Breton and the surrealists, *Littérature,* had posed their question to Valéry in December 1919: "Why do you write?" Valéry had answered: "out of weakness."[4] His answer reflected, as Merleau-Ponty says, an attitude of cynicism toward much of literature and writing as lacking in rigor, lacking in lucidity, produced out of consideration for the requirements of the reading public rather than as an exercise of intellect and pure form. Valéry had little respect for novels, including even Proust's *In Search of Lost Time* (*À la recherche du temps perdu*), consigning to them a "naturalism" of the everyday lacking that rigor of composition and calculation demanded of the self-conscious artist. The only major novelist he admired was Stendhal: "he is so reasonable."[5] He also admired the stories of Poe precisely for their rigor of composition and we will give attention to the influence of Poe below. In his *"Hommage à Proust,"* Valéry praises poetry as an "exercise in precision and continuous liaison between the sense of hearing, the form of the voice, and articulate expression." In contrast, he finds in the novel a "trick of the eye" (*trompe l'oeil*) that shares affinity with the tangible objects and natural descriptions of things in everyday life and languages. This is why we can give a résumé of a novel but not of a poem. What Valéry praises in Proust is that he "turned such a loose and simple structure to the most extraordinary account. . . . Proust analyzes—and gives us the feeling of being able to go on analyzing indefinitely—what other writers usually pass over. . . . an *infinity of* possibilities." This is a "treasure house," and it is this infinity of possibilities that Valéry thinks Proust means by "lost time" [*le temps perdu*] (CW, 9:296–99/O, 1:772–73). To me, this is an unusual and somewhat misdirected interpretation of the meaning of "lost time," which I would argue has much more to do with Proust's careful research and writing on involuntary memory. It likely reflects what Valéry admits at the beginning of his homage, that he has found the time to read very little of the *Recherche*. It also reflects Valéry's stress upon the intellect in poetry and poetics, and the contrast with Proust appears profoundly in the very first line of the Prologue of Proust's posthumous *Contre Saint-Beuve*. Proust's Narrator begins: "Every day I set less store on the intellect," and then adds: "What intellect restores to us under the name of the past, is not the past."[6]

Merleau-Ponty for and against Valéry: Monsieur Teste, Leonardo

Valéry developed these attitudes at length in his early work of 1896, beginning from "An Evening with Monsieur Teste" ("*La soirée avec Monsieur Teste*"). This work is as close as Valéry would come to writing his own novel: After its opening portrait of Monsieur Teste in the soirée, the fragmentary narrative is developed through two letters, a dialogue, extracts from Monsieur Teste's logbook, a walk, some sketches, and a concluding publisher's note regarding a letter from M. Teste's wife that the narrator suspects to be a fabrication. The central issue is the character of M. Edmond Teste, who was one who sought to be "all mind." The story bears a Latin dedication: "*Vita Cartesii res est simplicissima*" (The life of the Cartesian is a very simple affair). The forty-year-old M. Teste practiced his own "laws of the mind," among which were these: He expressed no opinions, he never laughed or displayed any distress or sadness, and he had banished a large number of words from his discourse that were not sufficiently precise. He never said anything vague. He attended the theater but spent his time developing a theoretical system of classification for the social order of the audience. His apartment was spartan—dreary, abstract, and banal. The soirée ended with bitter cigars and, just before bed, the soft and slow recitation by M. Teste of the numbers of the stock market, not for their monetary excitement, but strictly for the long sequences of the names of numbers like a poem.

The preface to *Monsieur Teste* describes an "acute ailment called precision" that renders literature suspect, including even many works of poetry. Valéry argues that the act of writing always imposes upon us a "sacrifice of the intellect," for literature is incompatible with precision of language, and not only literature but almost the "whole of philosophy" belongs among "those Vague and Impure things" rejected by M. Teste. He sought to reduce himself to "*real* properties" based upon an "infinite desire for clarity," making of himself "an inner island" (CW, 6:4–5/O, 2:12–13).

The writing of *Monsieur Teste* goes hand in hand with Valéry's study of Leonardo da Vinci published two years earlier in 1894 at the age of twenty-three as *Introduction to the Method of Leonardo da Vinci*. It is a surging, overflowing account of Leonardo as a "universal mind," the "monstrous brain or strange animal that wove a pure web connecting so many forms" (CW, 8:5/O, 1:1154). Valéry is preoccupied with studying the processes of a mind so creative in both the arts and sciences, and he wants nothing to do with those horrifying biographical moments in which we fail to be all that a rational life of the mind would require. Neither is he interested in a collection of "dubious anecdotes" or "a list of dates." He writes: "I am not ignorant of such matters, but my task above all is to omit them" (CW, 8:7–8/O, 1:1156) and rather, praise the artistic, literary, scientific, and technological works of Leonardo's intellect. Certain of Leonardo's scientific works are so limpid in their structure, he wrote, it is even "hard to believe they have an author. . . . There is something *inhuman* about them" (CW, 8:9/O, 1:1157).

We know that Merleau-Ponty disagrees profoundly with the story Valéry tells of Leonardo, for in "Cézanne's Doubt," Merleau-Ponty wrote that Valéry had made of Leonardo a "monster of freedom, without mistresses, creditors, anecdotes, or adventures" (SNS, 28/22). In fact, Merleau-Ponty has here quoted Valéry himself directly: "No mistresses, no creditors, no anecdotes, no adventures! One is led to adopt a more honest method, that of disregarding such details and of imagining a theoretical being" (CW, 8:106/O, 1:1231). Merleau-Ponty turns to Valéry's reflections upon Leonardo's meditations and drawings of love and death, in which Valéry finds "nothing more free, which is to say nothing less humane" (CW, 8:81/O, 1:1212). For in fact, Leonardo had expressed in his notebooks scorn for the ugliness of the acts of love in the full force of passion, and, now and again, had drawn "anatomical unions, frightful cross-sections of love's very act" (SNS, 28/22). Merleau-Ponty's commentary omits Leonardo's views on death, with which he would have found more sympathy, for Leonardo expressed the soul's great attachment and intertwining with the body. Valéry cites Leonardo's notebooks: "The organization of our body is such a marvelous thing that the soul, although *something divine*, is deeply grieved at being separated from the body that was its home. *And I can well believe*, says Leonardo, *that its tears and its suffering are not unjustified.* . . ." (CW, 8:82/O, 1:1213). Leonardo interprets death of the body as a disaster for the soul, as the diminution of something divine. "Death moving the soul to tears and destroying its dearest work, by the ruin of the structure that the soul had designed for its dwelling" (CW, 8:82–83/O, 1:1213). Valéry concludes: "Such is the feeling of Vinci. His philosophy is wholly *naturalistic*, outraged by *spiritualism*. . . . There is nothing more destitute than a soul that has lost its body" (CW, 8:83/O, 1:1214). Leonardo, and Valéry with him, gives us a paradoxical view of the body, for freedom—this "humane" freedom of detachment—is found in disdain for the ugliness of the acts of love, yet in the death of the body we witness its intertwining with the divinity of soul.

Twenty-five years after his youthful 1894 *Introduction to the Method of Leonardo da Vinci*, in 1919, Valéry would feel it necessary to qualify his account in a lengthy prefatory "Note and Digression." There, he continues to defend his preoccupation with observing the secret workings of the creative mind brought forth from "an intelligence so detached" (CW, 8:81/O, 1:1212). Yet, tellingly, Valéry writes that his early intellectualist account of Leonardo cast less light on the subject of Leonardo than on the person discussing it:

> In the end, it must be confessed that my only solution was to attribute my own agitation to the unfortunate Leonardo, transporting the disorder of my mind into the complexity of his. I inflicted all my desires on him, presenting them as aims he had realized. I ascribed to him many of the difficulties that haunted me at the time, as if he had met and surmounted them. I transformed my perplexities into his supposed power. I dared consider myself under his name and make use of my person. (CW, 8:106–7/O, 1:1232)

Valéry and the Logic of Creativity: Baudelaire, Mallarmé, Poe

The connection between Merleau-Ponty and Edgar Allan Poe is indirect through the Valéryan poetic that is influenced by the writings of Poe precisely during this early period of the creation of *Monsieur Teste* and rationalistic interpretation of Leonardo.[7] The "precepts of Poe" along with those of Mallarmé are sources for Valéry's concept of the "animal of words," which we will take up later.[8] Certainly, Merleau-Ponty could not have been unaware of the long tradition of Poe translation and interpretation in France beginning from Baudelaire to Mallarmé to Valéry. Baudelaire was not Poe's first translator in France,[9] though it was no doubt Baudelaire who brought Poe's name literary prestige by publishing his own translations of many of Poe's stories and poems, including "The Murders in the Rue Morgue" and "The Purloined Letter" in 1856, followed by a second collection in 1857 that included "The Tell-Tale Heart" and "The Fall of the House of Usher," among many others. He also wrote many critical essays and prefaces, such as Baudelaire's preface to "The Raven," preceding his prose translation of the poem (1853), and his translation of Poe's essay "The Philosophy of Composition" (1865).[10] Baudelaire made the American writer a vital part of the European literary experience. Valéry commented in "The Place of Baudelaire" (1924) that Poe "would today be completely forgotten if Baudelaire had not taken up the task of introducing him into European literature.... Every aspect of Baudelaire was impregnated, inspired, deepened by Poe" (CW, 8:204/O, 1:607). Mallarmé, as well, made his own translation of Poe's "The Raven" ("*Le Corbeau*") and published it in 1875 together with illustrations by Edouard Manet.[11] Altogether, Mallarmé created his own translations of thirty-six of Poe's poems, and translations of twenty are included in the Pléiade edition of Mallarmé's *Collected Works*, including "Ulalume," "Annabel Lee," and "For Annie."[12] In a tribute to Poe in Mallarmé's *Divagations*, he describes Poe as a writer from the far future: "very far from being our contemporary, someone we could only see burst into a sparkling cloud, creating a crown that fits no one now, meant for centuries hence. He is indeed that exception: the absolute literary case."[13] Mallarmé's poem "The Tomb of Edgar Poe" ("*Le tombeau d'Edgar Poe*") begins with the often-quoted opening line: "As into Himself at last eternity changes him" ("*Tel qu'en Lui-même enfin l'éternité le change*").[14] Understanding Valéry's fascination and engagement with Poe (as well as Baudelaire's and Mallarmé's) therefore enriches our understanding of Merleau-Ponty's engagement with Valéry. For Valéry's introduction to Leonardo, especially Poe's "Philosophy of Composition," was the crucial text in play, and for the character of Monsieur Teste, there are striking parallels with Poe's detective, M. Auguste Dupin.

In Valéry's first letter to Mallarmé presenting himself as a young poet, he addressed the letter "Dear Master" and appealed to "the cunning doctrines of the great Edgar Allan Poe," whom he names "the most subtle artist of this century!" The full paragraph from this letter of October 1890 is worth citing, since it offers a condensed account of Poe's "precepts" articulated in "The Philosophy of Composition":

> To make himself known in a few words he [Valéry addressing Mallarmé] ought to say that he prefers poems short, concentrated toward a final impact, in which the rhythms are like the marmoreal steps to the altar, crowning the final line! Not that he can boast of having realized this ideal! It is simply that he is deeply imbued with the cunning doctrines of the great Edgar Allan Poe—perhaps the most subtle artist of this century! (CW, 8:406/O, 1:1579)

This is an admirable crystallization of the aesthetic philosophy Poe set out for the creation of poetry in "The Philosophy of Composition," which, according to the author, offers us access to the inner workings of Poe's mind—"a peep behind the scenes," at "the wheels and pinions—the tackle for scene-shifting"—in creating "The Raven," no doubt his best-known poem. Poe presents the poetic principles according to which, he claims, he plotted out the poem. First among these is the notion of "writing backward," meaning the author must begin by elaborating the narrative plot to the dénouement. The end must clearly be in view before setting forth the development of incidents and intentions, thereby establishing a single, vivid effect that gives an "indispensable air of consequence, or causation."[15] Following on, Poe stipulates a distinct limit to extent or length, namely, the limit of a single sitting for the reader, meaning a length of about one hundred lines, for "The Raven" "in fact, a hundred and eight" (PC, 63). In order to render the work universally appreciable, "Beauty is the sole legitimate province of the poem" (PC, 63), therefore with regard to tone, sadness invariably touches the "sensitive soul," making melancholy the most legitimate poetical tone of the beautiful. Nothing could convey this province and tone more so than the refrain, with its returning identity and repetition, and no vowel within the refrain better than the "sonorous long *o*," in combination with "*r* as the most producible consonant" (PC, 64). Thus, in the search for the sound of the refrain, "it was absolutely impossible to overlook the word 'Nevermore,'" Poe writes, "in fact, it was the very first which presented itself" (PC, 65). Next follows the idea of either a parrot or Raven as non-reasoning creatures capable of speech and monotone repetition, the Raven "infinitely more in keeping with the intended *tone*" (PC, 65), finally death as the most melancholy poetical topic, most especially the death of a beautiful woman, and the bereaved lover expressing "the most delicious and most intolerable of sorrows" (PC, 66). Poe concludes his self-disclosure: "Here then the poem may be said to have its beginning—at the end, where all works of art should begin" (PC, 66), "Nevermore."

Is the disclosure of these workings of Poe's mind "behind the scenes" magic or logic? And why would Valéry have taken all this so seriously? Clearly Poe means for us to understand all of these step-by-step progressions as logical deductions, or, to capture the element of beginning from the end, retro-deductions. To give the Kantian name, they are transcendental deductions or the necessary conditions of possibility for the poem, "The Raven." Poe extends these logical progressions on to the selection of the locale of the bereaved lover's bedroom, the tapping of the raven against the shutters, its entrance through the window and alighting on the bust of

Pallas. His language stresses "indispensable" and "inevitable," and the word "must" occurs seven times, by my count; for example: "must be elaborated to its dénouement," "must be brief," "must be sonorous."

The editors of Poe's critical theory documents take a skeptical attitude: "no critic, no literary historian, no poet has ever believed that Poe literally produced 'The Raven' as systematically and cold-bloodedly as he says."[16] In fact, early in the essay, Poe himself makes a very different long listing of the workings of the poet's mind "behind the scenes," including the vacillations, fancies, despair, selections and rejections, erasures and interpolations, "the step-ladders and demon-traps—the cock's feathers, the red paint and the black patches" that afflict the literary process "in ninety-nine cases out of the hundred" (PC, 61). T. S. Eliot's landmark essay "From Poe to Valéry" (1949) argues that American critics have regarded Poe's analysis of the genesis of "The Raven" as "practicing either a hoax, or a piece of self-deception in setting down the way in which he wanted to think that he had written it."[17] On the other hand, we might note that Latin American critics have taken Poe seriously, no less than Jorge Luis Borges stating: "Perhaps naively, I believe Poe's explanations. Apart from a possible burst of charlatanism, I think that the mental process alleged by him corresponds, more or less, with the true process of creation. I am sure intelligence proceeds thus: by contradictions, by obstacles, by eliminations."[18]

Thus, we are brought back to the question of Valéry: What did he see in the essay and in Poe generally that he found so galvanizing? The first thing to remember is the long tradition of high regard for Poe in France that we have already outlined stretching over three generations from Baudelaire to Mallarmé, thus to Valéry. Mallarmé became a devotee of Poe's method of beginning from the end, finding the last word first, and the last line of his poem *"Un coup de dés,"* to which we will devote attention later, feeds itself all the way back into the beginning of the poem and even its title: "All Thought expresses a throw of the dice" (*"Toute Pensée émet un coup de dés"*).[19] Baudelaire also finds in Poe's "Philosophy of Composition" the touch of "a little charlatanism," yet argues the essay successfully articulates the poet's two greatest enemies, "the accidental and the unintelligible," moreover that Poe's "genius, however ardent and supple it may have been, was passionately fond of analysis, combinations, and calculations."[20] Baudelaire concludes his "Preface to The Raven" by comparing "the most magnificent rhythms of Victor Hugo" with "Poe's talents as a versifier."[21] Yet in truth, Baudelaire was especially drawn to Poe by "the flowers of evil (*les fleurs du mal*)" he finds there, by the "myth" of the poet's cursed, down and out life of misery, wretchedness, and wickedness (*le poète maudit*). Merleau-Ponty considers the phrase *"les poètes maudits"* in discussing the paradox of the relation between the author and the human being, between writing and living, but cautions against transforming failures of life into a title of glory for the poet as artist ("*sans transformer l'échec en titre de gloire comme faisaient les poètes maudits*") (ULL, 83). For example, one thinks of the almost immediate escalation of appreciation and public demand for the paintings of Van Gogh as soon as rumors of suicide or martyrdom began to circulate.[22] Of Poe, Baudelaire writes: "Today I add a new saint to the holy army of martyrs, for I have to write the history of one of those illustrious unfortunates, over-rich with poetry and passion.... A lamentable tragedy this Life of Edgar Poe! His death a horrible unravelling of the drama, where horror is besmutched [*sic*] with trivialities!"[23] Baudelaire attributes Poe's life and demise to the struggle between his interior life, "spiritual as a poet, spiritual even as a drunkard," and the "wild barbarous country" of the United States, which, for Poe, was only "a vast prison through which he ran, hither and thither."[24] One component of the "barbarous country" was the literary marketplace and moneymaking, of which Poe was keenly aware, for he wrote "The Raven," he confesses, to "suit at once the popular and the critical taste" (PC, 62).

We know that Valéry would not have found these failures of life and these gaps between the life and the works to be his main attraction to Poe, for he had dismissed them from his intellectualist construction of Leonardo, likewise their dismissal from consideration for Poe. We find only a passing reference to "the miserable shade of Edgar Allan Poe" in the context of Valéry's assessment of the Baudelaire-Poe relationship (CW, 8:204/O, 1:607). In his essay "On the Teaching of *Poetics* at the Collège de France," Valéry states that a "serious History of Literature should then be conceived not as a history of authors and the incidents of their lives, not as a history of their works, but as *a history of the mind in so far as it produces or consumes 'literature'*" (CW, 13:83–84/O, 1:1439). Therefore, one of the things Valéry admired in Poe was the latter's analysis of the psychological conditions of a poem (CW, 8:206/O, 1:609). Poe, like Valéry, was fascinated by the direct connection between the workings of the writer's intellect, his literary creation, and its likely singular effect on the reader. Valéry states: "Edgar Poe, who in this century of literary perturbation was the very lightning of the confusion, of the poetic storm, and whose analysis sometimes ends, like Leonardo's, in mysterious smiles, has clearly established his reader's approach on the basis of psychology and probable effects" (CW, 8:61–62/O, 1:1197–98).

Yet above all, Valéry was attracted by Poe's *theory* of poetry as a rational process of craftsmanship and intelligence. If Poe's philosophy of composition omits much about the literary art of poetry, it does disclose its craftsmanship, at least one approach to its craft. This distinction between art and craft is a tenuous one, equally between fine art and the useful arts, but what is missing from Poe's account of creativity in literary art will become clear as we proceed with Valéry's response, and that response will emphasize mystery and enchantment. On the positive side for now, with respect to art, Valéry found in Poe an aesthetic that values the poem itself as "pure poetry." In a statement inherited from Baudelaire, "a poem does not say something—it *is* something."[25] In the first place, "pure poetry" means the *elimination* from poetry of didactic, historical, or ethical concerns alien to poetic creation. This means the "pure poet" does not preach, engage in historical disputation, or offer a moral message. The "pure poem" eliminates such elements and limits itself to the pure elements of sound and sense. In the second place, Valéry believes that Poe, in defining "*pure poetry*" (*poésie absolue*) by way of "*elimination*," was "opening up a way, teaching a very strict and deeply alluring doctrine, in which a kind of mathematics and a kind of mysticism became one" (CW, 8:207/O, 1:609). In a letter to Mallarmé of April 1891, following his first presentation of himself, Valéry again writes tellingly of Poe's influence on himself as a young poet in forging a unique blend of mathematics and mystery: "A very special devotion to the work of Poe has led me to assign to the poet the kingdom of analogy. He defines the mysterious echo of things, and that secret harmony of theirs which is as real and certain as a mathematical equation to all artist[ic] minds.... constructed according to a rigorous architectonic order... liberating the poet from the encumbering aids of banal philosophies, sentimental falsities, and inert descriptions" (CW, 8:407–8/ O, 1:1721–22). From what we have seen of "The Philosophy of Composition" with its stress upon logical necessity in creative writing, we would have to say that an emphasis upon "mysticism" and the "mysterious echo of things" would come from the mind of Valéry more so than Poe, threads and phrases we also find in the poetics of Merleau-Ponty, to which we will come.

The alliance Valéry finds in Poe between the poet and mathematician affords us the opportunity to consider briefly Valéry's equal attraction to Poe's detective fiction and the relationship between *Monsieur Teste* and Poe's inspector, M. Auguste Dupin.[26] Valéry writes regarding *Monsieur Teste*: "It is, like everything else of mine, an occasional work. With the aid of notes quickly thrown together, I made up that pseudo portrait of nobody, a caricature if you like of someone who might have been invented by—Poe, once more."[27] Like Poe's "Philosophy of Composition," if we look at Poe's "The Murders in the Rue Morgue," we find that Poe uses the word "must" twenty times to convey the inner mental reasoning of Dupin in solving the murders.[28] Likewise, the interesting case of what might be called "mind reading" with which the narrative opens presents the detective engaged in what Poe describes as necessary deductions. The chain of silent mental wanderings of the narrator seem bizarre—"Chantilly, Orion, Dr. Nichols, Epicurus, Stereotomy, the street stones, the fruiterer"—yet Dupin arrives precisely at what the narrator was thinking, employing phrases such as "you could not avoid," "I certainly expected," "I was now assured," "you could not have forgotten it," and "I was sure."

We are thus brought back to the predilection for logical necessity in Poe's account of plotting out "The Raven" in "The Philosophy of Composition." What his account omits are the "preferences," we might say, both personal and cultural preferences, that led, for example, from the Beautiful as the province of the poem and melancholy its tone, to the death of a beautiful woman as the most beautiful poetical theme. Valéry's objection to Poe's mental self-disclosure in the essay is not that he offers a logical explanation of the poetic process but that he reduces the *entire* process of poetic creativity to logical deduction without any imaginative or metaphoric work whatsoever, science divorced from art. For Valéry, and certainly for Merleau-Ponty, creativity and the workings of "the kingdom of analogy" cannot be reduced to a deductive logical rubric. Commenting on the influence of Poe on Baudelaire and upon himself, Valéry argues: "The duty, work, and function of a poet are to bring to light and to utilize these powers of movement and enchantment, these stimulants of the emotional life and the intellectual sensibility . . ." (CW, 8:209/O, 1:611). For Valéry, movement and enchantment, emotional life and intellectual sensibility, find their harmonization both in the creative work of poetry and the philosophical work of poetics.

The Silence of Valéry: Crisis and Voluntary Solitude

The preface to *Monsieur Teste* is written in a voice that is a mixture of Teste, the character, and Valéry, the author, even something like a dialogue between them. Near the end, the voice that seems to be Valéry intervenes to say that M. Teste resembles himself, Valéry, at a moment of profound change. This would be that moment of intense personal crisis at age twenty that Valéry underwent on October 4–5, 1892, known as the "night of Genoa" (*la nuit de Gênes*), brought on by the rationalist attitudes mirrored in *Monsieur Teste* and in Valéry's interpretations of Leonardo and Poe, combined with a ravaging and unrequited love passion. The personal crisis of this night caused Valéry to resolve to turn away from literature, and indeed to a certain extent from life, in order to study the human intellect and cultivate his own mind. Nevertheless, of M. Teste, Valéry adds in the preface "a character of this kind could not survive in reality for more than a few quarters of an hour." He is a kind of "monster" and monsters die, yet "nothing is more instructive than to meditate on their destiny" (CW, 6:5–6/O, 2:13–14).

In the course of 1952–53, Merleau-Ponty was profoundly interested in this period of his life in which Valéry maintained a public silence. In fact, Merleau-Ponty writes that Valéry "kept quiet" ("*il s'est tu*") (ULL, 62), meaning that he did not publish any works as an author beginning from 1894 when he took up residence in Paris. Rather, he wrote only for himself in what would much later become the *Cahiers* (Notebooks). As we have already seen from the philosophy of Merleau-Ponty, silence has many facets: There is the silent expression of painting and there is the ontological silence of nature, which are life-affirming and life-giving, without which there can be no genuine expression. There is the silence of mind in the intuitive perception of deep listening and observing, such as Dupin. There is also the phenomenon of being silenced by another, by a *differend*, as Lyotard named it, which is a form of suffering since it is an incapacity to speak in the prescribed forms of legal or social power, therefore a kind of juridico-political mutism.[29] There is also another kind of negative silence that is the refusal to answer, the silence of dissimulation like the leaden silence of Heidegger, Lyotard contends, regarding the politics of National Socialism when questioned by Paul Celan. In the case of such a *differend*, silence is negative and oppressive rather than the fullness and expectancy of poetic silence, it is mute silence, leaden silence, Lyotard calls it.[30] There is also the "silence of the mad," another oppressive and negative silence brought to light and stressed by Foucault in his recently published work on literature.[31]

But the silence of Valéry was none of these. It is rather what Monsieur Teste calls a "voluntary solitude" ("*la solitude volontaire*"). It lasted for a period of twenty-five years from the crisis of 1892 until 1917, when Valéry was forty-six and Gide and Gallimard at last persuaded him to let them publish some of his earlier poems, to which Valéry worked for four years to add the masterpiece "*La jeune parque*" ("The Young Fate"), with its moving first stanza:

> Who is that weeping, if not simply the wind,
> At this sole hour, with ultimate diamonds? . . . But who
> Weeps, so close to myself on the brink of tears?[32]

More than forty dense, demanding stanzas stretching over fifteen pages follow in the French Gallimard Pléiade edition and nineteen pages in the English Bollingen Series translation.

Merleau-Ponty knows that Valéry's period of voluntary solitude was not a time of total self-silencing, for Valéry did publish some things during this period of time including the essay on Leonardo and *Monsieur Teste*, but by and large he wrote only for himself in his notebooks on themes of science, philosophy, psychology, sensibility, memory, time, and self (*ego scriptor*). Above all, he wrote almost no poetry. Out of the silence of this solitude Valéry cultivated and sharpened the powers of his own mind in a way similar to what Valéry attributed to Rilke. In his letter to Rainer Maria Rilke, Valéry wrote of the poet and writer with deep admiration, saying that he could not conceive a life of "such isolation, eternal winters spent in such excessive communion with silence" where freedom was given over to dreams, genius, and memory, where "thought was producing marvels out of that void and making time pregnant!" (CW, 9:290–91).[33]

In addition to the critical view he had taken of writing as weakness, Valéry was also troubled during this period, Merleau-Ponty comments, by incomprehensible paradoxes. Merleau-Ponty names the following in the course notes and includes them as well in the résumé of his lecture course, *Recherches sur l'usage littéraire du langage*. First, it is incomprehensible that our body can be at one and the same time the unmoving mass (*la mass inerte*) that marks our place during sleep and also the agile instrument at the service of painting, for example, everything that the mind would make of it. Next, it is incomprehensible that the mind is the power of doubt, questioning, reservation, and disengagement that makes us inaccessible and elusive while at the same time it merges ("*il se mêle*") and surrenders itself to everything that happens, and that precisely by its "indefinite refusal to be whatever it may be" ("*refus indéfini d'être quoi que ce soit*") it actually constructs and becomes something. Third, it is also incomprehensible that I, who am irreducibly foreign to all the images of who I am, feel affected by the image of myself I read in the look of others, and that I in turn reflect an image of them with which they are concerned. Thus is born between the other and me an exchange, a "chiasma of two destinies" ("*chiasma de deux destinées*")[34] where there are never quite two of us and yet, one ceases to be alone ("*où l'on n'est jamais tout à fait deux, et où pourtant on cesse d'être seul*") (ULL, 63, and RC, 25/82). Valéry recognizes, Merleau-Ponty argues, that these "absurdities" are most pronounced, most strongly felt ("*sont au plus haut point*") in language and literature (ULL, 63).

The Paradox of Merleau-Ponty's Attraction to Valéry

Why did Valéry hold such a powerful, magnetic attraction for Merleau-Ponty? There is much to question and even resist in the Valéryan poetic from Merleau-Ponty's philosophical point of view: its linguistic skepticism; its rather high-handed dismissals of much of literature such as Proust as well as philosophy that is too imprecise, perhaps an implied dismissal of Merleau-Ponty's own famous stress upon "ambiguity"; and the implacable Cartesian and intellectualist responses these provoked in Valéry's thought and writings. Though the paradox will not ease completely, there are some points of kinship to consider. For a first thing, Merleau-Ponty also wrestled with that very same "writing through weakness" we find in the poet. As Valéry would struggle toward a literature that Merleau-Ponty calls an "anti-literature in literature" (*"Anti-littérature d[an]s la littérature"*) (ULL, 86), so Merleau-Ponty created a "minority philosophy" that was an a-philosophy. "True philosophy," Merleau-Ponty wrote, is "a-philosophy" (NC, 275). Commenting on the preface to Nietzsche's *Gay Science*, Merleau-Ponty explains that a-philosophy is "faithful to what we live," and it does not end in a "total knowledge nor in despair, but in the 'will to appearance'" (NC, 275). In addition to Nietzsche, in the "history of a-philosophy" Merleau-Ponty includes Kierkegaard, Marx, and Heidegger. Thus, in Merleau-Ponty's "a-philosophy," as in Valéry's "anti-literature," both writers struggled with the problems of language and expression in similar ways.

Second, we have just arrived at the origin of Merleau-Ponty's central concept of "chiasma." It is found in Valéry. It has been documented by Emmanuel de Saint Aubert that the origin of Merleau-Ponty's concept of the "chiasma" is Valéry's *Tel quel*, in which he speaks of this "chiasma of two destinies." Merleau-Ponty cites this passage for the first time in "Man and Adversity," then repeats it in the course of 1952–53 as well as in the résumé of the course. When he first encounters the term, he comments that the "exchange" expressed by "chiasma" is exactly the right word ("*le mot est bon*") (S, 294/231). As there is a circuit of the touching-touched and seeing-seen, there is for both Valéry and Merleau-Ponty an equally inevitable and necessary circuit of self-other (*moi-autrui*).[35] Shortly, we shall also turn to another such idea from the Valéryan poetics that contributed deeply to Merleau-Ponty's philosophy of language, that of "implex" or the "animal of words."

For a third point regarding the fascination of Valéry for Merleau-Ponty, we can also see that Merleau-Ponty's focus on the life and work of Valéry centered on Valéry's long period of doubt and eventual return to language and poetry, just as Merleau-Ponty had also highlighted doubt and its creative importance in his studies of Cézanne. The philosopher, poet, and painter each in his own way learned to "work from doubt," making doubt a creative impetus for thought and art. Benedetta Zaccarello has highlighted the doubling between Valéry and Cézanne.[36] In the same way and for many of the same reasons that Merleau-Ponty was attached to Cézanne, Zaccarello argues, Valéry was attached to Degas, who was also "loutish to the point of misanthropy, terribly politically incorrect, tireless in his work, ready to devote unlimited time to each painting, ending sometimes by destroying it."[37] Merleau-Ponty also attributes to Valéry a kind of "anguish" experienced on the "night of Genoa" that links Valéry with both Cézanne and Descartes. Zaccarello points out that the self-doubt of Cézanne in working with paint also had its Valeryan linguistic double, for Merleau-Ponty spoke of Cézanne's art as a language of painting and portrayed it with repeated reference to language. This is most noticeable when Merleau-Ponty wrote that "on the basis of silent and solitary experience . . . the artist launches his work as a man launched the first word, not knowing whether it will be anything more than a shout" (SNS, 25/19). Merleau-Ponty wrote this about Cézanne, but it could also easily have been written about Valéry.

Emmanuel de Saint Aubert has written of Merleau-Ponty's engagement with Valéry that "this wrestling with Jacob seduces Merleau-Ponty" because "the itinerary of the writer offers a contemporary variant, more modern and more successful, of the Cartesian scenario."[38] Indeed, when one looks into what Valéry had to say about the meaning of Descartes for the twentieth century, we find that Valéry, too, was critical of Descartes's dualistic metaphysics, of his mechanistic view of nature, and the model of the animal as a machine that warrants much of the phenomenological opposition to Cartesianism (CW, 9:65–68/O, 1:833–35). What Valéry loved about Descartes was the rigor of his mathematical mind and his will to find his own Self and his own path out of scholasticism. Valéry writes that Descartes has been unlucky for there is no statue of him in Paris and his name has been given only to a poor street, but this is of no real consequence for his true monument is the *Discourse*. It is this work by Descartes that Valéry most admires. He admires it for its revolutionary language, namely, the use of "I" and "me," which are the sounds of the human voice, "to introduce us to ways of thinking in completely general terms." He admires it as well for its method, which Valéry names, borrowing a term from Stendhal, the method of "egotism" (CW, 9:31/O, 1:806). Valéry contends, rightly it seems to me, that in spite of the "*ergo*" (therefore), there is no syllogism in the *cogito ergo sum*. He claims additionally that there is not even any literal meaning of this revolutionary phrase. Rather, Valéry argues that the *Cogito* is a "piece of shock tactics" and "is like a clarion sounded by Descartes to summon up the powers of his ego" (CW, 9:31/O, 1:806–7). This is what made Descartes a most admirable "captain of the mind" for Valéry.

Finally, and most profoundly, I believe, Merleau-Ponty was attracted by Valéry's effort to work with silence and solitude, to discover how to move through and beyond silence to the poetic meaning of the world. Like Merleau-Ponty, Valéry too was seeking that "irrelative" of untamed being and untamed meaning beneath the surface of things, and he was also seeking the means of its expression. In a Working Note of February 1959, Merleau-Ponty wrote that "there would be needed a silence that envelops speech anew" and asks: "What will this silence be?" He writes: "As the reduction finally is not for Husserl a transcendental immanence, but the disclosing of the *Weltthesis*, this silence *will not be* the contrary of language" (VI, 230/179). Later that same year, on October 22, 1959, he noted "every philosophy is language and nonetheless consists in rediscovering silence" (VI, 267/213).

Valéry and the Return to Poetic Language

When Valéry made the return to poetic language following his lengthy period of silence, Merleau-Ponty focuses upon three main features that made the return possible. They are "embodied form," "semantic thickness," and the "animal of words," or implex. Let us study these in turn, beginning from embodied form.

Return to Poetic Language: Embodied Form—Breton

In order to discipline writing, language, and poetry, Valéry adopted the practice of writing his poems in the most difficult forms created in the history of poetry: not only the form of the sonnet he had at times employed in the early poems prior to the period of silence, but 8-syllable and 10-syllable lines. Valéry explains that "The Cemetery by the Sea" ("*Le cimetière marin*") began "by a rhythm, that of a French line . . . of ten syllables, divided into four and six. I had as yet no idea with which to fill out this form. Gradually a few hovering words settled in it, little by little determining the subject, and my labour (a very long labour) was before me" (CW, 7:80/O, 1:1338). "The Pythoness" ("*La Pythie*") "first appeared as an eight-syllable line whose sound came of its own accord. But this line implied a sentence, of which it was part, and this sentence, if it existed, implied many other sentences" (CW, 7:80/O, 1:1338). By adopting these most difficult of poetic forms that reach back to writers such as Victor Hugo, Valéry believed himself capable of changing the "soiled" everyday language into "a pure ideal Voice, capable of communicating without weakness, without apparent effort, without offense to the ear, and without breaking the ephemeral sphere of the poetic universe, an idea of some *self* miraculously superior to Myself" (CW, 7:81/O, 1:1339). Again, we encounter this Voice and Wisdom that is the voice of no one and which here is described as an "ideal purity" and a "pure poetry," as we have encountered it in Valéry's analysis of Poe's theory of poetry (see CW, 7:184–92/O, 1:1456–63).[39]

Of Valéry's adoption of the most difficult and labored poetic forms, in "Man and Adversity," Merleau-Ponty wrote of a great difference between Valéry's "academic image" and Valéry's comprehension of the real "essence of language." He writes that Valéry's poetry is not "simply a literature of exercises based upon linguistic and prosodic conventions which are more efficacious to the extent they are more complicated and, in short, more absurd" (S, 297/234). Rather, the true "essence of poetic language" disclosed by the work of Valéry, and even of all literary language, has three features, according to Merleau-Ponty's account. First, "it does not die out in the face of what it communicates to us." Second, the poem calls for the very words deployed, "and no others." And third, the ideas communicated are not the result of "lexical significations" but are the result of "more carnal relationships of meaning" (S, 297/234). In this regard, Valéry, Merleau-Ponty concludes, is not unlike the surrealists who were motivated by the search for a total meaning (S, 297/234), and with whom Valéry shares an understanding of the "pathos of language" (S, 295/233). Thus, Merleau-Ponty gives us one of the most surprising linkages of his poetics: Valéry (the often-named "rationalist") with surrealism (the often-named "absurdists"), and it is passion or suffering that provides the bridge.

Merleau-Ponty's engagement with surrealism, in particular with André Breton, is discussed in detail in the first section of Saint Aubert's Chapter 2 of this book, so comment here will be limited. Suffice it to say that Merleau-Ponty interacted seriously with Breton from the time of his early essays in *Sense and Non-Sense* through his 1948 radio lectures, *The Prose of the World*, and late interviews. He returned many times to Breton's central idea of "the sublime point." In spite of surrealism's early "insurrection against all language, against all meaning, and against all literature," Merleau-Ponty writes, in truth Breton sought to restore "a profound, radical usage of speech" (S, 296/233). Thus, his manifesto was *revolutionary*, but for Merleau-Ponty, more so in a constructive rather than destructive sense. "It was necessary," he writes, "to go back to that point of innocence, youth, and unity . . . to that 'sublime point' Breton speaks about elsewhere, at which literature, life, morality, and politics are equivalent" (S, 296/233).

In *Mad Love* (*L'amour fou*), Breton writes of the sublime point in geographic terms as the point on a mountain, upon which it would be impossible to dwell, but which could serve as a guide "in the direction of eternal love," which "had made me *see* and granted me the rarer privilege of *having others see*." He concludes: "I have never ceased to identify the flesh of the being I have loved and the snow of the peaks in the rising sun."[40] Thus, in this sublime point of Breton, Merleau-Ponty found mirrored many of his own desires for a unity of inner and outer, of enveloped—enveloping, the intertwining of self and other, of self and world. At the same time, he cautioned against a merely destructive surrealism, that in its excesses "is the art of farces and hoaxes. The Surrealism which endured was not satisfied to tear the customary world apart; it composed a different one" (S, 386/309). Breton's "mad love," he argues, is to be created beyond self-love and the pleasure of dominating and sinning, demonstrating that love need not wear out, rather love has its hidden depths. In this way, Merleau-Ponty finds Valéry quite close to Breton's experience of language (S, 297/234), even if Valéry's mature poetry took a more historic, academic form, even if Breton, originally attracted to Valéry's "silence" and *Monsieur Teste*, later rejected Valéry's "*La jeune parque.*"[41]

Once Valéry was himself confronted with his reputation for intellectualism, and it came in a conversation with Bergson. The philosopher spoke directly to Valéry of his "intellectualism," to which Valéry responded that Bergson was mistaken. Rather, Valéry named himself a "formist." The fact that his poetry begins from the form and proceeds to the subject matter or ideas of the works, he says, "gives the *impression* of intellectualism, by analogy with logic—but the forms are *intuitive* in origin" (CW, 9:344/C, 14:103). The use of the word "intuitive" is nothing about blind intuition or "inspiration," a notion Valéry rejects (see CW, 7:76/O, 1:1335). What Valéry means by the "intuition of form" is something quite visceral and muscular. He illustrates with a story of walking along the street and suddenly being "*gripped*" by a rhythm that took possession of him, then came a second rhythm that combined with the first creating certain transverse relations with it and growing increasingly complex (CW, 7:61/O, 1:1322). In Valéryan poetics, the embodied rhythm comes first, around which certain tones or sounds organize themselves, then gradually come the words. We recall that Merleau-Ponty began the important Part II of *Eye and Mind* with words from Paul Valéry: "The painter takes his body with him," says Valéry. "Indeed we cannot imagine how a *mind* could paint" (OE, 16/123). In *Signs*, Merleau-Ponty refers to Valéry's phrase: "Time is that 'body of the spirit' Valéry used to talk about" (S, 21/15).

Return to Poetic Language: Semantic Thickness—Ponge, Sartre

In "Man and Adversity," Merleau-Ponty also links Valéry with Francis Ponge in the same passage in which he links Valéry to Breton regarding the pathos of language. Ponge had himself been linked with surrealism briefly in the late 1920s as a young man, chiefly linked to Breton, and he remained in dialogue with Breton, culminating in a 1952 joint interview of Ponge, Breton, and Pierre Reverdy broadcast on French radio.[42] In spite of the stylistic differences between the expressionistic prose poems of Ponge and the more formed poetry of Valéry,[43] and because of this, in spite of Ponge's evident distaste for the poetics of Valéry as he interprets it, with its emphasis upon the "rules of traditional prosody" as frames for "an art of ideas,"[44] Merleau-Ponty links them through this idea of the "semantic thickness" of language (S, 297/234).

Ponge's early, now classic *Le parti pris des choses* (1942) is the work that brought him to the attention of the public and may be rendered in English in different ways, one of the most common and literal being "taking the side of things," but also "the voice of things" and "the nature of things."[45] Ponge engaged in literary definition-descriptions of the natural world (M, 14)[46]—the shrimp, the orange, the pebble, for example—and wrote, "if I define a butterfly as a *twice-spawned petal* (*pétale superfétatoire*), what could be *truer*?" (VT, 103/M, 37).[47] In another near-perfect definition-description, Ponge writes: "the wasp [bee] can be called the musical form of honey."[48]

Ponge imagines a brand-new kind of writing and a new poetic placed in between definition and description, taking from definition its precision and brevity, he even says "infallibility and indubitability," and from description its respect for the sensory aspect of things (VT, 83/M, 11). These Cartesian terms, especially indubitability, may seem to align Ponge with a Valéryan poetic of precision and purification of language, yet nothing could be further from comprehending Ponge's aims. Ponge's tools were the *Larousse* or the *Encyclopédie Larousse* and *Littré* (VT, 89/M, 19), thus his resources were precisely the everyday usages Valéry sought to purify in his own poetry and poetic writing. Ponge comments in "My Creative Method" that his *proèmes* are built up from and "replace" the encyclopedic dictionary, etymological dictionary, analogical dictionary (which he says does not exist), the dictionary of rhymes, the dictionary of synonyms, and all lyric poetry inspired by nature (VT, 106–7/M, 41). His poetry is processual, for he understands nature and things in terms of processes, movement, and development. "What is *being*?" Ponge asks. "It is only ways of being, in succession. It is as much so of objects. Or of opening and closing one's eyes."⁴⁹ Above all, Ponge attempted to capture the solidity, monumentality, and density of things in such a way as to awaken our own sensory contacts with the world of things, and this echoes the project of Cézanne. In fact, *The Making of the Pré* by Ponge includes a magnificent Cézanne painting as illustration alongside Ponge's remark: "Ah, what beautiful things one could say about the *pré*."⁵⁰ (*Pré* has multiple meanings: an approximation of "meadow," "prairie," "prayer," "sacred place.")

Merleau-Ponty speaks of Ponge in his Sorbonne lectures on child pedagogy and psychology and his radio addresses of 1948 subsequently published as *The World of Perception* (*Causeries*), and he writes of Ponge in his essay, "Indirect Language and the Voices of Silence" (1951–52) and "Man and Adversity" (1951), both published in *Signs*. To come to Ponge's concept of "semantic thickness," Merleau-Ponty writes that words have the "power to designate in excess of their accepted definition, through the muffled life they have led and continue to lead in us, what Ponge appropriately called their 'semantic thickness'" (S, 94/75; also 297/234). One of the sources from Ponge in which Merleau-Ponty found this concept is the *proème* (prose poem) titled "Introduction to the Pebble" ("*Introduction au galet*"). Ponge writes: "O infinite resources of the density of things (*l'épaisseur des choses*), *rendered* (*rendues*) by the infinite resources of the density of words (*l'épaisseur sémantique des mots*)" (T, 200).⁵¹ As one sees immediately, this symmetrical sentence pairs the density and richness of things with the density and richness of words. "The Pebble" is the long and final poem of *Le parti pris des choses* and begins from the point of view of classification: "A pebble is not an easy thing to define. If one is satisfied with a simple description, one can start out by saying it is a form or state of stone between rock and gravel. But this remark already implies a notion of stone that has to be justified" (VT, 69/T, 104). By the middle of the poem, Ponge turns from geology and history to the pebble's common universe with the human body: "If I now wish to examine a specific type of stone with greater attention, its perfection of form and the fact that I can hold it, roll it around in my hand, makes me choose the pebble" (VT, 74/T, 111). In his lectures of 1951–52 on "Method in Child Psychology," Merleau-Ponty writes that the pebble Ponge analyzes "is the pebble of the child (we ourselves are obliged to return to our childhood impressions of the pebble in order to recover the poetry of it). Therefore, the symbolization in the pebble is of a whole series of behaviors, as well as the evident relation between certain persons and the pebble. We thus understand that the spectator's conception of perception would not permit us to truly comprehend things" (Sorb, 134/421). Thus, a "thing" crystallizes all the qualities of its natural environment, geology, and biology as well as its phenomenology, psychology, psychoanalysis, legend, and mythology. All are essential parts of the poetic meaning of the thing. Crystallizing things in this way respects what Ponge, and Merleau-Ponty, mean by the "semantic thickness" of poetic language.

This notion brings us to the opposition between Merleau-Ponty and Sartre regarding phenomenology and poetic language. Philosophically, the name of Ponge is inevitably linked with that of Sartre who wrote a commentary on *Le parti pris des choses* in 1944, eventually published in 1947 as part of *Situations I,* titled "Man and Things" ("*L'homme et les choses*"). Ponge refers to Sartre in his own "This Is Why I Have Lived" (1961), specifically to Sartre's account of Ponge's way of "fixing, immobilizing, and petrifying" things for eternity (VT, 187). Ponge dedicated his poem "The Wasp" ("*La guêpe*"), which opens *La rage de l'expression*, to both Sartre and Simone de Beauvoir. Nevertheless, the interpretation of *Le parti pris des choses* Sartre offers overly reflects Sartre's own ontology and existential psychoanalysis; at least it marks out a sharp difference from the interpretation of Ponge by Merleau-Ponty. The tension or torsion in Sartre's rendering of Ponge stands out in his essay's final sentence: "For Ponge the thinker is a materialist and Ponge the poet—if we leave aside the regrettable intrusions of science—has laid the foundations of a Phenomenology of Nature."[52] Sartre wants to demarcate Ponge's thought or philosophy from his poetry, for Sartre interprets Ponge philosophically not only as a materialist but as an advocate of a mechanistic materialism of nature as machine. From the point of view of Merleau-Ponty, the singular mistake of Sartre's interpretation is the failure to distinguish between objects and things, and in his 1948 radio lectures Merleau-Ponty stressed: "The things of the world are not simply neutral *objects* which stand before us for our contemplation" (Caus, 28/63). Sartre's confusion of things with mere objects resulted from Sartre's own dualistic ontological template of for-itself being over against in-itself being, which is to say the radical freedom of subjects over against the total determinism of objects. In this way, Sartre refers to the "materialism" of Ponge, as well as mechanism, and attributes to him the "ontological desire" of becoming object, that is the desire for death. Sartre bases his analysis upon what Ponge has said about the mollusk in relation to the human. In "Notes Toward a Shell" ("*Notes pour un coquillage*") from *Le parti pris des choses,* Ponge tells us he most admires "a few restrained (*mesuré*) writers and musicians—Bach, Rameau, Malherbe, Horace, Mallarmé—and writers most of all" because, like the mollusk, they created monuments "made of the genuine human secretion common to the human mollusk, the thing most proportioned and suited to his body, yet as utterly different from his form as can be imagined: I mean words (*la parole*)"

(VT, 60–61/T, 86). Yet, when Ponge names the human the "mollusk-human," how mechanical, how passive, does this render the human's "secretion" of language? First, let us bear in mind that Ponge's poet as "mollusk-human" renders the nature-human continuum in terms of Life, not inert, inorganic matter. The poem "Snails" gives us the snail as a maker of works of art: "this shell, a part of their being, is at the same time a work of art, a monument. It lasts far longer than they" (VT, 45/T, 61). As well, Ponge emphasizes that the method of the snail is not pure passivity, rather an interpenetration of activity and passivity: "It [earth] goes through them. They go through it. An interpenetration in the best of taste, tone on tone so to speak—with a passive and an active element, the passive one simultaneously bathing and nourishing the active one, which displaces itself while it feeds" (VT, 42/T, 57). Here Ponge's thought accords with one of Merleau-Ponty's most insightful and delicate chiasms, the chiasm he analyzes between activity and passivity: "Philosophy has never spoken—I do not say of *passivity*: we are not effects—but I would say of the passivity of our activity, as Valéry spoke of a *body of the spirit*: new as our initiatives may be, they come to birth at the heart of being. . . . it is not I who makes myself think any more than it is I who makes my heart beat" (VI, 274/221).

This interpenetration of the active and passive is bifurcated in Sartre's ontology of objects and the psychoanalysis of death that he imposes upon Ponge. Sartre writes: "What gives the things in Ponge's lapidary their ambiguous originality is the very fact that they are not *animate*. They retain their inertia, their fragmentation, their 'stupefaction,' that perpetual tendency to collapse that Leibniz called their stupidity" (MAT, 441/283). Following on from the inanimate stupidity of things, Sartre pursues the argument by explicitly invoking his own ontology and existential psychoanalysis. He writes:

> It seems he [Ponge] has opted for a quick path to symbolically fulfilling our shared desire *to exist after the manner of the "in-itself"*. . . I have observed elsewhere that the desire of all of us is to exist *with complete consciousness* in the mode of being of things; to be entirely a consciousness and, at the same time, entirely a stone. Materialism provides a theoretical satisfaction of this dream since it tells human beings they are merely mechanisms. (MAT, 449/288)

It is true there are times in which Ponge divides humans from the world of nonhuman things and admires the nonhuman while criticizing the human. Examples appear in *Les parti pris des choses*: "The Gymnast" is portrayed as "the adulated paragon of human stupidity" (VT, 52/T, 72), and

"R. C. Seine No" shows no mercy to the "petty, ill-mannered, derby-hatted, briefcase-clutching little clerks" (VT, 53/T, 74). Nevertheless, all in all, to me this only means that Ponge has no patience for that vapid kind of humanism that would accord preciousness to all human activities no matter how self-centered and absurd.

Merleau-Ponty reacted immediately to Sartre's "Man and Things" (1947) and made his defense of Ponge and reply to Sartre during the summer of 1948 in an unpublished lecture titled "Man and Object" ("*L'homme et l'objet*").[53] His reply is indirect without naming Sartre out loud as his opponent, for the rupture in their friendship and end of their collaboration as editors of *Les Temps Modernes* was yet future (1951–52). The occasion was a cycle of lectures on "The Object and Poetry" ("*L'objet et la poésie*") given by Boris Vian, Jacques Lacan, and Jean Cocteau, for which Merleau-Ponty's lecture introduced the general theme. He begins by demarcating the classical world from the modern world, where the modern has the characteristics of ambiguity and openness rather than the classical fixed and finished, closed point of view. In this light, Merleau-Ponty invokes the name of Ponge alongside those of Cézanne, Breton, Bachelard, and Kafka—Sartre and Malraux as well (and here I presume Merleau-Ponty means to include Sartre as literary writer rather than existentialist philosopher). The address also stresses the way in which things are values: the thing is "at the same time an ethical category and the beginning of myth." Merleau-Ponty concludes by saying that the artist and writer of today want to "go further [*cherche plus loin*]." "They believe neither in finality nor preestablished harmony but are particularly sensitive to this vibration that gives birth to form in taking possession of matter."[54] In Emmanuel de Saint Aubert's study of Merleau-Ponty's philosophical development from 1945–51, we find his chapter on Ponge and Sartre, "*Le mollusque et la pierre*" ("The Mollusk and the Stone"). Saint Aubert sums up the conclusion toward which our argument leads:

> The preferences of Merleau-Ponty and Sartre diverge radically. . . . One easily imagines the reaction of Merleau-Ponty to Sartre's "Man and Things," the Merleau-Ponty who rightly already in 1936 defined the Cartesian look as "a specular attitude" that strips off from the object its human aspect (*dépouillait l'objet de son aspect humain*). . . . Thus, Ponge is rediscovered solidly within the framework of Bachelard, Breton, and even Claudel, the interpretation of Sartre purely and simply passed over in silence, to the benefit of the emphases of these lines of thought (*ces lignes*) regarding passion and desire.[55]

Return to Poetic Language: Implex—Mallarmé

Following on from embodied form and semantic thickness, we arrive at Valéry's concept of the implex. Everything in poetry, Valéry said, depends upon a collaboration among three great powers: "what we call the *External World*, what we call *Our Body*, and what we call *Our Mind*" (CW, 7:62–63/O, 1:1323). The collaboration among these three powers, *Corps-Esprit-Monde* (C.E.M.), yields our "*sensibility as a whole*," the cultivation of which was the long and laborious work to which Valéry devoted himself during the years of silence. This cultivation works to extend and deepen the implex or "animal of words" out of which arrives this ideal Voice that is the voice of no one. Merleau-Ponty spends several pages of the 1952–53 course notes analyzing the concept of implex (ULL 65, 129–35). The question that confronts Valéry and he does not stop interrogating, Merleau-Ponty indicates, is what is it that makes us capable of expression at certain moments and not others? ("*qu'est-ce qui fait qu'à certains moments, non quelconques, nous sommes capables d'expression?*") (ULL, 119). This is the question of the source, the fountainhead, or the origin, and we know that any answer to this question will be a divided and incomplete one filled with its own questions. This is the question of the limits of phenomenology against which Merleau-Ponty came up repeatedly and to which his response became his indirect philosophy. Let us suppose with Valéry that we are not to speak of some mysterious source of Inspiration. Let us also remember Valéry's rather intense rejection in *Idée Fixe* of anything like a Freudian Unconscious for its pansexualism, all its "dirty ins and outs" ("*toutes ces cochonneries*") (CW, 5:41/O, 2:223). "Do you want me to pitch you into the sea? . . . Don't you know I detest such dirty words?" (CW, 5:55/O, 2:234). Yet, it will remain the case that Valéry requires, just as does Merleau-Ponty, some notion of latency or passivity, out of which arrives genuine, original, and creative expression. This marvel that is both a presence and absence, an activity and passivity or latency, Valéry names implex. In the introduction to *Signs*, Merleau-Ponty refers to it directly: "Valéry was right to call this speaking power in which expression premeditates itself the 'animal of words'" (S, 26/18). This means that we have the acquisition of speech as we have arms and legs. "We make use of it without a thought, just as without thinking we 'find' our arms and legs" (S, 26/18).

"Implex" is a little-known and little-used word in English as well as French. The *Oxford English Dictionary* gives its meaning as "involved, having a complicated plot," being of Latin origin from *implectere*, to entwine; "implexed" means entwined, "implexion" means complication or intertwining, "implexure" is an infolding or fold (*un pli*). The *Oxford English*

Dictionary lists the first occurrences of "implex" in the writings Joseph Addison in 1710 and Ben Johnson in 1779–81. To my knowledge, Valéry does not tell us if he is aware of this English linguistic meaning and history or if, as stated in *Idée Fixe*, it is a neologism that is a bit of personal terminology from his own "private workshop" (CW, 5:55/O, 2:233). Nevertheless, these meanings—involved, complicated, intertwined, folded over—are suggestive of what Valéry has in mind. In other words, and as Derrida has phrased it, implex is that which cannot be simplex, it is complex.[56] The implex, Valéry tells us, is not an *activity*. Quite the contrary: "It's a *capacity*: our capacity for feeling, reacting, doing and understanding... individual, inconstant, more or less known to us... but always imperfectly and indirectly." He adds that implex is also "our capacity for resistance" (CW, 5:56/O, 2:234). "To sum up... implex is that by which and in virtue of which we remain contingent, conditional" (CW, 5:57–58/O, 2:236). Valéry illustrates: the implex of a muscle is very limited, either to stretch or contract; the implex of the retina is a certain range of lights and colors. The implex of memory is "the prize exhibit" that resists investigation and about which "we know nothing.... If we try to halt at the idea of memory, consider what it really is, at the heart... of consciousness, at that 'sunspot' (*la tache solaire*), that point of intensity and activity where ideas and questions find... or seek... and receive the maximum concentration" (CW, 5:58–59/O, 2:237). Memory is the sunspot of latency at the heart of the mysterious source of creativity.

Sunspots are not themselves intensely bright. Rather, they are dark spots on the sun that cause surrounding areas to be brilliantly illuminated. Such an insight from Valéry regarding the dark and light regions of memory makes one feel intensely the liaison that should have been possible between Valéry and Proust, to explore the relationship between the implex of memory and involuntary memory. But this is missing, left as one of Valéry's resistances alongside that of his resistance to Freud. Ultimately, the implex of memory brings us to the *intellectual* implex per se, which means "the greatest possible number of connections and associations" (CW, 5:59/O, 2:237). The intellectual implex frees words that are at the service of utility, repetition, and habit and imparts to them a special kind of energy or "perceptive [delicate] usage" (*l'usage délicat*). The poet coaxes words to express the flowing wholeness of things, their protean transformations and ambiguous relationships.

In developing his account of the meaning and achievement of implex in the 1953 lecture course notes *Research on the Literary Usage of Language*, Merleau-Ponty focuses on Valéry's concept of "extraordinary time" and its relation to knowledge, will, and desire discussed in a later passage of *Idée*

Fixe. Valéry claims that the poet performs a sort of mental labor in which the mind can recognize the word or thing it desired, and yet "it did not know what the object was that it now recognizes—but there was no mistaking it" (ULL, 132; see CW, 5:89/O, 2:260).⁵⁷ This "recognition of what one desired but did not know" occurs in a moment different from ordinary time, rather in a moment of "extraordinary time" that Merleau-Ponty describes as "the unity of event and desire" (ULL, 132).⁵⁸ Valéry compares it with a space in which a magnetic field is produced that has properties that are no longer those of ordinary space. "The role of will is only to maintain the charged elements in the field and a certain figure forms itself— that does not depend on us" (ULL, 132; see CW, 5:89/O, 2:260).⁵⁹ This is like the operation of focusing the eyes in vision, which depends upon a whole host of different muscles, nerves, and organs, all of which organize themselves beneath the level of conscious control.

Merleau-Ponty sums up by saying "implex is the operation of a meaning that is not yet thematized, liberated, posed for itself" (ULL, 133).⁶⁰ Unlike other commentators such as Derrida,⁶¹ Merleau-Ponty contends that implex is "not the Aristotelian concept of potency" but is rather that of "the imminent," that of "the horizon" (ULL, 133). "It is expressive of what has been prepared by this incubation, this impregnation" (ULL, 133). The implex is not the irrational, but a sort of hidden reason, for example, "risk-reason-implex" (ULL, 135).⁶² Merleau-Ponty stops here but it is possible to go so far as to say that the poem itself may be said to have or to be an implex.⁶³ Once its form, its rhythm, its first word, its first line are set in motion, it carries its own imminent energy, capacities, and limits. The world, too, is implex, no rigid, implacable, immobile *idée fixe*, but an energy and capacity for birth, metamorphosis, and dehiscence. In this way, implex is part of the constellation of ideas pointing the way toward a philosophy of Flesh.

Here we recall Valéry's statement that the notion of implex came to him from the poetic of Mallarmé, as well as Poe. When Valéry encountered Mallarmé's "A Throw of the Dice" ("*Un coup de dés*"), he was the first person to see it. The full title of the poem is "A Throw of the Dice will never abolish chance" ("*Un coup de dés jamais n'abolira le hasard*"). Mallarmé first read it aloud to Valéry in his own voice absent of artifice before showing him how the words were arranged on the pages, enormous blank spaces interspersed irregularly with words of different typeface and type size. On the first page, the entire top of the page is blank and at the very bottom appears "NEVER" ["*jamais*"] in very large, bold, capitalized typeface followed by the first three lines of the poem in much smaller, still capitalized type. Later "WILL NEVER ABOLISH" ["*n'abolira*"] appears as a single word at the very bottom of a blank page. Mallarmé had arranged the words of the poem carefully, even scientifically with graph paper, to visualize the spaces, the lacunas between the words, their "surrounding silence." Valéry writes that he was struck speechless by this unprecedented arrangement; nevertheless, he immediately recognized that he was in the presence of a new kind of silence. "With my own eye I could see silences that had assumed bodily shapes.... There on the very paper some indescribable scintillation of final stars trembled infinitely pure in an inter-conscious void; and there in the same void with them, like some new form of matter arranged in systems or masses or trailing lines, coexisted the Word!" (CW, 8:309/O, 1:624). A few pages later he continued with the same theme: "I was now caught up in the very text of the silent universe... that spoke and did not speak.... Where Kant, rather innocently, perhaps, had thought to see the Moral Law, Mallarmé doubtless perceived the Imperative of a poetry: a Poetics" (CW, 8:311/O, 1:626). The new silence of "*Un coup de dés*" is a silence of the universe, of the constellations in empty space; the arrangement of blanks and words, and the folds of the pages are the material embodiment of the ship, the Ocean, and the game of chance. The poem itself includes the word of a certain silence (cited here compressed without Mallarmé's blanks, and punctuated): "AS IF A simple insinuation into silence, entwined with irony, or the mystery hurled, howled, in some close swirl of mirth and terror, whirls around the abyss without scattering or dispersing and cradles the virgin index there AS IF" ("*comme si une insinuation simple au silence, enroulée avec ironie, ou le mystère précipité, hurlé, dans quelque proche tourbillon d'hilarité et d'horreur, voltige autour du gouffre sans le joncher ni fuir et en berce le vierge indice comme si*").

Mallarmé's brief preface to the poem urges an "agile reader" to read the blanks and pay close attention to the "spacing."[64] There is no completed thought in Mallarmé's poem; the poem is left unfinished, and its compositional structure is unclear. Merleau-Ponty scholar Rajiv Kaushik has written: "We are instead made to witness the way in which words are written down and formed in matter. In short, we are not given an attenuated representational image of things by the language but a production of language."[65] In "Man and Adversity" from *Signs*, Merleau-Ponty wrote: "In going from 'signifying' language to pure language, literature freed itself at the same time painting did from resemblance to things, and from the idea of a *finished* work of art. As Baudelaire already said, there are finished works which we cannot say have ever been *completed*, and unfinished works which say what they mean" (S, 295/233).

Valéry's own initial impression had captured the truth of the poem precisely: "I could see silences that had assumed bodily shapes" (CW, 8:309/O,

1:624). In "The Mystery in Letters," Mallarmé again wrote of the blanks on the pages that are the living body of poetic works:

> To lean, according to the page, on the blank, whose innocence inaugurates it, forgetting even the title that would speak too loud: and when, in a hinge [*dans une brisure*], the most minor and disseminated, chance is conquered word by word, unfailingly the blank returns, gratuitous earlier but certain now, concluding that there is nothing beyond it and authenticating the silence.[66]

Commenting on another of Mallarmé's texts, *Scribbled in the Theater*, Jacques Rancière writes of this "nothing": "There is certainly nothing pejorative in this 'nothing,' which opposes, gloriously, pure fiction to the banalities of representation. Yet its linkage with the infinite—'as far as a place merges with the beyond'—must be assured."[67] There is a linkage between the "nothing" or the emptiness of Mallarmé's pages and the infinite mystery and depth of the universe the poet had worked to express. Merleau-Ponty seldom used a word like "absolute," but he wrote that here we confront a "silence in principle," a "total silence," an "authentic" or "absolute silence" that is the stillness of empty space. In a Working Note of *The Visible and the Invisible*, he wrote: "Language realizes, by breaking the silence, what the silence wished and did not obtain. Silence continues to envelop language; the silence of absolute language, of the thinking language" (VI, 230/176).

Merleau-Ponty criticized Mallarmé in his course of 1958–59, *La philosophie aujourd'hui* (*Philosophy Today*), in contrast with Rimbaud, for Mallarmé's essentialist poetic and intellectualist project that sought the "reduction of things to their meaning or their pure working outline" ("*réduction des choses à leur sens ou leur épure*") (NC, 48). The last line of "*Un coup de dés*," "All Thought expresses a throw of the dice" ("*Toute Pensée émet un coup de dés*"), capitalizes "Thought" ("*Pensée*"), thereby referring to pure idea, free from time and place, as the cosmic sign of Poetry. An implicit part of this "Platonism" was Mallarmé's dream of writing the ultimate book, a dream he never completed, a dream we know Merleau-Ponty would have faulted, for he wrote in the concluding section of *Eye and Mind* regarding modern painting what he also ascribes to "the figurations of literature and philosophy" (OE, 91/149): "The idea of a universal painting, of a totalization of painting, of painting's being fully and definitively accomplished is an idea bereft of sense" (OE, 90/148). Merleau-Ponty writes of Mallarmé in this context in *The Prose of the World*, saying "he was fascinated by the empty page because he wanted to say everything. He postponed indefinitely writing The Book, leaving us in the name of his *works* writings which circumstances snatched from him—but which his weakness, his fortunate weakness, furtively allowed itself" (PM, 145/201). He adds, "the sorrow of language [*la passion du langage*]" is "the necessity of not saying everything if one is to say something" (PM, 201/145). Similarly, *Eye and Mind* concludes in arguing that the falsely imagined "disappointment" of the impossibility of a "total painting" or total book "is the regret of not being everything, and a rather groundless regret at that. For if we cannot establish a hierarchy of civilizations of speak of progress—neither in painting nor even elsewhere—it is not because some fate impedes us; it is, rather, because the very first painting in some sense went to the farthest reach of the future" (OE, 92/149).

Merleau-Ponty turned to Mallarmé in *Causeries* (*The World of Perception*) to express the distinction between the poetic use of language and "everyday chatter": "The poet by contrast, according to Mallarmé, replaces the usual way of referring to things, which presents them as 'well known,' with a mode of expression that describes the essential structure of the things and accordingly forces us to enter into that thing" (Caus, 59/100). The passage continues:

> To speak of the world poetically is almost to remain silent, if speech is understood in everyday terms, and Mallarmé wrote notoriously little. Yet in the little he left us, we at least find the most acute sense of a poetry which is carried entirely by language and which refers neither directly to the world as such, nor to prosaic truth, nor to reason. This is consequently poetry as a creation of language, one which cannot be fully translated into ideas. It is because poetry's first function, as Henri Bremond and Paul Valéry would later remark, is not to designate ideas, to signify, that Mallarmé and subsequently Valéry always refused either to endorse or reject prosaic commentaries on their poems. (Caus, 59–60/100–1)

In the version of his "Indirect Language and the Voices of Silence" essay published in *Signs*, Merleau-Ponty contrasts poetic language with what he names "empirical language," which is recollection and reuse of a "preestablished sign." "It is, as Mallarmé said, the worn coin placed silently in my hand. True speech, on the contrary—speech which signifies, which finally renders '*l'absente de tous bouquets*' present and frees the meaning captive in the thing—is only silence in respect to empirical usage, for it does not go so far as to become a common name" (S, 56/44). "What is absent from all bouquets" ("*l'absente de tous bouquets*") is a phrase Merleau-Ponty has here drawn from Mallarmé's essay "Crisis of Verse" ("*Crise de vers*"). In this text Mallarmé draws the distinction between "brute and immediate speech" and the "essential speech" of the poem, and he illustrates thus: "I say: a flower! And, out of the oblivion where my voice casts every contour, insofar as it is something other than the known bloom, there arises, musically, the very idea in its mellowness; in other words, what is absent from every bouquet." He adds this speech of the poet is "primarily dream and song" and the poet is able to give the hearer or reader the gift of a surprise, namely, "the surprise of never having heard that fragment of ordinary eloquence before, while the object named is bathed in a brand new atmosphere."[68] Here is the flower missing from all prosaic bouquets, the surprise of the musical poetic word uniting sound and sense, of the original and originating speech of dream and song. Milton's opening stanza of *Paradise Lost*, "Sing, Heavenly Muse," reminisces the opening line of Homer's *Iliad*, "Sing, goddess," and together they serve, as Merleau-Ponty scholar Jessica Wiskus has rightly written, as the "implicit opening of every poem, every creative use of language."[69]

Milton, Homer, Mallarmé, and Valéry are part of our poetic cultural implex: "Sing, goddess." In the end, this source named implex has been summoned by Merleau-Ponty as the extraordinary time of the unity of event and desire, that which we do not know but which we recognize. This latter is ever so close to that final description of the double formula of the unconscious that Merleau-Ponty cited from Jean Hyppolite: "I did not know" and "I have always known it," which the philosopher said "corresponds to two aspects of the flesh, its poetic and its oneiric powers" (RC, 179/198). In the commentary of Merleau-Ponty, implex has grown ever so close to the poetic and oneiric power of dream. *Eye and Mind* speaks of the "oneiric world of analogy" (OE, 41/132). In the end and in truth, implex is another name for that expressive power otherwise called silence. Implex is the silence that cracks open the self and is the revelation of that sunspot which is the fullness of the world. This silence is expressed in a stanza from Valéry's poem, "*La ceinture*":

> That vagabonding girdle
> In the aerial breath of sky
> Sets trembling the ultimate bond
> Of my silence with the world . . . [70]

PART II

Merleau-Ponty's Poetics

4

The Clouded Surface
Literature and Philosophy as Visual Apparatuses According to Merleau-Ponty

MAURO CARBONE

> Style for the writer, no less than colour for the painter, is a question not of technique but of vision.
> —Marcel Proust, *Time Regained*

"If phenomenology was a movement prior to having been a doctrine or a system, this is neither accidental nor a deception. Phenomenology is as painstaking as the works of Balzac, Proust, Valéry, or Cézanne—through the same kind of attention and wonder, the same demand for awareness, the same will to grasp the sense of the world or of history in its nascent state. As such, phenomenology merges with the effort of modern thought" (PhP, XVI/xxxv). As is well known, this is how Merleau-Ponty states the convergence of *modern* literature and painting with phenomenology in the lines concluding the preface to *Phenomenology of Perception*.

Three years after the publication of this work, Merleau-Ponty collects in the volume *Sense and Non-Sense* his main articles written during the previous years, distributing them into three parts respectively titled "Oeuvres" (rendered in English as "Arts"), "Ideas," and "Politics." In the four texts composing the first part, which had been previously published between 1945 and 1947, Merleau-Ponty highlights once more the deep convergence of some artistic experiences with "contemporary philosophy" (SNS, 75/59)—or rather, as he specifies at some point, with "phenomenological or existential philosophy" (SNS, 74/58). Such artistic experiences are painting in "Cézanne's Doubt," cinema in "The Film and the New

101

Psychology," and literature both in "Metaphysics and the Novel" and in "A Scandalous Author."

"The Tasks of Literature and Philosophy Can No Longer Be Separated"

In the important first section of "Metaphysics and the Novel," an essay originally published in the same year of *Phenomenology of Perception*, Merleau-Ponty seems to develop what we read in the conclusion of the preface to this latter work. Indeed, he explains once more that the "phenomenological or existential philosophy" (SNS, 36/27–28) "is the coming to consciousness of a movement older than itself whose meaning it reveals and whose rhythm it accelerates" (SNS, 35/27). On this subject, Merleau-Ponty emphasizes that "since the end of the 19th century . . . a new dimension of investigation was opened up" (SNS, 35/27), with the purpose of describing "the metaphysical in man,"[1] namely, the relationship of humans to themselves, to others, to things, and to the world in a time when "there is no longer any human nature on which to rely" (SNS, 37/28).[2] In this epoch, which Merleau-Ponty qualifies as *modern*, "the tasks of literature and philosophy can no longer be separated" (SNS, 36/28). Indeed, in such an epoch the "philosophical expression assumes the same ambiguities as literary expression, if the world is such that it cannot be expressed except in 'stories' and, as it were, *pointed out*" (SNS, 36–37/28; my emphasis), that is to say, literally *made seen*.

Moreover, Merleau-Ponty suggests that the aforementioned tasks are precisely the ones also joining literature and philosophy to cinema. On the one hand, he states that also the film "make[s] us *see* the bond between subject and world, between subject and others, rather than to *explain* it" (SNS, 74/58); on the other hand, he writes that "contemporary philosophy consists not in stringing concepts together but in describing the mingling of consciousness with the world, its involvement in a body, and its coexistence with others; and . . . this is movie material *par excellence*" (SNS, 75/59).

On this basis, we could state that Merleau-Ponty is suggesting that a peculiar dynamic is at work in Western culture since the end of the nineteenth century, making such culture "modern." This dynamic would intertwine with a new "metaphysical" condition, in which emerges what, in *Eye and Mind*, he will define as a "mutation within the relations of man and Being," (OE, 63/310) and a new relation to Visibility.[3]

In a short article titled "*Cinéma et psychologie*" and published on the weekly journal *L'écran français* in October 1945, Merleau-Ponty "summarizes"—such is the term used in the editorial premise—the 1945 lecture on film he had given a few months earlier. This would be published in 1947, under the aforementioned title "The Film and the New Psychology." Interestingly enough, in that short article, Merleau-Ponty writes that "cinema is precisely the art that, better than all others, is able to express human beings by their visible behavior."[4] The terms characterizing the new relation to Visibility in the cinematic domain sound close to the ones of the seminal and famous book titled *Der sichtbare Mensch, oder die Kultur des Films* (*Visible Man or the Culture of Film*), which the Hungarian film theorist Béla Balázs published in Vienna in 1924.[5] This book claims that film as an art form significantly retrieved the lost expressive capacities of the visual body and restored them to the center of Western civilization again after written culture had dominated for centuries. This new centrality of the visible would imply a crisis of the prevailing role of the concept in our culture. Even if it is very improbable that Merleau-Ponty directly read Balázs's book, it is important to remember that in the *Sense and Non-Sense* essays we are considering, he himself stresses not only the new importance of the visible in an age that he qualifies as "the film era" (SNS, 75/59), but also the consequent inadequacy of the traditional conceptual culture—and of philosophy's foundation on this very culture.

It is on such a background, which critically evokes "classical metaphysics" as merely working "by an arrangement of concepts," (SNS, 35/27) that Merleau-Ponty opens the first section of his essay titled "Metaphysics and the Novel" by repeating the names of the three French writers he had already cited in the closing lines of the preface to *Phenomenology of Perception*, with the addition of Stendhal.

In the whole of Merleau-Ponty's thought, it is hard to find a sentence that summarizes the ideas I have just examined better than the very often quoted phrase he writes in a November 1960 Working Note of *The Visible and the Invisible*: "Philosophy . . . cannot be total and active grasp, intellectual possession" (VI, 319/266), he claims, thus evoking once again the inadequacy of philosophy's traditional conceptual characterization. Then, a few lines below, he adds: "it makes us see by words. Like all literature" (VI, 319/266, trans. modified).

Here Merleau-Ponty proposes once more the idea we previously found in *Sense and Non-Sense*. Indeed, on the one hand, he states that the *tasks* of philosophy and literature at work in his epoch are converging; on the other hand, he claims that such tasks consist in making us see (by words) our relationship to ourselves, to others, to things, and to the world.

Therefore, we can state that such an idea crosses—sometimes more evidently than others—the whole path of Merleau-Ponty's thought. To use an expression that was born—and not by chance—in the field of film studies, we could assert that he sees literature and philosophy working in his epoch as convergent *apparatuses* (*dispositifs*) of vision, in turn understood as a *bodily* and not merely *ocular* practice.[6] These convergent visual apparatuses peculiarly function by words, and Merleau-Ponty stresses their varying efficiencies in expressing his epoch.[7]

The French literature theorist Stéphane Lojkine writes that conceiving literature as an apparatus of vision "implies the passage from a linear and textual modelling . . . to a spatial and iconic modelling, which includes the primacy of the image with respect to language, that is, the primacy of the medium with respect to the significant."[8] This is something similar to what I am proposing to consider concerning Merleau-Ponty's philosophy, on the basis of his own characterization of philosophy itself. Nevertheless, Lojkine's formulation suggests the separation of image from language *within language itself*, whereas I assert—as does Gottfried Boehm—that "the questioning of language is what emphasized the imaginary power inherent to language itself; it is what triggered the switch from the 'linguistic turn' to the 'iconic turn.'"[9] Boehm does not doubt the relevance of Merleau-Ponty's contribution to this switch.[10] I shall add that a component of this contribution—which is particularly important, yet so far not consequently developed—is the implicit idea, which I am discussing here, of *philosophy as a visual apparatus working by words* "like all literature." Furthermore, I shall point out that this perspective is crucial in our own time too, even though it is different from Merleau-Ponty's. Indeed, in my opinion, both our time and Merleau-Ponty's are characterized by a tension between the increasing importance of images and the traditional centrality of the concept in our culture.

There is no doubt that the idea of literature and philosophy as visual apparatuses becomes evident again in the last period of Merleau-Ponty's thought. In this phase—like in the concluding lines of the preface to *Phenomenology of Perception*, but also in some courses he gives at the Collège de France during the first half of the 1950s—he repeatedly evokes Marcel Proust and Paul Valéry among other writers. Indeed, Merleau-Ponty plans to devote to them, as well as to Paul Claudel and to some more recent writers such as Saint-John Perse and Claude Simon,[11] a part of "The Cartesian Ontology and the Ontology of Today," one of the two courses interrupted by his sudden death.

In that course, when summarizing the reasons for his particular interest in those literary samples, Merleau-Ponty mobilizes precisely an idea of literature understood as a visual apparatus. On the one hand, in my book *An Unprecedented Deformation*, I mostly characterize this idea by thematizing the French term *voyance*,[12] which he borrows from Arthur Rimbaud's

Letter of the Seer. Merleau-Ponty defines it as to "render . . . present to us what is absent," (OE, 41/132) in the mutual reference to visual perception and the imaginary. On the other hand, it is important to recall that this idea of literature as a visual apparatus "means to carry out a word's work,"[13] as Bernhard Waldenfels puts it. I will focus on this point later.

Like in the first section of the essay "Metaphysics and the Novel," the late Merleau-Ponty connects the idea of literature and philosophy understood as convergent visual apparatuses with the crisis of conceptual thinking he sees in his epoch. More precisely, in the course we are now considering, he links the configuration of literature he describes to what, in the title of this very course, he calls "the Ontology of Today."

In this course, he dates the beginning of that peculiar configuration of literature earlier than he had done before. As we know, in the first section of "Metaphysics and the Novel," he dated such a beginning at the end of the nineteenth century. In the summary of his 1953 course titled "Studies in the Literary Use of Language" and focused on Valéry and Stendhal, he corrects this periodization by stating that "*From a century now [Depuis cent ans]* writers have always been more aware of what is singular and even problematic in their calling" (RC, 22–23/80–81; my emphasis), thus raising what, in the preparatory notes of this very course, Merleau-Ponty qualifies as a "*modern* problem in its explicit form" (ULL, 69; my emphasis). Further correcting this periodization, in the course on "The Cartesian Ontology and the Ontology of Today," he writes that "it might be the case of a change of the relationship with Being in the writer starting from Romanticism" (NC, 187).

Nevertheless, despite this change in periodization, Merleau-Ponty develops in this last course what he wrote in the first section of "Metaphysics and the Novel," by suggesting the idea of a historical ontology (or, according to his earlier language, "metaphysics") of Visibility, which intimately links *what* is supposed to be visible and invisible in a certain epoch to *how* they are made visible and invisible. In other words, he describes *how* different cultural domains, understood as visual apparatuses, work in that epoch in order to provide us with a visible and an invisible. Since he writes that, starting with Romanticism, a "new bond between the writer and the visible" (NC, 190) takes shape, this means that, in his opinion, another bond was already at work then. This is precisely what the part devoted to the "Cartesian ontology" section of this course suggests from the beginning: "Descartes [is] aware that the fact of speaking of [the] vision of the mind is a novelty" (NC, 228).

Besides, it is in the perspective of the other historical novelty possibly opened by Romanticism that Merleau-Ponty interprets the work of the aforementioned writers—starting with Proust and onward—as "[a] reversal of the relations between the visible and the invisible; of flesh and mind" (NC, 392). Indeed, the course section he devotes to them is titled "The Philosophy of the Visible and Literature" (NC, 161), and a subsection of it is "The Visible and the Invisible: Proust" (NC, 191).

Merleau-Ponty's First Reading of Swann's Listening to Vinteuil's Little Phrase

In the subsection titled "The Visible and the Invisible: Proust" of the preparatory notes of his course on "The Cartesian Ontology and the Ontology of Today," as a first step, Merleau-Ponty transcribes the main passages of the first volume of Proust's *Recherche* in which Swann, the protagonist of this volume, during a *soirée* at the marchioness of Saint-Euverte's, happens to listen once again to the "little phrase" from Vinteuil's *Sonata*, which had been the "national anthem" of his romance with Odette.

Merleau-Ponty repeatedly returns to those Proustian pages throughout the course of his thinking. He evokes them for the first time in "The Body as Expression, and Speech," that is, the same chapter of *Phenomenology of Perception* in which we found the other main focus of his interest in Proust's novel, namely, the "function of the *body in memory*" (PhP, 211/187).[14]

Despite this constant reference, it is important to observe that the passage from Proust Merleau-Ponty evokes in that chapter of *Phenomenology of Perception* is skipped in the transcription he provides in his last course notes. This is a sign showing that the reasons for Merleau-Ponty's focus on those Proustian passages are not the same in these two cases.

In "The Body as Expression, and Speech," the goal of Merleau-Ponty's interest is to point out that language and its meaning are inseparable. What is expressed is inseparable from the way it is expressed, as the arts teach us. For this reason, the Proustian passage to which Merleau-Ponty seems to make a more direct allusion is the one in which

> when, after that first evening at the Verdurins', he [i.e., Swann] had had the little phrase played over to him again, and had sought to disentangle from his confused impressions how it was that, like a perfume or a caress, it [i.e., the little phrase] swept over and enveloped him, he had observed that it was to the closeness of the intervals between the five notes which composed it and to the constant repetition of two of them that was due that impression of a frigid and withdrawn sweetness; but in reality he knew that he was basing this conclusion not upon the phrase itself, but merely upon certain equivalents, substituted (for his mind's convenience) for the mysterious

entity of which he had become aware, before ever he knew the Verdurins, at that earlier party when for the first time he had heard the sonata played.[15]

Indeed, even though Merleau-Ponty does not quote this passage explicitly, what interests him is precisely Swann's failure "to disentangle" "the mysterious entity" expressed by Vinteuil's little phrase from the way in which the little phrase technically works. Thus, Merleau-Ponty states that

> the musical signification of the sonata is inseparable from the sounds that carry it: prior to having heard it, no analysis allows us to anticipate it. Once the performance has come to an end, we cannot do anything in our intellectual analyses of the music but refer back to the moment of the experience. During the performance, the sounds are not merely the "signs" of the sonata; rather, the sonata is there through them and it descends into them. (PhP, 213/188)

Merleau-Ponty continues: differently from music, language may seem to be limited to translating into words preexisting meanings, which are independent from such words, when we use language itself as a codified chain of signs related to established meanings. This causes us to focus on what Merleau-Ponty calls *spoken speech* (*parole parlée*), namely, "a secondary expression, a speech about speech that makes up the usual basis of empirical language" (PhP, 207n2/530n6). In this case, according to Merleau-Ponty, signs appear layered onto precodified significations, and the "spoken speech" consequently deceives us apropos of the origin and the real nature of language.

On the contrary, when a sentence introduces in the current language some variations—even the smallest—and establishes therein a previously unspoken signification, it provokes in those who receive the sentence (and even in him or her who pronounced it) a sort of *initiation* that is similar to the one experienced by Swann when listening to the "little phrase." In fact, the signification emerges precisely *in* that phrase: in this sense, signification and phrase are inseparable.[16]

Hence, according to Merleau-Ponty, what Swann finds out by trying to analyze the "little phrase" is also true for language: in every genuine expressive effort—that is, not limited to the use of the *spoken speech*'s established significations—the expression and the expressed reveal their mutual and inseparable inherence. Merleau-Ponty qualifies this use of language as *speaking speech*, in which "the meaningful intention is in a nascent state" (PhP, 229/202).[17]

However, concerning the specific topic of the present chapter, it is important to stress that music is not the only example of inseparability between the expression and the expressed that Merleau-Ponty provides in that passage. Still arguing on the same subject, immediately after quoting the example of Vinteuil's little phrase, animated by a sort of synesthetic purpose, he resorts to the visual example of theater, thus following once again Proust's own path. Indeed, the great fictional artists working as "models" for the *Recherche* narrator are, of course, the musician Vinteuil, the painter Elstir, the writer Bergotte, and precisely the renowned theater actress Berma. Hence, in order to stress once more the inextricable knot of expression and expressed, Merleau-Ponty, just after the reference to Vinteuil's little phrase, refers to the performance of Berma playing Racine's *Phaedra*, that Proust describes in *The Guermantes Way*: "Likewise, the actress becomes invisible, and it is Phaedra who appears. The signification absorbs the signs, and Phaedra has so fully taken possession of Berma that her ecstasy in Phaedra seems to us to be the pinnacle of naturalness and of facility" (PhP, 213/229).[18]

Switching from music to visual arts, this passage shows how Merleau-Ponty characterizes the body of the actress as a *medium* (and implicitly the human body as a *protomedium*) that becomes, as such, "invisible" (not differently from what normally does a "sign," but also a cinematic screen when making the moving images appear) in order to make us see the character's body. In the same sense, in another passage of *Phenomenology of Perception*, Merleau-Ponty describes our bodies as "the expressive space" (PhP, 171/147) par excellence. Yet, in this case he refers back to Swann's listening of Vinteuil's *Sonata* at the Saint-Euverte soirée in order to give an example of that expressive feature of our bodies. Indeed, at this aim, he quotes two phrases from Proust's description of the musicians playing that sonata: "As though the musicians were not nearly so much playing the little phrase as performing the rites on which it insisted before it would consent to appear"; "Its cries were so sudden that the violinist must snatch up his bow and race to catch them as they came" (PhP, 170n1/526 n117).[19]

Although music surely is, in *Phenomenology of Perception*, Merleau-Ponty's favorite example for showing the inseparability of expression and expressed, as I already pointed out, it is not the only one. Nevertheless, he admits that, in the case of language, the inseparability of expression and expressed seems to lose its evidence. In the chapter on the "Cogito," Merleau-Ponty lingers once more on this topic, so as to point out that we should not conclude that language is capable of grasping and fixing an order of nontemporal truths. As he explains, such an illusion is created by speech itself. Indeed, once it makes a meaning emerge, speech seems to dissolve in it, and appears to be but a vehicle of meaning itself. To succumb to such an illusion would be to conceive language as a mere translation of truths drawn from thought and independent from language itself.[20]

On the contrary, Merleau-Ponty reaffirms that "there is no fundamental difference between the modes of expression, and no privilege can be granted to one of them on the assumption that it expresses a truth in itself. . . . Expression is everywhere creative, and the expressed is always inseparable from it" (PhP, 448/411).

In view that the examined topics will be further developed in Merleau-Ponty's later reflection, it is important to stress that, on the bases of what we just read, "What we call an 'idea' is necessarily linked to an act of expression and owes its appearance of autonomy to this act. It is a cultural object, like the church, the street, the pencil, or the Ninth Symphony" (PhP, 447/410).

Of course, the "autonomy" of an idea cannot be but "apparent," since each idea actually lives "in the indefinite process of expression" (PhP, 446/409); in other words, it is inseparable from the peculiar cultural *becoming* of the expression itself.

After writing so, Merleau-Ponty mentions the name of Proust in order to temper the interpretation of some passages of his novel in terms that evoke what is usually understood as Platonism: "as much could be said about the Ninth Symphony, which subsists in its intelligible place, as Proust said, whether it is skillfully or poorly executed, or rather that leads its existence in a time more secret than natural time" (PhP, 447/410).[21]

In any case, according to Merleau-Ponty, it is true that "the existence of the idea does not merge with the empirical existence of the means of expression, but rather ideas endure or pass away, and the intelligible sky subtly changes color" (ibid.). Still, he continues, "it [also] remains true that in speech, more than in music or in painting, thought seems able to detach itself from its material instruments and to take on an eternal value" (PhP, 448/411). Nevertheless, he explains that speech's power to provide what it expresses with "an eternal value" simply consists in its peculiar capacity of *sedimenting*. In other words, "to express is . . . to ensure, through the use of already well-worn words, that the new intention takes up the heritage of the past; it is, in a single gesture, to incorporate the past into the present and to weld this present to a future, to open an entire cycle of time where the 'acquired' thought will remain present as a dimension without our needing to ever again summon it or reproduce it" (PhP, 449–50/413). In referring not necessarily only to speech, Merleau-Ponty resolutely claims what follows: "That which is called the 'non-temporal' within thought is that which, for having thus taken up the past and engaged the future, is presumptively of all times, and is thus anything but transcendent to time. The non-temporal is the acquired" (ibid.).

Merleau-Ponty's Second Reading of Swann's Listening to Vinteuil's Little Phrase

It is well known that Merleau-Ponty meant to analyze Proust's work in the second part of *The Prose of the World*, of which all we are left with are the unpublished Working Notes.[22] Nevertheless, we can find some traces of the research connected to this project in the summary and notes of two courses that Merleau-Ponty gave at the Collège de France in the years immediately following the interrupted writing of *The Prose of the World*. These are the 1953 course titled "Studies in the Literary Use of Language" (*Recherches sur l'usage littéraire du langage*) and the 1954 course titled "The Problem of Speech" (*Le problème de la parole*).

As I already mentioned, the first is focused on the work of Valéry and Stendhal. In these course notes, edited by Emmanuel de Saint Aubert and Benedetta Zaccarello, Proust's name appears mainly in Merleau-Ponty's "General Introduction" of the course itself, which immediately evokes its fundamental "problem: what is literature?" (ULL, 69).

More precisely, Proust's name appears first of all in the second of the two attitudes Merleau-Ponty sees as possible approaches to this problem, which he schematizes immediately afterward. The first is the attitude he names "classical," which he characterizes "by conception of literary language considered as something obvious" (ULL, 70); the second is the attitude he calls "modern" (ibid.)—a category that cannot but captivate our interest.

In light of the questions emerging in the present chapter, our interest is all the more increased by Benedetta Zaccarello's summary of the "modern" attitude in her "Avant-Propos" as she sees it arise from the course notes:

> The modern time is born out of the end of a belief, that of the possibility of delivering to a pictorial or verbal representation a given object pre-existing to the mimetic and communicative act that is at the origin of the [artistic or literary] work. The modern time begins when the artist or the writer ceases to believe that their work is all about representing [something] for a third party and by means of an established language assuring a correspondence between what is rendered and the image that the object itself leaves in the artwork.[23]

In the parallel between painting and literature that is hereby evoked, it is easy to find the idea of literature understood as an apparatus of vision functioning by words like the one I thematized earlier. The reconfiguration of this apparatus, following the crisis of its "classical" version, which is based on the notion of representation, urges Merleau-Ponty to return, six years after Sartre, to the question "What Is Literature?" and to try to answer via Proust, among others. Although in the 1953 course we have so far examined Merleau-Ponty could not focus his attention thereon, he will indeed the following year in his attempt to value the importance and the relative autonomy of "the Saussurian notion of speech" (RC, 34/88, trans. modified) with respect to that of language.[24]

In fact, as written by Stefan Kristensen, Merleau-Ponty "consecrates to Proust the last six lectures of his course on speech. They are to be read as the sequel of his course on literature from the previous year."[25] However, our reading cannot be limited to simply noticing this continuity. In the light of our findings thus far, Merleau-Ponty's attention concerning the Proustian answer to the question "What Is Literature?" is indeed our chance to gather precious clarifying aspects concerning the aforementioned, emblematic claim Merleau-Ponty formulated in 1960, according to which philosophy "makes us see by words. Like all literature." Besides, the connection between such a claim and the questions discussed in this course's pages on Proust is confirmed by the very question opening them: "Proust: A Philosopher?" (PbParole, [94](5)).[26]

Still, in these six lectures, the reprise of the questions that emerged in the previous year does not seem to be separate from the objectives Merleau-Ponty declares in the summary of the course, which those six lectures conclude: "The purpose of the course is to illustrate and to extend the Saussurian notion of speech as a positive and conquering function" (RC, 34/88, trans. modified). In other words, the search for Proust's answer to the question "What Is Literature?" allows Merleau-Ponty to also find feedback for his own characterization of speech (*parole*).

It is important to know that, in this phase of his reflection, Merleau-Ponty reformulates the distinction between *spoken speech* and *speaking speech*, in an attempt to find the ultimate interaction between the Saussurian notions of *language* (*langue*) and *speech* (*parole*). Of course, Merleau-Ponty confirms a historical and ontological primacy of speech, since he considers it to hold the power of instituting communication.[27] However, in *Phenomenology of Perception*, the transcendence that is expressed in language was situated in the *speaking speech*, understood as an individual act of expression that participates in the transcendence that animates the body proper by preserving a gestural meaning. Instead, here the transcendence at work in language acts precisely by virtue of the interaction of speech and language, i.e. by virtue of the mutual implication of *both* the elements composing it. In fact, the transcendence of language allows choosing from the sedimented patrimony of signs and significations those signifiers that, when encountered, make a new sense blossom, a sense that is implied in them and yet overcomes them, and also overcomes the intention of signification proper to the speaking subject, even when this sense is supposed to express the subject's very experience.

According to Merleau-Ponty, the mutual and inseparable bond between the experience and its linguistic expression, namely, the "vicious circle or prodigy" (RC, 41/94) connecting them, is what Proust put in light better than anyone else, by showing that "to speak or to write is truly *to translate* an experience which, without the speech that it inspires, would not become a text" (ibid., trans. modified). Here is highlighted, as Merleau-Ponty planned to do, the "positive and conquering" power of *speech*.

According to Merleau-Ponty, the Proustian literature succeeds in underlining the "vicious circle" of speech when describing *Recherche*'s narrator as he faces the creative experience of the three main artist characters that Proust, as I already mentioned, brings to life in his novel: namely, the writer Bergotte, the painter Elstir, and the musician Vinteuil.

By referring to the imaginary works of the painter and the musician—to which Proust devotes a series of elaborate reflections and which seem to progressively shape his own aesthetics—Merleau-Ponty emblematically discerns in Elstir's painting and in Vinteuil's music as many diacritical systems. Such diacritical systems creatively prolong the diacritical system that is at work in our sensible relation to the world, and hence answer this relation's call to be brought to expression. In this sense, on the one hand, Elstir's painting answers the call with its "metaphors." Indeed, the metaphors' *transfers* (such is the literal meaning of the term) from one sensible element to another are capable of displaying "the return to primary vision" (PbParole, [104](5)) in which, despite the distinctions introduced by intelligence and sedimented in the instituted language, we sense the co-belonging of things.[28] As we will see, the term "metaphor" will remain filled with important echoes even in Merleau-Ponty's subsequent reflection on the philosophical language.

On the other hand, as far as Vinteuil's music is concerned, Merleau-Ponty returns to the *Recherche* passages in which Swann listens to the *Sonata* during the reception at the marchioness Saint-Euverte's, yet he adds some further observations about Vinteuil's *Septet*. Proust characterizes this fundamental composition attributed to the imaginary musician, with respect to the *Sonata*, in an openly contrasting, even if intimately complementary way.[29]

In any case, Merleau-Ponty's focus is definitely on the pages concerning Swann's listening to Vinteuil's sonata, which this time he considers not only more broadly, but also from a deeper theoretical angle. He inserts in the notes of this course—as he does in those he will draft in 1961—a long transcription of those pages. However, in the two versions of this transcription, he includes and excludes different passages, sometimes highlighting the same expressions, at other times underlining different expressions. Generally speaking, we could say that, in the present transcription, Merleau-Ponty does not focus mainly on the visual elements of the Proustian description; rather, he explicitly questions the problem of the universal, and consistently titles the notes of this section "Vinteuil, the idea, the concept-less universal, the alogical essence, the objectivity through the individual" (PbParole, [107](8)).

The Proustian passage that seems to be at the very core of Merleau-Ponty's attention is the following:

> It was the charms of an intimate sadness that it [i.e., the little phrase] sought to imitate, to re-create, and *their* very *essence*, for all that it consists in being incommunicable and in appearing trivial to everyone except him who experiences them, had been captured and made visible by the little phrase. So much so that it caused their value to be acknowledged, their divine sweetness savoured, by all those same onlookers, if they were at all musical—*who then would fail to recognise them in real life, in every individual love that came into being beneath their eyes*. Doubtless the form in which it had codified those charms could not be resolved into rational discourse. But ever since, more than a year before, discovering to him many of the riches of his own soul, the love of music had, for a time at least, been born in him, Swann had regarded musical motifs as *actual ideas, of another world, of another order, ideas veiled in* shadow, unknown, impenetrable to the human mind, but none the less perfectly *distinct from one another, unequal among themselves in value and significance.*[30]

Here Proust highlights precisely that, to Swann, a peculiar "idea" of love is incarnated in the sound of the "little phrase" of Vinteuil's *Sonata*—to the extent that the former becomes inseparable from the listening of the latter. This idea, this "essence"—which is the way the Greek term *idea* is traditionally translated in most Western languages—has universally recognizable features even without their being strictly logical.

Thus, Merleau-Ponty sees in this passage the outline of a peculiar "order" of ideas, an order very different from the one that characterizes what

Proust qualifies, in the same passage, as the "ideas of the intellect"—meaning ideas in a Platonistic acceptation, on which our present notion of "concept" is also based. This is why Merleau-Ponty, while transcribing Proust's passage, emphasizes the words describing those ideas as peculiarly "*veiled*." In Proust's description, what is particularly relevant to Merleau-Ponty is that such a peculiarity makes those ideas "impenetrable to the human mind, but none the less perfectly *distinct from one another, unequal among themselves in value and significance*."[31]

Hence, with respect to *Phenomenology of Perception*, Merleau-Ponty's interest in the Proustian pages is in the notion of idea. He focuses on it by deepening the consequences of the indivisibility of the expression and the expressed as well as by deepening the bond between such indivisibility and the theme of the "time of ideas" (PhP, 447/410). In fact, it is precisely because these ideas do not preexist regardless of their expression, but are rather inseparable from it, that they cannot be considered as Platonistic.[32] Merleau-Ponty also faces more deeply and with a more engaged theoretical attitude the question of Proust's supposed Platonism, which we have seen implicitly evoked already in *Phenomenology of Perception*. Now he rather speaks of "pseudo-Platonism" (PbParole, [96]v(7)) and, as he explains in this course's summary, he proposes to interpret it as "an attempt at an integral expression of the perceived or lived world" (RC, 40/93).

Like painting and music, literature itself is, for Proust, "an attempt" aiming at the same goal. Its specificity is that it pursues this attempt beginning with the "everybody's language" (RC, 40/93, trans. modified), which the writer recreates in order to "deliver the prelogical participation of landscapes, dwellings, localities, and gestures, of men among themselves and with us" (ibid.). In this non-Platonistic or simply "pseudo-Platonistic" sense, Merleau-Ponty highlights that "the writer's work is a work of language rather than of 'thought'" (ibid.). Merleau-Ponty finds the Proustian answer to the question "What Is Literature?" precisely where Proust describes most paradoxically the "vicious circle" of experience and expression. Most powerfully, Proust's answer lies in his description of the conquering capacity of *speech*, evidenced in a sentence from *Time Regained*:

> As for the inner book of unknown symbols (symbols carved in relief they might have been, which my attention, as it explored my unconscious, groped for and stumbled against and followed the contours of, like a diver exploring the ocean-bed), if I tried to read them no one could help me with any rules, for to read them was an act of creation in which no one can do our work for us or even collaborate with us.[33]

In other words, the "vicious circle or prodigy" that Merleau-Ponty sees in this Proustian passage consists in highlighting that the experience only becomes text when and if the writer is able—as he explains in the previous page of the same summary—"to *produce a system of signs whose internal articulation* renders the landscape of an experience" (RC, 40/93, trans. modified; my emphases).

During this phase of his thought, Merleau-Ponty hence abandons the tendency to consider the experience as a text and the expression as its translation, which can still be found in *Phenomenology of Perception*.[34] In fact, in the phase of his reflection we are considering—more precisely in *Indirect Language and the Voices of Silence*—he points out that "the author himself has no text to which he can compare his writing, and no language prior to language" (S, 54/43). Speaking of "vicious circle," Merleau-Ponty aims at highlighting once more the *circular relation* that expression—be it language, music, or painting—engages with experience, for such a relation cannot be *archeological* without being *teleological* at once. In short: expression cannot recall an experience without recreating it at the same time.[35]

Merleau-Ponty's Third Reading of Swann's Listening to Vinteuil's Little Phrase

Seven years after "The Problem of Speech" course, as we already know, Merleau-Ponty opens the subsection titled "The Visible and the Invisible: Proust" of the notes he was preparing for his course on "The Cartesian Ontology and the Ontology of Today" with a new transcription of the Proustian pages devoted to Swann's listening of Vinteuil's *little phrase* at the Saint-Euverte soirée.

The passage concerning the universality of the ideas described in those pages is not included in the new transcription. Consistently with the title of this section and with that of this subsection of the course notes, the attention to the *visual elements* of that description is eventually strengthened and clarified.

In parallel, Merleau-Ponty had drafted a commentary on the same topic in the last pages of his unfinished book *The Visible and the Invisible*. In such a commentary, which is less developed than the one following the new transcription, he refers to the essences described by Proust in terms of "sensible ideas" (VI, 196/151). Such an expression powerfully underlines why Merleau-Ponty opens his commentary for *The Visible and the Invisible* by writing that "we touch here the most difficult point" (VI, 195/149). Indeed, the expression "sensible ideas" names an "entity" that is literally *unthinkable* in the tradition of the Western thought, since, starting with Plato, such a tradition has always tended and continues to think according to the separation and the opposition between the sensible and the ideas. In other words, the Western tradition has always tended to think according to the separation and the opposition of the visible and the invisible, which Merleau-Ponty points out in the "Cartesian ontology" too. Contrary to the Western philosophical tradition, Proust shows that, in our experience, certain ideas are not separable from and opposed to the sensible. In fact, they arise precisely thanks to our encounter with the sensible itself—like Swann's peculiar "*idea*" (NC, 191) of love is evoked when listening to the "little phrase" of Vinteuil's *Sonata*. This is the reason why Merleau-Ponty emphasizes and outlines in the pages where Proust describes Swann's experience a conception of ideas that would reverse the Platonistic theory of ideas. Thus, in his course notes he overtly writes, precisely in a *visual language*, that "One says Platonism, but these ideas have no intelligible sun, and are akin to the visible light" (NC, 194).

In other words—namely, the words of the parallel commentary on those Proustian pages, which Merleau-Ponty was drafting for *The Visible and the Invisible*—the sensible ideas ("musical ideas," as well as literary ones, and also "our notions of *light, of sound, of perspective*, of physical pleasure, the rich possessions wherewith *our inner temple is diversified and adorned*"),[36] not differently from the ideas of the intellect, are provided with a rigorous logic,[37] and aim at "the exploration of an invisible" (VI, 196/149). Still, now Merleau-Ponty fully emphasizes that, unlike the ideas of the intellect, they are "*veiled in shadow*" (NC, 191) and "cannot be detached from the sensible appearances and be erected into a second positivity" (NC, 194). This is why presently Merleau-Ponty also emphasizes that Proust qualifies them as "*notions without any equivalent.*"[38] Indeed, their sensible appearance is—as Proust explains and Merleau-Ponty points out—a sort of "clouded surface" presented "to the eye of reason."[39]

In short, as Merleau-Ponty summarizes in his course notes, "there are 1) [Descartes's] *intuitus mentis*, ideas of the intellect, and 2) ideas with a 'clouded [*obscure*] surface,' akin to notions of the sensible[,] in particular *light*" (NC, 194).

Thus, I think we have gathered now the main elements of the *visual apparatus* Merleau-Ponty finds at work in Proust's pages in order to "make us see by words"—rather than intellectually possessing—our relationship to ourselves, to others, to things, and to the world. Let us examine those elements more closely.

As we already saw, concerning the source of light, Merleau-Ponty points out that in those pages Proust describes the effects produced on the visible by a "visible light" (ibid.)—not an intellectual one. Indeed, Proust evokes *"the luminosity of a lamp that has just been lit, in view of the changed aspect of everything in the room, from which even the memory of the darkness has vanished."*[40]

On the other hand, we have what Proust qualifies as "a clouded surface," whose feature particularly interests Merleau-Ponty. Indeed, in his turn, he has always been interested in similar kinds of surfaces, that is, surfaces whose opacity is no longer understood as reducing or concealing the pure light of truth: in short, surfaces that, for these reasons, are no longer expected to be removed or even pierced, contrary to the tradition of Western metaphysics. Typically, this is the case with the "watermark [*filigrane*]," which Merleau-Ponty evokes in a note of *The Prose of the World*[41] in order to signify that "it is essential . . . to truth never to be possessed, but only transparent through the clouded [*brouillée*] logic of a system of expression" (PM, 52–53/37). Indeed, as the birth of cinema also testifies, the opacity of such surfaces, instead of forbidding vision, can rather *make us see* the images in which truth is manifested in its constitutive "ambiguity" (*Zweideutigkeit*),[42] thus reminding us that light and shade—traditionally opposed by our culture—simply cannot be separated. This is why Merleau-Ponty always saw, in the mutated status of those *mediation* surfaces, a major symptom of the mutations at work in his epoch.

From this perspective, I could not but see, in Merleau-Ponty's later research, the fragments of an ontological reflection on *mediation* understood as what *makes us see*, and, more widely, communicate. What I mean is an ontological reflection on the flesh understood as a synesthetic Visibility, as I proposed in *The Flesh of Images*. As Merleau-Ponty puts it in *The Visible and the Invisible*, "It is this Visibility, this generality of the Sensible in itself, this anonymity innate to Myself that we have previously called flesh, and one knows there is no name in traditional philosophy to designate it" (VI, 183/139).

On the other hand, an attentive analysis of the fragments of the later Merleau-Ponty's ontological reflection on the flesh understood as Visibility leaves unspecified some fundamental aspects of the rehabilitation of the opaque surface as a showing-surface. Let us examine closer how Merleau-Ponty characterizes the Proustian "clouded surface," precisely understood as a showing-surface, in his interrupted commentary concluding the fourth chapter of *The Visible and the Invisible*.

Making Us See by Words: Through a Veil or on a Screen?

First of all, we shall keep in mind that the case we are examining concerns a "clouded surface" composed of words.[43] In the chapter of *The Visible and the Invisible* preceding the one in which Merleau-Ponty comments on Proust's pages, he wonders precisely which kind of language could express our relationship to ourselves, to others, to things, and to the world. Of course, he focuses in particular on the philosophical language. Yet, by also evoking the "trading of the metaphor" (VI, 167/125) with regard to such language, he characterizes it in a way which is not essentially different from that of literature, and which echoes also Proust's characterization of Elstir's paintings as "metaphors." In this sense, it is important to remark that Merleau-Ponty makes use of *visual terms* in order to differentiate this language from the one traditionally used in philosophy. According to him, the latter relies on "the *manifest* meaning of each word and of each image" (a definition in which we can easily recognize the traditional characterization of the concept), whereas the former counts on "the *occult* trading of the metaphor" (ibid.; my emphasis).

As Merleau-Ponty explains, the literary language does not presume and claim to *disappear* in order to make us see the relationships at work in our experience. On the contrary, it is precisely *by not disappearing* that it can make us see them. Therefore, it does not compose a sort of surface forbidding vision, like a "screen" (Merleau-Ponty uses precisely this word) has traditionally been supposed to do.[44] In short, we could state that it is indeed by making us see itself that the literary language makes us see what exceeds it.

These are the main elements we can retain from the penultimate chapter of *The Visible and the Invisible* in order to better approach Merleau-Ponty's characterization of the Proustian "clouded surface" in the pages concluding the last chapter of that interrupted book. Here Merleau-Ponty refers to the function of that "clouded surface" by using alternately the terms *screen* and *veil*. Indeed, speaking of the sensible idea, he writes that we cannot "see it unveiled [*sans voiles*]" (VI, 197/150). Still, only a few lines earlier, he affirms that "there is no vision without the *screen* [*sans écran*]" (ibid.). Hence, on the one hand he uses the term *screen* in a totally different way from the acceptation of hiding surface we encountered in the previous chapter of *The Visible and the Invisible*. On the other hand, and what is much more important, he assimilates the "screen" and "veil" functions of showing without characterizing them respectively as a *fully* opaque surface and a *partially* opaque one. Yet, it is precisely such a characterization that determines their relative positioning with respect to the source of light projecting the images on the surfaces themselves, as well as with respect to the spectator. Indeed, a partially opaque surface, like a veil, is normally situated *between* the spectator and the source of light, which is therefore placed *behind* the surface. Whereas in the case of a totally opaque surface—

that is, a screen—it is the spectator that lays *between* the light source and that very surface—and nothing is or is supposed to be *behind* the surface itself.

Nevertheless, we heard Merleau-Ponty assimilate the "screen" and the "veil." This is why in the same page, he can write, once again without any differentiation, that a spectator could contemplate the sensible ideas "in transparency *behind* the sensible, or *in* its heart" (ibid.; my emphases).[45] And in the following page he insists that "they are there, *behind* the sounds *or between* them, *behind* the lights *or between* them" (VI, 198/150; my emphases).

Moreover, this first unspecified element produces a second one, since it prevents from distinguishing the veil's and screen's relative showing functions in a historical sense. But how did it actually work, the visual apparatus that, according to Merleau-Ponty, was *making the spectators see* back in his epoch? Did it work like a screen, as instituted by cinema at that time, or, much more traditionally, like a veil? And what about our epoch? Is the visual apparatus evoked by Merleau-Ponty still working in the same way also in the age of the "digital revolution"? And more particularly, is it still working in the same way as far as *words* are concerned? Or rather, are the relationships of the visual and the enunciable looking for a new balance in "mak[ing] us see by words"? And if this is the case, what does it imply for us, the readers, concerning our ways of perceiving, desiring, imagining, and thinking about our relationship to ourselves, to others, to things, and to the world?

For an ontology of Visibility like Merleau-Ponty's—which seems to have been increasingly attentive in seizing the historical mutations of Visibility itself—to leave the aforementioned elements unspecified is to continue to keep its project unaccomplished. On the other hand, the questions I raise point out how important it is to develop such a project according to contemporary concerns.

More generally but also more radically, concerning Merleau-Ponty's thought, I shall suggest that, despite his constant interest in cinema as a symptom of an epochal novelty in the ontological history of Visibility, the visual apparatus that remains the dominant visual model in his way of thinking is the veil, rather than the cinematic screen.

In its turn, the veil has an extremely long and rich history crossing that of human culture at least since the Jewish Tabernacle—which is meticulously described in the Bible—or the Egyptian statue of the goddess Isis. Merleau-Ponty does not take into account this history and its important variations, but his philosophical attitude surely rejects both the idea of veil as a metaphysical surface to be *overcome* (as the term *metaphysics* implies) and the idea of veil as surface that could be *seen-through* as if it did not exist (as the term *per-spective* tends to suggest). Merleau-Ponty's understanding of the veil seems to be close to that of Nietzsche, which he actually quotes in "Philosophy and Non-Philosophy Since Hegel," namely, the second of his last two courses: "we no longer believe that truth remains truth when the veils are withdrawn" (NC, 277).[46] Nevertheless, in Merleau-Ponty's understanding, this does not prevent him from still thinking of the veil as a surface referring to its "behind." Also when commenting on Proust's pages in his course notes, he insists that the sensible idea "becomes quasi-visible, but signifies beyond" (NC, 194) and again that such "an idea . . . is not *what* we see, but behind" (ibid.). Thinking according to such a visual model is precisely what prevents Merleau-Ponty's position from being consequently antimetaphysical. Or anyway, it is what makes it definitely belong to an epoch different from ours.

In any case, what we saw so far is that he does not care much about the peculiar characteristics of the visual apparatus to which he refers. His basic exigency is, on the one hand, to convince us that a medium is, in any case, necessary in order to make expression possible (even if it does not guarantee its success). On the other hand, he points out that such an expression cannot be reduced to what the medium directly transmits. In short, Merleau-Ponty affirms the necessity of mediation understood as an ambiguous *power of showing and concealing*, that is to say, the power to make us "see" in a direct, indirect, metaphorical, and even negative way,[47] no matter what wields it, whether a body, a veil, a screen, a watermark, or a literary passage. It is also in order to meet the need of affirming such a power without ignoring the need of accounting for the inevitable historic and cultural differentiations it can assume, that elsewhere I propose to talk in terms of "arche-screen."[48] This notion has to be understood as one would understand a (musical) theme—or, according to the meaning of the Greek term *arché*, a "principle"—which however, far from platonistically giving itself *before* the human time of history, does not cease to shape and reshape itself with and through its pre-historical and historical variations. As such, case by case, it will articulate in different ways its characteristic of surface that shows and conceals at once, as a transhistorical principle of visibilization and invisibilization. This could hence contribute in accounting for the historical mutations of visibility, and thus also for the "reversal of the relations of the visible and the invisible" (NC, 392) that, as we read, Merleau-Ponty sees at work in Proust just as in the ontology of his "today."

Translated by Marta Nijhuis

5

Metaphoricity
Carnal Infrastructures and Ontological Horizons

EMMANUEL DE SAINT AUBERT

How should we approach the relationship between Merleau-Ponty's philosophy and the question of *metaphor*? For those familiar with his work, the relationship is self-evident, the subject unavoidable. Yet the treatment, as well as the delineation of this issue, is complex. We might, of course, engage in a study of the originality of the philosopher's writing (especially in his later work); we might also review Merleau-Ponty's own explicit (albeit rare) assertions about metaphor, or perhaps even evaluate those aspects of his philosophy that lead us to a fresh understanding of metaphoricity. These complementary approaches would invite a reexamination of the most advanced dimensions of his anthropology and ontology, as well as their intimate intersection with his phenomenology of the flesh.

What interests Merleau-Ponty, however, as might well interest us in connection with his work, is not so much the provision of a possible linguistic definition of metaphor, or even a description of its linguistic functioning. From a Merleau-Pontian perspective, any definition would fall short of expressing what metaphor *is*, what makes metaphor so "alive." Merleau-Ponty is more interested in questions such as: Where does metaphor come from? How is it anthropologically, *naturally inscribed*? Why is metaphor so essential to the life of the mind, and what can it teach us about our mental life? In what ways is metaphoricity typical of our carnal being-in-the-world? Also: Where does metaphor take us; what is its *expressive power*? What can it tell us about humans, the world, and being? The ontological scope here is obvious.

Angles of Attack

These questions lead us in two directions: returning us to what lies "beneath" language and, going further, toward what lies "beyond" language; or rather, back to the flesh and toward being—via language. This transversal Merleau-Pontian dynamic is consistent with his overall philosophical objectives: We cannot isolate language and approach it directly, we must constantly return to the phenomenal body, starting with the body schema as a system of sensorimotor equivalences. Merleau-Ponty often seems to approach language as a form of corporeal sublimation-surrection,[1] a subtle flesh, a simply more glorious body—although his work on this issue remains incomplete, with the phenomenologist consistently postponing until "next year" his discussion of the irreducible specificity of language in relation to perceptual life and the body's natural symbolism. Merleau-Ponty's privileging of the concept of flesh, as opposed to incarnation, is also of note here. Metaphor is not a preexistent linguistic meaning that becomes incarnate, that dons a sensible garb: The body itself generates and orchestrates metaphoricity through its own fundamental analogicity. In the framework of this philosophy of the flesh, then, we might speak of the metaphorical power of the body, of the metaphoricity of the body. The issue here is not only how metaphor is formed, but also how metaphor *forms* the body, *from* the body.

For Merleau-Ponty, we need to consistently come back to perception; we can never really get beyond perception. The return to perception, to the phenomenal body as fundamental of our being-in-the-world, includes a return to the inextricable involvement of the *imaginary* in our perceptual life. Thought cannot escape the carnal (notably sensorimotor) reversibility that grounds and sustains it, nor can it escape the imaginary, which is fully tied up with our relation to the real. Thought remains irreducibly connected to perceived things, which are always already crystallizations of desire, as relief or impression (*en plein ou en creux*); things are always already imaginary bodies in relation to the body image: the flesh of my flesh. This hints at the structural complexity of Merleau-Ponty's own thought, in its originality and boldness, its fertility as well as its shortcomings. His concept of flesh attempts to encompass three mutual precessions characterizing the flesh and its expressive life, and its crowning achievement, the ability to forge and understand metaphors: the precessions between perception and *motor skills*, between perception and *desire*, and between perception and the *imaginary*. In certain places, Merleau-Ponty seems to outline a fourth precession, equally crucial to his theory of metaphor, but which, in our opinion, remains insufficiently developed: that is, between perception and *speech*.

Merleau-Ponty's reexamination of the issue of metaphor from the perspective of perceptual life is remarkable, particularly with regard to the relationship between visible and invisible (as in his treatment of depth, of shadow, of what he refers to more generally as "figuratives" [*les figuratifs*]).[2] So that we might even ask whether this is a genuine reexamination, or whether Merleau-Ponty is not completely shifting the issue, so as to approach it laterally, to return to that which lies at the foundations and horizons of metaphoricity—even though this is in fact partly something else, something he struggles to identify as, precisely, *something else*. It seems, incidentally, that the differentiation, or rupture, that grants speech its specificity, that grants autonomy to the institution of language, is in part lacking here. We might also mention two further distinguishing features of his thought that reinforce this investigation and its accompanying uncertainties: that is, the strong connection between his interest in *art* (with a privileged role given to painting) and *literature*[3] (a connection no doubt influenced, in part, by Surrealism),[4] as well as his explicit, recurring analogy between *speech* and *vision*—which, according to Merleau-Ponty, is more than an analogy.[5]

All in all, the boundaries of metaphor are somewhat destabilized; if any metaphor specialist were to read the following study, they might find themselves somewhat perplexed. Of course, this is not to be taken as a presentation of "metaphor in Merleau-Ponty." Instead, we are following in the philosopher's own indirect footsteps, in an attempt to provide an extensive and integrated overview—as we have suggested in our title—of the carnal infrastructure and ontological horizons of metaphoricity, as might be apprehended in (or inspired by) Merleau-Ponty's philosophy. So that these might in turn illuminate the oneiric-poetic dimensions of the relationship between *flesh* and *being*. For Merleau-Ponty, these dimensions need to be restored by philosophy itself, through a reconception of being and flesh, through an embrace of its own literary artistry and phenomenological description.

A Philosophy of the Flesh: Objectives and Requirements

In tackling this subject, we need to remember Merleau-Ponty's philosophical objectives, his desire to rethink the age-old question of the union of soul and body through the conception of flesh, his commitment to discovering the more spiritual dimensions of our animation, via a return to the living and expressive body. Which involves, incidentally, a better identification of the corporeal, perceptual, motor, as well as desirous, roots of intelligence. As I have shown elsewhere,[6] this philosophical intention is inextricably connected to a critical, anti-idealist and specifically anti-Cartesian scenario, as evident in the recurring debate over what Descartes refers to as "*commingling*" (*confusion*)[7] and what Merleau-Ponty prefers to call "encroachment."

The philosophy of the flesh hopes to encompass the three stages of this commingling-encroachment: the "mixture" that we are (anthropological commingling), as manifest in the ambiguity of perceptual and desirous life (phenomenological commingling), accessible only to a way of thinking that integrates commingling at an epistemological level. Metaphor comes full circle in this last register, in that of a "commingled thinking" dedicated to understanding our "mixed" being (the union of soul and body) and our being-in-the-world (our transactional being), in an espousal of the phenomenality that expresses them. As a feature of embodied intelligence, metaphor is the *expression* of the union of soul and body; of our own "way of being body."[8] But it is also the *exercise* of this way of being, an expression involved in the very construction of our flesh and its relations.

This philosophical objective cannot avoid a critical engagement with the classical conception of metaphor. Because here we are no longer dealing with the sensible and the intelligible, and their retrospective reconciliation in analogy, and neither are we dealing with body and soul, and their similarly retrospective unification. Instead, we are dealing with a corporeality that progressively animates itself in a dual movement of integration and differentiation, through the course of a complex history of attachments and separations, by the investment in, and the extension and conquest of, new territories. Metaphor is thus no longer a bridge over a previously established boundary, no longer a retroactive transgression, but a much more complex gesture, a single movement of differentiation and integration, separation and unification, delimitation and transgression. To affirm with Perelman that metaphor is a condensed analogy,[9] is both intelligent and deceptive in equal measure. No longer simply a retrospective clarification of the universal by means of a sensible analogue, metaphor is a participant in the blossoming of sense, at the very heart of the sensible world. No longer the illustrative accessory of an already established meaning, or the "participation in a prior idea,"[10] but a participant in the institution of meaning itself.

So that Merleau-Ponty cannot but agree with another author's fundamental critique of metaphor (and, by association, of scholastic analogy):

The idea of "transposing" and of metaphor is based upon the distinguishing, if not complete separation, of the sensible and the nonsensible as two realms that subsist on their own. The setting up of this partition of the sensible and nonsensible, between the physical and nonphysical is a basic trait of what is called metaphysics and which normatively determines Western thinking. Metaphysics loses the rank of the normative mode of thinking when one gains the insight that the above-mentioned partitioning of the sensible and nonsensible is insufficient. When one gains the insight into the limitation of metaphysics, "metaphor" as a normative conception also becomes untenable—that is to say that metaphor is the norm for our conception of the essence of language. . . . The metaphorical exists only within metaphysics.[11]

We are reminded of Ricoeur's comment, "In Heidegger himself the context considerably limits the import of this attack on metaphor, so that one may come to the conclusion that the constant use Heidegger makes of metaphor is finally more important than what he says in passing against metaphor."[12] Yet Heidegger's target is not metaphor per se, but its dualistic theorization—as characterized by the distinction, separation, scission (*Unterscheidung, Trennung, Scheidung*)[13] of physical and nonphysical, sensible and nonsensible. From a Merleau-Pontian perspective, however, Heidegger does not go far enough: He fails to push his rejection of the sensible/nonsensible distinction toward an ontological rehabilitation of the sensible—which means that he remains stuck in the encroachment of being and speech, without ever descending to the encroachment of being and flesh.[14] It is in this sense that, despite his pertinent critique of metaphysics, Heidegger still sees things "from above." While Merleau-Ponty fundamentally agrees with Heidegger's analysis of metaphor, then, he nevertheless pushes the fundamental aspects of this critique much further, toward the flesh.

Necessity and Limits of Figural Writing

Merleau-Ponty's writing evolves, unsurprisingly, along with his conception of the flesh, and through the gradual relinquishment of classical concepts, in favor of the descriptive power of certain "figures."[15] Aware of the semantic density of familiar words in his native tongue, Merleau-Ponty sets out to choose nonsubstitutable, new terms, without borrowing them directly or exclusively from any philosophical vocabulary. As is the case with original terms such as "flesh," "encroachment," "promiscuity," and many others—which, like so many comets, are never severed from the tails of their moral, political or spiritual meanings; from their psychological, erotic, or literary dimensions—and which are fueled throughout the progression of Merleau-Ponty's work. Merleau-Ponty's patient development of concepts falls in line with a certain style of French philosophical writing, one reluctant to incorporate neologisms or concatenated terms, but, as exemplified by Bergson, preferring to conquer new meanings by reclaiming familiar terms. Merleau-Ponty's own carnal vocabulary constitutes the matrix of a gradually emergent philosophical line of thinking. While not denying their empirical use, he employs them in the conquest of a suitably philosophical oversignification.

Merleau-Ponty's figures are thus not employed to recover a simple schematism whose sole function is to serve the logic of a pure idea (only to disappear behind it); on the contrary, they constitute a series of saturated structures, where an idea can crystallize, as if soaking in its mother liquor. From a classical perspective, these figures occupy an ambiguous position, midway between the sensible and the idea; in Merleau-Ponty's eyes, they *are* this very way. They serve as expressions of the thesis that an idea is only alive and valid within the horizons of a revelatory gesture, and through this very gesture. Each of Merleau-Ponty's figures *is* such a gesture, so that his philosophy becomes a continuous exercise of this gesture: an expressive practice in which metaphors serve not as illustrations but as a primordial symbolism, closely following the structures of the living and the sensible, the symbolism of the human body.

Dualistic thought—whether anthropological (soul and body) or ontological (subject and object)—condemns us to the pathetic task of retroactively gluing things together again, through the use of subtle but ultimately unsuccessful conceptual formulations. Of course, it is not so easy to free ourselves from dualistic thinking. Merleau-Ponty's aim is to overcome retrospective analogies and dead metaphors through the use of prospective figures that allow us to *think* differentiation, as it is "in the making." This cheerful naivety is a major feature of Merleau-Ponty's understanding of the "return to things themselves." Yet our logical and conceptual tools are only really suited to formulating the inverse movement, of uniting things *after* distinguishing them—even if our initial intention is to distinguish things *in order to* unite them. Hence the need for a somewhat preconceptual writing practice, one that attempts to apply itself to the movement of differentiation, by returning to a more elemental expressiveness. This is still, or more than ever, a matter of *thinking*; even though we can never fully escape the "view from above," the retrospective attitude of consciousness. No talk of transcending nondifferentiation is ever completely free from retrospection. And Merleau-Ponty's preferred figures fully betray this difficulty as well as this limitation: encroachment, entanglement, *Ineinander*, promiscuity, and others; intertwining, chiasm, and so forth cannot describe what leads to the formation of boundaries without employing schemas whose meaning depends on the existence of boundaries; without evoking parthood, suggesting the transgression of an established boundary, or even reference to the bipartition of inside and outside.

Metaphor as Flesh: Anthropological Aspects

Metaphor and Body Schema

I will not return here to the importance of Merleau-Ponty's work on the notion of the body schema, a theme I have developed extensively elsewhere.[16] I might, however, briefly recall some points that are essential to our subject. In the pioneering work on the body schema (in neurology, as well as developmental psychology and psychoanalysis), Merleau-Ponty discovers some essential sources for a new approach to the phenomenal body, one that highlights its intermodal and analogous unity, its dynamic praxis as fundamentally structured through incorporation, animated by a logic of desire—in other words, its deeply intercorporeal and relational nature.

In his first introduction to the concept of the body schema in *Phenomenology of Perception*, Merleau-Ponty takes up a theme that he will continue to cultivate for the rest of his life; a theme that is closely related to the question of metaphor: the body schema as a *system of equivalences*. We have our body, "not only as a system of current positions, but also, and consequently, as an open system of an infinity of equivalent positions in different orientations." As he continues: "What we called the 'body schema' is precisely this system of equivalences, this immediately given invariant by which different motor tasks are instantly transposable."[17] Almost as soon as he introduces this idea, Merleau-Ponty starts to employ it in more a generalized way. He understands that this capacity for transposition, these equivalences, can be extended to the entire intermodal (sensorimotor), intersensory, and intrasensorial cohesion of the body. The senses communicate via a body schema that lends itself fully to these exchanges, so that the philosopher describes it as a "system of immediate intersensory equivalences."[18]

This understanding of the body schema as a "general function of tacit transposition"[19] naturally leads Merleau-Ponty to address the issue of analogy with regard to the body, to consider the body schema as an operator of carnal analogies. Painting, modern painting in particular,[20] is a privileged expression of these bodily analogies mentioned in *Eye and Mind*: The painter takes his body with him, and the painting, from this moment, becomes a system of equivalences.[21] But it is in his analysis of the famous case of Schneider (in Gelb and Goldstein) that Merleau-Ponty first considers the *corporeal foundations* of analogy. Schneider—according to Gelb and Goldstein's presentation, putting aside the question of whether or not Schneider was pretending—is unable to understand analogy or metaphor. He is suffering from a condition that requires him to constantly filter everything through conscious analysis in order to coordinate his perceptual and motor life—a pathology that Merleau-Ponty also attributes, not without irony, to the intellectualism of idealistic philosophies.[22]

Merleau-Ponty notes that the patient does not understand analogies as simple as, "fur is to the cat as feathers are to the bird," or, "eye is to light and color as ear is to sounds." Schneider cannot access the metaphorical sense of common expressions such as "the foot of the chair" or "the head of a nail," although he understands each individual word. Normal subjects, including those of a similar background to Schneider, might not always be able to *explain* these analogies, yet they do nonetheless understand them. The normal subject can easily grasp or perceive an analogy without having to *analyze* it in any explicit way, yet in this patient's case, understanding is only attained through conscious conceptual and discursive explanation.

The body schema is at the origins of this com-prehension without ex-plication[23] of analogicity, a "synthesis" without analysis,[24] which is rigorous, even if the reasoning remains implicit—a carnal analogical power that Merleau-Ponty hopes to find at the heart of all "living thought."

> If we were to describe the analogy as the apperception of two given terms under one concept that coordinates them, then we would be giving as normal a procedure that is nothing other than pathological and that represents the detour through which the patient must go in order to offer a substitution for a normal understanding of the analogy. . . . Living thought, then, does not consist in the act of subsuming under a category.[25]

And of what does this consist?

> If the normal subject immediately understands that the relation between the eye and vision is the same as the relation between the ear and hearing, this is because the eye and ear are given to him immediately as ways of reaching a single world, and because he possesses a pre-predicative evidentness of a unique world, such that the equivalence of the "sense-organs" and their analogy is read upon the things and can be lived prior to being conceived. The Kantian subject posits a world, but, in order to be able to affirm a truth, the actual sub-

ject must first have a world or be in the world, that is, he must hold a system of significations around himself whose correspondences, relations and participations do not need to be made explicit in order to be utilized.[26]

The roots of this inherently analogical intelligence are not to be found in analogical *reasoning*—although it might be possible to retrospectively reason in this fashion—and neither is it rooted in analogical *concepts*—even if these are in part able to transcribe and preserve the structural complexity of the corporeal schematism. The endless and conflicting classical attempts to typologize and explain analogy fail to descend far enough, that is to say, to the depths of its original identity—to the topology of a flesh that operates as a system of corporeal and intercorporeal equivalences. Inaugurated in *Phenomenology of Perception*, we find this approach again in the late manuscripts, in connection with Schilder's descriptions of the topological equivalences of the human body as involved in the structuration of intercorporeality—and in connection with the Merleau-Pontian critique of Sartre's conception of the *analogon* in *L'imaginaire*.

This study of the body schema's transpositional capacity provides Merleau-Ponty with an alternative conception of universality, an ante-abstract generality the philosopher assigns to what he calls the "generality of the body," from *Phenemenology of Perception* onward. Merleau-Ponty forges this challenging concept through his analysis of habit, through his explorations in his work on the notions of "structure," "schema" (*typique*), and above all, "style."[27] Not content with applying this only to sensorimotor skills, linguistic comprehension is also seen as mobilizing the body schema.

> In fact, neither the word nor the sense of the word is *constituted* by consciousness.... By performing the critique of the verbal image, and by showing that the speaking subject throws himself into speech without representing to himself the words he is about to pronounce, modern psychology eliminates the word as a representation or as an object for consciousness, and uncovers a motor presence of the word, which is not identical to the knowledge of the word. The word "sleet," when I know it, is not an object that I recognize through a synthesis of identification; it is a certain use of my phonatory apparatus and a certain modulation of my body as a being in the world; its generality is not the generality of an idea, but rather that of a style of behavior that my body "understands" insofar as my body is a power of producing behaviors....

And Merleau-Ponty insists:

> One day I "caught on" to the word "sleet," just as one imitates a gesture, that is, not by breaking it down and by establishing a correspondence between each part of the word that I hear and some movement of articulation and phonation, but rather by hearing it as a single modulation of the sonorous world and because this sonorous entity appeared as "something to be pronounced" in virtue of the overall correspondence that exists between my perceptual possibilities and my motor possibilities, which are elements of my indivisible and open existence. The word has never been inspected, analyzed, known and constituted, but rather caught and taken up by a speaking power [*puissance parlante*], and, ultimately, by a motor power that is given to me along with the very first experience of my body and its perceptual and practical fields.

He concludes:

> The word's sense is . . . like a behavior of the world, a certain inflection of its style, and the generality of its sense, as much as the generality of the term is not the generality of the concept, but rather of the world as schema [*typique*].[28]

We note the slide here from the generality of the body, to that of the world. I grasp the meaning of a word in the same way that I recognize a "style of behavior." Initially described by Merleau-Ponty as "a certain modulation of my body as a being in the world"—this is later assimilated to "a behavior of the world, a certain inflection of its style": the generality of the *word* is that of "the world as schema [*typique*]." More than fifteen years before his reflections on "the flesh of the world," the philosopher is already lending the analogical logic of the body schema to the world.

From here it is simply a matter of transcribing the body schema's activity as a circular weaving of our being-in-the-world: as incorporation of the world, and projection onto the world. The body "flows over into a world whose schema it bears in itself."[29] And it is here that the influence of modern neurology is augmented by the discoveries of developmental psychology and, more so, those of psychoanalysis, the latter of which Merleau-Ponty praises for having uncovered the magnitude of the system of *incorporation* that animates us. Piaget's description of mobilization of the intelligence in this passive-active reciprocity of assimilation and accommodation, here becomes a more radically generalized carousel of introjection and projection: The whole of the flesh becomes an adaptive function, in its annexation of, and extension into the dimensions of the world.

This logic of incorporation thus replaces that of abstraction, according to this Merleau-Pontian understanding of carnal generality. The body schema possesses the power of "dilating our being in the world,"[30] through its capacity to annex things unto itself; things that are no longer objects but quasi-organs, contributing to our openness to the world, participating in a genuine "extension of existence."[31] The generality of the body also refers to its ability to lend its own structure to the world and to others, at the heart of this process of incorporation: It accesses *their* generality by generalizing *itself*, by lending them its *own* generality. This understanding of carnal generality forms the basis of the later Merleau-Ponty's daring limit notions of the thing's "flesh," of the "flesh" of the sensible, and of the world. The thing, the world and even being are described, along with the body, as systems of equivalences.[32] The body schema ensures the spatiotemporal cohesion of my body, in lending itself to the thing and to the world,[33] and these in turn become intersensorial beings,[34] genuine systems of equivalences: The world, under the influence of the analogicity of the flesh, becomes carnal, while being, under the influence of the flesh, becomes analogical.

Speech, and especially metaphor, can thus be seen as a continuation of the flesh's dynamic analogical investment, conquering the world through annexation and extension, through the exercise and extension of the body image. Things communicate "through me," "metaphorically"[35]—and Merleau-Ponty goes so far as to describe metaphor as this "participation of things with each other," the "participation of fragments of the world with one another."[36] In turn, "the act of writing, like the act of painting, attempts to express the metaphorical participation between things, between ourselves and things, and others." The "literary word" is already brewing in the "organization of our lives," as the "constitution of dimensions, analogies, equivalences," from the very foundations of the body schema.[37]

Metaphor and Body Image

Merleau-Ponty's interest in psychoanalysis is inextricably implicated in the evolution of his philosophy of the flesh. Even though he continues to translate Schilder's "body-image" as "body schema" (*schéma corporel*), it is clear that his conception of this schema increasingly integrates the essential influence of interpersonal relationships in the construction of the corporeal foundations of psychic identity, the importance of relations between body images, and the architectonic role of the life of desire. Merleau-Ponty thus sails close to the shores of what some psychoanalysts, beginning with Françoise Dolto, refer to (or will refer to) as the "body image" or "unconscious body image."[38]

His post-1955 work on the theme of "promiscuity" is revealing in this respect. Promiscuity becomes Merleau-Ponty's preferred figure for referring to the spatiotemporal, relational, introjected, and integrated multiplicity of the flesh; in other words, that which is constitutive of its identity and even its unity. The idea of promiscuity marks the climax of Merleau-Ponty's reflection on *intercorporeality*, taking account of the unconscious structural inscription of the interrelatedness and intertwining of body images. Integrating the promiscuity of space and time into itself—of my past, registered in the body schema, of space as imaginary body, starting with that of others—and haunted by the promiscuity of the body and bodies, the flesh becomes a "promiscuous body."[39] This promiscuity, in turn, is inevitably projected onto the world: As the caesura of the concepts of body and flesh, it also participates in what Merleau-Ponty's boldly calls the "flesh of the world"—with a nod here to Claude Simon and his descriptions of "human and inter-human magma."[40]

The flesh is the true bearer of the "corporeal generality" sought by Merleau-Ponty from the outset. And this is extended to the glorious body of language, of ideas, of metaphors. If the expressive flesh cannot but express *itself*, conveying the unconscious body image, then metaphor is itself animated by "Eros which has many pairs of arms and clusters of faces,"[41] thus coming to bear, in its most intimate contexture, this "pell-mell ensemble of bodies and minds, promiscuity of visages, words, actions, with, between them all, that cohesion which cannot be denied them . . . this inextricable involvement."[42] Living metaphor is inexorably transformed into the "promiscuous body"—in other words, metaphor itself is flesh.

If our apprehension of a simple word can mobilize the anthropologically transversal framework generated by the body schema (and/or body image), then language, especially in the case of metaphor, possesses the virtue of expressing this schema. By a play of overdeterminations and oversignifications, language conveys our primitive modes of knowledge, their postural impregnation by the perceived being's "style of existence," translating the coexistences inscribed in the body schema in such a way as to import the complexity of (what others prefer to call) the body image, into its own structure. This approach shines through in the unpublished preparatory notes for his 1946 course on the *Foundations of Psychology*, given at the Faculty of Arts in Lyon:

> "Everything has a sense"—seems at first arbitrary: we can explain the symbolic value of "rats" with puns, metaphors. But even so, this must be the case, or else we stop trying to explain. Acceptance by the patient, healing. But what sort of "sense" is this? The rat represents a

"being that bites," not because we *think* these representations, but because we grasp them as part of the animal's very physiognomy, by identification: same structure, coexistence with. Even more fundamentally: identification with the father ≠ mental operation, but same style of existence, sympathy.[43]

The body image is not itself an image-representation, although we find it *expressed* in images. Symmetrically, the imaginary is unconsciously structured along the axes and fault-lines of our relational identity; our images are always, to a certain extent, expressions and vehicles of the body "image." A philosophy of the flesh, for its part, can only be expressed through an image-language composed of figural tropes or metaphors, their role being more *expressive* than *illustrative*.

The Visible and the Invisible emphasizes that, according to its author, until then the "flesh" had "no name in any philosophy."[44] This concept is inaugurated in a similar passage in *Man and Adversity* (1951):

> None of the notions philosophy had elaborated upon . . . suffices for thinking about the body's relationships to life as a whole, about the way it meshes into personal life or the way personal life meshes into it. The body is enigmatic: a part of the world certainly, but offered in a bizarre way, as its dwelling, to an absolute desire to draw near the other person and meet him in his body too, animated and animating, the natural figure of the mind. With psychoanalysis mind passes into body as, inversely, body passes into mind.[45]

This absolute desire to unite with others in the "animated and animating" body, the "natural figure of the mind": the power of this formulation of the flesh should be emphasized. The *animating* (and not just animated) body, the *figure of the mind*. . . . One would expect a balanced formulation—the mind expressing corporeality, "the psyche is the metaphor of the physiological."[46] Here, as elsewhere, Merleau-Ponty is infused with the boldness of Claudel's flesh: "the body is the metaphor of the mind."[47] A formula that might lend itself to misinterpretation, if we were to understand metaphor in its traditional metaphysical sense. Or alternatively, if we reduced the flesh to a classical conception of incarnation, to the *animated* (and not animating) body. As Gérard Guillerault states, there is,

> a kind of retroactive loop wherein the body is nourished by the very language it helps to forge; it feeds on the very source of the linguistic effects it helps to produce. . . . In sum, the body itself is a "metaphorphor"—i.e., the *bearer* of the very metaphoricity it expresses, and by which it is expressed. It is the actualization of the very metaphor it

calls and galvanizes. And it is in this recursive twist that the unfolding of the body image plays out.[48]

Metaphor belongs to thought itself as carnal, as expression of the animated and animating body, and, hence, as sublimation of corporeality. In other words, far from betraying an ontological dualism, metaphor expresses—and in turn contributes to the composition of—an anthropological unity. In his first series of lectures at the *Collège de France*, Merleau-Ponty insists: "we don't think without the transfigured body, the body schema as bearer of meanings . . . the order of *logos* can only be understood as a sublimation of corporeality."[49] The term "figure" might indicate a fundamental dimension of metaphoricity that better translates this relation between image and flesh: to enfigure (*figurer*), to give face to, through an internal formation (pregnancy) "delivered" in an expressive effort that cannot return to itself without undergoing transfiguration and metamorphosis. Merleau-Ponty's writing seeks this expressiveness in figures that portray the structure of a behavior, a way of being, a style. The status of these figures is similar to that of the flesh itself, as defined in *The Visible and the Invisible*.[50]

Desire of Metaphor, Metaphors of Desire

During the course of the evolution of the concept of flesh, Merleau-Ponty begins to reconsider our being-in-the-world from a more radical intercorporeal perspective. The encroachment of things takes us back to the promiscuity of bodies; the depth of the world is primarily that of the flesh and the gaze of the other. This incorporation and expression, the implied play of exchanges between inside and outside, can never escape the subject of relationships, the life of desire. Because the question of metaphor is so tied up with that of the flesh, it must also secretly be tied to the stakes and expectations of interpersonal relationships. The power of its investment in, and incorporation into, the dimensions of the world inevitably mobilizes an intimate libidinal dynamics; its power of creating-expressing relationships must itself be reviewed from the perspective of a call to interrelationship. This provides an *intercorporeal*—and, to follow Merleau-Ponty, an *intersubjective*—dimension to metaphoricity.[51] At the price of its unity, the flesh—which is exposed to potential growth as well as possible breakdowns—advances in a space that is relational, between those abysses that are the secret and symmetrical equivalents of fusion and separation. Metaphor is at the forefront of its conquest of the outside world, its conquest of the unknown and unseen, of the depth of the world and other bodies. From this perspective, metaphor is a *transitional object*, in the Winnicottian sense. And "encroachment," the Merleau-Pontian figure par excellence, presents the carnal status of metaphoricity as a *mise en abyme*.

Metaphor, then, is not merely a fortuitous or necessary connection, the result of a secret dosage of contingency and necessity. It is also a *desired connection*. But a desire that cannot be attributed with the traditional features of the Freudian drive—as conservative, regressive, and divisive. Metaphoricity, then, is perhaps an interesting starting point for distinguishing desire from drive. Which is not to say that metaphor is totally stripped of drive, or that the drive is incapable of metaphor—the latter also benefits from the analogicity inscribed in the heart of the body schema's logic. But insofar as the drive is a force for return to the status quo, the release or elimination of a tension, an unbinding (with the death drive being the drive par excellence)—in this sense, it proves to be lacking in metaphor. When it comes to the drive, satisfaction involves exhaustion—going all the way, consuming, finishing with, to be completely "finished." With metaphor, on the other hand, pleasure (*jouissance*) operates in a completely different manner: here, satisfaction is a matter of self-intensification and self-recovery; metaphor involves an awakening and increasing of tension, rather than the relief of a prior tension. Metaphor is the deepening of the very depths it helps to reveal. Far from exhaustion, metaphor participates in the unveiling of the inexhaustible as such, launching an endless (nautical) rope (*un bout sans bout*), a taut chord that stretches out toward . . . the inaccessible, toward that which is given as such. Given, yet given as incomplete—and given only in the extent to which I give myself, to which I lend myself to metaphor's own tension.

Merleau-Ponty's manner of outlining the logic of desire within blind range of the Freudian drive,[52] his texts concerning that which is given as inexhaustible in the life of perception and desire,[53] resonates throughout the discussion of metaphor in relation to the flesh. The same applies to the resonance of his philosophical writing practice on a possible conception of desire. Merleau-Ponty does not construct his philosophy through treatises, and this is especially true of desire, an idea that gathers momentum through the course of his work. No one can tell whether he might have finally executed his project *De l'amour*,[54] but the title itself, borrowed from a writer (Stendhal), indicates the decisive role of literature for the philosopher. As we have seen, there is a surprising proximity between Merleau-Ponty's figures and certain texts by Claude Simon and Paul Claudel, one that helps to clarify the existential structures of desire in his philosophy.[55] This is no mere accident: It is through his engagement with literary works rather than another philosopher's theoretical treatises that Merleau-Ponty develops his notion of desire. And while Merleau-Ponty might have had no choice but to turn to literature, the result is that philosophy itself is put on trial by literary writing.[56]

We might nonetheless reproach Merleau-Ponty for his paradoxical treatment of the theme of desire, an approach that is at times unflinching (the content of a few direct assertions), at times very discreet (these same assertions are never fully developed), and at times very indirect (the question surfaces in a number of passages, even saturating the underlying imagination, without ever actually being thematized as such). One might have the impression that these indirect paths remain blocked in by imminence, the voices of an all-too silent desire, at risk of becoming nothing more than *substitutes*; or that these Merleau-Pontian figures (encroachment, chiasm, interlacing, promiscuity, enveloping-enveloped, and others) gravitate around desire as an ineffable core, consumed in a light that is never truly expressed. Indeed, to borrow a title from the philosopher, indirect language risks closing itself off in the voices of silence . . . Merleau-Ponty is here playing with the ambiguity of transitional objects, the ambiguity of figures that risk losing their transitional capacity if they do not figurate more than themselves. This pure autofiguration, of a flesh eventually absorbing everything, including being, into itself, would be the worst betrayal of metaphor's vocation.

Yet this is also a question of method: can one *directly* thematize desire, avoiding the *figurative*, without profoundly *disfiguring* desire? In his defense (and to some extent rewriting) of Freudian pansexualism, from *Phenomenology of Perception* onward, Merleau-Ponty is concerned with an anthropological dimension inaccessible to the abstraction of what he will later refer to as the "ontology of the object." Sexuality and desire, like vision, or even the hand, escape this abstraction, offering integral entrances into the *flesh*—the body as "structure of the whole" and intercorporeal tissue, the "promiscuous body" in *Ineinander* with the world, the "operating body," the "body of our experience," *my flesh* where phenomenal and objective are muddled. This is really what Merleau-Ponty, under the combined influence of certain authors (including Jean Wahl, Gabriel Marcel, Politzer, Hegel, and Blondel) refers to as the "concrete."[57] And this is the concern of Merleau-Ponty's ontology, which is specifically referred to as "concrete"—because it is only in returning to our most integral anthropological dimensions that we can open up new ontological paths. The *abstract* is relegated to objectivism as a variety of divisive thinking, a part-thinking that no longer points to the whole, a meaning that is no longer *figurative*. And desire is that which, par excellence, cannot be approached in the expression of its own meaning, without leading to all others, drawing out the contours of our relationship to being.

The Birth of Meaning: Epistemological Aspects

From Ambivalence to Ambiguity: Metaphor and Perceptual Logic

During his own lifetime, certain critics labeled Merleau-Ponty "a philosopher of ambiguity," without knowing what this really meant. Far from the Beauvoirian "vagueness," Merleau-Ponty's notion of ambiguity is relatively technical, an heir of the Gestaltist work on perceptual logic and three-dimensional recognition of "ambiguous figures." The author of *Phenomenology of Perception* is interested, from the start, in our perception of depth. He is particularly interested in how vision manages to mediate the conflictual and diplopic alternation of monocular images, so as to construct their coexistence—so as to avoid a cycloptic singular vision, the flatness of perspectival representation, the bird's eye-view of a Leibnizian god. Our vision of depth quickly becomes a true model of perceptual logic, and, subject to Merleau-Ponty's overdetermination of perception, an *analogatum princeps* of the functioning of embodied intelligence in general, and its metaphorizing power in particular—the intelligence that opens flesh to being, while still respecting its mystery. Depth thus becomes the paradigm of this deep and mysterious being.

This philosophical reading of depth is given more weight by his discovery of Melanie Klein's research on our "epistemophiliac tendencies," as well as his study of the psychology of "projective methods." The Merleau-Pontian approach to ambiguity is strengthened in its opposition to the notion of *ambivalence*, with Merleau-Ponty integrating those aspects of Frenkel-Brunswik's research that are connected to Rorschach's hypotheses, as found especially in the former's essay on the "Intolerance of ambiguity as an emotional and perceptual personality variable."[58] Frenkel-Brunswik studies the degrees of perceptual and intellectual rigidity pertaining to ambivalent subjects—those who avoid all ambiguity and can only proceed via trenchant dichotomies, walled in by their adoption of alternatives and categorizations that render them blind or ill-adapted to the perception of transitional phenomena, to the comprehension of passages and analogies.[59]

Merleau-Ponty might find here the overcoming of ambivalence in ambiguity operated by in-depth vision, but he generalizes this as a feature of our maturing relationship to the world and others. A maturation where the lives of desire and intelligence are closely intertwined, a "good ambiguity" taking the place of ambivalence's psycho-rigidity. Metaphor, we are to understand, belongs to this good ambiguity—which Merleau-Ponty will soon rewrite as "good dialectic" or "hyperdialectic." Here, as elsewhere, the philosopher is spurred on by his opposition to Sartre—the exemplar of ambivalence and the "bad dialectic"—as well as by the challenge of the three "comminglings" of the Cartesian scenario—particularly that of "commingled thinking," our only way of opening us to the mystery of our blended unity, to the depth of being, in contrast to the "ambivalences" of the ontology of the object. Merleau-Ponty is as opposed to what he refers to as thetic univocity (Descartes) as he is to ambivalent equivocity (Sartre's dialectic), which might be considered secretly equivalent—so that, in *Being and World*, we find the following cryptic formula: "It is the thetic that is ambivalent. My ambiguous-preobjective is unequivocal promiscuity."[60]

If ambiguity is a feature of mature intelligence—especially that of mature philosophical thought—this is not to be understood as merely a later achievement, with primitive thought relegated to the underworld of ambivalence and univocity. It is indeed an achievement, a struggle even, yet this regime of "good ambiguity" has been operating from the start, from the most archaic conjunctions of desire and perception in the unfolding of our being in the world. This is why, in opposition to Piaget's genetic epistemology, Merleau-Ponty defends the value of primitive analogical intelligence—especially the type of signification pioneered in so-called prelogical thinking, where metaphoricity is given full reign. Merleau-Ponty reproaches Piaget for summarily rejecting the child's prelogical intelligence (characterized as animism, finalism, artificiality, and realism), his consideration of this intelligence as though it were somehow rationally deficient. Piagetian constructivism is blinded by the retrospective illusion of the absence of . . . thus overlooking the first intimations of meaning, the coherence already at work in the foundations of our being-in-the-world and being-with-others—that is, in the foundations of our very identity. And thus overlooking, too, the genesis of an ultimate dimension of meaning, because prelogical thought inaugurates our poetic relationship with the world, a relationship that is borne in the sensorimotor and desirous bases of intelligence, and which, in its maturation, comes to constitute one of the most successful forms of human intelligence.

Metaphoricity and Reversibility

But let us explore Merleau-Ponty's debate with Piaget's epistemology a little further. Metaphor convokes the profound identity of intelligence as perceptual and judicative apprehension of *relationship*. This mode of knowledge, for Merleau-Ponty, is not first crystallized as or in a *representation*, but in the course of a relationship involving the sensorimotor base of intelligence, and the exercise of carnal *reversibility*. We are aware of the significance attributed to this "fundamental phenomenon of reversibility"[61] in the later writings; this "reversibility that defines the flesh."[62] I have explained elsewhere how and why Merleau-Ponty reclaims this notion from Piaget.[63] For the latter, access to this "logical reversibility"[64] liberates the intelligence from the inherent *irreversibility* of sensorimotor action, offering an escape from prelogical or "magical" thinking. This reversibility, for Piaget, is the primary characteristic of intelligence. For Merleau-Ponty, on the other hand, and contra Piaget, reversibility refers to a more fundamental feature of intelligence (secretly employed by logical reversibility itself): a reversibility inherent in sensorimotor intelligence, profoundly connected to the mutual precession of space and time in the mutual precession of perception and motor skills.

Merleau-Ponty's reversibility, in contrast to that of Piaget—and in accordance with the former's desire for a return from reflective consciousness to "carnal reflection"—offers us an insight into the way the world is set up for us. In his unpublished *Being and World* and the soon-to-follow *Eye and Mind*, Merleau-Ponty introduces this new concept through an analysis of perception as the experience of the "reversibility of dimensions."[65] This is true, in a certain sense, of our perception of the horizon and, more broadly, our vision of depth. The horizon is the "common seed" of all spatial dimensions,[66] and depth is not a "third dimension," nor even a primary dimension from which the other two would be derived.[67] Both ensure that the world is "around us," and "not in front of us," that "the thing exists as more than just a 'visual' film, an appearance."[68]

Depth cannot be captured by the "pure vision" (vision purified of movement, of all expression), the projection and "view from above" inherent in perspective drawing; it cannot be captured by representation, and yet it is "in all the modes of space."[69] Without depth, Merleau-Ponty explains, we would not understand the relationships between things, other than as simple separation or simple identity—the typical alternatives of logical thinking, resulting in dependence on the operation of (geometric or optical) projection, which just is the art of reducing the complexity of relations to pure fusions and separations. Depth is neither an "unmysterious interval" nor a case of things being "conjured away, one by another"; it lies in "their bond"; in other words, their "exteriority is known through their envelopment, and their mutual dependence in their autonomy."[70] Knowledge of this relationship cannot be delivered in a single visual snapshot, or even a combination of static visual images, but only through an agile, virtual change in orientation, through the variation of one's points of view.

Merleau-Ponty thus rewrites the logical reversibility as a *spatial* reversibility—a reversibility that cannot simply be constructed through the decentering of the sensorimotor, since it is also a sensorimotor achievement.

This ability to turn ourselves to different sides in order to see, to anticipate the next vision through movement, and the next movement through vision, this ability to experience the inextricable circularity of perception and motoricity described by Weizsäcker, is celebrated in *Eye and Mind*, which appeals to "this extraordinary overlapping, which we never give enough thought to," this extraordinary intersensory and intermodal complex on which we should meditate, so that we might "go back to the working, actual body . . . which is an intertwining of vision and movement"[71]—so that we might regain the flesh. This reversibility between dimensions is not constructed by the agility of representational life, but by the agility of the flesh, which establishes the world as a horizon of this virtual ubiquity and simultaneity deployed in our sensorimotor involvement. This reversibility is lost in the projectivism of representation, which fixes the world "around us" into a "world in front of us," petrifying the being of a thing into a "visual film," an "appearance"—petrifying being into an object, ignoring being as the *relationship* between beings.

For Piaget, the construction of logical reversibility is the exit turnstile out of prelogical thought and its ambiguities. Merleau-Ponty here discerns the weight of a philosophical mythology in the service of an ontology of the object (the perfectly observable separate being), where the mind is closed off to all mystery.[72] Space, here reduced to a nonmysterious extension, becomes an inert frame of neutralizable action and unambiguous meaning—thus securing objectivism, with its need for a fixed point and timeless permanence. For Merleau-Ponty, this is the eye of the cycloptic *inspectio mentis*, who sees without touching and without moving, who explains without understanding, a path that is contemplated but never actually traveled.

Metaphorical intelligence—typically portrayed as "prelogical"—is in fact an elevated expression of the use and sublimation of carnal reversibility. Neither based on an instantaneous representation, nor even a combination of representations, it benefits from the agility of perspectival/orientational variations and reversals. It extends and accentuates the exercise of dimensional reversibility that allows us to know the relationship between things, to com-prehend this relationship through involvement, without completely resolving it in pure explanation. It inhabits the tension of this chiasmatic gravitation, through which "exteriority is known through their envelopment, and their mutual dependence in their autonomy." Metaphor expresses and/or creates a connection, while leaving a sense of the imminence of other generated or generating relations—because this is never a solitary relation, but the enveloped-enveloping of an entire fabric of meaning.

While susceptible to the most subtle and "incorporeal" paths of intelligence, metaphor continues to live off the virtual ubiquity and simultaneity we find deployed in the sensorimotor foundations of analogical intelligence. It benefits from the highest degree of its agility, with which it still pulsates. This metaphorical intelligence belongs in full to Merleau-Ponty's overall philosophical objective: going from the most corporeal to the most "spiritual," by living the corporeal from beginning to end.

Metaphoricity and Divergence

We will now continue to explore the impact that Merleau-Ponty's analysis of perceptual logic has on a renewed conception of metaphor. Merleau-Ponty critically characterizes the classical approach to consciousness as involving a "conception of *meaning* as *essence*," the subjection of meaning to clear and distinct definitions.[73] Isolated and stable, meaning here obeys "an express statement, an 'I know *that*,'" a meaning possessed by consciousness, which is "ready-made to be put into words, translated into language, it is already the *positing* of an *express statement*."[74] The new sense of meaning, as initiated by perception, is quite different: the "modulation of a certain dimension," it is "practiced, rather than possessed as such"; it "manifests itself more in the exceptions where it's lacking than through its own position."[75] More an armature or infrastructure of the sensible, than a positive essence imposing itself in pure visibility, meaning is gradually hinted at or anticipated, in the continuous adjustment of my own infrastructure to that of the perceived.

We find this in one of Merleau-Ponty's privileged examples, the perception of a circle. Circularity is not given as an essence, but lived as a type of modulation of local space, a constant deviation, experienced as such through our motor simulation of this contour. "At every moment," he says, this line changes direction, but always in the same way. It is not located at a fixed point on the plane but recognized in the course of "a typical activity" that assumes the particular style of its change. Our premotor investment surrenders to a type of a divergence (*écart*), and this surrender is so complete that perception itself tends to regulate the small aberrations, to fill in the gaps, to resist the very variations of this style of variation.[76] The circular, Merleau-Ponty writes, is a "mode of divergence," and he specifies that this divergence, like that from which it diverges, is not explicitly presented to us in this way, or even thematized as such, but rather implied: we do not need to be aware of each respective tangent of each point covered, "their perception is *imperception*,"[77] and we are more sensitive to what is likely to diverge from the regularity of this mode of divergence.

Beyond this specific example, Merleau-Ponty finds that *any* sensible structure reveals itself, less in the direct announcement of its position, than in exceptions or divergences therefrom, in what might be considered effective or simply imminent "good mistakes." Perception functions through a simulated recognition of divergence or differential organization. Perception is not so much the awareness of an isolated abstract figure without a background; rather, it involves the tracking of a movement, a change: it can be characterized more as traction and attraction than abstraction, a positional and furtive judgment involved in a movement through space (and thus inseparable from time)—rather than the apprehension of an uninvolved atemporal and aspatial representation.

Merleau-Ponty finally describes this approach with the use of a recurrent formula, a "theory of perception as divergence [*écart*]," an idea that becomes the gravitational center of several themes of his writing: level, dimension, modulation, and in particular the qualifier "diacritical," which is liberally inspired by the work of Saussure. "Spoken or living language" reveals itself to be a relative and negative system of meaning: each word only means something in its difference from other words; its meaning is never grasped in isolation. In his analysis of perception as a type of divergence, Merleau-Ponty here develops an analogous logic.[78]

The mode of signification that corresponds to perceptual logic emerges from the tension of the interval grasped through a motor orientation, from a divergence between terms that are not positively given. Just as relief emerges from contrast, the respective identities of each term emerge through the tension of their differences, contours emerge from the encroachment of things. Merleau-Ponty thus moves beyond the classical approach to definition, typical of the retrospective view of projective intelligence: the defined always defined against an already positive background, the kind from which specific differences emerge. Diacritical perception also exposes the mythical status of the confrontation between consciousness and object: There is never *one* object, but always many *things*—if only figure and ground, with the possibility or even imminence of their reversal. Several things, which cannot even be fully described as objects, precisely because of the plurality that thwarts the face-to-face encounter between subject and object, the exclusivity of a dual relationship, or the solitude of the isolating attitude. Several things, each one of which is only perceived, received, recognized, through its tension in relation to other things.

This tension solicits our sensorimotor dynamism, which it requires in order to be grasped, scanned, and, in this sense, replayed, lived through its resonance within us, giving it to animate us. There is thus a motor dimension and hence a hint of transportation, of displacement, whenever we "grasp" a meaning. But also a relational dimension, inexorably accompanied by a vital aggressiveness, a putting to the test of similarities and differences that cannot be resolved through fusional identification, nor the severing of the relationship; neither through merging nor separation. And this relational tension cannot be lived except by reverting to the tension of relationship with others, to the originary motivational dimension of intelligence.

We could not account for these characteristics by the single inductive-abstractive process that moves from the sensible thing (or image) to the idea, or that gives a latently sensible being to all meaning: not only, or even primarily a vertical tension between *sensible* and *intelligible* dimensions, this is a horizontal tension between several meanings, a relation between meanings, each one of which possesses its own sensible comet-tail (or latency). This is hence a four-way relationship, but one in which, ultimately, no term is truly explicit, where each is always referring to two others—to its *sensible latency*, and to its *difference of meaning*.

Reading the Latent in the Manifest

I have analyzed elsewhere the noteworthy recurrence in Merleau-Ponty works of expressions such as "to take literally," "to take at his word," "to take seriously," all of which point toward what I have called the methodological principle of "*taking literally*."[79] These expressions should not lead us to believe that the phenomenologist is avoiding the figurative sense: to the contrary, it is the *figurative sense* that needs to be taken seriously, by taking the literal sense to the letter and at its word . . . Merleau-Ponty incorporates the virtues of our vision of depth into his own philosophical attention, the power of the perceptive focus vision. This trait is intensified under the influence of psychoanalysis, which has its own style of perceptive intelligence. In the eyes of the philosopher, Freud was one of the first to take the sensible world "seriously," that is, to believe in its promises by reading the *latent* in the *manifest*, and to thus pursue in our perception of the other an art of in-depth vision, an art of accessing the invisible in the visible. A somewhat forced interpretation, perhaps: It is primarily *language* that Freud takes seriously, while Merleau-Ponty is the one who finds within perceptual life a conception of the latent and manifest relationships initially applied to the verbal expression of the other.

In an unpublished note of March 1960 we find an incisive formulation of this Merleau-Pontian sense of a *taking literally* that is anything but literal: "Latent content is manifest content taken literally, taken, not as a symbol in the sense of analogy, but as identity. . . . The latent content is therefore not so latent."[80] Hence the seriousness with which Merleau-Ponty develops a figural style of writing that takes terms such as "encroachment," "promiscuity," "coupling" *literally* . . . because these are clearly not just metaphors.[81] Affirming that "latent content is not so latent," but rather the "manifest content taken literally," Merleau-Ponty does not intend to deny the density of latent meaning, to crush it into the flatness and univocity of the manifest. Conversely, the surface of things is always already revealed as depth, without requiring that anyone break it (or deny it) to gain access to the latter—the manifest expresses, shouts out, a latency that is well and truly its own, a latency of which it is the manifestation, even when it hides this.

Manifest and latent perpetuate this most intimate relationship between the visible and the invisible, where the visible is the manifestation of an invisible that works it from the inside. There is "no *metaphor* between the visible and the invisible"[82] in the sense of an analogicity that achieves similarity only after having secured the boundaries of dissimilarity. The invisible is not "really invisible,"[83] and neither is it "the contradictory of the visible"—it is its "secret counterpart."[84] More than this, it is in perceiving the visible that we have access to the invisible, because the latter "appears only within [the visible] . . . it is *in the line* of the visible, it is its virtual focus, it is inscribed within it (in filigree)."[85] The visible, therefore, "has an invisible inner framework"; "the visible is pregnant with the invisible."[86] The visible expresses the invisible. The focus is thus no longer solely, nor even primarily, on analogicity (the invisible as analogue of the visible); and neither is it solely, nor even primarily, on ontological participation (the visible as a participant in the invisible). The focus here is on the mutual expression of one by the other; on a form of relationship that is procreative, pregnant, and co-nascent. A relationship that goes both ways: because if "the visible is pregnant with the invisible," it is also its fruit: The latent is the infrastructure and matrix of the manifest. This relationship involves a process of transformation; it is no longer simply a matter of transporting forms or attributes, of transporting a way of being, a style (as in analogical resemblance or ontological participation). Far from a simple transposition, transportation here is metamorphosis and transfiguration.

In the world of the flesh, metaphors become "metamorphoses,"[87] and transference becomes "transubstantiation";[88] we are no longer dealing with the regulated correspondence between two epistemologically irreducible layers, but with an "effective resemblance."[89] As might be expected, Merleau-Ponty develops this idea less in his analysis of literature than of painting—or enters into the former through the latter. Whether figurative or not, painting does not *evoke* anything; that is, it does not present us with an *analogon* of an absent being; rather, it *makes visible*: Painting effects a metamorphosis, it delivers a being from its chrysalis, giving visible existence to the invisible; painting gives birth to the invisible by giving it flesh.[90] This birth is not simply a passage from inside to outside, from hidden to revealed. And neither is the visible only, nor even primarily, an incarnation of the invisible. The logic of the flesh here is not that of a descent into incarnation, but rather a *surrection* (upsurge), within the insurrectional and resurrectional movement of desire. Metaphor is thus not only, nor even primarily, the Logos made flesh, but also, and primarily, the very awakening and speaking of the flesh; the flesh that comes to Logos through its delivery (*enfantement*).

Figurative Being: Ontological Aspects

The Imaginary Texture of the Real

Having addressed the relations between manifest and latent, visible and invisible, it seems we are better prepared to tackle the ontological side of Merleau-Ponty's thought, while also considering another element involved in these relations: the *imaginary*. One might assume the philosopher of the primacy of perception would not be particularly interested in the imaginary. Yet this assumption is mistaken. If this issue remains under the radar in the work published during his lifetime, it nevertheless plays an essential role in the maturation of the anthropological dimension of his project, by the analysis of the relationship between the imaginary and perceptual life, as well as its ontological dimension, by the study of its relationship to the real.

In the late 1940s, Merleau-Ponty becomes attentive to Bachelard's "psychoanalysis" of the elements, his psychological and metaphysical approach to the imaginary. Thanks to Bachelard, and contra the early Sartre, Merleau-Ponty discovers the extent to which the imaginary is not without flesh, the extent to which being is not free of the imaginary; he intends to name this depth shared by reality and the imaginary as *oneiric being*. "We dream before contemplating. Before being a conscious spectacle, all landscape is an oneiric experience."[91] While the imaginary is certainly a deepening of the perceived, perception itself is strengthened by the oneiric experience that envelops it, contributing toward its success. "When we begin to open our eyes to the visible, we have already long been adherent to the invisible."[92] Avoiding the expression and development of this inner work, this imaginative figuration of reality, we are condemned to *disfiguring* it by not "figuring" it at all, under the illusion that we can access the things themselves independently of our imaginative and expressive relationships with them, independently of metaphor in particular.

Merleau-Ponty insists that perceptual success is not a matter of observation; observability is not a criterion of reality. Supported by motor skills, desire, and fantasy, perception "crystallizes" things—perceived things are not only preexistent beings waiting to be observed and recognized, but also the very fruit of this crystallization. In his courses at the Collège de France, Merleau-Ponty regularly takes up this notion of crystallization, which is freely borrowed from Stendhal's *De l'amour* (On Love), in order to counter Sartre's freedom without passivity, his reality free of the imaginary—against a fleshly donation that would complete itself without requiring any donation of flesh from my part.[93] In its irreducibly perceptual and expressive dimensions, the *flesh* operates the crystallization of the inexhaustible (that of the perceived thing, of the beloved) through the crystallization of desire (which animates the flesh). And the *thing* is "this crystallization of the inexhaustible that is wholly here, albeit inexhaustible."[94]

Perceptual recognition is more a *realization* than pure recognition—with both senses of "realization" at work here. In the work of expression, the real and the imaginary are so intertwined as to form a single fabric: the fabric of realization. I do not view my freedom and I do not observe the real, because these are *realizations*, births of being within me and of myself within being. The criterion of observability is distinctly incompatible with a phenomenological ontology: Being does not bring its signature and truth to bear unless I participate in its birth, which occurs beneath the surface of any observable separation. Yet this participation involves my own coming into being: realization, perceptual recognition is also co-nascence (*co-naissance*). Forged in the expression and realization of desire, in the effort of a *figuration* that culminates in metaphor. Metaphor itself is essentially a realizing and co-nascent crystallization.

Just as a crystal can only be born from and within its mother liquor,[95] so is crystallization sustained by that which constitutes its matrix, which Merleau-Ponty attempts to describe in various terms: the invisible, the incorporeal, the figurative. This mother liquor is the place of the inexhaustible, the trace of what the crystal has been, the seed of what it will become, and of what it will in the future bear. If we break the geode, however, everything stops, the crystallization process fossilizes, concretion becomes abstraction. Similarly, one cannot understand metaphoricity without considering the mother liquor that sustains it, without returning to the invisible as the imaginary texture of the visible, or to being as the "imaginary texture of the real."[96] Without returning to what Merleau-Ponty, following Bachelard, calls the "elements." Between being and flesh, these *elements* are not so much metaphors, as the cradle of all metaphoricity, the carnal-ontological and prelinguistic matrix of all metaphor.

From the Figurative to the Incorporeal

Merleau-Ponty's conception of mystery and his ceaseless reflections on perceptual depth converge in the final manuscripts, where we find a late breakthrough in his philosophy of expression and his ontology, in the notions of the "figurative" and the "incorporeal." Appealing to Cézanne and Klee, Merleau-Ponty claims that, if he wishes to open himself up to the "mysterious," the philosopher should haunt the visible, haunted by the invisible. Ontological mystery is not only the invisible as expressed in the visible. It is equally, if not primarily, the invisible as it expresses the visible, thereby expressing itself. Although we cannot observe this mysterious, pre-objective being, this does not mean that it is simply hidden: it is offered to us "through sensations," it is "at the source, hidden-revealed"—revealed, because the source is a spring (*source*), because these "unfathomable depths" are those of a "primordial breath" that animates us in its very expression.[97]

This is the case with all those things Merleau-Ponty refers to as "figuratives." This late concept, explored in the spring 1960 drafts of *Being and World*, might lend itself to misunderstanding if we think in terms of "figurative painting" or a "figurative painter," when in fact it refers to something completely different—so that "figural" might have been a more appropriate term here. "Figuratives" are those dimensions (shadow, lighting, atmospheric color, reflection, transparency, relief, contour, distance, and so on) that support the appearance of the figure, that contribute to what makes it a figure, but which are not themselves figures as such. To use a formula that Merleau-Ponty borrows from Paul Klee, a figurative "makes [things] visible,"[98] without being a visible thing itself. A shadow, for example, is not "something to see,"[99] although it facilitates better perceptual discrimination and connectivity, through its accentuation of depth and differentiation, contrast and relief.[100] Figuratives are thus not incidental to perception: the perceived world "only endures through the reflections, shadows, levels, and horizons between things (which are not things and are not nothing . . .)."[101] It depends on these figuratives, which are neither objective beings nor nonbeings, neither something nor nothing, neither visible nor purely in-visible. Between things, the figurative contributes to their differentiation and integration, participates in the construction of their respective identities, their common depth and bond.[102]

As the major example of this invisible that cannot be "detached from sensible appearances, or erected as a second positivity," *depth* is the "invisible *of* this world, that which inhabits it, sustains it, and renders it visible, its own and interior possibility, the Being of this being."[103] It is certainly not a secondary factor of the perceived world, but that which is "the most 'existential'" "of all the dimensions";[104] depth is the esthesiological inscription of the upward lift (*la portance*) of being unto which the flesh opens, the emblem of what we seek and desire, in a quest "that lasts 'an entire lifetime.'"[105] As the world's manner of being, as the flesh of the world that solicits in us a certain way of being, thus making us flesh, depth becomes a privileged figure of being in Merleau-Ponty's later writings. And our in-depth vision, the prime example of our perceptual relation to the world, becomes a model of the relationship between flesh and being. This analysis of in-depth vision thus presents us as having a unique relationship with the world: a relation of non-incorporating incorporation, a non-intercorporeal *corps-à-corps*. As the most carnal dimension of the world that goes so far as to solicit our flesh, depth is also *beyond the flesh*. Our vision of depth opens us to the upward lift of being, which is not beyond the world, that is, not of another world, but the horizon, the shadow or other side, most of all, depth: being as the depth of the world.

These invisibles—this depth, this shadow—offer us a figural or even Gestaltist model of being. Merleau-Ponty eventually uses a term that is somewhat surprising, given his status as a philosopher of the flesh: "incorporeals." An incorporeal is no longer the flesh of the world, and this highlights the limits of the signifying power of this metaphor. Discovered in the spring of 1959, as evident in his preparatory notes for *The Visible and the Invisible*, the notion of "incorporeal" refers to the invisible as "other side of the visible," as "its relief or structure," as that which sustains the invisible and renders it visible, as well as that onto which the visible opens.[106] This touches on some final aspects of Merleau-Ponty's reflection on the expressive relationship between *flesh* and *being*, on what expresses the flesh and what it is capable of expressing, including the exigencies and possibilities of language. In the autumn of 1960, Merleau-Ponty rereads his most recent work on *Being and World* and writes the following notes, typical of the precipitates of his most personal reflection:

> BEING *and* WORLD (= in-visible and visible). *Shadow* as model of true *negation*. Not the nothingness of corporeity, but its *other side*. A *figurative*. Language is full of them.[107]

The shadow is an incorporeal: the other side of corporeality, the other side of the visible, staging the latter by providing itself as relief, sustaining the visible, generating the visible, while also being that onto which the visible opens, and that which it itself engenders. The incorporeal is "not the nothingness of corporeity, but its other side," that without which flesh cannot come into the world, and to itself. In order to *be flesh*, the flesh needs depth and shadow, it needs being as incorporeal that sustains the world, while not being the world. Living language, the highest achievement of the flesh's expressivity, "is full" of these lacunar beings traversed by a genuine negativity, these lacunar beings desired by the very flesh they bear; a flesh that generates them, that attempts to express them, and is thereby expressed by them.

The body thus needs incorporeals if it is to be opened to metaphoricity, to let metaphor operate on itself, and vice versa, allowing metaphor to edify and sublimate its systems of equivalences. These incorporeals are *figuratives*, not figures; they are the matrices of figures,[108] not metaphors, but the condition of the possibility of metaphoricity. Beginning with the speech of others, as exemplary of those incorporeals on which the corporeal feeds, to open itself to the world, by opening itself to being, of those incorporeals called toward incarnation, not in the sense of the descent of a soul into a body, but—and this is completely different—in the sense of something that animates the (self-) animation of the body, that without which corporeality collapses into a body schema without body image, its systems of equivalences impoverished to the point of univocal closure.[109] "Language is full of them"—full of these figuratives, which are not linguistic elements as such, but what are *presupposed* by all linguistic expression: what language requires in order to function and to make sense, to avoid becoming necrotized in the "univocity of being."[110] Language, or rather speech, is full of these shadows and these silences, without which its expressiveness would be extinguished.

Merleau-Ponty intends to head toward the source, from metaphors to figuratives,[111] the esthesiological matrices of all metaphoricity, so as to better express being, itself figurative of the world. A being ill-adapted to the positivity and fullness of representation, and burdened with an inexhaustibility and negativity inherent in the toil of its own expression; being is no separate and separating third party, but the enveloping-enveloped and generating-generated of our relationships (relationships between ourselves, the world and others, and also between things), effecting the union of incompossibles. This ontology privileges two particular figuratives: *depth*, found throughout his work, and *shadow*, which features more in his later writing. Merleau-Ponty uses these figuratives to take his investigation of being in three complementary directions: being as the *common depth of beings*, as that which separates and unites them in a single gesture; being as the *other side of corporeality and intercorporeality*, that which inhabits the desirous dimensions of flesh, up to the glorious body of speech; and finally, being as the *shadow of the world*, as hidden and figurative, the latency that bears the visible and renders it visible. We find evidence of these three directions—sometimes separately, sometimes together—in his more ontological, later manuscripts: *Eye and Mind, The Visible and the Invisible, Being and World*, not to mention the course on *Cartesian Ontology and the Ontology of Today*. Which offer many insights into the proximity of the two final titles of Merleau-Ponty's oeuvre—*The Visible and the Invisible*, and *Being and World*—as well as his perpetual hesitation between the two.

These three directions offer us a more coherent bundle of meanings, more fruitful and more stable than the attempt to conceptualize the "flesh of the world." As though dealing with the best aspects of this idea, while avoiding its ambiguities. Merleau-Ponty's figuratives help us to escape the latent essentialism that threatens the "flesh of the world," if taken as a self-contained concept. Maintaining a descriptive diversity, they avoid the risk of totalization that comes with this concept, where the flesh no longer "enfigures" anything but itself, and a metaphoricity that has lost its transitional virtues, becoming instead a necrotic fetishism. Finally, they preserve and enhance a vital distinction between *flesh* and *being*. The "flesh of the world" is indeed depth, shadow, the other side of corporeality—but these latter denote something beyond the flesh: a transcendence that is clearly transcendence *of* the flesh, that cannot be conceived independently of the flesh, but that is indeed a *transcendence*, an opening to something . . . something *other than* the flesh.

Being is neither solely nor even primarily that which the visible represents, that to which the visible points, like the *metaphors* in a metaphysics that wishes to represent the intelligible through the sensible: It is itself, first and foremost, *figurative*, that which renders things visible and meaningful, and expresses itself in the same way. In its openness to being, the flesh desires and comprehends that by which it is borne. And this is indeed the ontological mystery that Merleau-Ponty discovers in its esthesiological inscription—our surrender to depth and to shadow, to the other side of the visible, to that which silently sustains the expression of the world—as in its relational inscription—our surrender to the "black portal" of another's eyes, to the silences of his speech, the other side of his corporeality, which intimately bear the expression of his flesh. In all of these cases, perception produces what "reflection will never understand"; it "sketches out what is accomplished by desire."[112]

The Encroachment (of Flesh) and the Analogy (of Being)

Merleau-Ponty portrays Descartes as someone who wants to exorcize all analogy, preferring to enclose himself in a univocal being, "on the edges of a world that doesn't equivocate"[113]—and he is equally critical of Sartre's use of the *analogon* as a protective measure against the intrusions of the imaginary. So that we find Sartre's face alongside that of Descartes in a group portrait of those who "refuse to haunt things."[114] Both are unable to perceive the invisible within the visible, incapable of opening themselves up to being as the imaginary texture of the real, as the depth of the world.

In his courses at the École Normale Supérieure, Merleau-Ponty begins to question the dichotomies in Sartre's *L'imaginaire*—"when I imagine something, not only is there an *analogon* of the absent being in front of me: this absent being seems mysteriously present, to have quasi-magical presence."[115] Images are not phantomlike representations, but genuine carnal doubles, generated in our corporeal exchange with the world. Sartre's separation of the real and the imaginary is vigorously contested in the Sorbonne lectures, where Merleau-Ponty starts with each term, only to discover the implicitness of the other. This opposition comes full circle in 1955, in his critique of the concept of the *analogon* (in Sartre, then Husserl), which is used to provide an intellectual explanation of the purity of the conscience and the nothingness of the imaginary,[116] a retrospective construction that gives an account of the presence of the absent, in a mode that no longer requires the body. Adopting a somewhat psychoanalytic perspective, this critique discerns in a certain use of analogy an example of consciousness's attempts at self-preservation. In its projective dimension, consciousness preserves an ontological integrity (of consciousness, of being, of God . . .) by ensuring a preexistent and irreducible separation. Analogy thus functions here in the service of a double *Noli me tangere*, addressed to both being and the flesh—a far cry from Merleau-Ponty's figuratives.

This critique is one of the more subtle issues of *Eye and Mind*, as confirmed in earlier versions of the manuscript. It is in fact against Sartre's *analogon* that Merleau-Ponty works out his idea of "effective resemblance," of analogy "according to the body," or "the oneiric world of analogy": which is a different type of analogicity; no longer an artificially erected bridge, with the impossible task of filling a prior categorical split (between visible and invisible, real and imaginary, me and others, etc.).[117] Analogicity in this instance is the fruit of an encounter between flesh and being, the common depth of their respective polymorphism—a polymorphism deployed by the flesh as a system of equivalences, deployed by being as the imaginary texture of the real and other side of the visible, the "internal double" descending into things, the invisible that radiates from within the visible itself.[118]

The evocation of analogy in Merleau-Ponty's late work constitutes a complex conceptual constellation, wherein the themes of the imaginary and the unconscious occupy a prominent place. In addition to his long engagement with Sartre's *L'imaginaire*, the philosopher also shares, along with Lacan and Hyppolite, his generation's enthusiasm for Freud's *Verneinung*, a small text that showcases Brentano's influence on the founder of psychoanalysis. This whole constellation contributes to the later evocation of a conception of analogicity as inscribed in both the topological structuring of intercorporeality, and in the very fabric of the unconscious—a "primordial unconscious" coextensive with our relation to being, so that the analogicity of flesh and the analogicity of being are mutually expressive.

In his unpublished manuscripts, we see how Merleau-Ponty's extensive work on Descartes from 1956 to 1961 leads him to a close reading of certain works by Etienne Gilson,[119] an author particularly sensitive to the Cartesian destruction of the analogicity of being. In the preparatory notes for his last course at the *Collège de France*, dedicated to the opposition of "the ontology of today" and the "Cartesian ontology," we find multiple traces of Gilson's detailed commentary on the *Discourse*, and more so, his impressive *Scholastico-Cartesian Index*, especially the entry on analogy.[120] This late reading echoes the fierce opposition to idealism (stemming from various intellectual currents at the time) encountered by Merleau-Ponty during his intellectual youth—starting with the fiery work of Maritain.[121] We are reminded that Merleau-Ponty published his first articles in the new Dominican journal *La Vie Intellectuelle* (Intellectual Life), and there is still a trace of this youthful fervor in his later work, especially in his portrait of Descartes as the high priest of the univocal, clasping in his hand "the breviary of a thought that wants no longer to haunt the visible," because it can no longer tolerate to be itself haunted by the "oneiric world of analogy."[122]

Despite his reading of these authors—whether earlier or later in his career—Merleau-Ponty never directly confronts the question of the *analogia entis*, which hails from a completely different philosophical continent and seems to hold little appeal. Merleau-Ponty's interest in the polymorphism of carnal being is shaped by his engagement with the human sciences, far removed from the context of the metaphysical problem of the analogicity of being.[123] Yet, as we have just seen, there are enough indirect links to legitimize some cautious remarks regarding a possible comparison—although anything more than a rough sketch might seem contrived.

We might reproach the complex adventures of the *analogia entis*—especially when they are orientated toward the question of the human modes of knowing God—for neglecting the fertility of Aristotle's focal structures (*pros hen* and *aph'enos*), and for favoring an already established dissemblance as the only possible ground of resemblance. Analogy in this case is thus only retrospectively transgressive in relation to an irreducible caesura (sensible/intelligible, physical/metaphysical) that is in fact emphasized by this very transgression. Frozen into a retrospective explanatory intelligence, analogicity loses its metaphorical power; its polymorphism becomes controlled. It becomes the bridge over an established boundary, a boundary that remains essentially unviolated; no encroachment can breach the immutable transcendence of an immovable Being. The figural and carnal genesis of metaphor is betrayed—metaphor itself is reduced to an implicit proportionality, a rational rewriting after the fact. In this retrospective logical reformatting, we lose sight of the imaginary and behavioral roots of metaphor, the manner of being in which it is generated, at the heart of the body schema's transfigurations.

Merleau-Ponty, for his part, manages to invert any conception of relationship as based on a presupposed separation. His later writings are more concerned with "this difference in identity, this metamorphosis or metaphor,"[124] with the "advent of difference on the ground of resemblance."[125] Rooted in his phenomenology of perceptual life, this perspectival inversion affects the ontological orientation of his thought. As we see in his work from 1948 to *Eye and Mind*, it is no stranger to the scenario of the opposition of the "modern world" and the "classical world." The world of classical thought is imprisoned in its retrospective attitude, frozen in an eternal past, in stark contrast to the Merleau-Pontian figures of modernity: "encroachment" and "adversity," the "blood of others" and "blood of things," the "flesh"[126]—a modernity that inflicts wounds, and is wounded in return, engaging a humanity who has retrieved its "sense of wonder and mystery."[127] The modern human believes in "neither a preestablished purpose nor preestablished harmony"[128]—these are nothing but artificial prospective assurances that somehow manage to explain everything, including evil itself, from the all-knowing perspective of hindsight.

Subject to the imperatives of an explanatory theology, the *analogia entis* takes the guise of a being that is virtually and imminently close (to us), while actually being primordially separate (from us) . . . and without ever really knowing how its imminent proximity will overcome this distance, how this metaphysical separation will ever be destabilized. At what point the incarnation is "followed out in all its consequences."[129] Merleau-Ponty's being, on the other hand, is carnal and brute, natural and even maternal—not separate, but enveloping-enveloped, a structuring rather than an overhanging entity, a being to which we have a prior and real attachment (as in a primordial indivision), and from which we are virtually and imminently differentiated . . . without really knowing at what point this pregnancy will lead to a real birth, or the extent of these "*differentiations* of one sole and *massive* adhesion to Being which is the flesh."[130]

The Twilight of the Idols: Metaphor and Mystique

Merleau-Ponty's ontology is thus anthropologized and (de)theologized in a completely different manner to that of ancient and classical metaphysics. In particular, his staunch opposition to the "ontology of object" reveals a break with any metaphysics of substance where the relation remains accidental, secondary to the issue of a being's permanent identity (as established through the assumption of separation). While Merleau-Ponty's line of thinking might be considered typically modern, he nevertheless stands out for his daring use of a quasi-psychoanalytic interpretative key, while pointing toward certain reflections that touch on the mystical. For Merleau-Ponty, not only does the ontology of the object fail to think identity and relationality together, but these are only considered in opposition, almost as though this ontology were based on a secret motivation to flee any relationship, or to despair of its possibility.[131] The ontology of the object is obsessed with the stabilization of the *substare*, a contemporary version of which Merleau-Ponty finds in the famous "permanence of the object" of Piaget's epistemology—a permanence initiating a succession of separations: the separation of subject and object, of space and time, and a radical decentering vis-à-vis the flesh.[132] A regime of separation where relationships are thought out retrospectively, where separation is never truly challenged, but always presupposed, and ultimately insurmountable. Merleau-Ponty, for his part, is looking for a "new ontology," an ontology where relational ties are essential to existential continuity (in the first instance, that of each person). The "relationship between beings," their "common depth" and "common transcendence"[133]—for Merleau-Ponty, being is never separate.

Throughout his subtle engagement with the question of analogy, Merleau-Ponty never explicitly addresses Thomism or neo-scholasticism. The latter are nonetheless implied in his recurring criticism of "explanatory theology," the major exemplar of which, in Merleau-Ponty's eyes, remains Leibniz (who, in his way, subjects the question of analogy to the demands of the logicians). Merleau-Ponty denounces the idolatrous remnants of a theology paradoxically ill suited to Christianity's central mysteries: a theology unable to think the incarnation all the way through, unable to fully assume kenosis, stuck with a Greek conception of being, impassive immutable—to which Merleau-Ponty opposes Pascal, Claudel, Bergson, Blondel, or even Teilhard de Chardin. Where one comes across furtive references to Maritain and Gilson, in the dock, cloaked in the ambivalence that our author is so fond of attributing to other philosophers: globally blind yet locally lucid, these philosophers seem to have at times perceived the possibility of an ontology other than the "primordial fullness of Being," the "retrospective thought of complete being,"[134] the possibility of an ultimately nonidolatrous conception of God, a God who is hidden and wounded, "perceived by the heart," who is "beneath" us, and "needs us."[135]

Those who question any theological turn need not worry: Merleau-Ponty is so critical of explanatory theology, as well as what he sees as the theological remnants of Sartre's thought,[136] that we know his approach is completely different. Those who object to any reference to Christianity have cause for concern: against certain theologians, the philosopher notes that he is not averse to the philosophical attempt to integrate a "transcription of Christian experience."[137] His own ontology, contrary to Heidegger's approach (as he sees it), is open to the exploration of all "mirrors of Being."[138] Whether neurology and psychoanalysis, the Bible or literature, Merleau-Ponty freely draws inspiration from these mirrors, in his attempt to find a philosophical word more appropriate to the paradoxes of our condition, our enigmatic and complex relationship with the world and others. A word that offers an "intelligible mouthful,"[139] bearing an "essence common to real and imaginary," "bearing meaning, not as 'an idea of the intelligence,' but meaning as *metaphor*."[140]

Merleau-Ponty's approach to being is thus partly linked to his critical reading of a particular conception of God and relation between man and God, less in the context of a close debate over a particular theological doctrine than in the context of a fierce critique of an idolatry that encumbers the mind and closes it off to the mysteries of our condition. For Merleau-Ponty, the very notion of an "objective being" is nothing but a fantasy, and paradoxically, this being reabsorbs the very margins of the imaginary, leaving neither time nor space for desire, faith, or hope. Objective being stretches out in the crushing explanatory space and time of Midday (as in the opening scene of Claudel's *Partage de Midi*), a shadowless time, a purity without recourse, where everything is crushed in a light that kills the depth of things and the depths of the other. The time of an absolute overflight of consciousness, the presence of Leibniz's overhanging God looming over us, his calculations having absorbed all contingency. A time of merciless judgment, where an omnipotent Third develops all invisibles, thus excluding us from ourselves. Yet while Merleau-Ponty's preobjective being is not "mystery in broad daylight,"[141] neither does it fall into the other extreme, into a false conception of mystery as a secret and reclusive truth, in the darkness of a moonless night.[142] A forbidden darkness, for which only a few select initiates possess the key—a key typically denied to the flesh, but reserved for a type of knowing that rejects the fertility of nonsense and cannot accept the role of faith and desire in intelligence. Seemingly opposed, these false conceptions of mystery nevertheless share a regressive tendency that has always threatened philosophy, a gnostic weakness where intelligence fails to break free from the tyranny of idols, desperately ignoring the human condition, from the passivity of the flesh to the truth of its desire.[143]

Preobjective being resides neither in the full explicative light of Midday's judgments nor in the total darkness and absolute unknowability of Midnight. Neither Being nor Nothingness, neither pure presence nor pure absence—which are equivalents in despair and solitude. This being resides in the Double Shadow—a term borrowed from the *Soulier de satin* (Satin Slipper)[144]—in the light and darkness that meet on a ragged edge, under a crescent moon.[145] Shadow, as the silence of the visible, which whispers its truth, participates in the world's staging, like the kind of silence that contributes to speech. Silence, as the shadow of speech, brings speech into relief. As the shadow of presence, it neither withholds nor imposes the latter, but offers and exposes it as lift, listening and gift: far from being an abandoning absence, it adopts a certain stance of withdrawal, as essential for the only presence who knows how to reunite with others, in the depths of their ontological solitude. Shadow, depth, silence: so many modalities of the invisible, far removed from the fullness of representation or the positivity of fantasy. Like so many lacunar spaces in being, which are no other than being itself, providing a space and time essential to the awakening of desire, to its growth and its expression.

Being, thought of as shadow and depth, as a figurative, escapes the God of Midday—who is already perfectly configured and thus completely *disfigured*—as well as avoiding the God of Midnight—who is secretly and surreptitiously controlled by our fear of representation. This conception of Being resonates with Merleau-Ponty's long-standing preference for the *deus absconditus* of Isaiah and Pascal, the genuine twilight of the idols. "If God is God, and not an Idol, then he must be hidden, the presence of an absence."[146] Thought of God is not an "intellectual *possession*":[147] "faith, not evidence," it is "the fact of the whole man."[148] This God is approached, "not through a positive intelligence, but through our very lives, in the thickness of our embodiment. . . . God as implication of existence, and this is why one believes in him with the body."[149]

In the draft of *Being and World* we find a striking defense of "the figuratives and the hidden God against the logic of Leibniz," further expressed in the programmatic formula: "Against this Leibnizian God, [we should] emphasize the hidden God and his 'figuratives.'"[150] Considering these two propositions together, we find a coherence between Leibniz's logic and his conception of God on one hand, and between Pascal's hidden God and Merleau-Ponty's figuratives on the other—as conceived within the framework of his phenomenology of perception.

I have examined elsewhere how (and how often) Merleau-Ponty expresses his general opposition to Leibniz—to his theodicy in particular, which blocks off any possible reflection on the human condition, of contingency and freedom, faith and hope.[151] Merleau-Ponty feels that Leibniz has overlooked the very paths he has chosen to take in his own thought. Prisoner of the overflight of objectivism,[152] Leibniz is blocked from understanding the flesh and its phenomenality[153]—in stark contrast to the "tremblings" that shook the author of the *Meditations*.[154] Unlike Descartes, in fact in direct opposition to him, Leibniz espouses his preestablished harmony, specific case of concomitance, against the Cartesian idea of the genuine mixing and mutual influence of soul and body.

Leibniz and Merleau-Ponty's paths cross before the sixth metaphysical *Meditation*, at which point they head in different directions, the latter wishing to take up and think through the "commingling" that the former simply erases in his idea of two parallel clocks, perfectly concordant "in their own exactness."[155] While Leibniz directs his attention to an axiomatized analogy, Merleau-Ponty focuses on the carnal foundations of metaphoricity. One reconstructs the view of a god looking down from above, the pure climactic essence of explanatory theology, which is also the death of biblical or mystical writing (since this god is already perfectly enfigured and expressed), while the other believes that we should consider the encroachment and expression of a being that, like "tangible [*sensible*] beings," "is a radiance, not an essence."[156] A being that is *omnitenens* rather than *omnipotens*,[157] that "bears us, bears us pell-mell with others," and that "holds everything together."[158]

This "Being where all things exist together,"[159] this relation between beings—"I am the tresses of everything that exists"[160]—in turn undergirds the more primitive roots of our sense of wonder in the face of "all these things existing together."[161] Its relationship to the world can be thought along the lines of the perceptual model of the phenomenological relationship between visible and invisible: As shadow and depth of the world, this being is anything but an object; it need not even first be enfigured, since it is itself, and the primary, *figurative*—figurative of the world and man, before the latter attempts to enfigure it in return.

While traditional theology most often focuses on an *enfigured God* (*le Dieu figuré*), Merleau-Ponty prefers to focus on a God who expresses himself in figures. As though God himself, assuming he exists, cannot speak about us, or himself, except in parables—parables that are, "not a way of presenting pure ideas in images; they are the only language capable of conveying the relations of religious life, as paradoxical as those of the world of sensation."[162] Fully enfigurable and enfigured, the idol points to nothing but itself, inexorably crushing all metaphoricity. The idol exempts us from "entering body and soul into an enigmatic life, the obscurities of which cannot be dissipated, but can only be concentrated in a few mysteries,"[163] releasing us from the only language capable of expressing our paradoxical relations, the paradox that we ourselves are. This fully transparent "great eternal diamond"[164] has no shadow, and nothing can overshadow it. Merleau-Ponty, on the other hand, evokes Pascal's "hidden God," Claudel's "God beneath us": a kenotic being, a shadow that has always crept into the horizons and depths of the world, stealing into our own shadows, so as to become the shadow of our shadow, so as to better express us.[165]

Translated by Janice Deary

On the Poetic and the True

GALEN A. JOHNSON

Two of the working titles Merleau-Ponty had considered for his posthumously published last work, *The Visible and the Invisible*, were *Genealogy of the True* and *The Origin of Truth*. The first three Working Notes for that book all bear the heading, "The Origin of Truth" (January 1959). Earlier in 1951, when Merleau-Ponty submitted his candidacy for the professorship of philosophy at the Collège de France, he mentioned two works in progress, one that would elaborate a theory of truth and the other a theory of literary language. The first was to have been called *The Origin of Truth*, the second, *Introduction to the Prose of the World*.[1] Though neither work was completed in his lifetime, we can draw two conclusions. The first is that the questions of truth and those of literary language were intimately linked in Merleau-Ponty's philosophical thinking. Additionally, we may conclude that there were two moments of his thought and work when the questions of truth were at the forefront of his attention, the time of *The Prose of the World* with the related course of 1953 at the Collège de France, *Recherches sur l'usage littéraire du langage*, and the time of his work on *The Visible and the Invisible* with the related essays in *Signs* and *Eye and Mind*. The focus of the first moment concerns clarifying the "mystery of language" in both literary and mathematical expression while the second moment introduces us to a new idea of truth and new vocabulary of truth centering on Merleau-Ponty's introduction and increasing use of the term *éclatement* (breaking forth, burst, spark, sparkle, shining). In a Working Note we will study in detail, in relation to "human enterprises" and poetry in particular,

Merleau-Ponty spoke of a "power to break forth, productivity, fecundity" (*pouvoir d'éclatement, productivité* [*praegnans futuri*], *fécondité*) (September 1959; VI, 262/208). The "power of breaking forth," its spark and shining in poetry and every human action and enterprise, Merleau-Ponty paired with the new ontological term, the "dehiscence" of Being. If Being is a becoming, truth is also event, happening, movement of thought and life.

We will study each of these moments of Merleau-Ponty's thinking in turn. Before doing so, we will need to make some orienting and contextualizing remarks regarding Merleau-Ponty's approach to the questions of truth and untruth in relation to the majority philosophical tradition.

Merleau-Ponty, Truth/Untruth, Illusion, Skepticism

For Merleau-Ponty, what is the "truth" of literature, the "truth" of fiction, the "truth" of poetry? To be more precise, how even should the question or questions of truth and literary truth be framed in the thought of Merleau-Ponty? Certainly it will not be a question or questions of the truth of beliefs, ideas, judgments, statements, or even propositions, as it is in many epistemological traditions that Merleau-Ponty calls "critical thought." Rather, truth will have to do with the truth of perception, the truth of life, and the truth of incarnate bodily movement. In a Working Note of *The Visible and the Invisible*, Merleau-Ponty writes: "One has to admit a sort of truth in the naïve descriptions of perception. . . . All that takes place in an order that is no longer that of objective Being, that is the order of the lived or the phenomenal which is precisely to be justified and rehabilitated as the foundation of the objective order" (September 1959; VI, 262–63/209). Thus, the calling of truth pertains to "being true" and "becoming true," more in the ontological-ethical sense of the truth of a life, the sense in which a person is or can become the truth as in the Latin expression *ecce homo* (behold the man).[2] The calling of truth also involves the sense in which an action is true, for example when a cabinetmaker is cutting for "the true" with practiced stillness of movement centering bodily motion with an ease of concentration and balance before a spinning lathe. The old-time cabinetmakers spoke of a fine work or building as square, plumb, level, and true. Square, plumb, and level each have precise instruments of measure. Nevertheless, even with these intact, the work or building is not "true" if it is warped, twisted, or racked, and for this, exact measures are either lacking or are less precise. We recall these words from the beginning of Merleau-Ponty's prospectus for his candidacy at Collège de France: "We never cease living in the world of perception, but we go beyond it in critical thought—almost to the point of forgetting the contribution of perception to our idea of truth. For critical thought encounters only *statements* which it discusses, accepts, or rejects. Critical thought has broken with the naïve evidence of *things*."³

Therefore, in an important sense, Merleau-Ponty's philosophy offers a critique of classical and modern theories of knowledge and truth, a critical genealogy of *truth as value* in the spirit of Nietzsche and Foucault. It is not accidental that one of the possible titles for what became *The Visible and the Invisible* was *Genealogy of the True*. Of history and truth, Foucault wrote: "If he [the genealogist] listens to history, he finds that there is 'something altogether different' behind things: not a timeless and essential secret, but the secret that they have no essence or that their essence was fabricated in a piecemeal fashion from alien forms."⁴ Nietzsche wrote in a famous aphorism from *The Will to Power*: "We possess *art* lest we *perish of the truth*."⁵

Merleau-Ponty's "minority philosophy" and even "a-philosophy" always retains a linkage and echo of the skeptical tradition in philosophy that we may approach through Merleau-Ponty's appropriations from Nietzsche. Merleau-Ponty's very first published article appeared in 1935 in *La Vie Intellectuelle* on the subject of Scheler and Nietzsche's typology of *ressentiment*,⁶ and his lecture course in the last year of his teaching, 1960–61, *Philosophie et non-philosophie depuis Hegel*, includes commentary on the preface to the second edition of Nietzsche's *The Gay Science*. In the fourth and final chapter of *The Visible and the Invisible* as well as several Working Notes we also find important Nietzschean influences on themes of truth and time.

In Merleau-Ponty's lecture course, *Philosophy and Non-philosophy since Hegel*, he entered into a discussion and commentary on Nietzsche's preface to the second edition of *The Gay Science* (1886). Merleau-Ponty worked from Nietzsche's German text and translated sections 2, 3, and 4 of Nietzsche's preface into French nearly in their entirety, with certain elisions. In *The Gay Science* preface, Nietzsche asks himself if philosophy has not been "merely an interpretation of the body and a *misunderstanding* of the body,"⁷ leading to two contrasting kinds of philosophy and two motivations for doing philosophy, sickness and health. From the sick body, its suffering and needs, arises a search for the "sunny places of thought" separated from life where there is mildness, patience, medicine, balm, and peace. This sick philosophy divorces body from soul, soul from spirit, and philosophy from life. It forgets, Nietzsche writes, that "we have to give birth to our thoughts out of our pain and, like mothers, endow them with all we have of blood, heart, fire, pleasure, passion, agony, conscience, fate, and catastrophe."⁸

Merleau-Ponty translates and cites Nietzsche's passage on the "sunny places of thought" (*les places ensoleillées*), and in his commentary on Nietzsche's text that follows, he says that true philosophy goes toward an "a-philosophy by fidelity to what we live; which does not culminate in 'all knowledge' (new positivism) nor in despair, but in the will to appearance.... Nietzsche holds on to the quality of the 'philosopher': the absolute of appearance" (NC, 278).[9] Thus, Merleau-Ponty affirms Nietzsche's critique of the dominant traditions of philosophy that Nietzsche argues falsely transform the contingencies of life into a kind of sunny thought and abstract philosophy like we find in Platonism and in Christianity. Merleau-Ponty further concurs with Nietzsche's praise of the "will to appearance" and incorporates the Nietzschean "absolute of appearances" right into the final statement of his ontology in Chapter 4 of *The Visible and the Invisible* titled "The Intertwining—The Chiasm": "What there is then are ... things we could not dream of seeing 'all naked' because the gaze itself envelops them, clothes them with its own flesh" (VI, 173/131). Nietzsche's text referenced here is included among the passages Merleau-Ponty translated from *The Gay Science*: "Today we consider it a matter of decency not to wish to see everything naked, or to be present at everything, or to understand and 'know' everything. One should have more respect for the bashfulness with which nature has hidden behind riddles and iridescent uncertainties."[10]

When Merleau-Ponty joins Nietzsche in linking truth with appearances, it is necessary to understand that appearance and truth—profundity—are not opposed in Nietzsche's thinking, nor in Merleau-Ponty's. Plato had established and authorized the opposition between truth and appearance in the "Divided Line" and "Allegory of Cave" in his *Republic*, and what we find in Nietzsche and Merleau-Ponty is a reversal of this aspect of Platonism in favor of the wisdom of the Greek tragedians, especially Aeschylus and Sophocles. Husserl had stated the phenomenological "principle of principles" in *Ideas* I: "every originary presentive intuition is a legitimizing source of cognition, that everything originarily (so to speak, in its 'personal' actuality) offered to us in 'intuition' is to be accepted simply as what it is presented as being, but also only within the limits in which it is presented there."[11] Merleau-Ponty argues that this well-known Husserlian call for the "return to the things themselves" must be distinguished from the idealist turn toward the inner consciousness of a subject such as we find in Descartes and Kant. Moreover, with respect to Husserl's stress upon "intuition," Merleau-Ponty argues that for Husserl, "noematic reflection" that remains within the object bringing to light its fundamental unity replaces a "noetic analysis" that bases the world on the synthesizing activity of the subject (PhP, iv/x). He proclaims a forceful revision of Saint Augustine's "inner man" and writes: "Truth does not 'inhabit' only 'the inner man,' or more accurately, there is no inner man, man is in the world, and only in the world does he know himself" (PhP, v/x). The "phenomenon" of phenomenology is that which manifests itself in our bodily engagements with the world and the phenomenon exhibits a structure of form and content that will be largely shared across cultures and times, though not completely so. Truth is a revealing that is also a concealing in the openness of "letting be" (*laisser être*). This accords with Nietzsche's stress in *The Birth of Tragedy* upon Apollo as *Schein* or shining in contrast with the turbulence and passion of Dionysus, both of which are necessary in the great Greek tragedies. *Schein* is sometimes translated as "appearance" or even "semblance," creating the troublesome suggestion of an appearance or semblance of something else that is the original and "causes" the appearance. In *Genealogy of Morals*, Nietzsche stressed that there is no cause or "substratum" behind events, "no being behind doing, effecting, becoming."[12] Rather, Nietzsche is already thinking phenomenologically in which the phenomenon is that which manifests itself and shines forth in itself. Merleau-Ponty scholar Frank Chouraqui has defended the implicit phenomenology of Nietzsche forcefully: "One of the most prominent connections between Nietzsche's thought and the entire phenomenological enterprise lies in Husserl's founding postulate that the thing-in-itself is an invalid concept. . . . A thing is, by definition and by essence, always an object of perception. This is also, of course, one of Nietzsche's most explicit, best established, and most consistently repeated claims."[13]

Many years before commenting on Nietzsche's *The Gay Science*, Merleau-Ponty had spoken of a kind of philosophical illusion that devalues appearances and contingency. In his essay titled "The Metaphysical in Man" published in *Sense and Non-Sense*, he had written that "the contingency of all that exists and all that has value is not a little truth for which we have somehow or other to make room in some nook or cranny of the system; it is the condition of the metaphysical view of the world" (SNS, 117/96). Contingency is no "little truth," it is "the big truth," and the truth of contingency cannot be reconciled with "positing an absolute thinker of the world" (ibid.).

This is a skeptical denial of absolute foundations as well as absolute origins consistent with the Apollonian-Dionysian dyad of *The Birth of Tragedy*, which Merleau-Ponty mentions explicitly in his lecture course: "Being superficial out of profundity (Apollo and Dionysus)" [*Être superficiel par profondeur (Apollon et Dionysos)*] (NC, 278/12). Merleau-Ponty is here referencing Nietzsche's passage from the last paragraph of *The Gay Science* preface: "Oh, those Greeks! They knew how to live. What is required for that is to stop courageously at the surface, the fold, the skin, to adore appearance, to believe in forms, tones, words, in the whole Olympus of appearance. Those Greeks were superficial—out of profundity."[14] In a previous paragraph of the same page, Nietzsche had written: "We no longer believe that truth remains truth when the veils are withdrawn" (NC, 277/11).[15] In terms of a classical and modern philosophy of perception and truth, the veil hides, it obscures the things. In Merleau-Pontian terms, the veil is precisely the instrument that reveals; but it never reveals all and everything, it reveals from within a tradition and perceptual faith.

Merleau-Ponty here shows us a limited form of skepticism that refuses absolute foundations for thought but nevertheless does not abandon perceptual truth and our attachment to Being. This means that Merleau-Ponty does not want everything Nietzsche wrote about truth and would decisively mark his distance from the very early Nietzsche who wrote the fragment "On Truth and Lie in an Extra-Moral Sense." There Nietzsche had asked the question Pilate had asked, and Nietzsche had responded cynically:

> "What, then, is truth?" And he had famously answered: "A mobile army of metaphors, metonyms, and anthropomorphism . . . which after long use seem firm, canonical, and obligatory to a people; truths are illusions about which one has forgotten that this is what they are; metaphors which are worn out and without sensuous power. . . . To be truthful means using the customary metaphors—in moral terms: the obligation to lie according to a fixed convention, to lie herd-like in a style obligatory for all."[16]

For this early Nietzsche, if faced with a choice between life or truth, we are to choose life; the opposition of this binary is irreconcilable in Nietzsche's early thought. To repeat the aphorism of *The Will to Power*, "We possess *art* lest we *perish of the truth.*"[17] To refer once again to Frank Chouraqui and his recent book, *Ambiguity and the Absolute: Nietzsche and Merleau-Ponty on the Question of Truth*, Chouraqui argues that Nietzsche's early position setting up this opposition between art and truth gave way to a more mature position in which he "undertook a passionate attempt to salvage truth from its own undercutting."[18] We can see such a view emerging in *The Gay Science* in a passage from the last section of its Book Two titled "Our ultimate gratitude to art," in which Nietzsche contrasts the truth of art with the so-called "objective truth" of science: "art as the *good* will to appearance."[19] As Chouraqui has put it, "if Nietzsche refuses to say that 'truth remains truth when the veils are withdrawn,' it does not mean that any veil will do"[20] (cf. Carbone, chapter 4, final section).

In both "The Metaphysical in Man" and the opening pages of *The Visible and the Invisible*, Merleau-Ponty makes clear that his assertion of contingency is not a "virulent skepticism," a Pyrrhonian skepticism that destroys the possibility of truth and knowledge through the loss of our relationship to Being. He writes, "the radical subjectivity of all our experience [is] inseparable from its truth value" (SNS 114/93). There is a "double sense of the *cogito* . . . I am sure that there is being—on the condition that I do not seek another sort of being than being-for-me" (SNS, 114/93). He adds: "It is our very difference, the uniqueness of our experience, which attests to our strange ability to enter into others and re-enact their deeds. Thus is founded a truth, which, as Pascal said, we can neither reject nor completely accept" (SNS, 114–15/93–94). This subjectivity as the condition for the possibility of truth is, indeed, double-sided or paradoxical. It is what Merleau-Ponty names the "perceptual faith" at the beginning of *The Visible and the Invisible*. He writes:

> The "natural" man holds on to both ends of the chain, thinks *at the same time* that his perception enters into the things and that it is formed this side of his body. Yet coexist as the two convictions do without difficulty in the exercise of life, once reduced to theses and to propositions they destroy one another and leave us in confusion. (VI, 23–24/8)

Pyrrhonism, Merleau-Ponty points out, "makes use of that faith in the world it seems to be unsettling" (VI, 19/5). This logical refutation or "winning on paper," is augmented by our experience. "We answer Pyrrhonism sufficiently," Merleau-Ponty writes, "by showing that there is a difference of structure and, as it were, of grain between perception or true vision, which gives rise to an open series of concordant explorations, and the dream, which is not *observable* and, upon examination, is almost nothing but blanks (*lacunes*)" (VI, 20/5). Each one of us and each of our perceptions begin from a faith in our perceptual contact with the world yet knowing that contact is contingent upon our birth, learning, language, history, and institutions. The key to the origin of truth in this perceptual faith comes in recognizing that subjectivity is not purely individual cut off from others, mine and only mine. Merleau-Ponty argues that the subject of perception is not an "I," rather it is the anonymous *one* that perceives through me. *Phenomenology of Perception* had stated:

> My first perception and my first hold on the world must appear to me as the execution of a more ancient pact established between X and the world in general; my history must be the sequel to a

> pre-history whose acquired results it uses; my personal existence must be the taking up of a pre-personal tradition. There is, then, another subject beneath me, for whom a world exists before I am there, and who marks out my place in that world. (PhP, 293–94/265)

This anonymity or pre-personal existence and tradition is the "natural mind" of my body that marks our place in the world and assures our adhesion to it. Our body in its relationship with the world and anchorage on the earth precludes a radical or virulent skepticism in which we would be imprisoned in Nietzschean illusions and phantasms. There is no coincidence with the things or a fusion with them, yet there is contact and adhesion that retains differences. In a crucial text from *The Visible and Invisible*'s chapter on "Interrogation and Intuition," Merleau-Ponty wrote: "What we propose here, and oppose to the search for essence, is not a return to the immediate, the coincidence, the effective fusion with the existent. . . . If coincidence is lost, this is no accident. If Being is hidden, this is, itself, a characteristic of Being" (VI, 162/122). Merleau-Ponty scholar Bernard Flynn has named Merleau-Ponty's position stated here a "weak universalism," not a full-blown universal philosophy "founded upon a domain prior to all interrogation and ambiguity, that is, a ground of certainty . . . not a universal that could 'once and for all' be achieved, but rather a universalism that precludes the closure of any particular system of signification."[21] Flynn clarifies that he means "weak universalism" in the sense of Gianni Vattimo,[22] not in contrast with strength, rather in the sense that philosophy in our age must comply with a multiplicity of interpretations, which is a hermeneutic notion of truth like that found in Ricoeur and Gadamer.[23] Flynn concludes: "The most singular, the most carnal, is the most universal."[24]

Another avenue for articulating this conclusion can be found in Merleau-Ponty's essay "Reading Montaigne," found in *Signs*. Montaigne is most often taken to be an entrenched skeptic without qualifications. Nevertheless, Merleau-Ponty takes a different approach that finds in Montaigne a recognition of the necessary linkage between truth and untruth. The skeptical position relies upon a premise that there is "a total truth with all the necessary facets and mediations," and this premise it denies. "Montaigne begins by teaching that all truth contradicts itself," Merleau-Ponty writes, "perhaps he ends up recognizing that contradiction is truth. . . . The first and fundamental of contradictions is that by which the refusal of each truth uncovers a new kind of truth" (S, 250–51/198). Véronique Fóti has clearly articulated this simultaneity and reversibility of truth/untruth in the thought of Merleau-Ponty: "The openness achieved in perception is always at the surface of a concealed depth; in this way it is primary truth/untruth."[25]

Whether we approach Merleau-Ponty's genealogy of the true through Nietzsche or Montaigne, we find a similar result, the critique of absolute knowledge, the critique of absolute skepticism, and the articulation of a "weak universalism" based upon the perceptual faith in our body's "natural mind" and adhesion to the world, together with its ambiguities, reversals, surface, and depth.

The Mystery of Language

Let us now turn explicitly to the first domain and moment of Merleau-Ponty's thought and writing concerning the truth of literary language, that from the time period of *The Prose of the World*, for the most part written during the summer of 1951, and Merleau-Ponty's course of 1953 beginning from January 1953 at the Collège de France on literary language (*Recherches sur l'usage littéraire du langage*). Both make clear that the questions of literary truth are embedded within the study and understanding of literary language. He states "our goal is not the problem of the professional writer . . . but our goal is 1) to know literary language itself, 2) . . . to confront it with its practice. To try, beyond its theories, in contact with its works, to define literary meaning, literary expression, and to see in what they consist" (ULL, 86–87). He finds in literary language a fundamental mystery best revealed through reading and incorporation of the poetry of Valéry and the fiction of Stendhal.

Merleau-Ponty's chapter titled "The Algorithm and the Mystery of Language" from *The Prose of the World* defines the mystery of language as the "metamorphosis" speech undergoes "through which words cease to be accessible to our senses and lose their weight, their noise, their lines, their space (to become thoughts)" (PM, 162–63/116). From the side of thought, it "renounces (to become words) its rapidity or its slowness, its surprise, its invisibility, its time, the internal consciousness we have of it. This is indeed the mystery of language" (PM, 163/116). This two-way exchange between words and thoughts means that when we speak, we do not think of the words we are saying or are being said to us but comprehend immediately their signification. Merleau-Ponty compares this to shaking another's hand, which is felt not as a bundle of flesh and bone, but "the palpable presence of the other person" (PM, 162/116). To put it another way, Merleau-Ponty says that "the mystery is that, in the very moment where language is thus obsessed with itself, it is enabled, through a kind of excess, to open us to a signification" (PM, 162/115).

Mathematical integers, geometry, and algorithms possess a purity, Merleau-Ponty argues (PM, 169/121), that causes us to assign them a timeless truth and a totality of meaning. This is "because knowledge uses the world-thesis which is its fundamental sound. We believe truth is eternal because truth expresses the perceived world and perception implies a world which was functioning before it and according to principles which it discovers and does not posit" (PM, 174/124). Nevertheless, because mathematical expression is an exploration of the world, an *event* that *opens* on a truth, "mathematical truth, reduced [brought back] to what we truly establish (*ramenée à ce que nous constatons vraiment*), is not of a different kind" (PM, 173/123) than perceptual truth. It is purer, cleaner, and less cluttered perhaps, yet it is not of a different order. Therefore, "mathematical thought rests upon the sensible but it is creative" (PM, 177/126). No expressive operation exhausts its object but retains "gaps and opacities" that new thematizations will fill in and clarify, which applies to mathematics equally with all other inquiries and disciplines. Thus, Merleau-Ponty concludes with a biological metaphor for the development of truth: "The awareness of truth advances like a crab, turned toward its point of departure, toward that structure *whose* signification it expresses. Such is the living operation that sustains the signs of the algorithm" (PM, 179/128).

The "movement of the crab" is a "laterigrade movement" which means a lateral or sideways movement rather than direct or frontal, a concealed approach of advance and regression yet with a deftness in the midst of supposed enemies. If one thinks of the prose of Proust, or of Flaubert, its length, its repetitions, its meditations circling back over the smallest details of everyday objects—cups, lamps, wallpaper, clothing, stone steps—we find the lateral, "indirect language" of literature. The "Indirect Language" chapter of *The Prose of the World* says this explicitly: "Personal life, knowledge, and history advance only obliquely. They do not go straight, without hesitation, toward goals or concepts. That which one too deliberately seeks, one does not achieve" (PM, 159/112). Merleau-Ponty adds the significance of this indirect kind of seeking for his understanding of truth: "even the purest of truths presuppose marginal views. Not being entirely in the center of clear vision, they owe their meaning to the horizon which sedimentation and language preserve around them" (PM, 159–60/113). "Horizon" and "sedimentation" are central phenomenological concepts inherited from Husserl. Perceptual experience is oriented toward a perceptual field in which the perceptual act, focused near or far, is tacitly oriented toward other aspects not given explicit attention or even actually present. Perceptual experience is temporal involving horizonal retentions of the past and protentions of the future. Our past experiences sediment into the perceptions of the present, just as language is a sedimented structure of past acts of speaking. In such ways through accounts of horizon and sedimentation, phenomenology creates a "thick" notion of experience.

In the "Indirect Language" chapter of *The Prose of the World*, Merleau-Ponty shows how the horizons and sedimentations of perceptual experience form a background for the novelist that is tacit, meaning that the silences are often as or even more important than what is explicitly written. He is commenting explicitly on Stendhal, *The Red and the Black*:

> What is important is not that Julien Sorel, after he has learned that he has been betrayed by Mme de Rênal, travels to Verrières and tries to kill her. It is that silence, that dreamlike journey, that thoughtless certainty, and that eternal resolution which follow the news. But there is no passage in which these things are said. . . . He [Stendhal] had only to decide to relate the journey in three pages instead of ten, to be silent about something rather than say such and such. . . . As though in a second life, he [Stendhal] made the trip to Verrières according to a cadence of cold passion which selects for itself the visible and the invisible, what is to be said and what is to remain unsaid. The desire to kill is nowhere *in* the words. It is between them, in the hollows of space, time, and the significations they delimit, the way movement in the film is between the immobile images which follow one another. (PM, 124–25/88; see also S, 95/76)

When Merleau-Ponty spoke of the "mystery of language" as the two-way conversion of words and thoughts, the one into the other back and forth, he cited Jean Paulhan, whom he says has expressed this "perfectly." Paulhan (1884–1968) was a writer and literary critic, older though roughly contemporary with Merleau-Ponty, who was director of the literary magazine *Nouvelle Revue Française*, on the fringes of André Breton's surrealist movement. Merleau-Ponty at first got off on the wrong foot with Paulhan at the beginning of *The Prose of the World*. He had puzzled Merleau-Ponty by saying the very opposite from Merleau-Ponty on the always unfinished nature of expression. In Paulhan's *Les fleurs de Tarbes* (*The Flowers of Tarbes*) he had adopted the statement of La Bruyère: "Of all the possible expressions which might render our thought, there is only one which is the best. One does not always come upon it in writing or talking: it is nevertheless true that it exists." Of this claim, tellingly, Merleau-Ponty asks: "How does he know this?" (PM, 11/6). That is a pointed question. Nevertheless, by the time of Merleau-Ponty's later chapter on the mystery of language, he credits Paulhan this way: "Paulhan is the first to have seen that in use speech is not content with designating thoughts the way a street number designates my friend Paul's house. Speech in use really undergoes 'a metamorphosis'" (PM, 162/116). In addition to *Les fleurs de Tarbes*, Merleau-Ponty's notes also cite Paulhan's *Clef de la poésie* (*The Key to Poetry*). The full title of the first is *Les fleurs de Tarbes ou La terreur dans les lettres* (*The Flowers of Tarbes or Terror in Literature*). This work is a consideration of the turning point in French literary history, around the time of the French Revolution and Terror, away from rule-bound imperatives of rhetoric and genre to the gradual abandonment of these rules in Romanticism and its successors searching for greater originality of expression. This opposing imperative is what Paulhan terms *Terror*, and it is double-edged in Paulhan's analysis. On the one hand it provides invention and renewal; on the other, its persuasive power can fall prey to an "optical illusion": revolutionary writers remain paradoxically as enslaved to language as rule-bound writers since they spend all their time trying to avoid its clichés.

Paulhan provides a way of clarifying what Merleau-Ponty meant by the "excess" of signification as part of the miracle of poetic language, namely, that language retains an untamed element, try to tame it as we might, or equally and paradoxically, try to celebrate it as we might. Merleau-Ponty cites the last page of *The Flowers of Tarbes*: "the signification of language consists in 'rays sensible to him who sees them but hidden from him who watches them,' while language is made of 'gestures which are not accomplished without some negligence'" (PM, 162/116).[26] After these words, Paulhan adds: "(like some stars, or stretching your arm out to its full length)."[27] Like nature and like philosophy itself, language also has a "back side" hidden from the light that remains untamed, a "baroque world" and baroque poetic. In "The Philosopher and his Shadow," Merleau-Ponty wrote: "Willy-nilly, against his plans and according to his essential audacity, Husserl awakens a wild-flowering world and mind (*un monde sauvage et un esprit sauvage*). This baroque world is not a concession of mind to nature.... This renewal of the world is also mind's renewal" (S, 228/180–81).

The Paradox of Expression

The last paragraph of the "Indirect Language" chapter of *The Prose of the World* speaks—for the first time, I believe, in Merleau-Ponty's philosophical writing—of the "paradox of expression." Merleau-Ponty writes: "When it is a matter of speech or of the body or of history, where there is a risk of destroying what one is trying to understand, for example, of reducing language to thought or thought to language, one can only make visible the paradox of expression" (PM, 160/113). He adds that "philosophy is the inventory of this dimension" (ibid.). The fourth and final chapter of *The*

Visible and the Invisible, "The Intertwining—the Chiasm," is explicit about a paradox in expression: "in the patient and silent labor of desire, begin the paradox of expression" (VI, 189/144). Therefore, this paradox in expression links the thought of *The Prose of the World* with that of *The Visible and the Invisible*. Moreover, if "philosophy is the inventory of this dimension," as Merleau-Ponty states, philosophy must be a philosophy of expression and a philosophy of language, of literary language in particular.

We might begin by noticing the paradox of expression has two sides or aspects: the first poses the delicate relation of words and things, that is, of the poetic expression and its meaning, as both an "equivalence" or "vibration" and a "deformation." And in the second aspect, the paradox contends that expression arises from desire. Both of these complicate—some might say "compromise"—the relationship of literature and truth.

To speak to the first aspect, Merleau-Ponty's *Phenomenology of Perception* had already rejected the theory of poetry as sheer onomatopoeia as "naive" for positing a purely natural sign in spite of the conventional variations in mother tongues (PhP, 218/193). For the theory of expression, there is a chiasm (crossing over) but also a gap or difference (*écart*) between the thing and its sign or expression, which means there must be heterogeneity all the while maintaining contact with the givens of the world (*les données*). The expressive word or work must speak or show differently or divergently yet simultaneously reveal the thing expressed. If the word or work were an imitation or exact replica, it would be a bare repetition that disclosed nothing; the word or work would be sheer redundancy. Merleau-Ponty's theory of expression has recently come to the forefront of scholars, each of whom formulates the meaning of expression in a singular, somewhat different way: *mise en forme*, excess, exscription.[28] These notions, each in its own way, point toward the paradoxical enigma of expression: painting and writing, whether prosaic or poetic per se, seek to maintain contact with the thing all the while creating new forms, which is to say authentic expression is "thing-image" in painting, photography, and cinema or "thing-word" in literary expression and this makes of expression an *event*, a happening of the new within the given.

In the "Indirect Language" chapter of *The Prose of the World* as well as the longer, augmented essay published in *Signs*, "Indirect Language and the Voices of Silence," Merleau-Ponty speaks of the equivalence that is yet heterogeneous between thing and expression as a "coherent deformation" (S, 68/54), and the phrase is an adaptation from Malraux.[29] In the central passage to which I wish to draw attention, Merleau-Ponty speaks first explicitly about painting and then moves toward language. He begins by saying that the picture of a woman is not in the woman seen, because that would mean the painting was already completed, yet the painter's expression must be "at least called for by her [*du moins appelés par elle*]" (S, 68/54). "Called for" in the sense of *appelés* connotes the way in which we are named, what we are called in introducing ourselves, for example, *je m'appelle*. The "call" expressed in the painting bears the same relationship and same kind of necessity as between the individual and her name. Thus, Merleau-Ponty immediately writes: "There is signification when we submit the data of the world [the givens, *les données*] to a 'coherent deformation'" (S, 68/54). Such a coherent deformation comprises the meaning of "style," which is not a subjective nuance of feeling, nor certain techniques of handling brushes and paint, nor even the name or signature of the painter. Rather, style is this unique relationship of both coherence and creativity (deformation) between an expression and the thing expressed, as called for by the thing. Merleau-Ponty puts it succinctly: "For each painter, style is the system of equivalences that he makes for himself for the work which manifests the world he sees. It is the universal index of the 'coherent deformation' by which he concentrates the still scattered meaning of his perception and makes it exist expressly" (S, 68/54–55).

Merleau-Ponty's essay moves from painting to poetry explicitly in terms of style as an "acquired voice . . . which announces itself in lightning signs (*des signes fulgurants*) as a spoken word or an arabesque" (S, 65/52). He asks: Why should expression of the world be limited to the prose of the senses or the concept? "It must be poetry; that is, it must completely awaken and recall our sheer power of expressing beyond things already said or seen" (S, 65/52). Lightning is a recurrent Merleau-Pontian metaphor for newness, miracle, mystery, and event, and we want to give it its due in our section on *éclatement* (explosion) that follows. Arabesque is conversely rare. While the arabesque may figure as the curved space in drawing, painting, and sculpture, it also is a figure of the body's flexible equilibrium in dance, a posture of the body bent forward supported on one leg with the other leg extended horizontally backward, one arm extended forward, the other backward. Merleau-Ponty asks us to consider the poetic line as similarly arabesque, a flowing, intricate, complex poise of balance stretching back and reaching forward. Poetic language is a "going beyond" and a "going further" in the voice and style of the writer, yet anchored and "called" by the things. Poetic words are the twinning of things, but the words are nonidentical twins that reveal the things in previously unseen and unthought-of ways.

Thus, Merleau-Ponty argues, when we rid ourselves of the idea of language and expression as imitation or the "translation" of an "original text," then we understand that "the idea of *complete* expression is nonsensical, and that all language is indirect or allusive—that it is, if you wish, silence" (S, 54/43). "Modern painters," Merleau-Ponty states, and by extension we would add modern poets, "want nothing to do with a truth defined as the resemblance of painting and world. They would accept the idea of a truth defined as a painting's cohesion with itself, the presence of a unique principle in it which affects each means of expression with a certain contextual value. . . . what replaces the object is not the subject—it is the allusive logic of the perceived world" (S, 71/57). In *The Visible and the Invisible*, Merleau-Ponty wrote of language as the power of rendering visible the invisibilities that he called the "lining and depth" of the visible (VI, 195/149): such invisibilities as hidden things, things not noticed but passed over, things elsewhere, and even more deeply, self and spiritual forms as well. The French word translated as "lining" is *la doublure*, literally the interior or lining of a garment, expressing the intimacy between outside and inside, between visible and invisible. Merleau-Ponty wrote of language as life: "Language is a life, is our life and the life of things . . . not a mask over Being but—if one knows how to grasp it with all its roots and all its foliation, the most valuable witness to Being" (VI, 167/127).

To return to Valéry for a moment and ideas we were developing in Chapter 3, we might consider this "living language" in relation to Valéry's succinct account of poetic language, which he presents as a poetic ideal more felicitous than achievable by any real person, himself included.

> The poet, then, dedicates and sacrifices himself to the task of defining and constructing a language within language . . . to constitute the speech of a man who is purer, more powerful and profound in his thoughts, more intense in his life, more elegant and felicitous in his speech, than any real person. This extraordinary speech we perceive and recognize in the rhythm and in the harmonies that sustain it, and that must be so intimately and even so mysteriously bound to its origins that the sound and sense, no longer separable, inexhaustibly correspond each to each in our memory. (CW, 8:209/O, 1:611)

These are remarkable phrases that Valéry attributes to the ideal poet: "language within language," "elegant and felicitous speech," and "extraordinary speech." Merleau-Ponty employed a very similar phrase, "the eloquent language," in *The Visible and the Invisible* and identifies it with the language of philosophy:

> the words most charged with philosophy are not necessarily those that contain what they say, but rather those that most energetically open upon Being . . . Hence it is a question whether philosophy as the

reconquest of brute or wild being can be accomplished by the resources of the eloquent language, or whether it would not be necessary for philosophy to use language in a way that takes from it its power of immediate or direct signification in order to equal it with what it wishes all the same to say. (VI, 139/102–3)

Here Merleau-Ponty attributes the resources of "the eloquent language" to philosophy, but he also seems to suggest that philosophical language must go beyond the eloquent language to one that has "the power of immediate or direct signification" with words that "most energetically open upon Being."

In opening this avenue of thought, there is a great temptation that should ultimately be resisted from the point of view of Merleau-Ponty and phenomenology. That is the suggestion of a kind of "pure poetry," or "pure philosophy" by extension. Valéry's text speaks of "the speech of a man who is purer, more powerful and profound in his thoughts." We have already considered the notion of "purity" in mathematics where Merleau-Ponty attributed it to the "clear relations of a system of signs that have no inner life" (PM, 169/121) and that get jumbled up when we consider the living, unfolding, and creative side of mathematical expression. Purity as this clear vision and thought is but one possibility; purity can mean almost as many things as the notion of "abstraction" in visual art—in fact abstraction itself may be considered a kind of purity. In modern painters of abstract expressionism like Newman and Rothko, abstraction or purity had to do with emptiness, a minimalism of the zip or band, that has a spiritual aspect; in another like de Kooning, it has to do with blurring the distinction between a specific image and its type, such as "woman," "door," or "river," a condensation of emotion into a swirl of paint and color. Klee defined abstraction as balancing the three formal elements of painting, line, shading (chiaroscuro), and color, "purely and logically so that each in its place is right and none clashes with the other."[30] Valéry was concerned and himself quite tempted by the thought of a "pure poetry" by which he meant something quite specific. In his lecture titled "Pure Poetry," Valéry considers the possibility and limits of pure poetic expression, using the word "pure" in the sense the physicist speaks of pure water. This would mean water that has been purified of contaminants through processes such as distillation and deionization. Such purified poetry might also be named "absolute poetry." "I have always held, and I still hold," Valéry writes, "that this aim is impossible to reach and that poetry is always a striving after this purely ideal state."[31] Valéry elaborates on the difficulty of pure poetry through an analogy with the musical universe of sounds within which, he believes, it is possible to speak of elements that are pure because they are well defined by instruments that are true instruments of measure, the tuning fork, the metronome, and the quality of the musical instruments themselves. Valéry means the analogy to highlight the distance between the means available to the musician in contrast with the poet, who is constrained by the practical and "clumsy" instrument of everyday language: "For him [the poet] there was no physicist to determine the relations between these means; there was no constructor of scales; no tuning fork, no metronome; no certainty in that direction; all he has is the clumsy instrument of the dictionary and grammar."[32] Extending the musical analogy with poetry, Valéry suggests one could only think of pure poetry as something that existed if the poet managed to create "poems in which the musical continuity was never broken, in which the relations between meanings were themselves perpetually similar to harmonic relations, *in which the transmutation of thoughts into each other appeared more important than any thought.* It is not so."[33] Though the pragmatic aspects of language having to do with everyday living and needs make the "creations of absolute poetry impossible . . . the notion of such an ideal or imaginary state is most valuable." Sounding like a Kantian regulative idea, Valéry concludes "the conception of pure poetry is that of an inaccessible type, an ideal boundary of the poet's desires, efforts, and powers."[34]

Valéry, though tempted, draws up short before the ideal of a "pure poetry." Rather than pure or purified poetry or philosophy, going further than the "eloquent language" brings us to language that is concrete, colorful, and anchored in sensible experience. The very condition of the possibility of philosophy is metaphor, or more precisely, "metaphoricity," as Emmanuel de Saint Aubert has defined it in the preceding chapter of this book. The most important ideas the poet and the philosopher seek to articulate are "sensible ideas," such as the musical idea, the literary idea, "the dialectic of love," and the painter's "articulations of the light." Sensible ideas cannot be detached from their sensible appearances and give us our knowledge, not only of painting, literature, and music, but also our knowledge of emotions, and indeed, "also the experience of the visible world" (VI, 196/149). Merleau-Ponty puts it this way: these are ideas that "could not be given to us *as ideas* except in a carnal experience . . . it is that they owe their authority, their fascinating, indestructible power, precisely to the fact that they are in transparency behind the sensible, or in its heart" (VI, 194/150). Such sensible knowing is less precise conceptually than intellectual ideas of "pure ideality" and necessarily are somewhat "veiled with shadows" (VI, 195/150).[35] Here again we come to the veil: "we no longer believe that truth remains truth when the veils are withdrawn," yet this does not mean that any veil will do.

The Explosion of Expression

The "slippage" or "play" that necessarily occurs between the thing expressed and the word or image of its expression is the first side of paradox of expression. But a second side is "the patient and silent labor of desire" from which expression begins. This claim that artistic and poetic expression grow from roots grounded in desire will bring us to considerations of truth in its branching aspects of intersubjectivity and love. We will approach these matters beginning from a new idea of truth.

We are now in a position to approach Merleau-Ponty's Working Note on *éclatement*. He writes: "*Pregnancy*: the psychologists forget that this means a power to break forth (*pouvoir d'éclatement*), productivity (*praegnans futuri*), fecundity" (VI, 262/208). Merleau-Ponty found himself increasingly drawn to the use of the nouns, *éclatement* and *éclat*, and the verb *éclater* throughout his last writings, especially *The Visible and the Invisible*. In addition to the Working Note of September 1959 just cited, among many other texts we find one such as this: "Lived experience is not flat, without depth, without dimension, it is not an opaque stratum with which we would have to merge. The appeal to the originating (*l'originaire*) goes in several directions: the originating breaks up (*l'originaire éclate*), and philosophy must accompany this break-up (*cet éclatement*), this non-coincidence, this differentiation" (VI, 165/124). *Éclat* and *éclatement* are often paired with the ontological notion of the "dehiscence" of Being: "The aesthetic world to be described as a space of transcendence, a space of incompossibilities, of explosion, of dehiscence, and not as objective-immanent space" (VI, 269–70/216). Thus, Merleau-Ponty gives an ontological weight to "dehiscence," a botanical term for the bursting open of seed pods when ripe to discharge their contents. Dehiscence and *éclatement* operate as a pair and the latter is the more forceful of the two, even violent, for *éclatement* means principally an "explosion or deflagration," particularly that of a bomb, and is directly related to the verb *éclater* meaning "to explode, to burst, to blow up, to break (thunderstorm)." The noun *éclat* means a "splinter, shard, sliver, brightness, glare, glitter, radiance, and sparkle," as the sparkle of a diamond. An essay by Jean-Luc Nancy found in *The Inoperative Community* is translated into English as "Shattered Love" ("*L'amour en éclats*"). The word "shatters" is *éclats* as we might speak of shattered glass. Nancy writes: "Love arrives in all the forms and in all the figures of love; it is projected in all its shatters. . . . Love flies into pieces as soon as it is sent."³⁶ Marta Nijhuis, artist as well as translator of Chapters 1 and 4 of this work, recently mounted an important exhibition of her painting, the catalog for which was titled *Éclats naissants* ("nascent radiances").³⁷

An explosion flashes, and the explosion of literary language that comes from "elsewhere" like the stars of the constellations lends it a radiance, radiation, brilliance, and light. In his last lecture course on *Philosophy and Non-Philosophy Since Hegel* that we have studied in relation to Nietzsche's *The Gay Science*, Merleau-Ponty referred to "a new idea of light" (*une nouvelle idée de la lumière*) that is closely connected with a new idea of truth (NC, 305/40). Here Merleau-Ponty is translating and commenting upon the first of the last four paragraphs of Hegel's *Phenomenology of Spirit* in which Hegel wrote about the nature of experience (*Erfahrung*) in relation to the meaning of dialectic, which, Hegel writes, "throws a new light" on the meaning of experience. If experience is understood dialectically, it must now be understood as a process of negation and renewal (*Aufheben*), and Hegel adds: "This is where the ambiguity (*Zweideutigkeit*) of this truth enters."³⁸ Merleau-Ponty's commentary takes the opportunity to seize upon Hegel's phrase, "throws a new light," to introduce his own concern with a "new idea of light," which must be characterized precisely in terms of the ambiguity Hegel describes. Merleau-Ponty writes: "A new idea of light is at work here. The true is of itself 'ambiguous.' . . . The 'polysemy' (*Vieldeutigkiet*) is not a shadow to eliminate true light. The true cannot be defined as coincidence and outside of all difference (*écart*) in relation to the true" (NC, 305/40). Polysemy emphasizes the multiplicity of meanings; ambiguity also has the sense of multiple meanings given at once. Merleau-Ponty illustrates the dialectical meaning Hegel assigns to "experience" with the example of "true friendship." As commonly understood, he writes, if experience encounters a new object, this devalues the old object. In Hegel's sense, on the contrary, "the knowledge of the old object becomes the new object. For example, what I projected about this friendship, once projected before me in the object, becomes the truth of this friendship" (NC, 307/41). The friendship becomes true, there is a process and a growth that involves both negation and renewal or deepening, a process of self-transcendence.

A New Idea of Truth (Light)

There is in Merleau-Ponty's late thought the search for a new idea of light that does not eliminate shadow and yields a new idea of truth that does not eliminate ambiguity and multiplicity (polysemy). Moreover, each of these is connected with the truth of a life, the truth of a friendship. About the new idea of light, Mauro Carbone has spoken of "the light of the Flesh" in Merleau-Ponty's later thinking, "to no longer conceive the giving of the true by following the traditional opposition—built by Plato in the Allegory of the Cave—between the deceiving shadows of what appears and the pure light emanating from truth. The giving of the true shall rather be conceived on the basis of an essential complementarity between light and shade."[39] Carbone associates this kind of light with the notion of the "diffused lighting of logos" in the nature philosophy of Schelling, as well as the "voice of light" that Merleau-Ponty speaks of in *Eye and Mind* drawn from the *Poimandres* by Hermes Trismegistus: "Art is not construction, artifice, the meticulous relationship to a space and a world existing outside. It is truly the 'inarticulate cry,' as Hermes Trismegistus said, 'which seemed to be the voice of the light'" (OE, 70/142). The creation story from *Pimander* begins from light and moves first to darkness and then to something of a watery nature out of which comes the inarticulate cry of the voice of fire (light). In the unfinished course of 1960–61, "Cartesian Ontology and Ontology Today," Merleau-Ponty repeats the phrase "the cry of light (*cri de lumière*)" that he contrasts over against the Cartesian notion of the "natural light" of reason (*lumière naturelle*) as its direct opposite (NC, 182).[40]

When we touch upon the metaphor of light, we are touching a founding metaphor of Western philosophy that we should not hurry by, for it persists from Plato through Descartes and the Enlightenment to Hegel and Schelling on to Merleau-Ponty and beyond. Plato analogized the highest Form, the highest truth of philosophy regarding the Good and the Beautiful (*kalagathon*), with the Sun, which has led Derrida to introduce the term "photology" to describe "the entire history of our philosophy."[41] Derrida is critical of this metaphor of darkness and light, and is also critical of metaphor in general, which he terms "the *analogical* displacement of Being" as "the essential weight which anchors discourse in metaphysics."[42] Here Derrida echoes Heidegger's critique of metaphor from *The Principle of Reason*, as discussed in Saint Aubert's previous chapter. Rather than reject out of hand light and metaphor, when Merleau-Ponty touches the topic of light he seeks to shift it to a new idea of light as various and varied "lightings" in which light is no longer portrayed as an ideal of truth with a direct and univocal analogical relationship with the Sun.[43] Varied and multiple "lightings" shift the fundamental idea of truth to a new idea of "the true" and "truthfulness" best found in literary and poetic language. Rather than the Sun, the softer, cooler, reflected lunar light of the night sky is more apt, as is the twilight of dusk when shadows lengthen and a contemplative, meditative feeling settles upon the landscape. Poetic truth is mobile rather than static, a truth of becoming rather than of being. Truth in art, life, and poetry are about movement, growth, and becoming. Poetic truth and truth in life will be characterized not by the universality of its language but by its particularity, which is to say a particularity or singularity that opens onto a universality, the kind of "weak" universalism discussed earlier. This kind of hermeneutic truth is known not for its stability but for its agility, its ability to remain subtle, supple, deep, and rich.[44]

Pursuing the analogy between language and light, poetic language offers multiple lightings, enlightenments, and different types of luminescence. The intense brightness of incandescent lighting all but eliminates shadows and generates almost as much heat as light. In addition to the natural lunar light of nightfall and the twilight of dusk, the luminescence of phosphorence may best express the genius of poetic language, for it glows with light without emitting heat and continues to emit light long after the source of radiation has ended, like the glow of phosphorescent stars on the ceiling of the room of a child at night. In the play by William Luce, *The Belle of Amherst*, about the life and poetry of Emily Dickinson, the well-imagined poet exclaims: "To find that phosphorescence, that light within, that's the genius behind poetry."[45] It is doubtful that this expression is literally that of the poet herself,[46] yet "phosphorescence" captures important qualities of poetic light and truth. Of truth, Emily Dickinson gave us this poem:

> Tell all the Truth but tell it slant—
> Success in Circuit lies
> Too bright for our infirm Delight
> The Truth's superb surprise
> As Lightning to the Children eased
> With explanation kind
> The Truth must dazzle gradually
> Or every man be blind—[47]

The "slant" of truth should not be taken in the sense of a slanted or "false" perspective, rather it is the mobility of the becoming of truth that Dickinson captures with the surprise of children dazzled gradually.

Stephen Spender, a member of the Oxford Group in the 1930s that included W. H. Auden, and who became poet laureate of the United States appointed by the Library of Congress in 1965, commented upon Gauguin's beautiful, much discussed, and controversial painting of his young mistress, *The Spirit of the Dead Walking*. Here phosphorescence plays an altered role in Gauguin's own account: "I lit the matches quickly and then I saw her quite still and naked, lying on her stomach on the bed; and her eyes immensely large in fear looked at me without seeming to know me. . . . I seemed to see a phosphorescence in the light from those fixed eyes."[48] Thus the poetic meanings of phosphorescence include a wider range also invoking feelings of fear, anxiety, and dread, as they appear in the Gothic literature of *Dracula* and H. P. Lovecraft and even Arthur Conan Doyle's *Hound of the Baskervilles*: "The huge jaws seemed to be dripping with a bluish flame and the small, deep-set, cruel eyes were ringed with fire. I placed my hand upon the glowing muzzle, and as I held them up my own fingers smoldered and gleamed in the darkness. 'Phosphorus,' I said."[49]

Stephen Spender wrote a stanza of one of his poems about time he spent with Merleau-Ponty by the lake in Geneva, Switzerland:

> Their voices heard, I stumble suddenly,
> Choking in undergrowth. I'm torn
> Mouth pressed against the thorns,
>   remembering
> Ten years ago here in Geneva,
> I walked with Merleau-Ponty by the lake.
> Upon his face I saw his intellect.
> The energy of the sun-interweaving
> Waves, electric, danced on him. His eyes
> Black coins thrown down from leaves. He who
> Was Merleau-Ponty that day is no more
> Irrevocable than the I that day who was
> Beside him—I'm still living![50]

Spender not only met the philosopher personally and was one of the discussants at the "East-West Encounter" (*Rencontre Est-Oest à Venice*), a major conference in Venice in 1956,[51] Spender wrote his poem in May 1964 following upon Merleau-Ponty's death in May 1961. It is clear that Spender also knew key aspects of Merleau-Ponty's later philosophy: Interweaving is particularly apt—interweaving, interlacing, chiasm.

If such polysemy of meaning and hermeneutic of truth may seem to render problematic any meaning of the "permanence" and "eternality" of truth, Merleau-Ponty takes up these questions in his course of 1959–60 titled "Husserl at the Limits of Phenomenology." He examined Husserl's essay on "The Origin of Geometry" within which there is a recurring emphasis on Husserl's use of the polyphonic term "interweaving" (*Verflechtung*), one of which is the interweaving of the Written and the ideal. This is the interweaving of writing with the traditions of thought and culture we inherit that make possible their endurance, permanence, and ideality. Merleau-Ponty writes: "*The Written*, foundation of the permanence and of the preexistence of ideality . . . we will see that there is *Verflechtung* and simultaneity between it and ideality" (HLP, 78/64).[52] Geometry, calculus, and literature are "permanent as meaning," as "sedimented sense" (HLP,

69/57). Therefore, "sedimentation, forgetfulness, is not a defect of ideality: it is constitutive of ideality" (HLP, 69/57). The danger of a kind of reductionist scientific writing and practice, "scientism," is to mistake the sedimentation of tradition for an ideality outside all time and place. In fact, the Written is a "more profound truth," a "militant truth," Merleau-Ponty says, that is larger than logical certainty and is "the interweaving of original formations and sedimentations of sense" (HLP, 80/66). Through these expressions, "more profound truth" and "militant truth," Merleau-Ponty arrives at one of the most salient and provocative statements of his own concept of philosophy. The *Wesen*, or essence, of philosophy, he writes, "can be grasped only in filigree (*filigrane*), as a secret or hidden connection. . . . Philosophy seeks in the archeology of the ground, in the depth and not in the height (the ideas) . . . philosophy as poetry" (HLP, 81/67).[53] The word "filigree" refers to a "watermark [*filigrane*]," the term Merleau-Ponty uses in a note of *The Prose of the World* (PM, 53/37)[54] in order to signify that "it is essential . . . to truth never to be possessed, but only transparent through the clouded [*brouillée*] logic of a system of expression which bears the traces of another past and the seeds of another future" (PM, 52–53/37). Customarily, Merleau-Ponty does not identify philosophy with poetry, as he suggests here, construing them to overlap in the usage of literary, poetic language, yet this text goes all in, we might say: "philosophy as poetry."

Merleau-Ponty continues this analysis to argue there is a retrospective illusion when any science or other form of knowledge is accorded the standing of "eternal truth" divorced from the primacy of experience and history. His statement in this regard is found in the 1953 course, *Le monde sensible et le monde de l'expression*:

> Even our reflection on perception belongs to culture. The truth of perceptual phenomena presents itself as truth *of* these phenomena in spite of the "retrograde movement" of thematized truth. The latter mustn't blind us to the structural changes that it introduces. The complete examination of the "world of expression" is also an examination of this examination. Consciousness can't ultimately be only of thematized truth, but of the latter + the perceptual {?}. Origin of the truth. (MSME, 64: "Development of a Theory of Rationality")[55]

Here Merleau-Ponty uses the phrase, "the origin of truth," to designate a mixture of tradition that we receive and ongoing perception, itself being the mixture of movement and expression. The "retrograde movement of truth" is an illusion Bergson had analyzed, whereby a truth once discovered, is retrojected backward in time to lend it an aura of eternality, forgetting that things and events happen at certain moments in time, that what is real is movement and duration. In Bergson's literary imagery from *The Creative Mind*: "Let us unfasten the cocoon, awaken the chrysalis; let us restore to movement its mobility, to change its fluidity, to time its duration."[56]

"A More Profound Truth": The Truth of Love

Merleau-Ponty's poetic of truth has taken us far beyond abstractions of propositional truth, what Heidegger called "mere correctness," toward mobility, fluidity, and intersubjective life. Merleau-Ponty knew all along from the beginning that developing a new idea of truth would require developing a new idea of intersubjectivity. He said so explicitly in the prospectus for his candidacy for the professorship at the Collège de France: "I found in the experience of the perceived world a new type of relation between the mind and truth. . . . We are obliged to answer these questions first with a theory of truth and then with a theory of intersubjectivity."[57] What we hold true is corroborated, questioned, further elaborated, and altered in the presence of others and in the speech of others, in our speaking together, which is dialogue. Merleau-Ponty wrote: "The foundation of truth is not outside of time; it is in the opening of each moment of knowledge to those who will resume it and change its sense" (PM, 200/144). Even in creating the presentation in 1950 for a new series of works in the Bibliothèque de Philosophie to be directed by himself together with Jean-Paul Sartre, Merleau-Ponty spoke of the necessity of intersubjective dialogue in the forging of philosophical truth: "One reflects in order to understand oneself, but one is sure to be understood only by explaining oneself before others, by entering into their perspective. Thus a particular situation is only finally understood in relation to all the others, whether they be philosophers, historians, or scholars of all inclinations entering into dialogue and establishing [*constituent*] effective philosophy."[58]

Merleau-Ponty's trajectory was to develop a theory of intersubjectivity through a new or renewed concept of the Unconscious as a perceiving consciousness, thus an enlargement of the phenomenology of perception and embodiment. In the résumé of his last *Nature* lecture course of 1959–60, in its section titled "Nature and Logos: The Human Body," we find the direction of this vector: "The double formula of the Unconscious ('I did not know' and 'I have always known it') corresponds to two aspects of the flesh, its poetic and oneiric power" (RC, 179/198). The oneiric and poetic desires of perception open onto "shatters" of life and the love of the world and others. Thus, through Freud and beyond in Merleau-Ponty, we are led to a conception of desire as "the openness to the world" (VI, 57/35). It is from such openness that expression is born. In the *Nature* lectures, developing the thought of Hegel that Nature is the weakness of the Idea, Merleau-Ponty argues that life is both fragility and obstinacy; it "will be, if nothing opposes it," a nearly inextinguishable will to life. However, this is not "a hard nucleus of being, but the softness of the flesh. . . . life is an investment, a singular point, a hollow in Being" (Natu, 302/238).

Merleau-Ponty increasingly turned to this term "hollow" (*le creux*) in his late philosophy to discuss the meaning of soul or subjectivity and openness. In a lengthy Working Note from January 1960 in which Merleau-Ponty takes up perception, movement, self-movement, and transcendence, he poses, once again, the problem of the relations between the soul (subjectivity) and the body. Rather than an "opacity of nature" or a parallelism between two positive substances, the soul–body relation "is the bond between the convex and the concave, between the solid vault (*la voûte*) and the hollow it forms (*du creux*)" (VI, 286/232). The "solid vault (*la voûte*)" is an architectural structure that is generally a concave work constructed of stone, brick, or concrete covering an empty space. It is a curved arch or set of curved arches to form a vault (roof, canopy) that is open below, often placed at the entrance to public buildings. The space below is a hollow or space of light and air, the concave of the convex, the hollow in the solid vault or arch through which one enters and exits the building or walks through laterally. "*Le creux*" is also the hollow of a horseshoe and "*le creux de la main*" is the hollow of the hand. This hollow of the arch, horseshoe, or hand is the space of light—also air—that is the meaning of subjectivity.[59] The point of Merleau-Ponty's image of the relation of body and soul is not only their inseparability, but the penetrability of soul that creates the permeability, the openness, of the body. A few sentences later he combines the image of vault and hollow with another: "The soul is *planted* in the body as the stake in the ground—or rather: the soul is the hollow of the body, the body is the distention of the soul" (VI, 286/233). The soul as "the stake in the ground" suggests the thought of the human as a vertical being in the landscape, but it is a more forceful metaphor that connotes pounding or driving the soul into the body, already bearing the connotation of the soul being vulnerable or wounded.

Desire understood and defined as the openness of the ensouled body to the world is a transcendental condition of possibility for human expression. Body without soul is impenetrable mass or matter; body with soul is life, self-movement, and creativity. In a rare moment of praise for Cartesianism, Merleau-Ponty wrote in a Working Note of February 1, 1960, titled "Human body—Descartes": "The Cartesian idea of the human body as human *non-closed*, open inasmuch as governed by thought—is perhaps the most profound idea of the union of the soul and the body. It is the soul intervening in a body that is *not of the in itself* . . . that can be a body and living—human only by reaching completion in a 'view of itself' which is thought" (VI, 288/234).

In a complication of this openness comes the vulnerability and woundedness love also makes possible. Merleau-Ponty incorporated the words *Noli me tangere* ("Do not touch me") into his lecture courses of 1954–55, *Institution and Passivity*, in relation to his interpretation of Proust's *The Fugitive*, the fifth volume of *In Search of Lost Time*, which raises many profound questions about the narrator and the nature of his love for Albertine. The narrator *knows* he loves Albertine only when she is absent from him with other people, which creates the ambivalence between love and jealousy, and finally when he learns that Albertine is dead, which creates the ambivalence between love and grief. And here this is actual and genuine ambivalence, not the "good ambiguity" (*Zweideutigkeit*) that frames Merleau-Ponty's account of "transitional objects."[60] Thus, whether the ambivalence of love is with jealousy or with grief, it was not the existence of Albertine that Marcel desired, and thus one might easily speak of the "impossibility of love, the 'error' of love" (IP, 73/36). However, the true error, Merleau-Ponty writes, "lies in believing that it [love] is only an error" (IP, 74/37). The implicit background is Sartre's arguments for the impossibility of love in the section of *Being and Nothingness* describing our being-for-others. Against Sartre, Merleau-Ponty extends the argument:

> Love entails a beyond oneself, the very beyond of the false desire of possession . . . the truth is beyond what would please me or what would calm my anxiety. Like death, love is what reveals the "personality." It allows us to see everything that someone is, how someone is the world itself, being itself, a world, a being from which we are excluded; in the experience undergone of this pain, one is beyond desire and domination. (IP, 74/37–38)

If the narrator loves Albertine only in her absence from him, either absent in place and time while present with others or absent in death, then his love is hopelessly intertwined with jealousy and grief. To the narrator, Merleau-Ponty concludes, "Albertine is present at a distance like the little phrase in its sounds, not separable from them and yet intangible, *noli me tangere*. Cf. Proust, *Time Regained*: grief teaches you how to see" (IP, 74/38). The "little phrase in its sounds" is the musical phrase from Vinteuil's posthumous *Septet* that the narrator heard in an evening filled with premonitions of their imminent breakup. Merleau-Ponty writes that "we do not possess the musical or sensible ideas . . . they possess us" (VI, 198/151). This is not the musical phrase from Vinteuil's *Sonata* that was the "national anthem" of the love of Swann in his romance with Odette.⁶¹ In this musical phrase from the *Septet*, Albertine was present to the narrator, but only at a distance, intangible, as Merleau-Ponty says, resonant with grief. Here in the context of Proust's novel the command *noli me tangere* is functioning in relation to the distance between the narrator and Albertine, which, if it be love at all, expresses the pain and grief of absence, of a breakup without the promise of reunion. Merleau-Ponty writes, "the love for Albertine was the anticipation of separation and of death, the 'binary rhythm' was a prenotion, a 'more profound' truth" (IP, 75/38). He concludes with this account of this more profound truth of love:

> In exchange for what we had imagined, life gives us something else, and something else that was secretly willed, not fortuitous. Realization is not what was foreseen, but nevertheless what was willed. We advance by recoiling, we do not choose directly, but obliquely, but we nevertheless do what we want. Love is clairvoyant; it addresses us precisely to what is able to tear us apart. (IP, 75/38)

Love like truth, love as truth, advances obliquely, like the laterigrade, sideways movement of the crab. Yet love is also clairvoyant, it sees further and beyond; it is a distant vision but also "a vision from up close": "realization is not what was foreseen, but nevertheless what was willed" (IP, 75/38).

From the instituting of a love, Merleau-Ponty extends the analysis to the instituting of an artwork. He writes: "Institution of a work, like the institution of a love, [intends a] sense as open sense, which develops by means of proliferation, by curves, de-centering and recentering, zigzag, ambiguous passage, with a sort of identity between whole and parts, the beginning and end. A sort of existential eternity by means of self-interpretation" (IP, 87/48–49). Love and art are both movements and developments that move off center and then center again, curving and zigzagging from a shared beginning to a shared end.

In the lecture course on "The Problem of Passivity," Merleau-Ponty approached the "last problem" of his expanded ontology, "which is truth and subjectivity, freedom." The true is here joined with the "me-others hinge" (IP, 179/134). This is about the "coexistence of subjects who are gathered together through truth as *a-letheia*" (IP, 180/135). He names this the *Vernunftproblem*, which is the "problem of reason." In this openness onto truth in the region of intersubjectivity, we come to common life, which requires "that no one claims to be absolutely in the right or absolutely wrong" (IP, 180/135). Merleau-Ponty calls this a "probabilism," not as the calculation of probabilities such as the chances of an event occurring, but "probabilism in the sense of the maximum of truth at the moment." He concludes: "Perception as the revelation of a new sense of truth, not of adequation, which suppresses the plurality of subjects and of perspectives, but as movement toward integration, openness" (IP, 180–81/135).

Love is not pure, like poetry and poetic truth itself, philosophy also. In a Working Note of November 1960, Merleau-Ponty states clearly regarding philosophy: "It shows by words. Like all literature. . . . No absolutely pure philosophical word" (VI, 319/266).[62] There is openness and there is openness; openness to the world is confirmed and raised to a higher power in openness to the other, with its constellation of complicated and complex feelings. Merleau-Ponty elaborated further these complications in the "Indirect Language" chapter of *The Prose of the World*, speaking even of "obsession":

> We are saying that in the same cultural world everyone's thoughts lead a hidden life in the others, as a kind of obsession, each being moved by the other and entangled with him the moment he begins to offer resistance. This is not a skeptical principle; on the contrary, it is a principle of truth. We really inhabit the same world and are open to truth precisely because there arises this diffusion among thoughts, this osmosis which makes the cloistering of thought impossible and deprives of all meaning the question of to whom a thought belongs. (PM, 133/94)

Perhaps this is one reason among others why the love poem is the apex of poetry and poetic feeling, the content one does not attempt until life and language have seasoned and matured. Likewise, the philosophy of love has always been the highest point of philosophical thought, yet it is the most difficult to approach without trivializing, cliché upon cliché. This is how Nancy begins his essay on "Shattered Love," the shatters, splinters, bursts, and splendors of love (*éclats*), wondering if a philosopher will be able to say or write anything that does not merely skate on surfaces without depth or profundity. "The thinking of love, so ancient, so abundant and diverse in its forms and in its modulations, asks for an extreme reticence as soon as it is solicited. It is a question of modesty, perhaps, but it is also a question of exhaustion: has not everything been said on the subject of love?"[63] Yet Nancy argues that thinking itself is love, certainly the kind of thinking that is philosophy: "Love does not call for a certain kind of thinking, or for a thinking of love, but for thinking in essence and in its totality. And this is because thinking, most properly speaking, is love. . . . Without this love, the exercise of the intellect or of reason would be utterly worthless."[64]

We find further elaboration of the nature and meaning of dialogue and intersubjectivity in the chapter of *The Prose of the World* titled "Dialogue and the Perception of the Other." At the beginning of the chapter, Merleau-Ponty seems to be thinking of intersubjectivity as a movement building from the self outward to the other, in which the other person will be made in my own image, we might say. He writes, for example: "The other's body is a kind of replica of myself, a wandering double which haunts my surroundings more than it appears in them. The other's body is the unexpected response I get from elsewhere, as if by a miracle things began to tell my thoughts" (PM, 186/134). Nevertheless, from this beginning Merleau-Ponty wonders how to reverse the directionality and genuinely enter into the thought and life of others. He asks himself, "how can I decenter myself?" (PM, 188/135). There comes a glimmer of that decentering for which Merleau-Ponty was searching: "Myself and the other are like two *nearly concentric* circles which can be distinguished only by a mysterious slippage" (PM, 186/134). He adds that this decentering and slippage will be inconceivable if our approach to an other is direct, "like a sheer cliff," which means a one-to-one faceoff.[65] Our relationship with an other is not a relation of two positivities but a relation of "two opennesses" that are charged and together create an attraction, an expectancy. Merleau-Ponty writes: "In reality there is neither me nor the other as positive, positive subjectivities. There are two caverns [*antres* = caverns, lair, den, hideout], two opennesses, two stages where something will take place—and which both belong to the same world, to the stage of Being. . . . They are each the other side of the other. This is why they incorporate one another" (VI, 317/263).

He points out that if a book or another person really teaches us something, we must come to a juncture at which we are "surprised, disoriented": "In the perception of the other, this happens when the other organism, instead of 'behaving' like me, engages with the things in my world in a style that is at first mysterious to me but which at least seems to me a coherent style because it responds to certain possibilities which fringed the things in my world" (PM, 197–98/142). Such a decentering and slippage of self portends a different account of rationality, that "does not require that we all reach the same idea by the same road, or that significations be enclosed in definitions. It requires only that every experience contain points of catch for all other ideas and the 'ideas' have a configuration. This double requirement is the postulation of a *world*" (PM, 198–99/143). When Merleau-Ponty says "world" in this context, he means the cultural world, chief among which is our power of speech and poetic language.

The last paragraph of Merleau-Ponty's "Dialogue" chapter asks this remarkable question: "In the end, what should we call this power to which we are vowed, and which, however we feel, pulls significations from us?" "This power to which we are vowed,"[66] what is this power, this charge and magnetism? He answers this way:

> Certainly, it is not a god, since its operation depends upon us. It is not an evil genius, since it bears the truth. It is not the "human condition"—or, if it is "human," it is so in the sense that man destroys the generality of the species and brings himself to admit others into his deepest singularity. It is still by calling it speech and spontaneity that we best designate this ambiguous gesture which makes the universal out of singulars and meaning out of our life [*et du sens avec notre vie*]. (PM, 203/146)

Speech and dialogue, "make meaning out of our life," or more simply, if we are willing to risk, they make the meaning of life. At the end of his Sorbonne lecture "The Child's Relations with Others," Merleau-Ponty speaks of adult or mature love and says this: "From the moment when one is joined with someone else, one suffers from her suffering. . . . One is not what he would be without that love, the perspectives remain separate—and yet they overlap. One can no longer say, 'This is mine, this is yours'; the roles cannot be absolutely separated. . . . [Love] tears me away from my lone self and creates instead a mixture of myself and the other."[67]

While stressing the conjuncture of truth with love and dialogue, Merleau-Ponty was not blind to the "truths" of his times, and ours, which are increasingly polarized and absent from the kind of dialogical rationality he articulated. At the end of "Man and Adversity," he noted that "conversation is becoming difficult" between Christians and non-Christians, Marxists and non-Marxists. He was thinking about an altered reality and altered happiness: "Sometimes one starts to dream about what culture, literary life, and teaching could be if all those who participate, having for once rejected idols, would give themselves up to the happiness of reflecting together" (S, 308/242). Wistfully it seems, he then adds: "But this dream is not reasonable. The discussions of our time are so convulsive only because it is resisting a truth which is right at hand, and because in recognizing—without any intervening veil—the menace of adversity, it is closer perhaps than any other to recognizing the metamorphoses of Fortune" (S, 308/242–43). This plea for reasonable discussion and dialogue based upon a truth that is "right at hand" (*une vérité toute proche*) is left unspecified. Nevertheless in the context of the essay, it is plausible to suggest that Merleau-Ponty understands this truth in terms of the experiences and realities of artistic expression and creation,[68] successes and failures, a "militant truth" demanded by his times and ours, facing the "menace of adversity" and "metamorphoses of Fortune." In 1951, when Merleau-Ponty wrote this text, we see that he was already anticipating the commingling of hope and the tragic, of light with shadow, that we have encountered in his later thought. Here again, too, is the ambiguous meaning of the "veil," both hiding and showing.

In the end, the truth of poetic and literary language is the truth of a world. We might appropriate Merleau-Ponty's words written of love and death and say that great poetry and literature "allow us to see everything that someone is, how someone is the world itself, being itself, a world" (IP, 74/37–38). The truth of literature is its power (*éclatement*) to join our world with the world of others. Sometimes it may be a world from which we may be excluded by pain and suffering, a world far from our own experience, or it may also be a world very near at hand. Dufrenne has written about this in relation to the music of Bach: "When we say that the joy expressed by a fugue opens Bach's world to us, the word 'world' indicates a relation to the real."[69] In this sense, Bach's world is true, and it is possible and painful that some may be barred from its truth. "Suppose that a captive in his prison," Dufrenne continues, "delivered to hatred and seeing the sky only 'beyond the rooftop,' hears a Bach fugue. He knows clearly that the music is not meant for him. Someone has banned him from the world of Bach, or he may have banned himself."[70] On the other hand, we may be introduced to a world into which we are able to be joined and enlarged, transformed and transfigured in shared experience, sympathy, and feeling, the joining of souls across times and places. This is the truth of literary worlds, their nobility and mobility, subtlety, suppleness, depth, and richness.

Acknowledgments

This work has been supported by many individuals and institutions to whom we are deeply grateful, and we wish to acknowledge them here, if all too briefly and inadequately. We acknowledge and deeply thank the book's precious translators, Janice Deary, who rendered the French texts of Emmanuel de Saint Aubert into beautiful English, and Marta Nijhuis, who has done equally beautiful English translation work for the chapters of Mauro Carbone, all the while successfully meeting her own demanding personal and professional engagements. We also thank Amy A. Foley for her many fruitful ideas and suggestions as well as her clear-sighted and finely detailed editorial work on all of the chapters of the book as their progress unfolded. We acknowledge and thank Naama Malomet for her work as research assistant in summer 2018 and Gianna Chaves in winter 2020.

The University of Rhode Island (URI) has supported this work financially in a number of ways, with the award of a sabbatical leave to Galen Johnson and award of financial grants from the URI Office of Research and Economic Development and from the URI Center for the Humanities. A two-year appointment to the Jane C. Ebbs Endowed Philosophy Professorship provided critical support in both time and funding. Travel grants have also been received from the URI Provost, Donald H. DeHayes, the consecutive deans of the College of Arts and Sciences, Winifred E. Brownell and Jeannette E. Riley, the Richard Beaupre Hope and Heritage Endowment, and the URI Alumni Association. We also thank the RI Council for the Humanities (RICH) for providing grant funding for a conference, "Phenomenology and the Arts Today," in spring 2017 where two of the book's authors were present and some of these ideas were shared and developed. All three coauthors have been privileged to present their work at conferences of the International Merleau-Ponty Circle and the Society for Phenomenology and Existential Philosophy (SPEP), and we thank all of our colleagues for their encouragement, support, and creative critiques on these occasions. For assistance with Greek texts and etymology as well as a visiting residency, I thank my brother, Tim Johnson, Dean of the School of Languages, Cultures, and World Affairs at the College of Charleston, South Carolina. Finally, we express profound thanks to Marjorie L. Johnson, fellow Merleau-Ponty scholar and daughter, for her interest, ideas, and assistance with French texts and translations, including the creation of the French transcription of our concluding Nyons workshop.

Emmanuel de Saint Aubert's research group, Archives Husserl de Paris (UMR 8547 Pays germaniques, CNRS-ENS), has provided crucial financial support for the translation work of Janice Deary. We gratefully acknowledge that this book has received the support of Translitteræ (École universitaire de recherche, program "Investissements d'avenir" ANR-10-IDEX-0001-02 PSL* and ANR-17-EURE-0025).

The Institut Universitaire de France Seniorship appointment was crucial in providing Mauro Carbone with the conditions to continue his research even in a period affected by health issues. Hence, he deeply thanks this most prestigious French institution. He is also extremely grateful to his coauthors and the publisher for waiting for a good resolution of these health issues with friendly understanding and warm support. Furthermore, for the enriching exchanges about the topics of his chapters, he would like to thank in particular Rajiv Kaushik and Claudio Rozzoni.

The two nonnative English authors of the present book cannot but be extremely grateful to the third coauthor for being the soul of this project's realization.

Finally, our deepest gratitude is to Jean, Hélène, and Marta, who have lent their support and encouragement and shared in the discovery and creation of these ideas.

—GAJ

Notes

Introduction

1. Merleau-Ponty (1908–61) is likely best known within aesthetics and its related ontology for his writings on modern painting: "Cézanne's Doubt" (1945), "Indirect Language and the Voices of Silence" (1951–52), and "Eye and Mind" (1960). See *The Merleau-Ponty Aesthetics Reader: Philosophy and Painting*, ed. Galen A. Johnson (Evanston, IL: Northwestern University Press, 1993). One finds in that work this final sentence of my preface: "A detailed and systematic study of these works [i.e., *Sense and Non-Sense* and *The Prose of the World*] and the philosophical questions of literary meaning would be a welcome complement to this philosophy of painting for rounding out the complete picture of Merleau-Ponty's aesthetic theory" (xv).

2. See ULL, 131, note 1, written by the directors of the transcription, Benedetta Zaccarello and Emmanuel de Saint Aubert.

3. In *Poetics* 1457b, Aristotle had given the classical definition: "A metaphor is a word with some other meaning which is transferred either from genus to species, or from species to genus, or from one species to another, or used by analogy." See also Paul Ricoeur, *The Rule of Metaphor: Multi-disciplinary Studies of the Creation of Meaning in Language*, trans. Robert Czerny, with Kathleen McLaughlin and John Costello SJ (Toronto: University of Toronto Press, 1977), 14; French original: *La métaphore vive* (Paris: Seuil, 1975).

4. The Greek infinitive *pherein* means "to carry, transport, or transfer," from the verb *phero*, meaning "bear or carry." See H. G. Liddell and R. Scott, *Greek-English Lexicon, with a Revised Supplement* (Oxford: Clarendon Press, 1996), 1922–24.

5. See Mikel Dufrenne, *Le poétique* (Paris: Presses Universitaires de France, 1963), esp. 1–6, 183–94.

6. Cited in Jean Hytier, *The Poetics of Paul Valéry*, trans. Richard Howard (Garden City, NY: Anchor Books, 1966), 66. French original: *La poétique de Valéry* (Paris: Librairie Armand Colin, 1953). Valéry also wrote: "Where Kant, rather innocently, perhaps, had thought to see the Moral Law, Mallarmé doubtless perceived the Imperative of a poetry: a Poetics" (CW, 8:311/O, 1:626). Also cited in Chapter 3.

7. CW, 1:229 "Pour autant qu'elle se plie / À l'abondance des biens / Sa figure est accomplie, / Ses fruits purs sont ses liens. / Admire comme elle vibre / Et comme une lente fibre / Qui divise le moment, / Départage sans mystère / L'attirance de la terre / Et le poids du firmament!" (O, 1:154).

8. "*poésie = métamorphose d'une chose en une autre en tant qu'elles ont la même manière de moduler l'être*" (ULL, 141).

9. The comparison between economic and literary value in these terms is that of Valéry. Cf. "Opening Lecture of the Course in Poetics" (CW, 13:94ff/O, 1:1344).

10. Merleau-Ponty read and studied French literary figures nearly exclusively, and our insertion of Edgar Allan Poe in Chapter 3 as well as Emily Dickinson and Stephen Spender in Chapter 6 provide some deviation. Simone de Beauvoir is important for Merleau-Ponty, and he writes at length about her novel *L'invitée* (translated as *She Came to Stay*) in "Metaphysics and the Novel," as well as her novel of the French Resistance, *Le sang des autres* (*The Blood of Others*), which is discussed in his Mexico Lectures of 1948. Emmanuel de Saint Aubert has devoted extensive time and depth to *Le sang des autres* in his *Du lien des êtres aux éléments de l'être* (Paris: Vrin, 2004), 61–103. In the same book, Saint Aubert also considers her *Les mandarins* and *Mémoires d'une jeune fille rangée*. Saint Aubert refers to Beauvoir in Chapter 2, along with Elizabeth Lacoin, and Beauvoir's views on "ambiguity" are discussed in his Chapter 5 herein, on metaphor. In addition to Emily Dickinson, an art exhibition by one of our translators, Marta Nijhuis, is also referred to in Chapter 6. Even with this said, the study of Merleau-Ponty and literature could well be extended in a follow-up volume to related writers beyond Merleau-Ponty's own preferences bounded by cultural and historical context.

11. The modernist focus therefore omits Balzac (1799–1850) and Stendhal (1783–1842). Balzac's *Le chef-d'oeuvre inconnu*, with its main character of Master Frenhofer, plays a role in Merleau-Ponty's "Cézanne's Doubt," where it provides an image of how Cézanne understood his own work as unfinished. Stendhal's *The Red and Black* provides an important text for the conclusion of "Indirect Language and the Voices of Silence," and Stendhal's overall oeuvre is the focus of much of Part II of the course of 1953, *Research on the Usages of Literary Language*. In this book, Stendhal's essay "De l'amour" (On Love), with its concept of "crystallization," enters into the discussion in Saint Aubert's Chapter 5.

12. Cited earlier in this introduction in the context of Merleau-Ponty's course of 1953: "And in a sense, as Valéry said, language is everything since it is the voice of no one, since it is the very voice of the things, the waves, and the forests" (VI, 203–4/155).

13. Francis Ponge, *The Voice of Things*, ed. Beth Archer (New York: McGraw-Hill, 1972), 107; from Francis Ponge, *Méthodes*, vol. 2 of *Le grand recueil* (Paris: Gallimard, 1961), February 26, 1948. Here it is helpful to refer explicitly to footnote 33 of Carbone's Chapter 1: "my suggestion is to see the *analogy*—in which the power of creating *correspondences* characterizes the sensible world—as the common origin of metaphoricity and conceptuality, understood as styles of thought and expression that have traditionally been opposed to one another. In this way, not only could one consider an intimately metaphorical origin of the concept itself, as does, among others, Hannah Arendt. . . . Indeed, one could go so far as to trace the roots of both the metaphor and the concept in the polymorphism of Being itself, that is to say in the *analogizing excess* of the sensible, as well as of language."

14. It has not been possible previously because we did not have his second reading found in the transcription of Merleau-Ponty's notes for his 1954 course titled "The Problem of Speech," especially its section titled as a question: "Proust: A Philosopher?" (PbParole, [94](5)). The first reading occurs in "The Body as Expression, and Speech" of *Phenomenology of Perception*, and the third reading comes in the subsection titled "The Visible and the Invisible: Proust" of the preparatory notes of his course on "The Cartesian Ontology and the Ontology of Today" in NC, 191–98.

15. Translation modified by Carbone.

16. This term, "metaphoricity," is not a neologism or coinage by Saint Aubert but has a lineage of use that includes Renaud Barbaras, who has written of general metaphoricity: "Far from metaphor bearing on objects already circumscribed, things proceed from a general 'metaphoricity,' from a universal *participation* that they concentrate or crystallize in order to be constituted into things." See Barbaras, *The Being of the Phenomenon: Merleau-Ponty's Ontology*, trans. Ted Toadvine and Leonard Lawlor (Bloomington: Indiana University Press, 2004), 195. French original: *De l'être du phénomène: L'ontologie de Merleau-Ponty* (Grenoble: Editions Jerôme Million, 1991). "Metaphoricity" is a term also used by the psychoanalyst Gérard Guillerault cited by Saint Aubert as well as North American scholars Glen A. Mazis, *Merleau-Ponty and The Face of the World: Silence, Ethics, Imagination, and Poetic Ontology* (Albany: State University of New York Press, 2016), Chapter 6, "Toward a Poetic Ontology," 289–92, and Rajiv Kaushik, *Merleau-Ponty between Philosophy and Symbolism: The Matrixed Ontology* (Albany: State University of New York Press, 2019), Chapter 5, "Philosophical Language—Literary Language."

17. See Chapter 5, note 2.

18. In the last pages of his most recent book, Saint Aubert considers the question of the relationship between metaphors and figuratives (*figuratifs*). He

argues that two figuratives are privileged in Merleau-Ponty's writings, always throughout them "depth," and in the late writings, "shadow." See *Être et chair: Du corps au désir—l'habilitation ontologique de la chair* (Paris: Vrin, 2013), 407.

19. There is a different word in French, *grossesse*, that expresses the pregnancy of the female, and the *prégnance* of the metaphor is specifically a literary term referring to a quality of thought that is creative, fecund, and open. It is in this sense, to cite but one passage, in which Merleau-Ponty wrote in *The Prose of the World*, "Finally, I would need to understand how speech can be pregnant (*prégnante*) with a meaning. Let us try, then, not to explain this but to establish more precisely the power of speaking, to get close to that signification which is nothing else than the unique movement of which signs are the visible trace" (PM, 165/118). This French term, *prégnance*, is also found in Gestalt theory as the "law of pregnancy," referring to a perceptive structure that makes a strong, powerful impression. The Latin phrase Merleau-Ponty uses, *praegnans futuri*, is found in Leibniz and refers to the "now" that is saturated with its future. The Leibnizian connotations of the phrase in which all truth turns out to be analytic and all of reality a "preestablished harmony" are objectional to Merleau-Ponty. The previous paragraph of the Working Note refers more appropriately to "a crystallization of time, a cipher of transcendence" found in every painting and human enterprise. "Symbolic *pregnance*" also plays an important role in Cassirer's account of creative intelligence in the *Philosophy of Symbolic Forms*, cited by Merleau-Ponty in *Phenomenology of Perception*.

20. The term is that of Jean-Luc Nancy. See *Corpus*, trans. Richard A. Rand (New York: Fordham University Press, 2008): "A writer doesn't touch by grasping, by taking in hand (from *begreifen* = seizing, taking over, German for 'conceiving') but touches by way of addressing himself, sending himself *to* the touch of something outside, hidden, displaced, spaced. His very touch, which is certainly *his* touch, is in principle withdrawn, spaced, displaced" (19).

1. "The Proustian Corporeity" and "The True Hawthorns": Merleau-Ponty as a Reader of Proust between Husserl and Benjamin

1. For this passage from Proust, see *Swann*, 6/6–7. [We have cited from the English translation of Proust, rather than from *Phenomenology of Perception*. —Trans.]

2. See Gerd Brand, *Welt, Ich und Zeit: Nach unveröffentlichten Manuskripten Edmund Husserls* (The Hague: M. Nijhoff, 1955), 25.

3. Edmund Husserl, *Die Krisis der europäischen Wissenschaften und die transzendentale Phänomenologie*, ed. Walter Biemel (The Hague: M. Nijhoff, 1954); trans. David Carr, *The Crisis of European Sciences and Transcendental Phenomenology* (Evanston, IL: Northwestern University Press, 1970), 109.

4. Ibid., 108.

5. The difference between Merleau-Ponty's and Husserl's perspectives has also been remarked by one of the German philosopher's last collaborators, namely Ludwig Landgrebe, who illustrates it as follows: "Husserl also talks

about a sedimented and accustomed knowledge, about the imprint of previous experiences, in whose light the perceived appears as this or that particular thing. Still, he considers it as a possession of the Ego. Contrarily, Merleau-Ponty means to point out that, rather than being a possession of the Ego, this is a possession of the body, which has learned to move in the world according to an aim and without any reflection, and which however synthesises the actual and the past. Such a past is proper to the body as something it has acquired, as a synthesis thanks to which we can talk about a perception." Ludwig Landgrebe, "Merleau-Pontys Auseinandersetzung mit Husserls Phänomenologie," in *Phänomenologie und Geschichte* (Gütersloh: Gütersloher Verlagshaus Gerd Mohn, 1968), 178.

6. In the first chapter of my book *The Thinking of the Sensible* (Evanston, IL: Northwestern University Press, 2004), I insisted on the feature of continuity that, in this phase of his meditation, Merleau-Ponty attributes to our originary experience of time.

7. Emmanuel de Saint Aubert, personal correspondence, November 20, 2010.

8. See Walter Benjamin, introduction to *The Origin of German Tragic Drama* (1928), trans. John Osborne (New York: Verso, 1998).

9. See Walter Benjamin, "Sur quelques thèmes baudelairiens" (1940), in *Essais II 1935–1940*, French trans. Maurice de Gandillac (Paris: Denoël/Gonthier, 1983), 150n2. [Of all the English editions of this essay by Benjamin we consulted, none reported the note quoted by Carbone. We hence took the liberty of translating it directly from the French edition used by Carbone himself. —Trans.]

10. Gilles Deleuze also will insist on this latter characterization, in an openly antiphenomenological sense, in *Proust and Signs*.

11. As it is well known, the last section of the first chapter of *Sodom and Gomorrah*, the fourth volume of Proust's novel, is titled "The Intermittences of the Heart." Proust had considered this as a title for the entire novel.

12. Benjamin, *The Origin of German Tragic Drama*, 36, my emphasis.

13. Giorgio Agamben, *Infanzia e storia: Distruzione dell'esperienza e origine della storia* (Turin: Einaudi, 1978); trans. Liz Heron, *Infancy and History. The Destruction of Experience* (New York: Verso, 1993), 42.

14. On this translation of the term *Leib* and on the theoretical misunderstandings that followed, see the chapter titled "Flesh: Toward the History of a Misunderstanding" in my book *The Flesh of Images: Merleau-Ponty between Painting and Cinema* (Albany: State University of New York Press, 2015), 10 ff.

15. See the passage from *Signs* quoted below as well as NC, 194 and 196.

16. See S, 292/230.

17. See Edmund Husserl, *Formale und transzendentale Logik* (1929); trans. Dorion Cairns, *Formal and Transcendental Logic* (The Hague: M. Nijhoff, 1969), 292.

18. Walter Benjamin, "The Image of Proust" (1929), in *Illuminations: Essays and Reflections*, trans. Harry Zohn, ed. Hannah Arendt (New York: Schocken Books, 2007), 205, trans. modified.

19. In fact, according to Benjamin, for Proust in "the world distorted in the state of analogy . . . the true surrealist face of existence breaks through." Ibid., trans. modified.

20. Ibid., 204, trans. modified.

21. Ibid., trans. modified.

22. Ibid., 211.

23. Benjamin, "On Some Motifs in Baudelaire" (1940), in *Illuminations*, 160.

24. Ibid., 188.

25. Ibid., trans. modified.

26. *Swann*, 43/59, trans. modified.

27. Walter Benjamin, "Central Park," in *Selected Writings, Volume 4: 1938–1940*, ed. Howard Eiland and Michael W. Jennings, trans. Edmund Jephcott (Cambridge, MA: Harvard University Press, 2003), 161–99, here at 183, trans. modified.

28. Benjamin, "On Some Motifs in Baudelaire," 188.

29. See Walter Benjamin, "The Work of Art in the Age of Its Technological Reproducibility," in *The Work of Art in the Age of Its Technological Reproducibility and Other Writings on Media*, ed. Michael W. Jennings, Brigid Doherty, and Thomas Y. Levin, trans. Edmund Jephcott, Rodney Livingstone, Howard Eiland, and others (Cambridge, MA: The Belknap Press of Harvard University Press, 2008), 23.

30. Benjamin, "On Some Motifs in Baudelaire," 157.

31. Ibid., 160.

32. On the basis of what I have claimed so far, my suggestion is to see the *analogy*—whose power of creating *correspondences* characterizes the sensible world—as the common origin of metaphoricity and conceptuality, understood as styles of thought and expression that have traditionally been opposed to one another. In this way, not only could one consider an intimately metaphorical origin of the concept itself, as does, among others, Hannah Arendt. See Arendt, *The Life of the Mind* (1971) (New York: Harcourt Brace Jovanovich, 1978), "Language and Metaphor," 99ff.; indeed, one could go so far as to trace the roots of both the metaphor and the concept in the polymorphism of Being itself, that is to say in the *analogizing excess* of the sensible, as well as of language.

33. *Swann*, 43/59.

34. Benjamin writes: "Is not the involuntary recollection, Proust's *mémoire involontaire*, much closer to forgetting than what is usually called memory? And is not this work of spontaneous recollection, in which remembrance is the woof and forgetting the warp, the contrary of Penelope's work rather than its likeness? For here the day unravels what the night has woven. When we awake each morning, we hold in our hands, usually weakly and loosely, but a few fringes of the tapestry of lived life, as loomed for us by forgetting. However, with our purposeful activity and, even more, our purposive remembering each day unravels the web and the ornaments of forgetting. This is why Proust

finally turned his days into nights, devoting all his hours to undisturbed work in his darkened room with artificial illumination, so that none of those intricate arabesques might escape him." Benjamin, *Illuminations. Essays and Reflections*, 202, trans. modified.

35. See Merleau-Ponty, "The Problem of Passivity: Sleep, Unconsciousness, Memory," IP, 117 ff.

36. "This notion of Time embodied, of years past but not separated from us, it was now my intention to emphasise as strongly as possible in my work. And at this very moment, in the house of the Prince de Guermantes, as though to strengthen me in my resolve, the noise of my parents' footsteps as they accompanied M. Swann to the door and the peal—resilient, ferruginous, interminable, fresh and shrill—of the bell on the garden gate which informed me that at last he had gone and that Mamma would presently come upstairs, these sounds rang again in my ears, yes, unmistakably I heard these very sounds, situated though they were in a remote past." *Temps retrouvé*, 351/529.

37. See IP, 256/196.

38. See VI, 247/193 ff.

39. For more about this point, see my *The Thinking of the Sensible*, 7ff.

40. "Farther than India and China" ("plus loin que l'Inde et que la Chine") is a line precisely drawn from *Grieving and Wandering*. Also, it has to be recalled that Nietzsche, in turn, qualifies history as "monumental" in his second *Untimely Meditation*, *On the Advantages and Disadvantages of History for Life* (1874). As for the intertwining of architectonic time and mythical time in this Working Note and, more generally, in Merleau-Ponty's interpretation of Proust, see Rajiv Kaushik's chapter "Proust and the Significant Event" in his book *Art and Institution: Aesthetics in the Late Works of Merleau-Ponty* (New York: Continuum 2011), 91ff.

41. *Swann*, 182/260.

42. See ibid., 181–83/259–62.

43. See NC, in particular 191–98.

44. See Merleau-Ponty, "Merleau-Ponty répond à Claude Simon 'écrivain et penseur'" (March 23, 1961), *Critique* 414 (November 1981): 1147; trans. Celia Britton, "Merleau-Ponty Replies to Claude Simon 'Writer and Thinker,'" in *Claude Simon*, ed. Celia Britton (New York: Longman, 1993), 39.

45. For Claude Simon, see NC, 204 ff. As for Merleau-Ponty's interest in Claude Simon's work, see Chapter 2.

46. See Mauro Carbone, *An Unprecedented Deformation: Proust and the Sensible Ideas*, trans. N. Keane (Albany: State University of New York Press, 2010), chap. 2, sec. 1.

47. This also implicates the consequence that, already in 1957, Merleau-Ponty indicated with respect to the phenomenological reduction: "After all, it was Husserl who said that there was no transcendental reduction that would not first have been an eidetic reduction. And then, from the fact that every reduction is first eidetic, does it not follow that it can never be adequate to

actual experience, since there is always between the *eidos* and the actual experience this distance that precisely provides the clarity of reflective or philosophical thought?" Merleau-Ponty, "Excerpt from the Discussion Following De Waelhens, 'L'idée de la phénoménologie,'" Troisième Colloque philosophique de Royaumont titled *L'oeuvre et la pensée de Husserl* (April 23–30, 1957), in Marc-André Béra, ed., *Husserl: Troisieme Colloque philosophique de Royaumont (23–30 avril 1957): L'oeuvre et la pensée de Husserl* (Paris: Minuit, 1959), 158; trans. Ted Toadvine in *Chiasmi International* 20 (2018): 241–42.

48. Merleau-Ponty, "Cinq notes sur Claude Simon," in *Médiations* 4 (Winter 1961–62), then in *Esprit* 66 (June 1982), 66, trans. modified; trans. Celia Britton, "Five Notes on Claude Simon," in *Claude Simon*, 38.

49. The Working Note of *The Visible and the Invisible* titled "Rays of past of world" says: "Perhaps valid in general: there is no association that comes into play unless there is overdetermination, that is, a relation of relations, a coincidence that cannot be fortuitous, that has an *ominal* sense.... Overdetermination *always* occurs: the retrograde movement of the true (= the pre-existence of the ideal) ... furnishes always still other reasons for a given association" (VI, 294/240–41). Apropos of the Bergsonian expression that, in this Merleau-Pontian passage, substitutes the one I evoked in my text, see the important explication given by Merleau-Ponty himself: "Bergson took account that there was not necessarily a fault in retrospection, and in the introduction to *The Creative Mind*, after the work, he no longer speaks of retrospective illusion, but of a 'retrograde movement of the true': when we think something true, it is only retrospectively that the true appears to us as true." Natu, 101/69.

50. About Merleau-Ponty's notion of (mutual) precession, see my book *The Flesh of Images: Merleau-Ponty between Painting and Cinema*, 56 ff.

51. Walter Benjamin, *Aus einer kleinen Rede über Proust, an meinem vierzigsten Geburtstag gehalten* (1932), in *Gesammelte Schriften*, vol. 2, ed. R. Tiedemann and H. Schweppenhäuser (Frankfurt: Suhrkamp, 1972–77), 1064, my emphasis. [We use the translation of the Benjamin passage as it appears in John McCole, *Walter Benjamin and the Antinomies of Tradition* (Ithaca, NY: Cornell University Press, 1993), 273. Indeed, apparently the lecture from which the passage is drawn has no translation in English. —Trans.]

2. A Poetics of Co-Naissance: Via André Breton, Paul Claudel, and Claude Simon

I thank my friend Galen Johnson for honoring me with an invitation to participate in this wonderful project. I would also like to express my gratitude to Janice Deary, who has undertaken the long and difficult task of translating my work.

1. [Given the significant and intentional play on words here—*co-naissance* as "co-birth" and *connaissance* as "knowledge"—this word will be left untranslated throughout this chapter. —Trans.]

2. See Emmanuel de Saint Aubert, *Du lien des êtres aux éléments de l'être* (Paris: Vrin, 2004) and *Être et chair I* (Paris: Vrin, 2013).

3. See, e.g., MSME, 182.

4. See Saint Aubert, *Du lien des êtres aux éléments de l'être*, sec. B, chap. 2.

5. See Emmanuel de Saint Aubert, *Vers une ontologie indirecte* (Paris: Vrin, 2006) and *Être et chair I*.

6. OntoC, 209.

7. [The French *surrection* is a geological term referring to tectonic "upsurge." It will not be translated in this chapter, however, since the author occasionally depends on "surrection" as the shared semantic root of "resurrection" and "insurrection." —Trans.]

8. Surrealism is explicitly mentioned in a number of texts. See SC, 181; SNS, 186; Caus III, 31; PM, 156; PM-ms, [225], [224], [224]v, [257], [257]v, [258], [220], [214], [210]; S, 296–297, 386; HoXX, 344; ULL, [22](I8), [24](II2), [72](VI10); Natu, 62; PhAuj, 48; RC, 146; NTi, [283]; OE-ms, [154]; OE, 30; OntoC, 189.

9. *Le dossier du surréalisme*, coll. "La Tribune de Paris," broadcast on July 29, 1947 (I.N.A. archives).

10. We have unfortunately been unable to locate the text or preparatory notes among Merleau-Ponty's papers.

11. PM-ms, [190], in black, late writing: 1955, 1959, or 1960.

12. See the remnants of these interviews, boxes 7 to 9.

13. See SNS, 186; HT, 236; HO, 151; Caus III, 31; Mexico, [157](45), [158](44); PM-ms, [225], [224], [224]v, [257], [261]v, [220], [216], [217], [191], [192], [190]; S, 296; ULL, [26](II4), [27](II5); NMS, [118](10); PhAuj, 48.

14. André Breton, *Second manifeste du surréalisme* (1930), in *Oeuvres complètes* (Paris: Gallimard, 1988), 1:781.

15. OE, 25/169.

16. See AD, 12, 99.

17. SNS, 55/43.

18. See S, 296.

19. The most celebrated examples in France are the Verdon and Tarn gorges.

20. Breton, *L'amour fou*, VII, in *Oeuvres complètes*, 2:782–83; trans. Mary Ann Caws in *Surrealist Painters and Poets: An Anthology* (Cambridge, MA: MIT Press, 2002), 139–40. Breton spent some time in Castellane in 1931 and 1932, near the gorges of Verdon and the natural site of the "sublime point."

21. PM-ms, [257].

22. Ibid., [257]v.

23. See S, 386, October 1954.

24. See PhAuj, 48, beginning of 1959.

25. Before giving up his medical studies to devote himself to his literary vocation, Breton served as a military nurse and assistant doctor during the First World War. Yet the experience that made the greatest impression on him was his time as an extern at the Centre Neurologique de la Pitié, in 1917, working under hysteria specialist Dr. Babinski, Charcot's great successor.

26. See PM-ms, [220], [224]v; S, 386.

27. PbPassiv, 220.

28. Breton, *L'amour fou*, 1:681.

29. *Oeuvres complètes* (Paris: Gallimard, 1992), 2:832.

30. S, 296/233.

31. "Perhaps with an analysis of Breton in §IV: Breton and surrealism as failed attempt to reach a sur-objectivity. Failed, because they revert from the 'omnipotence of human desire' (*L'amour fou*), to objective chance, i.e. finality, occultism—a reversion from the surreal to the puerile, from inspired speech to automatic writing. They don't understand that it is not simply a matter of repeating our infancy, but of sublimating it beyond the objective." PM-ms, [220].

32. See S, 305.

33. "To find out whether a conception of Nature and natural man doesn't still, in assuming an ontological mystery, tacitly presuppose (as with Breton) the space necessary for a gnosis—Or whether on the contrary we can succeed in making mystery an *element*. . . . I would like to achieve the second attitude." NMS, [118](10), probably autumn 1957.

34. Breton, *L'amour fou*, I, 682.

35. HO, 151.

36. Caus III, 31/65–66.

37. Caus II, 23–24/56.

38. Caus III, 29/63.

39. "For the surrealists, the object = crystallization of desire. A. Breton at the flea market, reading what he wants into the emotion provoked by an object. Poetry of the found object, of the human object reclaimed by nature (abandoned locomotive in the forest, covered by plants). . . . All objects reside in us." Mexico, [157](44). See also Mexico, [159](39).

40. "The thing is not in front of us, but with us, it wounds our body. In a certain sense, it is even in us . . . we are completely in things and they are in us. Impossible to distinguish what comes from us and what comes from things." Mexico, [158](44).

41. We should add here, in connection to Bachelard's influence on Merleau-Ponty, that our access to the reciprocal envelopment of visible and invisible, real and surreal, is also dependent on the mutual precession of *perception* and *imaginary*.

42. "BEING *and* WORLD (= in-visible and visible)." EM3, [245](27).

43. Breton, *Dictionnaire abrégé du surréalisme*, in *Oeuvres complètes*, 2:846.

44. See Jean Wahl, "Maurice Merleau-Ponty et la présence de Claudel," *Bulletin de la Société Paul Claudel* 11 (October 1962): 7–10; *Défense et élargissement de la philosophie: Le recours aux poètes—Claudel, Valéry* (Sorbonne lectures, 1958–59) (Paris: Centre de Documentation Universitaire, 1959); "'Cette pensée . . . ,'" in *Les Temps Modernes* (October 1961), 399–436. See also Nicolas Castin, "Le promeneur claudélien," in *Merleau-Ponty et le littéraire* (Paris: Presses de l'École Normale Supérieure, 1997), 83–92.

45. Merleau-Ponty's library has some surprising gaps in it with regard to both literary texts and those of other fields, especially philosophy. Mme Merleau-Ponty has confirmed that an indeterminate number of books were given away after the philosopher's death. Certain Claudelian texts mentioned in the testimonies of Simone de Beauvoir and Elisabeth Lacoin, for example, are no longer in the library.

46. *Mercure de France*, 1907; reprinted in *Oeuvre poétique* (Paris: Gallimard, 1967).

47. According to the date in Merleau-Ponty's copy.

48. See, e.g., ChRe, 23.

49. PhP, 94.

50. Ibid., 245/219.

51. Ibid.

52. EM1, [128].

53. See in particular NPVI, [135](1).

54. This influence, much more significant than we might be led to believe by Merleau-Ponty's rather sparse references, was more liberally expressed in his courses. For more on this subject, see the account offered by Jean Wahl, or even that of Michel Oriano in "A Personal Recollection," *Journal of the British Society for Phenomenology* 25, no. 1 (January 1994): 5. For some explicit references to Claudel in Merleau-Ponty's oeuvre, see SC, 213; PhP, 446, 469, 479; SNS, 216, 53; Caus III, 28–29, IV, 41–42; PM, 118, 157; PM-ms, [208], [211], [232]v, [260]v; S, 88, 297, 391–97; MSME, [201]; PbParole, [65](16), [68], [74](19), [77](1); PbPassiv, [246], 256; PhDial, [40](2); Natu, 132; EM1, [5]v(5); PhAuj, [13](13bis–16bis); NPVI, [162]; VI, 140, 233, 272; EM2, [152](10), [169](9), [231]; NTi, [299]; EM3, [244](25); OE-ms, [4](6), [15]v(12), [40](9), [162]; OE, 32; S-ms, [7](3), [17](11); Brou, [98](105); VI, 161, 174; NPVI, [190]; NTi, [353]; OntoC, [9](10bis), [22](18), 191, 194, 198–201, 248, 390–92. Merleau-Ponty dedicated a relatively ambiguous—we might say prudent—text to the French writer, on the occasion of the latter's death, a "death that changed the world." See EM1, [5]v(5); EM2, [152](10), [169](9): "Claudel était-il un génie?" in *L'Express* (March 5, 1955), 3–4, reprinted under the title "Sur Claudel," in *Signes* (Paris: Gallimard, 1960), 391–97.

55. "What makes him move so many men who are nevertheless alien to his beliefs is that his is one of the rare French writers who have made the din and prodigality of the word tangible." S, 395/317.

56. André Vachon, *Le temps et l'espace dans l'oeuvre de Paul Claudel* (Paris: Seuil, 1965). See in particular 218, 339, 358, 359, 370, 390, and 410–22. For Claudel, "the genesis of man and genesis of the world take place simultaneously. This is the fundamental theme of *Traité de la Co-naissance au monde et de soi-même*. Do we even need to point out how far we are from Thomist philosophy here? This way of envisaging the relation between man and world seems closer to the phenomenological perspective. Man and world are here indissociably committed to each other, at the heart of a system Merleau-Ponty refers to as 'Myself-others-things'" (218).

57. Reading *Les illuminations* on their publication in 1886, Claudel often mentions the "seminal influence" of Arthur Rimbaud, particularly in two texts devoted to the "man with soles of wind," reprinted in *Oeuvres en prose* (Paris: Gallimard, 1965), 514–28. Claudel claims the continuous "surrection" (upsurge), in each *Illumination*, of a world co-born along with its perceiver, the reformulation of the world through perception and imagination, in the "unbreakable fabric" constituted by soul and body together. Claudel characterizes this Rimbaldian discovery as a violent refutation of any kind of positivism and Kantianism—the poet was one of Auguste Burdeau's unhappy students.

58. For more on this point, see my book *Le scénario cartésien* (Paris: Vrin, 2005), esp. chap. 2.

59. Wahl, "Maurice Merleau-Ponty et la présence de Claudel," 10.

60. Vachon, *Le temps et l'espace dans l'oeuvre de Paul Claudel*, 414.

61. "I am. I feel, I listen to the beating of the machine inside me, between my bones, that which ensures my continued existence . . ." Claudel, *Art poétique*, 141. "I am seeing and hearing, I see, I taste, I smell . . ." (165).

62. "Does the body not end there, where it feels itself in contact with another body?" Claudel, *La cantate à trois voix*, in *Oeuvre poétique*, 372. In *Le père humilié*, the blind "Pensée de Coûfontaine" cannot see that she is seen, she cannot see herself, so she concludes that she doesn't exist. "Alone, I am like someone who has no body, no focal point, no face. It is only when someone comes, holds me, takes me in their arms—this is the only time I exist in a body. It is only through him that it is known. I do not know my body unless I have given it to him. I only begin to exist in his arms." Claudel, *Le père humilié*, in *Théâtre II* (Paris: Gallimard, 1965), 541.

63. OE-ms, [162]. See also OE-ms, [4](6), [15]v(12), [40](9); OE, 32; OntoC, 390, [9](10bis).

64. *Cinq grandes Odes* (Paris: N.R.F., 1913), 78.

65. *Le soulier de satin*, in *Théâtre II*, 683.

66. *L'histoire de Tobie et de Sara*, in ibid., 1313.

67. *Connaissance de l'Est*, in *Oeuvre poétique*, 99–100.

68. *Paul Claudel interroge Le Cantique des cantiques* (Paris: Gallimard, 1948), 113. See also 407–8. See as well *Un poète regarde la Croix* (Paris: Gallimard, 1935), 73, 220.

69. Claudel, *L'oeil écoute*, in *Oeuvres en prose*, 170.

70. "We must consider that the state of motion applies, in fact, not only to tangible things, is synonymous not only with a local displacement. There is movement wherever there is a variation in existence." Claudel, *Art poétique*, 152. "Everything is movement, or, to say the same thing in a different way, everything is expressed by movement" (153). "It is not space that allows for movement; movement is the condition of everything that exists, and, in realizing itself, creates dimension and space." Claudel, *Présence et prophétie* (Fribourg: Librairie de l'Université, 1942), 290. "As beings, we share a fundamental trait with all being: movement. There is only knowledge because there is movement, just as

there is only being because there is movement." Wahl, *Défense et élargissement de la philosophie*, 280.

71. *La jeune fille Violaine*, Act III, in *Théâtre I* (Paris: Gallimard, 1967), 618.
72. Claudel, "Traité de la co-naissance," in *Art poétique*, 149–53.
73. PhAuj, 88, 1959.
74. NMS, [27](5)–[27](6), probably autumn 1957.
75. S, 30/22.
76. VI, 141/104.
77. See especially the course on March 9, 1961, OntoC, 198ff.
78. OntoC, [22](18).
79. "Hommage à Maurice Merleau-Ponty," broadcast on Service des Émissions Culturelles, May 17, 1961 (I.N.A. Archives). Merleau-Ponty's development of the notion of ontological simultaneity is itself mediated by Jean Wahl. For his 1961 courses, the philosopher consults a typographic copy of Wahl's 1958–59 lessons (*Défense et élargissement de la philosophie*), as well as an article on Claudel by the same author, "Simultanéité: Peinture et nature," *Cahiers Paul Claudel* 1 (1959): 221–49. See OntoC, 198 and 391. Wahl's interest in the idea of simultaneity can be traced to his 1920 thesis *Du rôle de l'idée de l'instant dans la philosophie de Descartes*. He is also deeply impressed by Claudel's perceiving *exsisto*, "I exist among the things that are," by a fundamental sense of philosophical wonder before "this infinitely subtle and diverse flow of things, existing together, all around us," which are "reciprocally penetrated" in "deep being" ("Simultanéité: Peinture et nature," 223, 244, 246).
80. Claudel, *Connaissance de l'Est*, 93.
81. "This simultaneous presence to experiences that are nevertheless mutually exclusive, this implication of the one in the other, and this contraction into a single perceptual act of an entire possible process are what make up the originality of depth; depth is the dimension according to which things or the elements of things envelop each other." PhP, 306/276.
82. "Being anchored in one of them, I felt the solicitation of the others which made them coexist with the first. Thus, at every moment I was swimming in the world of things and overrun by a horizon of things to see which could not possibly be seen simultaneously with what I was seeing but *by this very fact* were simultaneous with it." PM, 74/52.
83. OE, 84/187. "Vision . . . teaches us that different or even incompatible beings can exist *together*, without concession or compromise—in sum, simultaneity as a dimension of being, and this mystery is already involved in our most prosaic everyday distance perception." OE-ms, [35]v(51). See also OE-ms, [15](11), [39]v(8), [52]v(34); OE, 29.
84. PbPassiv, [246].
85. See PhP, 306; PM, 74; NTi, [145]; PhAuj, 79; HLP, [121]; OE-ms, [15](11), [19](19), [35]v(51), [39]v(8), [52]v(34); OE, 29, 84; S-ms, [17]v(12); S, 22; OntoC, 174, 207.
86. NaPer, 21.
87. SC, 213/197.

88. EtAv, 35.
89. PhP, 246/220.
90. Mexico, [159](39); [157](45).
91. Ibid., [158](44).
92. Caus II, 21/53–54.
93. Ibid., 19/52.
94. See *Connaissance de l'Est*, 102; Paul Claudel and Jean Amrouche, *Mémoires improvisés* (Paris: Gallimard, 1954), 193–94.
95. *Cinq grandes Odes*, in *Oeuvre poétique*, 238.
96. "Simultanéité: Peinture et nature," 244. Citation from Claudel, *L'oeil écoute*, 189.
97. Wahl, *Défense et élargissement de la philosophie*, 280.
98. Ibid., 177.
99. Ibid., 174–75, 280. See also "Simultanéité: Peinture et nature," 225.
100. PhP, 245.
101. Ibid., 245–46/219.
102. "Between God and ourselves . . . there is a sharing of substance." Claudel, *Les aventures de Sophie* (Paris: Gallimard, 1937), 88. "The painter 'takes his body with him,' says Valéry. Indeed we cannot imagine how a *mind* could paint. It is by lending his body to the world that the artist changes the world into paintings. To understand these transubstantiations we must go back to the working, actual body . . ." OE, 16/162.
103. *Art poétique*, 150.
104. PhP, 247–48/221–22.
105. This collusion of the erotic and sacramental meanings of *co-naissance* is typical of Claudel's "flesh." As, for example, we find in the following extract from one of Sara's tirades—Sara being one of the most extraordinary female characters in Claudel's entire oeuvre: "All food, compact, profound, exquisite, I am bread, I am the fruit between the teeth to be bitten, I am the fig, the grape's inseparable companion, and the ambrosia next to this nectar! I am the fig tree, food of Israel, with leaves on all sides like long fingers. Whoever eats me will be filled with the flesh and seed of God. Whoever breaks me open from under this black bark, I will raise them up, for my flesh is true food." *L'histoire de Tobie et de Sara*, in *Théâtre II*, 1298). This final phrase is a direct reference to Christ's Eucharistic speech (John 6:55).
106. PhP, 370/334.
107. See *Être et chair I*, chap. 2, §2d and §3.
108. "Sensation is not a passive process; it is a special state of activity. I compare it to a vibrating string, where a note is formed by the correct finger position." *Connaissance de l'Est*, 105.
109. "Vibration is movement imprisoned by form." "Traité de la co-naissance," 149.
110. "Where am I and where are you? Together and apart. Far from you, and with you. But to make you penetrate this union . . . I need this music . . . a

fragile mixture, palpitating with being and nothingness in each second . . . this desire, that goes straight down, against the current of the stream, whose ebb and flow I have experienced so many times." *Le soulier de satin*, 815.

111. "We now turn to vibration in itself. I understand this as a movement that is double and one, where a body departs from a point so as to return to it. And this is the 'element,' a radical symbol for that which, in essence, constitutes every life." *Connaissance de l'Est*, 106.

112. *Mémoires improvisés*, 194–95.

113. For the poet, as for Merleau-Ponty, this "union" is one of his most pressing concerns; Claudel is also seeking what we might call the metasubstantial entanglement of soul and body, along the expressive paths associated with perception, movement, and desire. See *Art poétique*, 151–52; *Le père humilié*, 556.

114. At the risk of some raised theological eyebrows, Claudel adopts an original perspective concerning the human body, drawing his inspiration from the potentialities of the *glorious body*, a Christian image from Paul's First Epistle to the Corinthians (15:42–44), and interpreting these properties in a carnal, erotic way; see Vachon, *Le temps et l'espace dans l'oeuvre de Paul Claudel*, especially 415–22. The glorious body is already on the horizon of the human body, this penetrating and penetrated body of clay. In perception, as in love, the body is creator of simultaneity and ubiquity, already agile as air, subtle as water and fire.

115. "Living action par excellence is vibrational development. . . . Our entire nervous apparatus is dedicated to vibrational development. This is what quivers in contact with Being. In each moment, our being is born and co-born with other bodies of which it takes cognizance." "Traité de la co-naissance," 159.

116. HO, 151. "The universe most obviously opposed to Claudel's is that of Leibniz, where every monad is in itself complete, containing within itself, in a sense, the entire universe. The central idea of Claudel's world, on the other hand, is the incompleteness of any fact." Wahl, *Défense et élargissement de la philosophie*, 157.

117. See, e.g., PhP, 245, 248, 262, 273, 465, 514; SNS, 23; HO, 151; Caus II, 21; PM, 169, 208; S, 54; EP, 28; MSME, [20](I4), [27](II3); PbPassiv, 217, 264; VI, 22; OE-ms, [165], [171]v, [50](29); OE, 77; Brou, [112](128), [112](129); VI, 155, 190; OntoC, 173; NTontoc, [117], [118]v.

118. "Simultaneous movement = vibration" (OE-ms, [171]v), "simultaneity of movement: vibration" (OE-ms, [165]). "Forms [are the] 'scars' of forces, and forces vibrate within forms" (OntoC, 173). "Just as it has created the latent line, painting has made itself a movement without displacement, a movement by vibration or radiation" (OE, 77/184).

119. By subjecting everything to linear perspective, "he fashions on the canvas a representation of the landscape which does not correspond to any of the free visual impressions. This controls the movement of their unfolding yet also kills their trembling life [*la vibration et la vie*]" (Caus II, 21/53). "Priority

given to intaglio prints, to drawing (over colour): the object is rendered by its exterior, its external packaging, not by its internal vibration" (NTontoc, [117]).

120. "The perceived does not reveal itself except through its vibration in me, it is always beyond" (MSME, [20](I4)), "the thing, precisely because it makes me vibrate physically, reaches me from within, obsesses me, is always beyond" (MSME, [27](II3)). "The perception itself . . . not an intuition, but a vibration of the field" (PbPassiv, 264/204). "Thus, each perception is a vibration of the world, it touches well beyond what it touches, it awakens echoes in all my being in the world, it is super-significant" (PbPassiv, 217/165). See also PhP, 245.

121. "And if true philosophy dispels the vertigo and the anxiety that come from the idea of nothingness, it is because it incorporates them into being and conserves them in the vibration of the being which is becoming." EP, 28/21.

122. SNS, 23.

123. Brou, [112](129). See also VI, 155/115.

124. Claudel insists on desirous knowledge as *respiration*, all the way to knowledge of God, and even God's self-knowledge. "Man's entire character lies in respiration." *Journal I* (Paris: Gallimard, 1968), 527. "We worship a breathing God" (*Le Livre de Tobie*, 72). "God's inhalation [*aspiration*] takes from me this fragrance He has communicated to me, and my desire requests it back from His mouth. . . . Even today we can resist a reasonable argument, but we cannot resist a perfume! From God's mouth, a gust of myself on my face!" (*Paul Claudel interroge Le Cantique des cantiques*, 32–33). "God inhales her, and she breathes God in, exhales him through all her pores. . . . Thus in the Holy Trinity, God inhales and breathes himself. We worship a living, desiring, breathing God." *Journal II* (Paris: Gallimard, 1969), 151. "We attract God inside ourselves, and breathe him . . ." (ibid., 9). Etc.

125. OE, 30/167 and 28/166.

126. "In truth, every 'thing' loses the property of being simply 'visible' or simply 'material' the moment it enters into the circuit of perception, and more so, when it enters the field of poetic knowledge. As soon as it is seen, a thing takes on a 'meaning,' it can no longer hide behind the smooth shell of objectivity: it bursts, pushes its extensions towards the knowing subject, on the one hand, and towards all other things in the world, on the other . . . Claudel never says that the visible evokes the invisible, but that both the one and the other . . . hint at the Presence that prevents them from being separate. . . . In short, visible and invisible are not opposed to each other, as created and uncreated—both belong to the realm of creation. . . . If we attentively scrutinize the visible, we 'apperceive' the invisible." Vachon, *Le temps et l'espace dans l'oeuvre de Paul Claudel*, 412. Claudel wrote to one of his correspondants that his poetic universe was not the "flat little two-dimensional world . . . but the real, complete universe, visible and invisible." Letter from 1905, *Correspondance Paul Claudel/Francis Jammes/Gabriel Frizeau*, in *Oeuvres complètes*, 76.

127. See OE, 30–32.

128. Jean Wahl, *Hommage à Maurice Merleau-Ponty* (I.N.A. Archives).

129. OE, 31–32/167–68.

130. "There is a profound space-time unity in 'deep being' (Claudel)" (EM2, [231], 1959).

131. "Claudel goes so far as to say that God is not above but beneath us . . ." (PM, 118/83). "The universal is not above, it is beneath (Claudel)" (VI, 272/218). "Claudel says that God is not above us, but beneath us. Philosophy does not survey the world and being from above, it penetrates it, precisely so as to be a *radical* thought." (S-ms, [7](3)).

132. Sartre, *L'Être et le Néant* (Paris: Gallimard, 1943), 50.

133. EM1, [128], autumn 1958.

134. VI, 116/84.

135. Aimé Césaire, "Cahier d'un retour au pays natal," *Volontés* 20 (August 1939); reprinted with a preface by André Breton (Paris: Bordas, 1947; Paris and Dakar: Présence Africaine, 1983), 47.

136. Emmanuel Mounier, "Traité du caractère (la lutte pour le réel)" (1946), in *Oeuvres d'Emmanuel Mounier* (Paris: Seuil, 1961), 2:389–90. For more on the relationship between Merleau-Ponty and Mounier, see *Le scénario cartésien*, chap. 2.

137. René Huyghe, *Dialogue avec le visible* (Paris: Flammarion, 1955), 404. Huyghe, psychologist and art historian, an acquaintance of Merleau-Ponty from *hypokhâgne*; both were associated with the Collège de France, where Huyghe occupied the chair of the psychology of fine arts from1950 to 1976.

138. OntoC, 209, course on March 16, 1961; the "flesh of the world" is implicitly attributed to Claude Simon throughout this course.

139. Ibid., 205.

140. Ibid., 204.

141. Interview between Madeleine Chapsal and Claude Simon (November 1960), in *Les écrivains en personne* (Paris: U.G.E., 1973), 285–91.

142. OntoC, 205–6.

143. See *Du lien des êtres*, sec. B, chap. 1.

144. Ibid., chap. 3, §2.

145. See *Le scénario cartésien*.

146. OntoC, 213.

147. Breton, *Second manifeste du surréalisme*, 1.

148. See Claude Simon, "Discours de Stockholm" (December 9, 1985): "I am an old man now. Like the lives of many others who inhabit our old Europe, my early life was no little disturbed. I witnessed a revolution. I went to war in singularly murderous circumstances. . . . I have been taken prisoner. I've known hunger. Have been forced to exhaust myself with physical labor. Escaped. Been gravely ill, several times at the point of a violent or natural death. I've rubbed shoulders with all sorts and conditions of men, both clergy and incendiaries of churches, peaceable bourgeois and anarchists, philosophers and illiterates. I've shared my bread with tramps, in a word, I've been about the world . . . all, however, without finding any sense to all this, unless it should be the one

assigned to it, I believe, by Barthes, following Shakespeare: that 'if the world signifies anything, it is that it signifies nothing'—except that it exists." Nobel Foundation, *The Nobel Prizes 1985* (Stockholm: Wilhelm Odelberg, 1986), English translation from the Nobel Prize website.

149. Claude Simon attended the lecture at the Collège de France on March 16, 1961. At the end of the course, he admitted to Merleau-Ponty he felt perplexed by the philosopher's reading of his work. Despite certain significant resonances, this "very intelligent" Claude Simon seemed a stranger to him . . . To the writer's "that just isn't me," Merleau-Ponty responded in a letter, dated March 23 and published under the title "Merleau-Ponty Replies to Claude Simon, Writer and Thinker," *Critique* 414 (November 1981): 1147–48. He thanks Simon for sharing his reflections, "as disenchanted as they might be," and tries to explain the writer's impressions ("someone else does all that—or: what talent I *had*—or: I don't believe I have put all that in these pages") are the inevitable impressions "of any writer": "I do not think you could avoid that kind of surprise, discomfort, and melancholy." But also mentioning their agreement—"in these courses I said things in direct agreement with your way of seeing things"—Merleau-Ponty makes a weighty confession: "It is true that I hesitated to interpret your work: precisely because in your books I found many things congruent with my own work, I felt some qualms about annexing them, incorporating them into my personal ruminations."

150. Claude Simon, *Le vent* (Paris: Éditions de Minuit, 1957), 98; *The Wind*, trans. Richard Howard (New York: George Braziller, 1959), 103–4.

151. OntoC, 209, course on March 16.

152. See *Être et chair I*, chap. 2.

153. Ibid., chap. 4.

154. See EM2, [175](20).

155. *La route des Flandres* (Paris: Éditions de Minuit, 1960), 237; *The Flanders Road*, trans. Richard Howard (London: John Calder, 1985), 190.

156. Ibid., 238–39/192.

157. Ibid., 241–42/193–94.

158. See, e.g., OntoC, 204, course on March 9.

159. "The interlocking bodies . . . all our limbs shivering closely interlaced entwined . . . groping for her flesh for the entrance for the opening of her flesh among that tangled."

160. "It was as if I could hear something in all of it, something like breathing, like the respiration of her own flesh." See also Merleau-Ponty, OntoC, 215, course on March 16: "everything starts to breathe with 'a respiration as imperceptible and total as that of plants.'"

161. "feeding on me becoming me or rather me becoming it," "as though under a milk-giving goat," "feed on me my flesh nourishing the earth," "it was as if we were drinking each other slaking each other's thirst gorging on each other feasting famished."

162. "The world's flesh is female by the very fact that it can engender and create without even knowing it."

163. See "Metaphorical Figures of Passivity-Activity."

164. "or undressing, stretching their tired bodies, or already in bed, inert, sweating, and some struggling for pleasure with sighs and gasps," "there was nothing left of my body but a shrunken wizened foetus lying between the lips of a ditch as if I could melt into it disappear there engulf myself there," "I carefully stepped over the interlocking bodies (they looked like corpses)."

165. On the distinction between drive and desire, and Merleau-Ponty's strange silence with regard to the former, see *Être et chair I*, chaps. 8 and 9.

166. Natu, 288/226.

167. Claude Simon, for his part, tends to accentuate the opposite: that is, a strong association of promiscuity and death drive. The writer is haunted by his experience of war, death, and destruction, by the fatigue and fear that drive the body toward dimensions that don't seem to fit into the human, or even animal, condition. This discrepancy between Simon's and Merleau-Ponty's conception of promiscuity continues until the writer's last books. See, e.g., *L'acacia* (Paris: Éditions de Minuit, 1989), 91, 231–32.

168. It is noteworthy that this involves an encounter with literature, rather than a confrontation with other philosophers: as an investigation of desire, in its existential dimensions, it seems writers and their metaphors are able to go beyond the level of "illustration," so that this literary engagement is simply necessary. It is perhaps impossible to thematize desire directly, bypassing metaphorical figures, without profoundly *disfiguring* it. This reflects on the epistemological status of the concept of flesh itself and our ways of approaching it. So that, once again, we find ourselves faced with an investigation requiring the exploration of issues pertaining to imagination and metaphor. See Chapter 5 herein.

169. For more on this dialectical engagement between Being and beings, see *Vers une ontologie indirecte*, chap. 3.

170. See *Être et chair I*, chap. 7, §§2 and 4; chap. 8, §3.

171. Ibid., chap. 1, §3.

172. "The Father is in me, and I in him" (John 10:38; see also 14:10–11), "Abide in me, and I in you" (John 15:4; see also 15:5), "He that eateth my flesh, and drinketh my blood, dwelleth in me, and I in him" (John 6:56), etc.

173. In Claude Simon's cited texts we find references to this fantasy of "eating the other," the flesh-food of incorporation—just as we do in Paul Claudel (who is also referenced in the 1961 courses), and with Claudel exploring this theme in its triple directions: erotic, knowing, and mystical.

174. "They incorporate my flesh, and I absorb them . . . my body is comprised of foreign segments, just as others are made with my substance." (OE-ms [40]v(10)), "my substance passes into them" (OE, 34/168), "this other is made from my flesh and blood" (PM, 187/134), etc.

175. For more on the Merleau-Pontian meaning of reversibility, cf. *Être et chair I*, chap. 6, particularly §4.

176. PbPassiv, [182](48).

177. Ibid., 230–31/176.

178. Ibid. [235].

179. NMS, [27]v(6).

180. See OE, 31–32. See also OE-ms, [15]v(12), [40](9); OntoC, 171.

181. "The coherence of a life—Whatever happens, it will make sense in relation to what came before. . . . I do not make time. I am on board with time—Even my initiative, my creative role, in the sense that things are not complete, I have things to do, this is only the requisite, the postulation of a life that has already begun—The meaning of the words 'to be born' and 'to die': I can never say, even to myself, I am yet to be born, or I am already dead; I can only say that I am born and that I will die. *I.e.* I continue, I am always between . . . a life that has always continued between the one and the other, whose substance has always been a continuous *surrection*, as prescribed by birth." PhDial, [39](1)–[40](2), course on February 23, 1956.

182. NMS, [51]v(6).

183. Ibid. [95].

184. EM1, [128], autumn 1958.

185. See *Être et chair I*, sec. A, esp. chap. 1, §4, and chap. 3, §2.

186. For further discussion on the theme of the "blood of others" and "bleeding" objects, see *Du lien des êtres*, esp. sec. A, chap. 2, and sec. B, chap. 1.

187. OntoC, 211, course on March 16.

188. "All objects, everything visible, all people, 'transparent' to each other, inhabiting each other, involved or nested, one within the other . . ." (OntoC, 215). "Like nested time, nested space . . . proliferative space . . . ubiquitous space, where bodies are superimposed on each other . . . where places are nested, one within the other" (209). "*Human magma [Le magma des hommes]* . . . humans and time, space, are made of the same magma. For example, just as time is a nested time, so there is a sort of encroachment [*empiétement*] of bodies over each other . . ." (OntoC, 211). Etc.

189. See Jean Guillaumin, *Le rêve et le Moi: Rupture, continuité, création dans la vie psychique—Sept études psychanalytiques sur le sens et la fonction de l'expérience onirique* (Paris: Presses Universitaires de France, 1979).

190. See *Être et chair I*, chaps. 7 and 8, esp. §3.

191. "Woman's flesh, i.e. mother, containing the master-copy-man [*l'homme-témoin*], that is, protecting him from time, and now, by death, giving him birth, into the 'void'" (OntoC, 211).

192. EM2, [173]v(16), 1959.

193. See *Le soulier de satin*, Second Day, scenes 13 and 14.

194. "The new logic the *Art poétique* spoke of has nothing to do with that of classical theodicies. Claudel does not take it upon himself to prove that this world is the best of all possible worlds, nor to deduce Creation. Taking it as it is

with its wounds, its bruises, and its staggering gait, he simply affirms that from time to time we find encounters in it that we had not hoped for, that the worst is not always certain." S, 395/317.

195. OntoC, 201.

196. Ibid., 202.

197. "Passion . . . is to transfer onto a being our indistinction with all being" (OntoC, 201). "Two human souls, in nothingness, who are able to give themselves to each other, and in a single second, like the detonation of time's self-annihilation, who are capable of replacing all things with each other!" Claudel, *Le pain dur,* in *Théâtre II*, 158; cited ibid.).

198. OntoC, 201.

199. PbPassiv, [246], 1955.

200. OntoC, 201.

201. Claudel, *Paul Claudel interroge Le Cantique des cantiques*, 204.

202. *Le soulier de Satin*, Second Day, scene 13.

203. OntoC, 201.

204. Ibid.

205. Ibid., 201–2.

206. Ibid., 202.

207. Ibid., 198.

208. Ibid., 202.

209. VI, 189/144.

210. Paul Valéry, *Choses tues*, VI, *Tel Quel*, I, in *Oeuvres* (Paris: Gallimard, 1960), 2:490. Cited in S, 294; ULL, [43](III11).

211. Natu, 287/225.

3. From the World of Silence to Poetic Language: Merleau-Ponty and Valéry

1. "Voici parler une Sagesse / Et sonner cette auguste Voix / Qui se connaît quand elle sonne / N'être plus la voix de personne / Tant que des ondes et des bois!" CW, 1:136–37/O, 1:136.

2. "Indirect Language and the Voices of Silence" was first published in *Les Temps Modernes* (June–July 1952) and was included in *Signs* (1960). An abbreviated version of the essay without the opening section on Saussure was originally written as the third chapter of *The Prose of the World* (1951) published posthumously. For analysis of the differences among the three versions of "Indirect Language and the Voices of Silence," see Galen A. Johnson, "Structures and Painting," in *The Merleau-Ponty Aesthetics Reader*, ed. Galen A. Johnson (Evanston, IL: Northwestern University Press, 1994), 14–15.

3. The introductory pages of this *inédit* have been transcribed and published by Emmanuel de Saint Aubert. See *Merleau-Ponty* (Paris: Hermann, 2008), 41–53.

4. See Henry A. Grubbs, *Paul Valéry* (New York: Twayne, 1968), 84.

5. *Correspondance Gide-Valéry* (1897), 291; Cited in Charles G. Whiting, *Paul Valéry* (London: Athlone Press, 1978), 132n32.

6. Marcel Proust, *Contre Saint-Beuve*, in *Marcel Proust on Art and Literature*, trans. Sylvia Townsend Warner (New York: Carroll and Graf, 1984), 19. French original: Proust, *Contre Sainte-Beuve* (Paris: Gallimard, 1954).

7. To our knowledge, we have no direct comments from Merleau-Ponty on the writings of Poe. Nevertheless, Poe has been taken up in a significant way in recent continental philosophy owing to Jacques Lacan's seminar on Poe's detective story "The Purloined Letter." See Jacques Lacan, "Seminar on *The Purloined Letter*," trans. Jeffrey Mehlman, *Yale French Studies* 48 (1972). Lacan dwells upon the etymological meaning of "purloined" (*volée*) and links it with an interpretation of the meaning of "repetition automatism" in Freud. Derrida published a response to Lacan's reading of "The Purloined Letter" in "The Purveyor of Truth" (1975) in terms of his critique of the "metaphysics of presence." Lacan's seminar together with Derrida's critique, along with many essays by others, are collected in *The Purloined Letter: Lacan, Derrida, and Psychoanalytic Reading*, ed. John P. Muller and William J. Richardson (Baltimore: Johns Hopkins University Press, 1987). More recently, Deleuze commented briefly on Poe's "The Purloined Letter" in terms of presence and absence. See Gilles Deleuze, *Difference and Repetition*, trans. Paul Patton (New York: Columbia University Press, 1994), 102. Most recently, Bernet has brought Heidegger into the interpretation of "The Purloined Letter" in relation to Heidegger's seminar on Parmenides. See Rudolf Bernet, "The Secret according to Heidegger and 'The Purloined Letter' by Poe," *Continental Philosophy Review* 47 (2014): 353–71.

8. See ULL, 65n2. The reference to Poe and his linkage with Mallarmé as sources for Valéry's concept of an "*animal Langage*" comes in an article by Pius Servien, who had assisted Valéry at the Collège de France. See Pius Servien, "Au Collège de France," in "Paul Valéry vivant," *Cahiers du Sud* (1946): 169: "En Valéry, cet implexe, cet animal de mots, jeune fauve autrefois, se domptant suivant les préceptes de Poe et de Mallarmé [In Valéry, this implex, this animal of words, formerly a wild youth, tames itself following the precepts of Poe and Mallarmé]." Servien also mentions lessons on Edgar Poe that Valéry had given on rhythm and lyrical language. See 167–68.

9. William Tomas Bandy's research cites four French translators of Poe prior to Baudelaire, the most significant being Isabelle Meunier's translation of "The Black Cat" in 1847. See Bandy, *The Influence and Reputation of Edgar Allan Poe in Europe* (Baltimore: Cimino, 1962). Cited in Lois David Vines, *Valéry and Poe: A Literary Legacy* (New York: New York University Press, 1992), 13–14.

10. The list of Poe's works translated into French by Baudelaire is found in *Baudelaire on Poe: Critical Papers*, ed. Lois and Francis E. Hyslop Jr. (State College, PA: Bald Eagle Press, 1952), 167–68. See also *Edgar Poe et la critique française de 1845 à 1875* (Paris: Presses Universitaires de France, 1928).

11. Stéphane Mallarmé, *Le corbeau/The Raven: Poëme par Edgar Poe*, trans. Stéphane Mallarmé (Paris: Richard Lesclide, 1875).

12. Stéphane Mallarmé, *Oeuvres complètes*, ed. Henri Mondor and G. Jean-Aubry (Paris: Gallimard, 1945), 190–212. See Vines, *Valéry and Poe*, 32.

13. Stéphane Mallarmé, *Divagations*, trans. Barbara Johnson (Cambridge, MA: The Belknap Press of Harvard University Press, 2007), 96. French original in Mallarmé, *Oeuvres complètes*, 531.

14. Stéphane Mallarmé, *Poems*, trans. C. F. McIntyre (Berkeley: University of California Press, 1957), 88. French original in Mallarmé, *Oeuvres complètes*, 189. "The Tomb of Edgar Poe" was written by Mallarmé in 1876 to honor the twenty-fifth anniversary of the poet's death.

15. Edgar Allan Poe, "The Philosophy of Composition," in *Edgar Allan Poe: Critical Theory—The Major Documents*, ed. Stuart Levine and Susan F. Levine (Urbana: University of Illinois Press, 2009), 60. Hereafter cited in the text as PC.

16. Ibid., 57–58.

17. T. S. Eliot, "From Poe to Valéry," *The Hudson Review* 2, no. 3 (Autumn 1949): 333.

18. See Emron Esplin, "Borges's Philosophy of Poe's Composition," *Comparative Literature Studies* 50, no. 3 (2013): 458–69, here at 463.

19. See Virginia A. La Charité, *The Dynamics of Space: Mallarmé's "Un coup de dés jamais n'abolira le hasard"* (Lexington, KY: French Forum Publishers, 1987), 171.

20. Charles Baudelaire, "Preface to 'The Raven,'" in *Baudelaire on Poe*, 155.

21. Ibid., 157.

22. Fellow artist Emile Bernard was the originator of the claim of Van Gogh's suicide by wound from a revolver written in a letter to art critic, Albert Aurier, two days after Van Gogh's funeral in Auvers. See Steven Naifeh and Gregory White Smith, *Van Gogh: The Life* (New York: Random House, 2012), "Appendix: A Note on Vincent's Fatal Wounding," 877.

23. Charles Baudelaire, *Edgar Allan Poe: His Life and Works*, trans. H. Curwen, in *The Works of Edgar Allan Poe, including Poetical and Prose Writings* (New York: W. J. Widdleton, 1876), 2.

24. Ibid.

25. See Eliot, "From Poe to Valéry," 337.

26. See "Dupin–Teste: The Poe Connection," in Vines, *Valéry and Poe*, 77–103.

27. Paul Valéry, *Lettres à quelques-uns* (Paris: Gallimard, 1952), 97–98. Cited in Vines, *Valéry and Poe*, 79.

28. See Esplin, "Borges's Philosophy of Composition," 466.

29. Jean-François Lyotard, *The Differend: Phrases in Dispute*, trans. Georges Van Den Abbele (Minneapolis: University of Minnesota Press, 1988), xi. Lyotard defines the *differend* as a case of conflict in which there are not the words to express a wrong in one language such that it could find an equivalent in the other language; between the two languages there is incommensurability. Famously, the first example is that of the Jewish victims of the camps who are now as survivors placed in the position of proving the existence of gas chambers

where the only acceptable proof in a court of law is direct first-person testimony, "seeing with one's own eyes" (3). The only acceptable proof that the gas chamber was used to kill is that one died from it, but if one is dead, one cannot testify as an eyewitness. As another case, Lyotard understands perfectly why some feel more grief over damages inflicted upon an animal even than those inflicted upon a human "because the animal is deprived of the possibility of bearing witness to the human rules for establishing damages," and thus the animal is a "victim *ipso facto*," "a paradigm of the victim" (28).

30. Jean-François Lyotard, *Heidegger and "the jews,"* trans. Andreas Michel and Mark S. Roberts (Minneapolis: University of Minnesota Press, 1990), 52.

31. See Michel Foucault, *Language, Madness, and Desire: On Literature*, trans. Robert Bononno (Minneapolis: University of Minnesota Press, 2015). Foucault's discussion ranges from figures of the literature of the classical age, Lear and Quixote, to modern figures such as Sade, Antonin Artaud, and Jacques Rivière. In the classical age, "as for madness, it will remain silent, the pure object of an amused gaze" (13). As for the modern age, Foucault concludes: "our culture finally developed an ear for this language, which never flagged and unsettles our own. And it did so through this subterranean work of madness in language, against language; the work of madness in recovering its own language; it seems to me that all this subterranean work enables us now to listen with new ears" (23).

32. "Qui pleure là, sinon le vent simple, à cette heure / Seule, avec diamants extrêmes? . . . Mais qui pleure, / Si proche de moi-même au moment de pleurer?" CW, 1:68/O, 1:96.

33. According to Valéry's *Collected Works*, the original French source for Valéry's letter to Rilke is the literary review *Les Cahiers du Mois* (August 1926). See CW, 9:385.

34. Emmanuel de Saint Aubert argues that by using the term "chiasma" and not "chiasm," Valéry makes reference to the rhetorical sense and not the physiological [ocular] meaning of chiasm: "*Tout en disant 'chiasma' et non 'chiasme,' Valéry fait bien référence au sens rhétorique et non physiologique du chiasme.*" Emmanuel de Saint Aubert, *Le scénario cartésien: Recherches sur la formation et la cohérence de l'intention philosophique de Merleau-Ponty* (Paris: Vrin, 2005), 171. *The Visible and the Invisible* does speak of the blind spot in vision created by the crossing of the optic fibers, and in one passage speaks of the blind spot in our relations with others. See VI, 109/78.

35. Saint Aubert comments: "Chiasm designates here an exchange that is resolved neither in fusion nor in separation" ("*Le chiasme désigne ici un échange qui ne se résout ni dans la fusion ni dans la séparation*"). Ibid., 170.

36. "Le doute de Valéry: Pensée, existence, écriture dans les *Recherches sur l'usage littéraire du langage*," in *Du sensible à l'oeuvre: Esthétiques de Merleau-Ponty*, ed. Emmanual Alloa and Adnen Jdey (Brussels: La Lettre Volée, 2011), 161–84, esp. "*Ut pictura scepsis*," 169–80.

37. Ibid., 170. "*Au Degas de Valéry justement: rustre jusqu'à la misanthropie; terriblement politiquement incorrect; inlassable dans son travail, et prêt à consacrer un temps démesuré à chaque tableau, finissant parfois par le détruire.*"

38. Saint Aubert, *Le scénario cartésien*: "*L'itinéraire de l'écrivain lui offre une variante contemporaine, plus moderne et plus aboutie, du scénario cartésien*" (174).

39. See Paul Valéry, "Pure Poetry, Notes for a Lecture" (CW, 7:184–92/ O, 1:1456–63): "The conception of pure poetry is that of an inaccessible type, an ideal boundary of the poet's desires, efforts, and powers. . . ." CW 7:192/O, 1:1463.

40. André Breton, *Mad Love*, trans. Mary Ann Caws (Lincoln: University of Nebraska Press, 1998), 114–16.

41. See Whiting, *Paul Valéry*, 114.

42. On Ponge's early encounters with Breton, see Martin Sorrell, *Francis Ponge* (Boston: Twayne, 1981), 20, 43. The joint interview of 1952 is found in Francis Ponge, *Méthodes*, vol. 2 of *Le grand recueil* (Paris: Gallimard, 1961), 287–302. Hereafter, this work will be cited in the text as M.

43. For a side-by-side analysis of the poetry of Ponge and Valéry, see Robert L. Mitchell, "Valéry and Ponge: Rheuminations," in *From Dante to García Marquez: Studies in Romance Literatures and Linguistics*, ed. Gene H. Bell-Villada, George Pistorius, and Antonio Giménez (Williamstown, MA: Williams College, 1987), 313–22. Mitchell compares Ponge's "Pluie" (Rain) and Valéry's "Neige" (Snow).

44. Ponge expressed his opposition to Valéry in *Pour un Malherbe* (Paris: Gallimard, 1965), 254–55. Regarding Valéry's view of the traditional rules of prosody as creative for the expression of ideas, Ponge writes: "It is absolutely necessary to "work" against this conception. . . . Give ideas! What a pity! Alas! Valéry proves here that he is not a poet. That seems evident, too evident." ("*Il faut absolutement 'fonctionner' contre cette conception. . . . 'Donne des idées!' Quelle pitié! Hélas! Valéry prouve ici qu'il n'est pas poète. Cela me semble évident. Trop évident.*") Ponge continues to say that for the poet to communicate an emotion, one must oppose all rules and obstacles. On Valéry's poetic, Ponge cites Valéry's *Cours de Poétique au Collège de France*, December 10, 1937, 142, coll. Ygdrasill, 1937–38.

45. Francis Ponge, *Le parti pris des choses*, in *Tome premier* (Paris: Gallimard, 1965), 62. Hereafter cited in the text as T. (This work was originally published separately by Gallimard in 1942.)

46. English translation, Francis Ponge, *The Voice of Things*, ed. and trans. Beth Archer (New York: McGraw-Hill, 1972). Hereafter, this work will be cited in the text as VT.

47. "Twice-spawned petal" ("*pétale superfétatoire*") is found in the last line of Ponge's poem "The Butterfly" (VT, 46). French original, "Le papillon": T, 62.

48. "The Wasp," in *Things: Francis Ponge*, 97–102; French original: T, 261–70. The wasp as the "musical form of honey" is found at 101; French original: T, 270. Nevertheless, has the author here confused the wasp (*la guêpe*) and the honeybee (*l'abeille*)?

49. "The Object Is the Poetics," in *Things: Francis Ponge*, ed. and trans. Cid Corman (New York: Grossman, 1971), 94. French original: "L'objet, c'est la poétique," in *Nouveau recueil* (Paris: Gallimard, 1967), 145–46. Hereafter cited in the text as NR. Ponge notes that the expression "*l'objet, c'est la poétique*" is from Braque.

50. Francis Ponge, *The Making of the Pré*, trans. Lee Fahnestock (Columbia: University of Missouri Press, 1979), 62–63. French original: *La fabrique du pré* (Geneva: Éditions d'Art Albert Skira, 1971), unnumbered, approximately 110–11. The Cézanne painting is not titled. Among other possibilities, it resembles *Large Trees at the Jas de Bouffan* (1885–87).

51. English translation by Sorrell, *Francis Ponge*, 50.

52. Jean-Paul Sartre, "Man and Things," *Critical Essays (Situations I): Jean-Paul Sartre*, trans. Chris Turner (New York: Seagull Books, 2010), 457. French original: *Situations I* (Paris: Gallimard, 1947), 293. Hereafter cited in the text as MAT.

53. We have only a written summary of Merleau-Ponty's lecture published as "L'homme et l'objet" ("Man and Object"), an unpublished lecture given by Merleau-Ponty at the Pavillon du Marsan, in introduction to a cycle on "L'objet et poésie" ("The Object and Poetry"), résumé by J. L. Dumas, "Les conférences," in *La Nef* 45 (August 1948): 150–51. I express my thanks to Emmanuel de Saint Aubert for a digital copy of this text.

54. Merleau-Ponty, "L'homme et l'objet": "*Les artistes d'aujourd'hui ne croient ni à la finalité ni à l'harmonie préétablie, mais ils sont particulièrement sensibles à cette vibration que suscite la forme en prenant possession de la matière*" (151).

55. Emmanuel de Saint Aubert, *Du lien des êtres aux éléments de l'être: Merleau-Ponty au tournant des années 1945–1951* (Paris: Vrin, 2004), 279, 284–85, 286.

56. See Jacques Derrida, "*Qual Quelle*: Valéry's Sources," in *Margins of Philosophy*, trans. Alan Bass (Chicago: University of Chicago Press, 1982), 302.

57. "*Il ne connaissait pas ce qu'il reconnaît . . . Mais il ne pouvait pas s'y tromper.*"

58. "*Ce temps extraordinaire d'unité de l'évènement et du désir.*"

59. "*Le rôle du vouloir est seulement de maintenir dans ce champ les éléments 'en charge' et il voit se former 'une certaine figure—qui ne dépend plus de nous.'*"

60. "*L'implexe est l'opération d'un sens qui n'est pas encore thématisé, libéré, posé pour soi.*"

61. Derrida writes: "Such a system [implex] covers that of the classical [Aristotelian] philosopheme of *dynamis*." *Margins of Philosophy*, 303.

62. "*d'une sorte de raison cachée: par exemple hasard-raison-implexe.*"

63. See Philip Wheelwright, introduction to *Idée Fixe*. CW, 5:xxi.

64. Mallarmé, *Oeuvres complètes*, 455.

65. Rajiv Kaushik, *Art, Language, and Figure in Merleau-Ponty: Excursions in Hyper-Dialectic* (London: Bloomsbury, 2013), 117.

66. Mallarmé, "The Mystery in Letters," in *Divagations*, 236. French original: Mallarmé, *Oeuvres complètes*, 387. Rather than "hinge," the French word *brisure* might also be translated as "break," "fold," or even "difference."

67. Jacques Rancière, *Mallarmé: Politics of the Siren*, trans. Steven Corcoran (London: Continuum International, 2011), 56. See Mallarmé, "Scribbled in the Theater," in *Divagations*, 120–21. French original: Mallarmé, *Oeuvres complètes*, 296.

68. Mallarmé, "Crisis of Verse," *Divagations*, 210–11. French original: Mallarmé, *Oeuvres complètes*, 368. "Crise de vers" is the second part of Mallarmé's "Variations sur un sujet."

69. See Jessica Wiskus, *The Rhythm of Thought: Art, Literature, and Music after Merleau-Ponty* (Chicago: University of Chicago Press, 2013), 9.

70. "Cette ceinture vagabonde / Fait dans le souffle aérien / Frémir le suprême lien / De mon silence avec ce monde . . ." CW, 1:136–37/O, 1:121.

4. The Clouded Surface: Literature and Philosophy as Visual Apparatuses According to Merleau-Ponty

1. This expression appears twice in the examined page (SNS, 36/27–28). Another essay in *Sense and Non-Sense* also bears a corresponding title. However, it has to be remarked that the English translation of the volume does not account for this repeated occurrence.

2. See also *Indirect Language and the Voices of Silence*: "henceforth expression must go from man to man across the common world they *live*, without passing through the anonymous realm of the *senses* or of Nature" (S, 64/51).

3. May the reader allow me to note that the proposal to characterize the later Merleau-Ponty's notion of Flesh precisely as "Visibility" is at the basis of my book *The Flesh of Images: Merleau-Ponty Between Painting and Cinema* (2011), trans. Marta Nijhuis (Albany: State University of New York Press, 2015).

4. Published for the first time in *L'écran français* 17 (October 24, 1945): 3–4, then reproduced in Mauro Carbone, Anna Caterina Dalmasso, and Elio Franzini, eds., *Merleau-Ponty e l'estetica oggi / Merleau-Ponty et l'esthétique aujourd'hui* (Milan and Paris: Mimesis, 2013), 21–24, here at 22. For remarks on this article, see my book *Philosophy-Screens: From Cinema to the Digital Revolution* (2016), trans. Marta Nijhuis (Albany: State University of New York Press, 2019), 10–12.

5. Béla Balázs, *Early Film Theory: Visible Man and The Spirit of Film*, ed. Erica Carter, trans. Rodney Livingstone (New York: Berghahn Books, 2010), 1ff.

6. In the field of film studies, the use of the French term *dispositif*, usually translated as *apparatus*, is introduced in the 1970s, for the purpose of defining the specificity of cinema at a time when the "seventh art" was menaced by other media, like television and videos. See Jean-Louis Baudry, "Effets idéologiques produits par l'appareil de base" (1970), trans. Alan Williams, "Ideological Effects of the Basic Cinematographic Apparatus," in *Film Theory and Criticism, Introduction Readings*, ed. Gerald Mast, Marshal Cohen, and Leo Braudy, 4th ed. (New York: Oxford University Press, 1992), 302–12, as well as "Le dispositive: Approche métapsychologique de l'impression de réalité" (1975), trans. B. Augst, "The Apparatus: Metapsychological Approaches to the Impression of Reality in

Cinema," in *Narrative, Apparatus, Ideology: A Film Theory Reader*, ed. Philip Rosen (New York: Columbia University Press, 1986), 299–318. In a different historical context, yet sharing the same purpose, Raymond Bellour has typically defined the cinematic apparatus or *dispositif* as follows: "The living projection of a film in a cinema, in the dark, for the prescribed time of a more or less collective session, becomes and remains the condition for a unique experience of perception and memory, defining its spectator, and that any other situation of vision more or less alters. And only this experience is worth being called 'cinema.'" Raymond Bellour, *La querelle des dispositifs* (Paris: P.O.L., 2012), 14. On these bases and more generally, a visual apparatus or *dispositif* is meant to be a set of material elements and cultural practices allowing a particular viewing experience. Basically, such an experience is provided by the specific kinds and the mutual positioning of three elements: the surface showing images; the space and conditions hosting the viewer(s); and the light source.

7. At the beginning of his course at the Collège de France titled "The Cartesian Ontology and the Ontology of Today" (1960–61), on which I will focus later, Merleau-Ponty points out an epochal "backwardness of the official philosophy" (NC, 163).

8. Stéphane Lojkine, ed., *L'écran de la representation: Théorie littéraire—Littérature et peinture du 16ᵉ au 20ᵉ siècle* (Paris: L'Harmattan, 2001), 37.

9. See Gottfried Boehm, "Die Wiederkehr der Bilder," in *Was ist ein Bild?*, ed. Gottfried Boehm (Munich: Fink, 1994), 11–38, here at 14.

10. On the impossibility of reducing Merleau-Ponty's phenomenology of language to the linguistic turn, see also Bernhard Waldenfels, "Faire voir par les mots: Merleau-Ponty et le tournant linguistique," *Chiasmi International* 1:57ff.

11. See NC, 391. Apropos of Merleau-Ponty as a reader of Paul Claudel and Claude Simon, see Chapter 2.

12. See Mauro Carbone, *An Unprecedented Deformation: Marcel Proust and the Sensible Ideas* (2004), trans. N. Keane (Albany: State University of New York Press, 2010), esp. 16ff.

13. Waldenfels, "Faire voir par les mots," 57.

14. See Chapter 1.

15. *Swann*, 343/496.

16. "A piece of music or a painting that is not immediately understood ultimately creates its own public—so long as it truly *says* something—which is to say, by secreting its own signification. In the case of prose or poetry, the power of speech is less visible because we have the illusion of already possessing within ourselves, with the common meaning of words, what will be necessary for understanding any text whatsoever. . . . But in fact, it is less the case that the sense of a literary work is built from the common meanings of the words than that the literary work contributes to modifying that common meaning. There is, then, either for the person listening or reading, or for the person speaking or writing, a *thought in the speech* of which intellectualism is wholly unaware" (PhP, 209/185).

17. The distinction proposed by Merleau-Ponty between "speaking speech" and "spoken speech" seems to be inspired by the Saussurian distinction between "speech" (*parole*) on the one hand, and "language" (*langue*) on the other hand. Still, at the same time, Merleau-Ponty's own distinction is in fact autonomous as it resolutely focuses on the mobile and creative characteristic of language. Besides, the distance separating Merleau-Ponty's and Saussure's distinctions has been highlighted by several commentators. In any case, and quite rightly, it is commonly agreed that the actual influence of Saussure's linguistics on Merleau-Ponty's philosophy is subsequent to *Phenomenology of Perception*.

18. See *Guermantes*, 41/54: "[Vinteuil's] playing has become so transparent, so imbued with what he is interpreting, that one no longer sees the performer himself."

19. As for Proust's two phrases, see respectively *Swann*, 342/494 and 346/500.

20. "Language has, in fact, installed in us this certainty that we have of reaching, beyond its expression, a truth separable from that expression, and of which this expression is only the clothing and the contingent manifestation. Language only appears to be a simple sign when it has taken on a signification, and the coming to awareness, in order to be complete, must uncover the expressive unity in which signs and significations first appear." PhP, 459/422.

21. Neither I nor other specialists of Proust's work whom I consulted could clearly identify to which Proustian passage Merleau-Ponty is referring here.

22. In his "Editor's Preface," Claude Lefort—as the editor of the posthumous publication of this text, which Merleau-Ponty decided to leave unfinished—gives some precious information concerning the history of the book, and casts a light on a particularly important moment in Merleau-Ponty's intellectual itinerary. As for the writing periodization of *The Prose of the World*, Lefort tends to think that the pages that were found—which supposedly constituted the first part of the book—were written, on the basis of previous solicitations, in a year's time, namely during 1951, and that the decision to suspend the writing was made the following year. Lefort also points out that, between 1950 and 1951, Merleau-Ponty decided to reduce the inquiry domain of *The Prose of the World* with respect to the preliminary projects. This, Lefort suggests, might have been due to Merleau-Ponty's intention of subordinating the inquiry domain of this book to that of *The Origin of Truth*, namely the book that, in his plan, was to unveil the metaphysical sense of his theory of expression. The reflection on the subjects that this latter work was to deal with, would eventually end up in the unfinished pages of *The Visible and the Invisible*. Moreover, in his "Editorial Note" to *The Prose of the World* (see PM, xv–xvi/xxiii–xxiv), Lefort explains that the Working Notes concerning this writing suggest that Merleau-Ponty meant to consecrate the second part of the book to the analysis of some literary experiences, including precisely that of Proust.

23. Benedetta Zaccarello, "Pour une littérature-pensée: Avant-propos." ULL, 20–21.

24. "Speech, as distinguished from language, is that moment when the significative intention (still silent and wholly in act) proves itself capable of incorporating itself onto my culture and the culture of others—of shaping me and others by transforming the meaning of cultural instruments" (S, 115/92).

25. Stefan Kristensen, *Parole et subjectivité: Merleau-Ponty et la phénoménologie de l'expression* (Hildesheim: Olms, 2010), 146–47. I would like to thank Kristensen for sharing with me his unpublished transcription of "The Problem of Speech" course notes. I also wish to thank Emmanuel de Saint Aubert for allowing me to compare Kristensen's transcription with his own. Concerning my references to these course notes, from now on I will follow Saint Aubert's system of references to the unpublished manuscripts stored at the Bibliothèque Nationale de France. In my turn, I shared Kristensen's transcription with the participants of a seminar I directed in 2009 at the State University of Milan, Italy. One of them was Claudio Rozzoni, who took that opportunity to write a very thoughtful and rigorous article on those course notes, which has been published under the title "Intorno a una domanda 'inedita' di Merleau-Ponty: Proust philosophe?," *Chiasmi International* 12 (2010): 183–201.

26. See Rozzoni, "Intorno a una domanda 'inedita' di Merleau-Ponty: Proust philosophe?," 183.

27. This aspect is highlighted by J. M. Edie, who points out that, according to Merleau-Ponty, "the structures of *la langue* . . . are, though logically presupposed in analysis, historically and ontologically generated by speech itself." J. M. Edie, "Was Merleau-Ponty a Structuralist?," *Semiotica* IV (1971): 315n4.

28. The Proustian narrator refers to the "chaos that is everything we see" (*Jeunes filles*, 398/565) or evokes the experience "to gaze delightedly at a belt of liquid azure without knowing whether it belonged to sea or sky" (ibid., 399/566). About the senses and the importance of "metaphoricity" in Merleau-Ponty's philosophy, see Chapter 5.

29. See Mauro Carbone, "Composing Vinteuil: Proust's Unheard Music," *Res* 47 (Autumn 2005): 163–65.

30. *Swann*, 343/495–96; Merleau-Ponty's emphases.

31. Merleau-Ponty's emphases.

32. See PbParole, [109]v.

33. *Temps retrouvé*, 186/274.

34. In the preface of this book, Merleau-Ponty affirms that the "operative intentionality is the one that provides the text that our various forms of knowledge attempt to translate into precise language" (PhP, XIII/xxxii).

35. Therein lies the very sense of Proust's *Recherche*. Indeed, as Paul Ricoeur writes, this novel "posits an equation which, at the end of the work, should be completely reversible between life and literature, which is to say, finally, between the impression preserved in its trace and the work of art that states the meaning of the impression. This reversibility, however, is nowhere simply given.

It must be the fruit of the labor of writing. In this sense *Remembrance* could be entitled *The search for the lost impression*, literature being nothing other than the impression regained." Paul Ricoeur, *Temps et récit*, vol. 2, *La configuration dans le récit de fiction* (Paris: Seuil, 1984); trans. Kathleen McLaughlin and David Pellauer, *Time and Narrative* (Chicago: University of Chicago Press, 1985), 2:150–51. It is indeed of "equation" that we need to speak, as Ricoeur does quite rightly, rather than of identity, for the reversibility of life and literature will not generate a mutual coincidence anyway.

36. This Proustian passage from *Swann*, 344/496 is not quoted in the "The Problem of Speech" unpublished notes, whereas it appears both in *The Visible and the Invisible* and in the "The Cartesian Ontology and the Ontology of Today" course notes. Merleau-Ponty's emphases, which I am reproducing, are only in the latter version.

37. "Never was spoken language so inexorably determined, never had it known questions so pertinent, such irrefutable replies." *Swann*, 346/500.

38. See *Swann*, 344/497. Merleau-Ponty's emphasis in NC, 192.

39. Ibid.

40. Ibid. Merleau-Ponty's emphasis in NC, 192.

41. See PM, 53/37, footnote *, where the French word *filigrane* is translated as "adumbration." About Merleau-Ponty's use of that word, see also Chapter 6, note 54.

42. "Truth is itself *zweideutig*. . . . The *Vieldeutigkeit* is not a shadow to be eliminated by true light" (NC, 305.) See also Maurice Merleau-Ponty, "Philosophy and Non-Philosophy Since Hegel," trans. and ed. Hugh J. Silverman, in *Philosophy and Non-Philosophy since Merleau-Ponty* (New York: Routledge, 1988), 9–83, here at 40.

43. As I already did in Chapter 1, note 34, it is inevitable, but also very important, to remind ourselves that Walter Benjamin too compares Proust's work to a sort of "clouded surface" composed of words: the surface of a "tapestry" where writing weaves involuntary memory and forgetting. See Walter Benjamin, "The Image of Proust," in *Illuminations* (New York: Schocken Books, 1970), 202–3. In other words, for Walter Benjamin, as well as for Merleau-Ponty, it is impossible to think of Proust's work as articulated in two distinct phases, namely, *first recollecting and then writing*. In fact, these two experiences—recollecting and writing—are mutually entangled, precisely like the yarns in a tapestry. In this sense, I cannot but disagree with Andrew Benjamin, who considers "recognition" as "preliminary" with respect to "the intermediary act of writing" and bases on this opinion his critical remarks concerning my book on Proust in his article, "Writing on Proust Today: Notes on Mauro Carbone's *An Unprecedented Deformation*," *Research in Phenomenology* 44 (2014): 421–31, in particular 429 for the quoted expressions.

44. See VI, 166/125.

45. I shall flag that Merleau-Ponty is using here the term *transparency* without any critical implication (as for instance, in the aforementioned quotation from

PM, 53/37, and again in VI, 138/101) on the basis of the Latin etymological meaning of that very term, which is "to appear through" a medium. Therefore Merleau-Ponty cannot be considered as criticizing the notion of "transparency" as such. Rather, he can be considered as criticizing "*any ideology of transparency*," as Emmanuel Alloa states, meaning that ideology as the promise of "the return to the immediate, the coincidence" (VI, 162/122), namely, an ideology of *immediacy* in the sense of abolition of any possible medium. See Alloa, *La resistance du sensible: Merleau-Ponty critique de la transparence* (Paris: Kimé, 2008), 16.

46. See Friedrich Nietzsche, *Die frohliche Wissenschaft* (1887), in *Nietzsche Werke: Kritische Gesamtausgabe*, part 5, vol. 2, ed. G. Colli and M. Montinari (Berlin: Walter de Gruyter, 1973); trans. W. Kaufmann, *The Gay Science* (New York: Vintage Books, 1974), 38.

47. This happens when, by concealing the visible, one ends up magnifying it.

48. See Carbone, *Philosophy-Screens: From Cinema to the Digital Revolution*.

5. Metaphoricity: Carnal Infrastructures and Ontological Horizons

1. [As noted in Chapter 2, in French, *surrection* is often used in a geological sense to refer to tectonic upsurge or uplift. This term has not been translated here, since it is recognizable as the root of a number of familiar English words, words such as "resurrection" and "insurrection," which are indeed used by the author as closely related to *surrection*. —Trans.]

2. [As in English, the French term *figuratif* (figurative) is normally used as an adjective. Its nominalization is not unheard of, for example, figurative painters might be referred to as *les figuratifs* ("figuratives"). The Merleau-Pontian *figuratif* bears little relation to this latter example, however; it might be understood as similar to "connective," that is, as that which serves to *connect*, or a "fixative," which is used to *fix* things. In a similar way, "a figurative" is that whose function is "to figurate." —Trans.]

3. See in particular the 1953–54 course, *Le problème de la parole* (The Problem of Speech), where the analogy is pushed so far as to directly associate, with Proust, metaphor and painting—e.g., PbParole, [102]v(4), [105]v(6), [112](12), [125](4). See also Chapters 1 and 4.

4. For more on this point, see Emmanuel de Saint Aubert, *Du lien des êtres aux éléments de l'être* (Paris: Vrin, 2004), sec. B, chap. 2.

5. See in particular OntoC, 182–86.

6. See Emmanuel de Saint Aubert, *Le scénario cartésien* (Paris: Vrin, 2005).

7. [Emmanuel de Saint Aubert is here referring to Descartes's *Meditation VI* on the union of mind-body "*confondu et mêlé*," over against the caricature of Cartesian mind-body dualism of separate and distinct substances. Here is Descartes's text from the French edition of 1647 from which Merleau-Ponty has been reading:

> La nature m'enseigne aussi par ces sentiments de douleur, de faim, de soif, etc., que je ne suis pas seulement logé dans mon corps, ainsi qu'un pilote

en son navire, mais, outre cela, que je lui suis conjoint très étroitement et tellement confondu et mêlé, que je compose comme un seul tout avec lui. Car, si cela n'était, lorsque mon corps est blessé, je ne sentirais pas pour cela de la douleur, moi qui ne suis qu'une chose qui pense, mais j'apercevrais cette blessure par le seul entendement, comme un pilote aperçoit par la vue si quelque chose se rompt dans son vaisseau; lorsque mon corps a besoin de boire ou de manger, je connaîtrais simplement cela même, sans en être averti par des sentiments confus de faim et de soif. Car en effet tous ces sentiments de faim, de soif, de douleur, etc., ne sont autre chose que de certaines façons confuses de penser, qui préviennent et dépendent de l'union et comme du mélange de l'esprit avec le corps.

(*Oeuvres*, ed. Charles Adam and Paul Tannery [Paris: Cerf, 1897–1909; reissue, Paris: Vrin, 1964–1974], 9:64.) The first problem for the English translator with the crucial Cartesian phrases "*confondu et mêlé*," "*sentiments confus*," and "*façons confuses de penser*" is that the English "confusion" meaning "fusion together" is obsolete or rare. Therefore, it must not be taken as a cognate of the French word, since in English, "confusion" has a primary meaning of mental discomfiture, perturbation, agitation, or disorder. In his *Le scénario cartésien*, which he references, Saint Aubert pointed this out: "*La 'confusion' n'est pas d'abord chez Merleau-Ponty l'indicatif péjoratif du manque de rigueur*" (24) ("Confusion is not in the first place, for Merleau-Ponty, a pejorative term indicative of lack of rigor").

The second problem is that translating "confusion" as "mixture" or "blend" overlooks that Descartes wrote both words, "*confondu et mêlé*," where *mêlé* would have the meaning of mixture. Furthermore, "*confondu*" is the stronger of the two terms, meaning more than mixing together two distinct substances, but intermingling them throughout the *lived experience* of the mind-body union. Here Descartes comes closest to the phenomenological insight that he fails to pursue but becomes the hallmark of Merleau-Ponty's phenomenology of embodiment.

After lengthy correspondence and face to face conversations between us, I have chosen mainly the English noun "commingling" to translate the French "confusion," for two reasons. It is a word distinct from either mixture or blend, and I believe it has the stronger, more radical meaning intended. As well, it is a term used by the English translators, Laurence J. Lafleur (1951) and Donald A. Cress (1993). Jonathan Bennett uses "intermingling" (2017, online: "Early Modern Texts"). In the second occurrence of "confusion" in Saint Aubert's chapter, I have attempted to show the Cartesian vs. Merleau-Pontian meaning by hyphenating: commingling-encroachment, thereafter using "commingling" to show the threefold repetition: anthropological, phenomenological, epistemological. Finally, in the last occurrence in the all-important note 131, I have left the word "confusion" as Merleau-Ponty wrote it in contrast to encroachment. By that point, I think the reader should be well informed. —Galen A. Johnson]

8. "... before being reason, humanity is another corporeity. The concern is to grasp humanity first as another manner of being a body." Natu, 269/208.

9. Thanks to the merging of the theme and the phor. [The "theme" is that which is conveyed by the "phors"; e.g., in "Juliet is the sun," the *phors* are Juliet and the sun, while the *theme* is beauty. —Trans.] If analogy takes the form "A is to B as C is to D," then metaphor would take the form "A of D," "C of B," or even "A is C." See Chaïm Perelman, *Traité de l'argumentation: La nouvelle rhétorique* (1958) (Brussels: Éditions de l'Université de Bruxelles, 2008).

10. PbParole, [112](12), course on March 11, 1954; see also [102]v(4).

11. Martin Heidegger, *Der Satz vom Grund* (Pfullingen: Günther Neske, 1957); *The Principle of Reason*, trans. Reginald Lilly (Bloomington: Indiana University Press, 1996), 48.

12. Paul Ricoeur, *La métaphore vive* (Paris: Seuil, 1975), 357; *The Rule of Metaphor*, trans. Robert Czerny (London: Routledge, 1978), 280.

13. Heidegger, *Der Satz vom Grund*, 88–89.

14. For more on this point, see Emmanuel de Saint Aubert, *Vers une ontologie indirecte* (Paris: Vrin, 2006).

15. [The French term *figure* encompasses what we refer to in English as to "figures of speech," "rhetorical figures," or "figural tropes" more generally. I have decided to use the word "figure" in its simple form throughout this chapter, since the author, like Merleau-Ponty, frequently plays on a variety of senses of "figure"—as referring, for example, to figures of speech, figurative drawing, and shapes and images, among other senses of the term. —Trans.]

16. See Emmanuel de Saint Aubert, *Être et chair I: Du corps au désir— l'habilitation ontologique de la chair* (Paris: Vrin, 2013), sec. A.

17. PhP, 165/142.

18. MSME, 129. See also PhP, 175, 377; Sorb, 311; MSME, 135; Natu, 279.

19. PhP, 196/172.

20. See RC, 146.

21. See PM, 86, 89, 90, 99; S, 68, 69, 71, 76; TiTra, 29; OE-ms, [13](7); OE, 71.

22. "If we wish to see what underlies the 'symbolic function' itself, we must first understand that even intelligence does not fit well with intellectualism. What compromises thought for Schneider is not that he is incapable of perceiving the concrete givens as exemplars of a unique *eidos*, or of subsuming them under a category; rather, it is that he can only link them through an explicit subsumption." PhP, 148/129.

23. [Saint Aubert intends to highlight a spatiostructural opposition here between "com-prehension" (from *com-prendre*, a play on words meaning "to understand" and "to take with") and "ex-plication" (suggesting an unfolding movement, in contrast to the inwardly directed "im-plication"). —Trans.]

24. "Not intellectual conjuring ... not deciphering of signs by interpretive understanding ... but bodily intentionality ... immanent sense of the 'metamorphosis,' gestural sense for a body that knows the syntax of gesture, synthesis without analysis." MSME, 166.

25. PhP, 149/129–30. For the opposition between metaphor and categorical subsumption, See PbParole [98]v.

26. PhP, 150/131.

27. See *Être et chair I*, chap. 1, §§3 and 4.

28. PhP, 461–62/424–25. See also PhP, 272/244–45.

29. PM, 110/78.

30. PhP, 168/145.

31. Ibid., 178/154.

32. See, e.g., EM2, [149](4), [178](IV), [228](1); VI, 258, 301.

33. "With the notion of body schema, it is not only the unity of the body that is described in a new way, but also, through it . . . the unity of the object. . . . My body is the common texture of all objects" (PhP, 271–72/244). The identity of the thing "is thus of the same nature" as the identity of the body schema (see PhP, 216/191).

34. See PhP, 260, 270, 366, 367, 377; EM2 [156], [164](1); etc.

35. PbParole, [98]v, course on March 4, 1954.

36. Ibid., [105]v(6) and [102]v(4).

37. Ibid., [125](4), course on March 25, 1954.

38. For more on this point, see *Être et chair I*, sec. A.

39. NCorps, [85]v(4).

40. OntoC, 213.

41. PbPassiv, 242/185.

42. VI, 116–17/84.

43. FP [3a]. In the margins of this paragraph, we can just make out a note left during a rereading of the text: "Imago, emblem, overdetermination."

44. VI, 193/147. See also VI, 183/139.

45. S, 290/229 (translation slightly modified).

46. Dolto's recurrent formula, quoted by Gérard Guillerault, *Les deux corps du moi: Schéma corporel et image du corps en psychanalyse* (Paris: Gallimard, 1996), 215.

47. Paul Claudel, November 1911, *Journal* (Paris: Gallimard, 1968), 1:208.

48. Guillerault, *Les deux corps du moi*, 216.

49. MSME, 162.

50. See in particular VI, 184.

51. It is debatable, however, whether Merleau-Ponty goes far enough in his quest for the foundations of intersubjectivity. His wager on the ascending dynamic—from the body to the flesh, from the body to its progressive animation and sublimation—risks blinding him to metaphorphoses in the other direction. He does not seem to take full stock of the retroactive impact of language here, the impact of others' speech on our corporeal institution: the extent to which our flesh is edified or undermined, disfigured, or transfigured by the words of others. Yet to be fully open to metaphoricity, our systems of equivalences require that the life of desire animating them benefits from the symboligenetic power (*la puissance symboligène*) of this

word, its essential contribution to the edification of the body image in Dolto's sense. In other words, this philosophy of the flesh has failed to identify as such the differentiations that it has initiated between body schema and body image, and this lack is not without consequences when it comes to theorizing the anthropological foundations of our capacity for forging and understanding metaphors—a body schema without body image remains closed to metaphoricity.

52. For more on this point, see *Être et chair I*, sec. C, in particular chaps. 8 and 9.

53. That is, in the context of his reconsideration of *Leibhaftigkeit*.

54. See NTi, [343], April 1960.

55. See Chapter 2.

56. We should not forget that, during his first year at the Collège de France, Merleau-Ponty included a course on the "literary use of language" (*Recherches sur l'usage littéraire du langage*).

57. For more on this point, see *Le scénario cartésien*, chap. 2, and *Vers une ontologie indirecte*, 119–34.

58. "Intolerance of ambiguity as an emotional and perceptual personality variable," in *Journal of Personality* 18 (September 1949): 108–43.

59. See in particular RAE, 152–64, and Sorb, 304–7. More broadly, see *Être et chair I*, chap. 7.

60. EM2, [189]v(2).

61. VI, 203/155.

62. Ibid., 189/144.

63. See *Être et chair I*, chap. 6.

64. Logical reversibility designates a capacity for regrouping actions together in thought alone, more precisely, the mental cancellation of a transformation: the capacity to imagine a transformation (leading from state A to state B), followed by a reciprocal transformation (which cancels the preceding), but without ever passing through action.

65. EM3 [245]v(28); OE 65.

66. Ibid., [245]v(28).

67. OE, 65/172.

68. EM3, [245]v(28).

69. OE, 65/180.

70. Ibid., 64–65/180.

71. Ibid., 17/162.

72. Circumscribing time, so as to not have more than one relationship of mastery with space, approaching transformation from above by neutralizing its irreversibility, comes to envisage action per se as a *given*, in the projective status of the latter, without any of the epistemological encroachment and existential implication that define mystery. This is a case of observing action without participating in it, simulation without involving the sensorimotor, of playing at it without having to deal with its consequences. For the ways in which Merleau-

Ponty is liberally inspired by Gabriel Marcel's conception of mystery, see *Le scénario cartésien*, chap. 3.

73. MSME, 48.
74. Ibid., 57 and 49.
75. Ibid., 56 and 49.
76. See ibid., 49–50 and 56–57.
77. Ibid., 56.
78. "*Diacritical conception of the perceptual sign.* It's the idea that we can perceive differences without terms, divergences [*écarts*] in relation to a level that is itself not an *object*,—the only way to have an awareness of perception that is faithful to it and that does not transform the perceived into an ob-ject, into the meaning it has in the isolating or reflective attitude" (MSME, 203). The next Working Note, titled "Diacritical perception," continues on the same theme: "To perceive a physiognomy, an expression, is always to make use of diacritical signs, as well as to make an expressive gesticulation with one's body. Here each sign has no other value than to differentiate itself from the others, and differences appear for the onlooker or are used by the speaking subject that are not defined by the terms between which they occur, but which on the contrary define them" (MSME, 203–4).
79. See *Vers une ontologie indirecte*, 47ff.
80. NCorps, [88](9). See also PbPassiv, 201–2.
81. Husserl's own relationship with writing is markedly different. The case of *Paarung* ("pairing") is perhaps emblematic of this difference. Ignoring the mathematical origins of this term, as well as the subjective and asymmetrical nature of Husserl's *Paarung*, Merleau-Ponty confirms, on a number of occasions, his own literal meaning of "coupling" (*accouplement*) as a totally reciprocal action *à deux* (for two), between my own body and that of the other. "Husserl said that the perception of the other is like the 'phenomenon of coupling.' The word is barely a metaphor. In the perception of the other, my body and the other's body are paired together, accomplish an action *à deux*" (RAE, 178). See *Être et chair I*, chap. 2, §§2 and 3.
82. VI, 275/221; Working Note, November 26, 1959.
83. Ibid.
84. VI, 269/215; Working Note, November 1959.
85. Ibid.
86. Ibid., 216.
87. See PbParole, [105]v(6), [165].
88. See Desc, [77](2); OE-ms, [57](4); OE, 16.
89. See NTi, [286]; EM3, [232](2); OE-ms, [15](11), [18]v(18), [24]v(29), [41]v(12), [162]; OE, 35, 40; NTontoc, [115], [117].
90. See PbParole, [112](12); OE-ms, [14]v(10), [39](7), [49]v(28); OE, 27, 74.
91. Gaston Bachelard, *L'eau et les rêves: Essai sur l'imagination de la matière* (Paris: José Corti, 1942), 6.
92. D'Annunzio, cited in ibid., 24.

93. From 1955 to 1959, these three directions are progressively united under "crystallization." The manuscript *La Nature ou le monde du silence* hopes to "replace the notion of decision with that of crystallization. This is what differentiates me from Sartre" (NMS, [136], probably autumn 1957). "Sartre's thought does not adhere to this crystallization. It is essentially a thought that likes to talk, that does not enter into the silence of the perceiver" (NPVI, [136](3)–[136]v(4), spring 1959).

94. EM2, [156]; see also [164](1)–[164](2).

95. See OE, 19–20/163.

96. Ibid., 24/165; see also OE-ms [38]v(6).

97. See OntoC, 167; PhAuj, 56–57, [70]; OE, 85.

98. Paul Klee, in Will Grohmann, *Paul Klee* (Paris: Flinker, 1954), 160. "Art does not reproduce the visible; rather, it makes visible." Klee, "Credo du créateur," in *Théorie de l'art moderne* (Paris: Gallimard, 1998), 34. In Merleau-Ponty, see particularly PhAuj, 57; OE-ms, [49]v(28); OE, 74; VI, 198; OntoC, 171, [7]v(7bis).

99. PhP, 358/324.

100. "Some shadows and lights in a flat painting are thus sufficient to give it relief. . . . The painting's shadows and lights give relief by mimicking 'the original phenomenon of relief.'" PhP, 28/21.

101. S, 202/160.

102. This notion is perfectly in line with Merleau-Ponty's comprehension of perceptual logic, particularly with regard to his "theory of perception as divergence [*écart*]."

103. VI, 196–98/151.

104. PhP, 296/267.

105. OntoC, 167.

106. Ibid., 195.

107. EM3, [245](27).

108. "Incorporeals are either pre-things or figuratives (matrices)." Ibid., [243]v(24).

109. This does not mean that there are "two bodies," an organic body and a breath-body, the possible gnostic conclusion that might be derived from a dualistic reading of Merleau-Ponty or Dolto. There is only a corporeity that animates itself, and animates its own animation; the notion of the "incorporeal" is thus important for avoiding either a *dualism* or a *monism* of the flesh.

110. EM3, [245]v(28).

111. "Figuratives are not *metaphors*; they are where metaphors come from." EM3, [254].

112. S, 24/17.

113. OE, 36/169.

114. OE-ms, [41](11); see also OE, 36; the "refusal to *haunt* the visible," NTontoc, [117], course on February 2, 1961.

115. UAC, 28.

116. "... analogon—non-elucidated concept in Sartre's *L'Imaginaire*, and in Husserl, when he says that life, the organism are thought of as '*analogon*' of *Ichlichkeit* (*Krisis, Beilage* on biology).... In Sartre, one unloads onto the *analogon* everything positive in the image, so as to be free to define the imaginary negatively (as is the case with Husserl: to be free to define *Ichlichkeit* as pure consciousness)." PhAuj, 124.

117. "The theory of the *analogon* is inadequate. It assumes a disconnect between the observable and the unobservable, or the imaginary and the real. While also throwing away the bridge" (OE-ms, [158]). "Painting is not an *analogon*, but an acquired body. Culture = imaginary body" (NArn2, [5](3), probably spring or summer 1960). "Painting itself here generates the corporeal-existential reprise that nevertheless alone gives it its meaning.... This is what Sartre called the *analogon*—but it is an *analogon that itself generates the very analogy* of which, in retrospect, it appears to be the bearer" (NTi, [346], May 13, 1960, unpublished Working Note titled "Peinture (Chastel)"). "Critique of the *analogon*: support [*point d'appui*] for referring to the absent In-Itself" (OntoC, [8](8bis)).

118. "This is how we have a being that is not an 'in itself,' and neither is it nothing: paintings—icons. This is the internal double of things, descending in them, a returned vision, that which weaves it internally, descending into the visible. The imaginary, in the true sense (in what makes it free, beyond the seen *analogon*) is not the sign of an absent in-itself (and valued as present by forgetting the entire in-itself, nothingness valued as being). It is the carnal double, the internal equivalent, the secret cipher of the real." OntoC, 174.

119. In particular his *Index scolastico-cartésien* (Paris: Félix Alcan, 1912; Paris: Vrin, 1966); *La liberté chez Descartes et la théologie* (Paris: Félix Alcan, 1913; Paris: Vrin, l982); *René Descartes: Discours de la méthode, texte et commentaire* (Paris: Vrin, 1925). Merleau-Ponty read also *Introduction à l'étude de Saint Augustin* (Paris: Vrin, 1929) and *L'esprit de la philosophie médiévale* (Paris: Vrin, 1932).

120. See NTontoc, [101], [151]–[154], [168], [172].

121. For more on this context, see *Le scénario cartésien*, chap. 2, particularly 56ff.

122. OE, 36/169 and 41/171 (translation slightly modified).

123. If there were a sufficiently close conceptual relationship between Merleau-Ponty's philosophy and Heidegger's thought, this confrontation would be indirectly relevant. Yet this is not the case. For further discussion, see *Vers une ontologie indirecte*.

124. NArn1, [14](8).

125. VI, 269/217; Working Note, November 1959.

126. For more on this opposition between the "modern world" and the "classical world," and how Merleau-Ponty employs this in the outline of his own ontology, see *Du lien des êtres aux éléments de l'être*, sec. B.

127. HO, 151.

128. Ibid.

129. SNS, 214/176, 1946.

130. VI, 324/270; Working Note, December 1960.

131. On the evening of May 3, 1961, the philosopher passed away, leaving on his desk the following words, obviously read over numerous times, underlined and annotated in the margins: "*Encroachment*, which for me is philosophy, is nothing but *confusion* for Descartes, that is, *nothingness* [*néant*]. The philosophy of distinct thoughts . . . philosophy founded on God, i.e. assuming God without even wishing to see him, even using him to find reasons not to see him . . . is a philosophy of an objective, horizontal being, the opposite of our own philosophy of vertical Being. And this is the very philosophy that renders the other inaccessible . . . because it seeks the other *behind* an impassable objective Being." Desc, [84](9).

132. See *Être et chair I*, chap. 6.

133. EM1, [16](F), autumn 1958.

134. NMS, [79] and [78].

135. For a more extensive analysis of Merleau-Ponty's critique of theology, see Emmanuel de Saint Aubert, "'L'Incarnation change tout': Merleau-Ponty critique de la 'théologie explicative'," in *Archives de Philosophie* 71, no. 3 (2008): 371–405.

136. See, e.g., NTi, [226].

137. SNS, 214/176.

138. See RC, 156.

139. See PM, 42; S, 297; OntoC, 202. Merleau-Ponty borrows the expression from Claudel, "Traité de la co-naissance," *Art poétique*, in *Oeuvre poétique* (Paris: Gallimard, 1967), 149.

140. OntoC, 202.

141. Jean-Paul Sartre, *L'Être et le Néant* (Paris: Gallimard, 1943); "Tel," 1980, 631. Consciousness "is penetrated by a great light . . . all is there, luminous; reflection is in full possession of it, apprehends all . . . 'mystery in broad daylight' . . . without shading, without relief" (*Being and Nothingness*, trans. Hazel Estella Barnes (New York: Philosophical Library, 1956), 570–71.

142. See *Vers une ontologie indirecte*, chap. 4.

143. See, e.g., Natu, 122; NMS, [104](D) and [118]v(10).

144. Paul Claudel, *Le soulier de satin* (Paris: Gallimard, 1929), Second Day, Scene XIII.

145. For a theory of metaphor that might be delivered by an analysis of the Double Shadow in the *Soulier*, cf. Valérie Deshoulières, "La métaphore vive ou la représentation de l'Irreprésentable," *Argumentation* 6, no. 4 (1992): 461–71.

146. PhDial, [241](5), course on March 19, 1956.

147. "Not an intellectual *possession*: in truth God is hidden." PhDial, [248], course on April 16, 1956.

148. Ibid., [246](3), course on April 16, 1956.

149. Ibid., [248].

150. EM3, [256] and [244]v(26), April or May 1960.

151. See *Le scénario cartésien*, chap. 7.

152. Merleau-Ponty considers Leibniz the major representative of "surveillant" thought from above (*la pensée de survol*), to echo an expression borrowed from the Leibnizian Raymond Ruyer, "absolute overflight" (*survol absolu*).

153. "To explain how I differ: in that Leibniz speaks of the monad he is, as though he were not—Like something surveyed by his mind from above—The world is overflown in the same way. . . . He does not see the world as *erlebt*, vertical, the *Erfahrung*; neither the *fungierende* intentionality opening to time, the carnal world, nor the chiasm and the *Ineinander*, he finds himself above all of this—Neither the silence of the visible and the originality of the world of *lekta*. Whatever he says about expression, perspective, or signs, even when true, is always seen through the medium of objectivity." NTontoc [127], beginning of 1961.

154. See *Le scénario cartésien*, chap. 1.

155. See Gottfried Leibniz, *Die philosophischen Schriften von Gottfried Wilhelm Leibniz*, ed. Carl Immanuel Gerhardt, 7 vols. (Berlin, 1875–1890), 5:500–501.

156. S, 239/190.

157. To reclaim the older, more appropriate translation of the Greek "pantocrator."

158. NMS, [27](5)–[27](6), probably autumn 1957.

159. PhAuj, 88, 1959.

160. Claudel, *L'histoire de Tobie et de Sara*, in *Théâtre II* (Paris: Gallimard, 1965), 1543.

161. For further discussion on Merleau-Ponty's cultivation of this emblematic Claudelian expression, see Chapter 2. See also the course on March 9, 1961 (OntoC, 198ff), titled "*La cohésion de l'Être et la simultanéité: Claudel*" (OntoC, [22](18)).

162. SNS, 213/175.

163. Ibid.

164. SNS, 212/175.

165. "It is now more than two thousand years since Europe abandoned so-called vertical transcendence, and it is a little extravagant to forget that Christianity is for the most part the recognition of a mystery in the relation of man to God. This derives precisely from the Christian God's refusal of any vertical relation of subordination. He is not simply a principle of which we are the consequences, a will whose instruments we are. There is a sort of impotence of God without us. Claudel goes so far as to say that God is not above but beneath us—meaning that we find him not as a suprasensible model which we must follow but as another self in ourselves which dwells in and authenticates our darkness. Transcendence no longer hangs over man; strangely, man becomes its privileged bearer." PM, 118/83–84.

6. On the Poetic and the True

1. "An Unpublished Text by Maurice Merleau-Ponty: A Prospectus of His Work," presented by Martial Gueroult, Collège de France, in *The Merleau-Ponty Reader*, ed. Ted Toadvine and Leonard Lawlor (Evanston, IL: Northwestern University Press, 2007), 288–89. An earlier version of this text in English translation appeared in *The Primacy of Perception*, trans. Arleen Dallery (Evanston, IL: Northwestern University Press, 1964), 3–11. Original French: "Un inédit de Maurice Merleau-Ponty," *Revue de métaphysique et de morale* 4 (1962): 401–9. Reprinted in *Parcours deux, 1951–1961* (Lagrasse: Verdier, 2000), 36–48.

2. "What is truth?" Pilate had asked, then proclaimed, "behold the man" (*ecce homo*). See John 18:8 and 19:5.

3. "An Unpublished Text by Maurice Merleau-Ponty," 283.

4. Michel Foucault, "Nietzsche, Genealogy, History," in *The Foucault Reader*, ed. Paul Rabinow (New York: Pantheon Books, 1984), 78.

5. Friedrich Nietzsche, *The Will to Power*, ed. Walter Kaufmann, trans. Walter Kaufmann and R. J. Hollingdale (New York: Vintage Books, 1967), 822 (1888).

6. Maurice Merleau-Ponty, "*Christianisme et ressentiment*," in *La Vie Intellectuelle* XXXVI (1935): 278–306; English: "Christianity and *Ressentiment*," trans. Gerald G. Wening, *Review of Existential Psychology and Psychiatry* 9, no. 1 (Winter 1968): 1–22.

7. Friedrich Nietzsche, *The Gay Science*, trans. Walter Kaufmann (New York: Vintage Books, 1974), preface, sec. 2, 34–35.

8. Ibid., preface, sec. 3, 35–36.

9. My translation of Merleau-Ponty's French text: "Idée qu'il y a une philosophie qui n'interroge pas assez, qui fuit l'interrogation dans 'places ensoleillées'—toute philosophie est 'transfiguration' (cf. Marx); que la vraie philosophie est au-delà: grand soupçon, abîme, a-philosophie par fidélité à ce que nous vivons; que ceci se termine non par 'tout savoir' (nouveau positivisme) et non par désespoir, mais par la volonté de l'apparence. . . . Nietzsche tient à la qualité du 'philosophe': l'absolu de l'apparence" (NC, 278). An English translation by Hugh J. Silverman of Merleau-Ponty's *Philosophy and Non-Philosophy Since Hegel* is found in *Philosophy and Non-Philosophy Since Merleau-Ponty*, ed. Hugh J. Silverman (New York: Routledge, 1980), 9–83. See page 12 for Silverman's translation of this passage of Merleau-Ponty's commentary. Further references to Merleau-Ponty's lecture course will include citation of the page number of Silverman's English translation following the citation of the French original.

10. Nietzsche, *The Gay Science*, 38.

11. Edmund Husserl, *Ideas Pertaining to a Pure Phenomenology and to a Phenomenological Philosophy*, First Book: *General Introduction to a Pure Phenomenology*, trans. F. Kersten (Dordrecht: Kluwer Academic, 1982), 44.

12. Friedrich Nietzsche, *On the Genealogy of Morals*, trans. Walter Kaufman and R. J. Hollingdale, in *On the Genealogy of Morals and Ecce Homo* (New York: Vintage Edition, 1967), First Essay, sec. 13, 45.

13. Frank Chouraqui, "Originary Dehiscence: An Invitation to Explore Resonances Between the Philosophies of Nietzsche and Merleau-Ponty," in *Nietzsche and Phenomenology: Power, Life, Subjectivity*, ed. Élodie Boublil and Christine Daigle (Bloomington: Indiana University Press, 2013). In this volume, one finds extensive considerations of the linkages between the thought of Nietzsche and the entire phenomenological tradition including Husserl, Heidegger, and Merleau-Ponty. Some of the material of this part of this chapter is drawn from my own essay in this volume titled "Nietzsche and Merleau-Ponty: Art, Sacred Life, and Phenomenology of Flesh," 195–214.

14. Nietzsche, *The Gay Science*, 38.

15. Ibid., 38.

16. Friedrich Nietzsche, "On Truth and Lie in an Extra-Moral Sense," in *The Portable Nietzsche*, edited and translated by Walter Kaufmann (New York: Penguin Books, 1954), 46–47.

17. Nietzsche, *The Will to Power*, 822 (1888), 435.

18. Frank Chouraqui, *Ambiguity and the Absolute: Nietzsche and Merleau-Ponty on the Question of Truth* (New York: Fordham University Press, 2014), 65.

19. Nietzsche, *The Gay Science*, 107, 163.

20. Chouraqui, *Ambiguity and the Absolute*, 83. Martin C. Dillon makes a similar distinction between the early Nietzsche of "On Truth and Lie in an Extra-Moral Sense" and a later Nietzsche of *The Gay Science* and *Thus Spake Zarathustra*. See M. C. Dillon, "Art, Truth, and Illusion: Nietzsche's Metaphysical Skepticism," in *Symposium: Canadian Journal of Continental Philosophy* 8, no. 2 (Summer 2004): 299–308. Dillon summarizes: "As early as *The Gay Science* and *Thus Spake Zarathustra*, Nietzsche deliberately shifts to the logic of becoming . . . [which] allows Nietzsche to acknowledge the finite truth of appearances, and it is this that allows him to abandon the epistemological and moral nihilism of his early years" (308).

21. See Bernard Flynn, "Merleau-Ponty and the Philosophical Position of Skepticism," in *Merleau-Ponty and the Possibilities of Philosophy*, ed. Bernard Flynn, Wayne J. Froman, and Robert Vallier (Albany: State University of New York Press, 2009), 124–25. Flynn writes, "in the first chapter of *The Visible and the Invisible*, he first considers a form of skepticism which he readily dispatches, namely, Pyrrhonism, which is a form of skepticism that begins with the priority of doubt" (124).

22. See Gianni Vattimo, *Art's Claim to Truth*, trans. Luca D'Isanto (New York: Columbia University Press, 2008), xii. Originally published as *Poesia e ontologia* (Milan: Urgo Mursia Editore S.p.A., 1985). See also *Weakening Philosophy: Essays in Honor of Gianni Vattimo*, ed. Santiago Vabala (Montreal: McGill-Queens University Press, 2007).

23. See Paul Ricoeur, *The Conflict of Interpretations*, ed. Don Ihde (Evanston, IL: Northwestern University Press, 1974); Hans-Georg Gadamer, *Truth and Method*, ed. and trans. Garrett Barden and John Cumming (New York: Seabury Press, 1975).

24. Flynn, "Merleau-Ponty and the Philosophical Position of Skepticism," 126–27.

25. Véronique M. Fóti, "On Truth/Untruth in Heidegger and Merleau-Ponty," *Research in Phenomenology* 13 (1983): 185–98. "We will first consider Merleau-Ponty's account of truth/untruth in perceptual experience. Perception inscribes itself in a horizonal field which is opened up by the perceiver's connaturality to and bodily participation in the perceptible world, and structured by the body's response to the solicitation of the sensible. This structure emerges as equivocal and latent. . . . The openness achieved in perception is always at the surface of a concealed depth; in this way it is primary truth/untruth" (190).

26. Jean Paulhan, *Les fleurs de Tarbes ou la terreur dans les lettres* (Paris: Gallimard NRF, 1941), 168; English translation, 94.

27. Ibid.

28. See Bernhard Waldenfels, "The Paradox of Expression," in *Chiasms: Merleau-Ponty's Notion of Flesh*, ed. Fred Evans and Leonard Lawlor (Albany: State University of New York Press, 2000); Veronique Fóti, *Tracing Expression in Merleau-Ponty: Aesthetics, Philosophy of Biology, and Ontology* (Evanston, IL: Northwestern University Press, 2013), 106, 112; Leonard Lawlor, "Nascency and Memory: Reflections on Véronique Fóti's *Tracing Expression in Merleau-Ponty*," *Chiasmi International: Trilingual Studies Concerning Merleau-Ponty's Thought* 16 (2014): 294; Leonard Lawlor, *Thinking Through French Philosophy: The Being of the Question* (Bloomington: Indiana University Press, 2003), 91; Donald A. Landes, *Merleau-Ponty and the Paradoxes of Expression* (London: Bloomsbury, 2013), 8–9, 18; Lawrence Hass, *Merleau-Ponty's Philosophy* (Bloomington: Indiana University Press, 2008), 155.

29. See André Malraux, *The Voices of Silence*, trans. Gilbert Stuart (Princeton: Princeton University Press, 1978), 324; French original: *Les voix du silence* (Paris: Gallimard, Bibliothèque de la Pléiade, 1951), 322. The Pléiade edition collects together Malraux's three-volume history of art titled *Psychologie de l'art*, published in Switzerland by Albert Skira. The volumes were respectively subtitled *Le musée imaginaire* (1947), *La création esthétique* (1948), and *La monnaie de l'absolu* (1949). Merleau-Ponty's citation from Malraux on "coherent deformation" is from the second volume. Though Malraux stresses the coherence of an artist's style, the phrase "coherent deformation" is Merleau-Ponty's own, a creative deformation of Malraux's text, one might say.

30. Paul Klee, *On Modern Art*, trans. Paul Findlay (London: Faber & Faber, 1948), 31.

31. Paul Valéry, "Pure Poetry: Notes for a Lecture," in *The Art of Poetry*, trans. by Denise Folliot (New York: Pantheon Books, 1958), 185.

32. Ibid., 190.

33. Ibid., 192.

34. Ibid.

35. In *Ideas I*, Husserl himself had stated that for a genuinely descriptive phenomenology, in contrast with exact geometrical concepts, essences necessarily often retain a quality of vagueness or inexactness. Husserl, *Ideas* I, sec. 74, 166. See also secs. 67–69, 153–57.

36. Jean-Luc Nancy, "Shattered Love," in *The Inoperative Community*, trans. Lisa Garbus and Simon Sawhney (Minneapolis: University of Minnesota Press, 1991), 101, 109. French original, "L'amour en éclats," in *Aléa* (Paris: Vrin, 1986).

37. See Exposition Marta Nijhuis, *Eclats naissants: Errances et évanescences du figural*, Université Jean Moulin Lyon 3, April 3–12, 2013.

38. See Georg Hegel, *Phenomenology of Spirit*, "Introduction," trans. A. V. Miller (Oxford: Oxford University Press, 1977), paragraph 86, 55. J. N. Findlay's analysis of paragraph 86 on the meaning of dialectical experience and ambiguity says this: "For consciousness to negate what at first seemed absolutely objective, and for it to regard this absolute truth as a mere truth-for-consciousness, is for consciousness to have lived through an experience (*Erfahrung*) in the phenomenological sense, which always involves self-transcendence" (507).

39. Mauro Carbone, *The Flesh of Images: Merleau-Ponty Between Painting and Cinema*, trans. Marta Nijhuis (Albany: State University of New York Press, 2015), 63.

40. Also see my *The Retrieval of the Beautiful: Thinking through Merleau-Ponty's Aesthetics* (Evanston, IL: Northwestern University Press, 2010), 33, 108–10.

41. Jacques Derrida, *Writing and Difference*, trans. Alan Bass (Chicago: University of Chicago Press, 1978), 27.

42. Ibid.

43. See Cathryn Vasseleu, *Textures of Light: Vision and Touch in Irigaray, Levinas, and Merleau-Ponty* (Andover, MA: Routledge, 1998). Vasseleu stresses the "texture of light" as a fabric in which touch is always implicated in vision. In her review of Vasseleu's book, Kelly Oliver states: "Cathryn Vasseleu takes issue with Martin Jay's thesis in his expansive volume *Downcast Eyes: The Denigration of Vision in Twentieth Century Thought* (1994). Vasseleu persuasively argues that rather than denigrate vision, French theorists—Merleau-Ponty, Levinas, and Irigaray—are trying to reconceive of vision in more productive terms." See review by Kelly Oliver, *Hypatia* 16, no. 1 (Winter 2001): 106.

44. Dennis J. Schmidt has described a "hermeneutic concept" of truth that "is defined not by its universality or stability but by its agility." See *Between Word and Image: Heidegger, Klee, and Gadamer on Gesture and Genesis* (Bloomington: Indiana University Press, 2013), 71.

45. William Luce, *The Belle of Amherst* (Boston: Houghton Mifflin, 1976), 9.

46. The expression does not sound like Dickinson's syntax and cadence of expression and, in fact, Dickinson's own account of poetic feeling emphasizes the cold rather than the light and heat of fire: "If I read a book and it makes my whole body so cold no fire can warm me, I know *that* is poetry. If I feel physically as if the top of my head were taken off, I know *that* is poetry. These are the only ways I know it. Is there any other way?" Cf. *The Letters of Emily Dickinson*, ed. Thomas H. Johnson (Cambridge, MA: The Belknap Press of Harvard University, 1965), Letter 342a, 2:473–74. This is an early letter the poet addressed to Thomas Higginson in August 1870, written when she was forty. I express my thanks to my colleague at the University of Rhode Island, Mary Cappello, for this reference and these opinions regarding Luce's attribution of "phosphorescence" to Dickinson.

47. *The Complete Poems of Emily Dickinson*, ed. Thomas H. Johnson (Boston: Little, Brown, 1960). In the authoritative numbering of the 1775 poems of Dickinson by Thomas H. Johnson, this is poem 1129, 506–7.

48. See Stephen Spender, "Painters as Writers," in *Poets on Painters: Essays on the Art of Painting by Twentieth Century Poets*, ed. J. D. McClatchey (Berkeley: University of California Press, 1988), 142.

49. Arthur Conan Doyle, "The Hound of the Baskervilles," in *Sherlock Holmes: The Complete Novels and Stories, Volume II* (New York: Bantam Books, 1986), 132.

50. Stephen Spender, "One More New Botched Beginning" in *Selected Poems* (New York: Random House, 1964), 80.

51. See "East-West Encounter," trans. Jeffrey Gaines, in *Texts and Dialogues: On Philosophy, Politics, and Culture—Maurice Merleau-Ponty*, ed. Hugh J. Silverman and James Barry Jr. (Amherst, NY: Humanity Books, 1992), 26–58. The transcript of the conference was originally published in *Comprendre*, September 16, 1956. Spender's comments in the English translation are at 32 and 49.

52. In this appeal to writing as the storehouse of permanence and ideality Merleau-Ponty predates but adopts the same position as Derrida in his own introduction to Husserl's "The Origin of Geometry," published in 1962. On the linkage of Merleau-Ponty and Derrida on this point, see the foreword to the English translation of *Husserl at the Limits of Phenomenology*, written by the translator, Leonard Lawlor, and titled "*Verflechtung*: The Triple Significance of Merleau-Ponty's Course Notes on Husserl's 'The Origin of Geometry,'" esp. xxi–xxxii.

53. There is some hesitation by the transcribers of the Course Notes regarding this term "filigree" (*filigrane*). In the original transcription of the fifty-five sheets preserved at the Bibliothèque Nationale de France, prepared by Franck Robert and published as *Merleau-Ponty: Notes de cours sur* L'origine de la géométrie *de Husserl* (Paris: Presses Universitaires de France, 1998), the term "filigrane" does not appear, but there is an {?} to indicate an illegible word (81). In a revised French version by Dominique Darmaillacq of Robert's original

transcription, the {?} is replaced by the French word that Lawlor has translated as "filigree." I thank Leonard Lawlor for his elucidation of this matter.

54. See PM, 53/37, where the French word *filigrane* is translated as Husserl's notion of "adumbration" (*Abschattungen*): "The thing emerges over there, while I think I am grasping it in a given variation of the *hylé* where it is only in adumbration (*où elle n'est qu'en filigrane*)." About Merleau-Ponty's use of this word, see also, Chapter 4 of this book on "the clouded surface." I am grateful to Mauro Carbone for the cross reference he has pointed out to Merleau-Ponty's use of the term "*filigrane*" in *The Prose of the World*.

55. Translation by Bryan Smyth, to whom I express thanks for sharing his English translation of Merleau-Ponty's course notes in advance of publication by Northwestern University Press. I have also consulted on the translation with Marjorie. L. Johnson: "Même notre réflexion sur la perception appartient à la culture. La vérité des phénomènes perceptifs s'offre comme vérité *de* ces phénomènes en dépit de 'mouvement rétrograde' du vrai thématisé. Celui-ci ne peut nous rendre aveugles aux changements de structure qu'il introduit. L'examen complet du 'monde de l'expression' est aussi examen de cet examen. Conscience dernière ne peut être seulement du vrai thématisé, mais de celui-ci + la {?} perceptive. Origine de la vérité" (MSME, 64).

56. Henri Bergson, *The Creative Mind: An Introduction to Metaphysics*, trans. Mabelle L. Andison (New York: Carol Publishing, 1946, 1992), 11.

57. "An Unpublished Text by Maurice Merleau-Ponty: A Prospectus of His Work," 286.

58. *Les Temps Modernes* 55 (May 1950). My translation of the French text is from the back cover of the journal: "On médite pour se comprendre, mais on n'est sûr de s'être compris qu'en s'expliquant devant les autres, en entrant donc dans leur perspective. Ainsi une situation particulière ne se comprend finalement qu'à travers toutes les autres et, bon gré mal gré, philosophes, historiens, savants de toutes les tendances entrent en dialogue et constituent la philosophie effective." This brief text by Merleau-Ponty is published in the original French with new English and Italian translations in *Chiasmi International: Trilingual Studies Concerning Merleau-Ponty's Thought* 20 (2019),199–204.

59. See Mauro Carbone's discussion of the "hollow" in *The Thinking of the Sensible* (Evanston, IL: Northwestern University Press, 2004), xv.

60. See Emmanuel de Saint Aubert's explication of Merleau-Ponty's account of metaphor in terms of "transitional objects" in Chapter 5: "Metaphor is at the forefront of its conquest of the outside world, its conquest of the unknown and unseen, of the depth of the world and other bodies. From this perspective, metaphor is a *transitional object*, in the Winnicottian sense."

61. Merleau-Ponty's three readings of Proust's pages devoted to Swann's listening to Vinteuil's little musical phrase have been analyzed very precisely in their occurrences across Merleau-Ponty's oeuvre in Chapter 4 of this volume. Also see the recent book by Mauro Carbone, *An Unprecedented Deformation: Marcel Proust and the Sensible Ideas*, trans. Marta Nijhuis (Albany: State

University of New York Press, 2010), in which he has given us a detailed and exact analysis of the musical work of Vinteuil as the musical pillar of Proust's *Recherche*, both the *Sonata in F Sharp* for piano and violin prominent in Swann's love affair with Odette and the *Septet* at play in the relationship and breakup of the narrator with Albertine. See esp. 75–81. Stefan Kristensen has also given us an account of Merleau-Ponty's discussion of Elstir, Vinteuil, and Proust in his 1953–54 course at the Collège de France on *The Problem of Speech*, in which Merleau-Ponty poses the "necessity to reexamine language as if it were music." See Stefan Kristensen, "*Valéry, Proust et la vérité de l'écriture littéraire*," in *Chiasmi International: Trilingual Studies Concerning Merleau-Ponty's Thought* 9 (2007): 331–49, at 339.

62. In Chapter 4, Mauro Carbone has also quoted this citation, appropriating it within the context of philosophy and literature as "visual apparatuses" that "show by words."

63. Nancy, "Shattered Love," 82.

64. Ibid., 84. Merleau-Ponty scholar, Martin C. Dillon, wrote something quite similar of love and truth: "Truth is one among many life values. So is love. In my view, they are inseparable. The thought of their inseparability is philosophy." See Martin C. Dillon, *Beyond Romance* (Albany: State University of New York Press, 2001), 11.

65. Rosalyn Diprose has commented on the transition and double bind in which Merleau-Ponty finds himself in this chapter and defends him against critics who take his position as egocentrism: "Upon close scrutiny," she writes, "it is not so clear that for Merleau-Ponty the self as a perceiving body comes before and so dominates the other." See Rosalyn Diprose, *Corporeal Generosity: On Giving with Nietzsche, Merleau-Ponty, and Levinas* (Albany: State University of New York Press, 2002), 182.

66. See Scott Marrato, "'This Power to Which We Are Vowed': Subjectivity and Expression in Merleau-Ponty," in *Time, Memory, Institution: Merleau-Ponty's New Ontology of Self*, ed. David Morris and Kym Maclaren (Athens: Ohio University Press, 2015), 160–79.

67. Maurice Merleau-Ponty, "The Child's Relations with Others," in Toadvine and Lawlor, *The Merleau-Ponty Reader*, 182; French original: RAE, 228.

68. See the discussion of this passage by Emmanuel de Saint Aubert, "*L'imminence de la vérité*," in *Vers une ontologie indirecte: Sources et enjeux critiques de l'appel à l'ontologie chez Merleau-Ponty* (Paris: Vrin, 2006), 257–60.

69. Mikel Dufrenne, *The Phenomenology of Aesthetic Experience*, trans. Edward S. Casey with Albert A. Anderson, Willis Domingo, and Leon Jacobson (Evanston, IL: Northwestern University Press, 1973), 518.

70. Ibid., 519.

Index

abstraction, 174
Adam (Biblical character), 64
Addison, Joseph, 93
Alexander, Samuel, 46
ambiguity, 137, 138
ambivalence, 137, 184
Amrouche, Jean, 206n94
analogia entis doctrine, 152–53
analogical reasoning, 129
analogicity, 151, 153
analogon, concept of, 151, 231nn116,117
analogy, 23, 127, 128, 129, 195n13, 198n32
apparatus (cinematic, visual), 9, 101–20; definition of, 219–20n6
a-philosophy, conception of, 82, 161, 162
Arendt, Hannah, 195n13
Aristotle, 153, 193n3
art: *vs.* craft, 78
association, 29–30
Auden, W. H., 179
Augustine, of Hippo, Saint, 163
Aurier, Albert, 215n22

Babinski, Joseph, 201n25
Bachelard, Gaston, 33, 91, 145, 146, 202n41

Balázs, Béla, *Visible Man or the Culture of Film*, 103
Balzac, Honoré de, 1, 2, 101, 194n11
Bandy, William Tomas, 214n9
Barbaras, Renaud, 195n16
Barthes, Roland, 210n148
Baudelaire, Charles, 2, 73–74, 76, 77, 95; *The Flowers of Evil*, 26; *Previous Existence*, 17
Beauvoir, Simone de, 2, 89, 194n10, 203n45; *She Came to Stay*, 194n10
being: co-existence of, 43; creation and, 13; dehiscence of, 11, 160, 176; depth as figure of, 34, 51, 148; desire and, 62–67; dimensions of, 8–9; in the Double Shadow, 156; as figurative, 150, 158; flesh and, 31, 32–33, 67, 150; floating in, 67; God and conception of, 156–57; knowing and, 44–46; metaphoricity of, 10; notion of "objective," 155; notion of primary, 11–12; poetics of, 67; qualities of, 154; relationship between, 154, 157; as shadow of the world, 150; three directions of investigation of, 149–50; truth and, 146
Bellour, Raymond, 220n6

241

Benjamin, Andrew, 223n43
Benjamin, Walter: analysis of Proust's work, 7, 20, 21, 23–4, 198nn19,34, 223n43; "On Some Motifs in Baudelaire," 20, 26; *The Origin of German Tragic Drama*, 21
Bennett, Jonathan, 225n7
Bergotte (character), 108, 112, 240n61
Bergson, Henri, 30, 86, 182, 200n49; *The Creative Mind*, 182
Berma (character), 108
Bernard, Emile, 215n22
Bernet, Rudolf, 214n7
blind spot in vision, 216n34
Blondel, Maurice, 136, 155
body: Cartesian idea of, 183–4; dualistic reading of, 230n109; as "expressive space," 108; generality of, 129, 131; incorporeal and, 149; Leonardo da Vinci on, 73; as medium, 23, 107; memory and, 20–21, 22, 25, 27, 29; as metaphor, 10, 122, 133–34; mind and, 22, 92; notion of glorious, 207n114; notion of other's, 187; ontology of, 81; in relation to the sensible world, 19, 92; soul and, 183, 207n113
body image, 131–34
body schema, 127, 128, 129, 130–31, 227n33, 228n51
Boehm, Gottfried, 104
Borges, Jorge Luis, 76
Brentano, Franz, 152
Breton, André, 2; *Abridged Dictionary of Surrealism*, 38, 40; on crystallization, 34; on desire, 38, 39; idea of the sublime point, 8, 85, 86; influence on Merleau-Ponty, 52, 85–86; *Mad Love*, 86; medical career, 201n25; on poetry of found object, 202n39; *Second Manifesto of Surrealism*, 35, 54; surrealism of, 85
Brunschvicg, Léon, 40
Burdeau, Auguste, 204n57

Carbone, Mauro, 7, 9, 177, 178, 191, 195n13, 199n46, 220n12, 222n29, 224n48, 237n39, 239nn54,61, 240n62

carnal generality, 131
Cassirer, Ernst, 196n19
Castin, Nicolas, 202n44
Celan, Paul, 80
Césaire, Aimé, 52
Cézanne, Paul, 1, 51, 53, 72, 82–83, 87–88, 91, 101, 147, 194n11
Chapsal, Madeleine, 209n141
Charbonnier, Georges, 35
Charcot, Jean-Martin, 201n25
Chastel, André, 231n117
chiasm, concept of, 81, 82, 171, 216nn34,35
Chouraqui, Frank, 163, 164
cinema, 102, 103. *See also* apparatus
circularity, 61, 141
Claudel, Paul, 2; *Art poétique*, 40–41, 47, 212n194; on body as metaphor of mind, 133; on desirous knowledge, 208n124; discussion of co-naissance, 2, 8, 41, 43, 64; on entanglement of body and soul, 207n113; on equation of being and being perceived, 42; on experience of desire, 207n110; on genesis of man and the world, 203n56; on glorious body, 207n114; on God, 206n102, 208n124, 209n131, 233n165; idea of existence, 204n62, 205n79; idea of flesh, 63, 206n105, 211n173; idea of the world, 207n116, 212n194; influence of, 40, 52, 63, 203n55, 204n57; *vs.* Leibniz, 64; *Le soulier de satin*, 63–5, 66; on movement, 204n70; *Partage de Midi*, 63; on perception, 43; on problem of knowledge, 45, 46; "Profound Novelty," 52; on reformulation of the world through perception, 204n57; on respiration, 50; on sensing and sensation, 206n108; *vs.* Simon, 63; on simultaneity, 34, 64, 205n81; on union and separation, 65; on vibration, 49, 206n109, 207n111; on visible and invisible, 208n126
clouded surface, 10, 116, 117, 118
Cocteau, Jean, 91
coexistence, 43
coincidence and non-coincidence, 69

communion, 46–47
"com-prehension," *vs.* "ex-plication," 226n23
co-naissance: of beings, 35; conception of, 2, 8, 32, 35, 41, 42; of flesh, 35; phenomenology of, 40–42; sensation as, 47; sublime point, 51
concept, metaphorical origin of, 195n13, 198n32
consciousness, 141, 237n38
contingency, 163
corporeity, 20, 22, 26, 148–49
Coûfontaine, Pensée de (character), 204n62
coupling: conception of, 46, 47–48, 56
Cress, Donald A., 225n7
crystallization, 34, 146, 230n93

D'Annunzio, Gabriele, 229n92
Deary, Janice, 67, 158, 191, 192
death, 61–62, 72
dehiscence, 176
Deleuze, Gilles, 214n7
depth: as figurative, 149; as invisible of the world, 147–48; perception of, 137, 139; poetics of, 32
Derrida, Jacques, 93, 178, 214n7, 218n61
Descartes, René, 7, 23, 83, 105, 124, 151, 152, 157, 162, 178, 224n7, 232n131
Deshoulières, Valérie, 232n145
desire: to be and to be with, 57–59; catalysts of, 38, 39; Claudel on experience of, 207n110; crystallization of, 53; development of notion of, 135–36; disfiguring, 136; drive *vs.*, 56–57, 135; exchanged, 66, 67; existential structures of, 56–60; fertility of, 59; flesh and, 32, 37, 52–62; investigation of, 211n168; metaphorical figure of, 35, 134; mystical horizon of, 58; omnipotence of, 37–40; as openness to the world, 182, 183; potency and, 37; radical capacity for surrection, 37; sexuality and, 136
desirous knowledge, 208n124
Dickinson, Emily, 179, 194n10, 238n46
differend: notion of, 80, 215n29

Dillon, Martin C., 240n64
Diprose, Rosalyn, 240n65
dispositif (cinematic, visual). *See* apparatus
divergence, 141–43
divine freedom, 59–60
Dolto, Françoise, 131, 228n51
Doyle, Arthur Conan, *Hound of the Baskervilles,* 180
drive, 56–57, 135
dualistic thinking, 126
Dufrenne, Mikel, 189
Dupin, M. Auguste (character), 74, 78, 79, 80

éclatement (breaking forth), 11, 159, 160, 172, 176, 189
Edie, J. M., 222n27
Eliot, T. S., "From Poe to Valéry," 75
Elstir (character), 108, 112, 240n61
embodied form, 69, 84, 92
encroachment, 61, 151, 153, 232n131
Erfahrung (experience), 24
Erlebnis (experience), 20, 24
Eros and *Thanatos,* 56, 57
Eve (Biblical character), 64
existence: Claudel's idea of, 204n62, 205n79; coexistence and, 43; perception and, 42–44; vibration as mode of, 49–50
experience, 20, 23–24, 101, 112, 115
expression: experience and, 115; explosion of, 176–77; and expressed, 108, 109; idea of complete, 172–73; paradox of, 170–76; as poetics of depth, 32; theory of, 171–72, 221n22
exscription, 13, 196n20
extraordinary time, 93–94

figural writing, 125, 126–27
figuratives: concept of, 66, 147, 150; incorporeal as, 149; meaning of, 224n2; metaphor and, 195n18; types of, 149
figure: ambiguity of, 136; around desire, 136; as gesture, 126; meaning of the term, 226n15; of modernity, 153; status of, 134
filigrane, 10, 117, 181, 223n41, 238n53, 239n54

Findlay, J. N., 237n38
flesh: as bearer of "corporeal generality," 132; being and, 8, 31, 32–33, 34, 39, 40, 51, 57, 62, 150; Claudel's idea of, 206n105, 211n173; concept of, 10, 60, 122, 211n168; depth and shadow of, 149; encroachment and, 61; logic of, 145; ontology of, 5, 117; philosophy of, 63, 123–25, 133; poetics of, 8, 32; as synesthetic visibility, 117; woman's, 212n191
flesh of the world: *vs.* being, 62; desire and, 52–62; ontology of, 62; in philosophical works, 52, 53; reciprocal envelopment of flesh and, 39, 40, 54–55
Flynn, Bernard, 166, 235n21
food and sexuality, 49
forgetfulness, 24, 25, 29
Fóti, Véronique, 166
Foucault, Michel, 161, 216n31
Frenkel-Brunswik, Else, 137
Freud, Sigmund, 25–26, 57, 93, 143, 182, 214n7

Gadamer, Hans-Georg, 166
Gauguin, Paul, 179
Gelb, Adhemar, 128
Gestalt theory, 196n19
Gilson, Etienne, 152, 155; *Scholastico-Cartesian Index,* 152
God: being and, 156–57; Christian, 233n165; Claudel's idea of, 209n131; expressed in figures, 158; hidden, 155, 157, 158; knowledge of, 208n124; philosophy founded on, 232n131; relation between man and, 155, 233n165; in traditional theology, 158
Goethe, Johann Wolfgang von, 46
Gogh, Vincent van, 215n22
Goldstein, Kurt, 128
Grohmann, Will, 230n98
Guillaumin, Jean, 212n189
Guillerault, Gérard, 133, 195n16

Hegel, Georg Wilhelm Friedrich, 136, 177, 178, 183
Heidegger, Martin, 11, 80, 82, 125, 182, 214n7, 235n13

Higginson, Thomas, 238n46
Homer, *Iliad,* 98
horizon, concept of, 139, 168, 169
Hugo, Victor, 84
Husserl, Edmund: on act of intentionality, 19; on adumbration, 239n54; *Cartesian Meditations,* 48; conception of retention, 26; *The Crisis of European Sciences and Transcendental Phenomenology,* 19; on genuinely descriptive phenomenology, 237n35; on knowledge, 196–97n5; on the "operative," 19; "The Origin of Geometry," 180; on perception of the other, 229n81; on phenomenological "principle of principles," 162; on phenomenology of the constitutive ego, 20; on reduction, 199–200n47; on relation of body and totality, 19
Huyghe, René, 52, 209n137
Hyppolite, Jean, 98, 152

ideas: expression of, 114; of the intellect, 114, 116; order of, 113–14. *See also* sensible ideas
idol, 158
Iliad (Homer), 98
illusion, 163, 164, 166
imaginary: as oneiric being, 145; perception and, 122; separation of real and, 151
imaginary texture of the real, 145–57
imaginative figuration of reality, 145–46
implex ("animal of words"), 69, 82, 84, 92–94, 98, 218n61
incorporation: desirous, 38–39; knowledge as, 48; poetics of, 33
incorporeal, notion of, 147, 148, 149, 230n109
Ineinander, 29, 33, 34, 55, 57, 59, 60
initiation, 26, 27, 29–30
intellectualism, *vs.* intelligence, 226n22
intentionality, 19–20, 21
intercorporeality: being as the other side of, 149–50; flesh as interwoven, 60; Merleau-Ponty's reflection on, 132; promiscuity and, 54–56
intercorporeity, 33, 34, 60

intersubjectivity, 182, 187, 227n51
invisible, relation to visible, 32, 38, 65, 208n126
involuntary memory: corporeal feature of, 20–21, 22, 25; experience of, 23–26; forgetfulness and, 24, 25, 29; Proust on, 23–24; temporality in, 26
Isaac (Biblical character), 47
Isolde (mythological character), 63

Jay, Martin, 237n43
Johnson, Ben, 93
Johnson, Galen A., xiv, 191, 213n2, 237n20

Kafka, Franz, 91
Kandinsky, Vassily, 46
Kant, Immanuel, 5, 42, 75, 95, 128, 162, 175, 194n6, 204n57
Kaushik, Rajiv, 95
Klee, Paul, 147, 174, 230n98, 236n30
Klein, Melanie, 55, 58, 137
knowledge/knowing: being and, 44–46; as coupling, 47–48; as incorporation, 48; relationship with the sensible world, 58
Kristensen, Stefan, 111, 222n25, 240n61

Lacan, Jacques, 91, 152, 214n7
Lacoin, Elizabeth, 194n10, 203n45
Lafleur, Laurence J., 225n7
Landgrebe, Ludwig, 196n5
language: attributes of, 221n20; beneath and beyond, 122; eloquent, 173–74; figuratives of, 149; as form of corporeal sublimation-surrection, 122; functions of, 28; imaginary power of, 104; and its meaning, 106, 107; as life, 173; literary, 4, 118; vs. music, 107; operative intentionality of, 222n34; poetic vs. empirical, 97–98; as power for error, 70; qualities of living, 13, 69–70, 142; separation of image from, 104; silence and, 70; vs. speech, 107, 111–12, 222nn24,27; and things, 69; as translation of truths, 108–9. See also mystery: of language
latent and manifest relationships, 143–45
La Vie Intellectuelle (Intellectual Life) journal, 152

Lefort, Claude, 221n22
Leibniz, Gottfried Wilhelm, 64, 90, 157, 196n19, 233nn152,153
Leonardo da Vinci, 72, 73
life: as hollow of being, 183; language as, 173; meaning of, 188, 212n181
light: analogy between language and, 179; of the flesh, 177–78; new idea of, 177, 178
literary expression, 3, 4, 9, 102, 171
literary truth, 160
literature: anti-literature and, 82; cinema and, 102; Foucault's discussion of, 216n31; parallel between painting and, 110–11; philosophy and, 2, 5, 102, 103–4, 105; tasks of, 102, 103; as visual apparatus, 104, 105, 240n62
logos, 23, 28
Lojkine, Stéphane, 104
love: art and, 185; "error" of, 184; impossibility of, 184; as mixture of oneself and the other, 188; more profound truth of, 185; philosophy of, 186; shattered, 176–77; thinking as, 186; truth and, 185, 188, 240n64
Lovecraft, H. P., 180
Luce, William, *The Belle of Amherst*, 179
Lyotard, Jean François, 80, 215n29

magma, metaphorical figure of, 52, 132
Mallarmé, Stéphane, 2; "Crisis of Verse," 97; *Divagations,* 74; on language, 97–98; "The Mystery in Letters," 96; poetics of, 95–96; *Scribbled in the Theater,* 96; "A Throw of the Dice," 5, 76, 94–95, 96; "The Tomb of Edgar Poe," 74; translations of Edgar Poe's stories, 73–74, 76; Valéry's letter to, 74
Manet, Edouard, 74
Marcel, Gabriel, 23, 40, 136, 229n72
Maritain, Jacques, 152, 155
meaning: conception of, 137, 141
mediation, 117, 120
memory: of the body, 29; as chiasm of remembering and forgetting, 29; consciousness of the past and, 18–19; experience and, 23–24; forgetfulness and, 24, 25, 29; function of body in,

memory (*continued*)
25, 27; implex of, 93; notion of true, 29; reality and, 27, 28, 30. *See also* involuntary memory

Merleau-Ponty, Maurice: analysis of Proust, 7, 9, 17, 18–19, 109, 110, 111, 120, 184–85; attitude to religious faith, 40–41; Breton's influence on, 34, 85–86; on Cézanne's art, 82–83; Claudelian influence on, 34, 40–41, 42, 51, 63–64, 203n55; comment on Stendhal, 169; comparison to Benjamin, 24; courses given at the Collège de France, 2; criticism of explanatory theology, 154–55; critique of Leibniz, 157, 233nn152,153; critique of Sartre, 230; death, 180; engagement with literary works, 2, 135, 194n10; engagement with surrealism, 35–36, 85, 86; first published article, 152, 161; influence of literary authors on, 6; interpretation of Bergson, 200n49; interpretation of Husserl, 162–63, 199n47; interpretation of Nietzsche, 163–64; interpretation of Ponge, 88–89, 91n93; interpretation of Valéry, 8, 71–73, 80, 85, 86; last written words of, 232n131; lectures, 4; on Leonardo da Vinci, 72; library of, 203n45; Mexico Lectures, 39; Nietzschean influence on, 161–62; ontology of, 41, 136, 154; periodizations of the "modern," 7, 9, 105; as philosopher of ambiguity, 137; philosophical objectives of, 123–24; poems about, 180; poetics of, 6, 11, 31–32, 33–35; polemics with Sartre, 91, 151; radio talks, 39; reference to Paulhan, 169–70; on Saussure's theory of signs, 1; Simon's influence on, 27, 52, 210n149; Sorbonne lectures, 88; style of writing, 144; weak universalism of, 166; work on Descartes, 151, 152

Merleau-Ponty's courses and lectures: "The Cartesian Ontology and the Ontology of Today," 4, 27, 52, 104, 105, 115, 178; *Causeries* radio talks, 35, 38–39; "The Cohesion of Being and Simultaneity: Claudel," 44; *Foundations of Psychology*, 132; "Husserl at the Limits of Phenomenology," 180; *Institution and Passivity*, 184; "Man and Adversity," 2, 22, 36, 82, 85, 88, 133, 188; "Man and Object," 91; "Metaphysics and the Novel," 17–18, 102, 103, 105; "Method in Child Psychology," 88; *Nature* lectures, 182–83; *Philosophy and Non-philosophy since Hegel*, 161, 177; *Philosophy Today*, 96; "The Problem of Passivity," 27, 185; "The Problem of Speech," 2, 115; *Research on the Literary Usage of Language*, 2, 3, 8, 11, 70, 110; *The Sensible World and the World of Expression*, 2

Merleau-Ponty's philosophical works: *Being and World*, 34, 60, 138, 139, 147, 148, 150, 157; "The Body as Expression, and Speech," 106; "Brouillon d'une redaction," 68; "Cezanne's Doubt," 72, 194n10; "Cinema et psychologie," 102; *Eye and Mind*, 13, 23, 36, 42, 44, 47, 86, 96–97, 98, 139, 140, 150, 151, 153, 159; "Film and the New Psychology," 9; *Genealogy of the True*, 11, 159; "Indirect Language and the Voices of Silence," 1, 69, 97, 115, 213n2; *Introduction to Ontology*, 36, 51; *Nature, or the world of silence*, 43, 230n93; "The Novel and Metaphysics," 1; *The Origin of Truth*, 11, 159, 221n22; *Phenomenology of Perception*, 1, 2, 12, 18, 20, 21, 23, 24, 25, 44, 46–47, 49, 101, 108, 115, 127, 136, 137, 171; *The Prose of the World*, 2, 11, 12, 35, 44, 52, 85, 96–97, 110, 159, 167, 168, 169, 170, 171, 185, 221n22; "Reading Montaigne," 166; *Sense and Non-Sense*, 9, 85, 101, 219n1; *Signs*, 92, 159, 166, 171; *Structure of Behavior*, 35, 44; "The Film and the New Psychology," 103; "The Metaphysical in Man," 102, 163, 165; "The Philosopher and his Shadow," 170; "The Voice of Silence, or the Philosophical Question," 68; *The World of Perception*, 7, 88, 97

metaphor: body image and, 131–34; body schema and, 127; as co-nascent crystallization, 146; as condensed analogy, 124; of darkness and light, 178; definition of, 121, 125, 131, 193n3, 239n60; of desire, 134; as desired connection, 135; drive and, 135; etymology of the term, 5; as expression of the union of soul and body, 124; figuratives and, 195n18; as flesh, 127, 132, 135; function of, 112; as "metamorphoses," 144–45; ontological significance of, 6; perceptual logic and, 137–38; from perspective of perceptual life, 123; philosophy and, 10, 13; *prégnance* of, 196n19; as sublimation of corporeality, 134; as transitional object, 135
metaphorical intelligence, 140–41
metaphoricity: of the body, 122; conceptuality and, 195n13; and divergence, 141–43; intercorporeal dimension of, 134; ontological, 6; philosophical works on, 195n16; reversibility and, 138–41
Meunier, Isabelle, 214n9
Milton, John, *Paradise Lost*, 98
minority philosophy. *See* a-philosophy
mixing, idea of, 53–54, 56
modern world, *vs.* classical world, 7, 64, 91, 153, 231n126
modernity (modernism), 6, 153
Montaigne, Michel de, 166–67
Mounier, Emmanuel, 52
movement: notion of, 204n70
music: audience, 220n16; of Bach, 189; and its expression, 108; as many diacritical systems, 112; and its sound, 107
mystery: false conception of, 147, 156; of language, 159, 167, 169

Nancy, Jean-Luc, 196n20; "Shattered Love," 176–77, 186
Nature, as weakness of the idea, 183
Nietzsche, Friedrich: *The Birth of Tragedy*, 163; *The Gay Science*, 82, 161, 162, 163, 164, 177; *Genealogy of Morals*, 163; on history, 199n40; phenomenological thinking, 163; philosophical views, 161–62, 235n20; on truth, 164, 235n20; on will to appearance, 162
Nijhuis, Marta, 177, 194n10
nothingness, idea of, 208n121

object, 202nn39,40
Oliver, Kelly, 237n43
ontology, 27, 53, 154
operative intentionality, 19–20
Oriano, Michel, 203n54
overdetermination, notion of, 200n49

painting: abstract expressionism, 174; *vs. analogon*, 231n117; body schema and, 127–28; expression and, 172; formal elements of, 174; idea of universality of, 96, 97; style of, 172; truth as resemblance of, 173
Paradise Lost (Milton), 98
Pascal, Blaise, 155, 156, 157, 158, 165
passion: notion of, 213n197
passivity-activity: communion, 46–47; coupling, 46, 47–48; metaphorical figures of, 46–51; reciprocity of, 46–47; respiration, 46, 47, 50; vibration, 46, 47, 49
Paul, Saint, 49
Paulhan, Jean, *The Flowers of Tarbes*, 169, 170
Pensée de Coûfontaine (character), 204n62
perception: as communication, 48; definition of, 236n25; desire and, 33, 122; existence and, 42–44; imaginary and, 122; motor skills and, 122; of the other, 229n81; speech and, 123; theory of, 42, 142; as type of divergence, 229n78; as vibration, 208n120
perceptual faith, 165–66
perceptual logic, 137, 141, 142–43
perceptual recognition, 146
perceptual truth, 164, 168–69
Perelman, Chaïm, 124
Perse, Saint-John, 104
phenomenological anthropology, 64
phenomenological ontology, 64
phenomenological philosophy, 102

phenomenology, 1, 20, 40–42, 89, 101, 237n35
philosophy: cinema and, 102; of the flesh, 123–25, 133; founded on God, 232n131; of language, 12–13; literature and, 2, 5, 102, 103–4, 105; meaning of, 13; tasks of, 102, 103; as visual apparatus, 104, 105, 240n62
phosphorescence, poetic meanings of, 179–80
physical and nonphysical, separation of, 125
Piaget, Jean, 130, 138–39, 140, 154
Plato, 65, 96, 109, 114, 115, 116, 178; *Republic,* 162
Poe, Edgar Allan: "The Black Cat," 214n9; on creativity in literary art, 78; "The Fall of the House of Usher," 73; French translations of, 73–74, 214nn9–10; literary reputation, 76–77; Mallarmé on, 74; "The Murders in the Rue Morgue," 73, 74, 78; "The Philosophy of Composition," 74, 75, 76, 78–79; on poetic principles, 75–76; "The Purloined Letter," 73, 74, 214n7; "The Raven," 74, 75–76, 77, 79; studies of, 214n7; "The Tell-Tale Heart," 73; theory of poetry, 77; Valéry's fascination with, 74–75
poetic language, 4, 70, 84–86, 87–91, 97–98, 172, 179, 181
poetics, 3, 4, 32, 33–34, 87
poetic truth, 178–79
poetry, 5, 97, 172, 220n16, 238n46. *See also* pure poetry
Politzer, Georges, 136
Ponge, Francis, 2, 8; on being, 87–88; engagement with surrealism, 87; "The Gymnast," 90, 91; interpenetration of active and passive, 90; "Introduction to the Pebble," 88; *Le parti pris des choses (Taking the Side of Things),* 53, 87, 88; literary definition-descriptions of natural world, 87; *The Making of the Pré,* 88; "My Creative Method," 87; "Notes Toward a Shell," 89; poetic of, 69, 87; "R. C. Seine No," 91; on rules of prosody, 217n44; semantic thickness, 88, 89; "Snails," 90; "This Is Why I Have Lived," 89; "The Wasp," 88, 217n48; on writers and musicians, 89–90
Poulet, Georges, 42
power of breaking forth. See *éclatement* (breaking forth)
power to which we are vowed, 187–88
prégnance (literary "pregnancy"), 11, 35, 56, 176, 196n19
primitive analogical intelligence, 138
probabilism, 185–86
promiscuity, 54–56, 61, 132, 211n167
Prouhèze (character), 63, 64, 65
Proust, Marcel: Benjamin's reading of, 20–21, 24, 198nn19,34, 223n43; concept of corporeality, 20–21, 22; *Contre Saint-Beuve,* 71; on effects produced on the visible, 116–17; *The Fugitive,* 184; on hawthorns on the Méséglise Way, 27; idea of clouded surface, 118; *In Search of Lost Time,* 18, 70, 222n35, 223n36; influence on Merleau-Ponty, 2, 7, 21, 24; on literature, 111, 112; on memory and experience, 23–24; notion of embodied time, 199n36; philosophical ideas of, 7, 17, 18; pseudo-Platonism of, 114; on question of literature, 114; *Recherche,* 106, 107, 112, 239n61; scholarship, 9; on sensible ideas, 115, 116; *Time Regained,* 101
pure poetry, 174–75, 217n39
purity: notion of, 174
Pyrrhonism, 165, 235n21

Rancière, Jacques, 96
reality: memory and, 28, 30
Rebecca (Biblical character), 47
reciprocal envelopments, 39–40
reduction, 199n47
respiration, 46, 47, 50–51, 208n124
retention, 26
retrospective illusion, 30
Reverdy, Pierre, 87
reversibility: as characteristic of intelligence, 139; construction of logical, 140; of dimensions, 139; metaphoricity and, 138–41; spatial, 139–40

Ricoeur, Paul, 125, 166, 222n35
Rilke, Rainer Maria, 81
Rimbaud, Arthur, 2, 50, 104, 204n57
Rodrigue (character), 63, 64, 65
Rorschach, Hermann, 137
Rozzoni, Claudio, 222n25
Ruyer, Raymond, 233n152

Saint Aubert, Emmanuel de: on Cartesian mind-body dualism, 225n7; on chiasm, 216nn34,35; concept of metaphoricity, 175, 195n16; on metaphors and figuratives, 195n18; on opposition between "com-prehension" and "ex-plication," 226n23; study of Beauvoir's oeuvre, 194n10
Sara (character), 206n105
Sartre, Jean-Paul: analysis of "double incarnation," 41; conception of divine freedom, 59; idea of *analogon*, 129, 151, 231nn116,117; interpretation of objects and things, 89; *L'imaginaire*, 151, 152; "Man and Things," 89, 91; polemics with Merleau-Ponty, 91, 151, 230n93; on Ponge, 89, 90–91; separation of real and imaginary, 151; theology of, 155
Saussure, Ferdinand de, 1, 142, 213n2, 221n17
Scheler, Max, 40
Schilder, Paul, 55, 129, 131
Schmidt, Dennis J., 237n44
Schneider, Johann, 128, 226n22
screen: 10, 108, function of, 118–20; *vs.* veil, 119
sedimentation, 168–69, 181
semantic thickness, 69, 84, 87, 88, 89, 92
sensation, 47, 206n108
sensible, 47, 48, 125
sensible ideas, 7, 10, 115, 116
sensible latency, 143
sentient, 47, 48
separation, 61, 65
Servien, Pius, 214n8
sexuality, food and, 49
shadow, 148, 149, 156
Shakespeare, William, 210n148
silence, 8, 68–69, 80, 96, 156

Simon, Claude: and Claudel, 63; conception of the flesh of the world, 8, 54, 55; development of poetics of incorporation, 34; on human and inter-human magma, 132; idea of flesh, 56, 57, 211n173; idea of promiscuity, 211n167; influence on Merleau-Ponty, 27, 52, 210n149; on initiation, 29–30; *Le Vent*, 52; Merleau-Ponty Note on "The 'Association' as Initiation," 29; Nobel Prize speech, 209n148; novelty of, 52–53, 54–55
simultaneity: idea of, 34, 44, 205nn79,81–83
skepticism, 11, 164, 165
soul, entanglement of body and, 183, 207n113
speech: *vs.* language, 221n17, 222nn24, 27; power of, 112, 114; speaking *vs.* spoken, 111–12, 221n17; vicious circle of, 112, 115; vision and, 123
Spender, Stephen, 179, 180
Stendhal (Henri Beyle), 2, 70, 83, 103, 105, 110, 135, 167, 194n11; *De l'amour* (On Love), 146; *The Red and the Black*, 169, 194n11
sublime point, 8, 35–37, 40, 51, 85, 86
surfaces: notion of clouded, 117
surrealism: *Abridged Dictionary of Surrealism*, 40; Breton's work on, 35–36; defense of, 38; Merleau-Ponty's engagement with, 85, 86; Ponge's engagement with, 87; relation to reality, 38, 202n31; view of object, 202n39
surrection, 35, 59, 60, 66, 201n7, 224n1
Swann (character), 106, 107, 108, 110, 112–13, 115

taking literally, methodological principle of, 143
Teilhard de Chardin, Pierre, 59, 155
temporality: chapter of *Phenomenology of Perception*, 20; critique of Husserl, 26; Freudian interpretation of, 26; mythical, 28; spatiotemporality, 60
theology, 154–55, 158
thetic univocity, 138

Thomas Aquinas, Saint, 154, 203n56
time: as absolute overflight of consciousness, 155–56; common idea of, 26; embodied, 199n36; extraordinary, 94; lost, 71; simultaneity of, 29
transparency, notion of, 223n45
Trismegistus, Hermes, *Poimandres,* 178
truth: absolute, 237n38; appearance and, 162; being and, 146; biological metaphor for development of, 168; comparison to love, 240n64; Dickinson's poem on, 179; eternal, 11, 168, 181; exploration of question of, 159–60, 161, 188–89; genealogy of, 161, 167; hermeneutic of, 180, 237n44; as illusion, 164; intentionality and, 21; life and, 164, 177; of literary language, 167; of love, 185; of painting, 173; mathematical, 168; militant, 181; more profound, 181, 182–89; new idea of, 176, 177–82; Nietzschean notion of, 164; origin of, 11, 181; in perceptual experience, 236n25; of poetic and literary language, 189; retrograde movement of, 181–82; stability of, 179; subjectivity as the condition for possibility of, 165; untruth and, 166

ubiquity of intercorporeity, 34
unconscious, concept of, 32, 182

Vachon, André, 42
Valéry, Paul: admiration of Stendhal, 70; on alliance of philosophy with poets, 6; on body of the painter, 206n102; *Cahiers* (Notebooks), xvii, 80, 206n79, 214n8, 216n33; conversation with Bergson, 86; correspondence of, 74, 81; on creativity, 72, 79; critique of Descartes, 83; difficult poetic forms of, 84–85; on "extraordinary time," 93–92; "An Evening with Monsieur Teste," 71–72, 79, 80; on history of literature, 77; "Hommage à Proust," 70, 71; on ideal poet, 173; idea of chiasm, 2, 216n34; idea of implex, 73, 92–94; *Idée Fixe,* 92, 93; influence on Merleau-Ponty, 8, 71–73, 80, 85, 86; *Introduction to the Method of Leonardo da Vinci,* 72, 73; "La ceinture," 98; on language, 3, 69, 82, 195n12; "La Pythie," 4, 8, 68, 69, 84; logic of creativity, 73; "Note and Digression," 73; "On the Teaching of Poetics at the Collège de France," 77; "Opening Lecture of his Course in Poetics," 3; "Palm," 5; paradoxes of, 81–84; personal and creative crisis, 79–81; on poetic language, 84–98, 173; on poetics of Mallarmé, 94–95; on poetry, 4, 6, 69, 70, 82, 174–75; Ponge and, 87; silence of, 80; study of Edgar Allan Poe, 70, 74–75, 77, 78–79, 214n8; study of Leonardo da Vinci, 72–73; surrealism of, 85; on traditional rules of prosody, 217n44; view of writing and literature, 71
Vasseleu, Cathryn, 237n43
Vattimo, Gianni, 166
veil: 10, 118, 119, 120, 164, 175, 176, 188,189
Vetch, Rosalie, 63
Vian, Boris, 91
vibration, 46; as element of life, 207n115, 208n121; as image of the encounter of desires, 50; as joint act of soul and body, 49; as mode of existence, 49–50; perception as, 208n120; as simultaneous movement, 206n109, 207nn111,118
Vinteuil (character), little phrase from *Sonata* of, 9, 108, 110, 112–13, 116, 185, 240n61
visible: poetic of, 8; relationship between invisible and, 38, 40, 116, 144, 208n126; shadow of, 66
Visible and the Invisible, The (Merleau-Ponty): on blind spot, 216n34; on characteristic of being, 166; on concept of truth, 160; on eloquent language, 173–74; on experience of initiation, 26, 27, 29; on flesh of the world, 52, 66–67; formulation of the Proustian corporeity, 22; on function of screen, 118–19; investigation of

being, 150; on language as life, 1, 173; on linguistic "paradox of philosophy," 12; on manifesto format and surrealism, 36; on mystery of language, 11; notion of incorporeal, 148; on paradox of expression, 171; on perception, 43–44; on perceptual faith, 165; philosophical language of, 118; on primary being, 11–12; reference to Valéry, 68, 69; on relation of words and seeing, 9; on scepticism, 165; on "sensible ideas," 115–16; on silence, 69, 96; on skepticism, 235n21; on status of figures, 134; on temporality, 26
Visible Man or the Culture of Film (Balázs), 103

Wahl, Jean, 42, 44, 45, 46, 50, 136, 205n79
Waldenfels, Bernhard, 105
Weizsäcker, Viktor von, 140
Whitehead, Alfred North, 46
Winnicott, Donald Woods, 135, 239n60
Wiskus, Jessica, 98
world: Claudel's idea of, 207n116, 212n194; modern *vs.* classical, 153; in the state of analogy, distortion of, 23
writing, act of, 131

Ysé (character), 63
Yseult (mythological character), 63

Zaccarello, Benedetta, 82, 83, 110

Galen A. Johnson is Professor of Philosophy at the University of Rhode Island. He has been General Secretary (Executive Director) of the International Merleau-Ponty Circle (2005–2015) and Jane C. Ebbs Endowed Professor of Philosophy (2016–2018). He is the author of *The Retrieval of the Beautiful: Thinking through Merleau-Ponty's Aesthetics* (Northwestern University Press, 2010) and editor of *The Merleau-Ponty Aesthetics Reader: Philosophy and Painting* (Northwestern University Press, 1993).

Mauro Carbone is Professor of Aesthetics at the Faculté de Philosophie of the University Jean Moulin Lyon 3 and an Honorary Member of the Institut Universitaire de France. He is the founder and the coeditor of the journal *Chiasmi International: Trilingual Studies Concerning Merleau-Ponty's Thought*. His present research focuses on the connections between philosophy and contemporary visual experience. Among his books are *The Flesh of Images: Merleau-Ponty between Painting and Cinema* (SUNY Press, 2015) and *Philosophy-Screens: From Cinema to Digital Revolution* (SUNY Press, 2019).

Emmanuel de Saint Aubert is Research Director at the Husserl Archives in Paris (National Center for Scientific Research, École Normale Supérieure). His research bears most particularly on the work of Merleau-Ponty, rereading him through the lens of an overall knowledge of numerous unpublished writings. Among his books are *Vers une ontologie indirecte: Sources et enjeux critiques de l'appel à l'ontologie chez Merleau-Ponty* (Vrin, 2006) and *Être et chair I: Du corps au désir—L'habilitation ontologique de la chair* (Vrin, 2013).

Perspectives in Continental Philosophy
John D. Caputo, series editor

Recent titles:

Galen A. Johnson, Mauro Carbone, and Emmanuel de Saint Aubert, *Merleau-Ponty's Poetic of the World: Philosophy and Literature.*
Ole Jakob Løland, *Pauline Ugliness: Jacob Taubes and the Turn to Paul.*
Marika Rose, *A Theology of Failure: Žižek against Christian Innocence.*
Marc Crépon, *Murderous Consent: On the Accommodation of Violent Death.* Translated by Michael Loriaux and Jacob Levi, Foreword by James Martel
Emmanuel Falque, *The Guide to Gethsemane: Anxiety, Suffering, and Death.* Translated by George Hughes.
Emmanuel Alloa, *Resistance of the Sensible World: An Introduction to Merleau-Ponty.* Translated by Jane Marie Todd. Foreword by Renaud Barbaras.
Françoise Dastur, *Questions of Phenomenology: Language, Alterity, Temporality, Finitude.* Translated by Robert Vallier.
Jean-Luc Marion, *Believing in Order to See: On the Rationality of Revelation and the Irrationality of Some Believers.* Translated by Christina M. Gschwandtner.
Adam Y. Wells, ed., *Phenomenologies of Scripture.*
An Yountae, *The Decolonial Abyss: Mysticism and Cosmopolitics from the Ruins.*
Jean Wahl, *Transcendence and the Concrete: Selected Writings.* Edited and with an Introduction by Alan D. Schrift and Ian Alexander Moore.
Colby Dickinson, *Words Fail: Theology, Poetry, and the Challenge of Representation.*
Emmanuel Falque, *The Wedding Feast of the Lamb: Eros, the Body, and the Eucharist.* Translated by George Hughes.

Emmanuel Falque, *Crossing the Rubicon: The Borderlands of Philosophy and Theology*. Translated by Reuben Shank. Introduction by Matthew Farley.
Colby Dickinson and Stéphane Symons (eds.), *Walter Benjamin and Theology*.
Don Ihde, *Husserl's Missing Technologies*.
William S. Allen, *Aesthetics of Negativity: Blanchot, Adorno, and Autonomy*.
Jeremy Biles and Kent L. Brintnall, eds., *Georges Bataille and the Study of Religion*.
Tarek R. Dika and W. Chris Hackett, *Quiet Powers of the Possible: Interviews in Contemporary French Phenomenology*. Foreword by Richard Kearney.
Richard Kearney and Brian Treanor, eds., *Carnal Hermeneutics*.

A complete list of titles is available at http://fordhampress.com.

www.ingramcontent.com/pod-product-compliance
Lightning Source LLC
Chambersburg PA
CBHW030437300426
44112CB00009B/1037